Isaac Jennings

Memorials of a Century

Embracing a Record of Individuals and Events, chiefly in the early history of

Bennington

Isaac Jennings

Memorials of a Century
Embracing a Record of Individuals and Events, chiefly in the early history of Bennington

ISBN/EAN: 9783337425586

Printed in Europe, USA, Canada, Australia, Japan

Cover: Foto ©ninafisch / pixelio.de

More available books at **www.hansebooks.com**

MEMORIALS OF A CENTURY.

THE EARLY HISTORY OF BENNINGTON, VT.

FIRST CHURCH.

BY

ISAAC JENNINGS,

PASTOR OF THE CHURCH.

BOSTON:
GOULD AND LINCOLN,
59 WASHINGTON STREET.
1869.

Rockwell & Rollins, Printers and Stereotypers.
122 Washington Street, Boston.

To

THE PEOPLE OF HIS PASTORAL CHARGE,

WITH AFFECTION AND ESTEEM,

AND TO

All interested in the Early History of Bennington,

THIS VOLUME

IS RESPECTFULLY INSCRIBED,

BY

THE AUTHOR.

To REV. ISAAC JENNINGS.

Dear Sir: Having listened with much pleasure to your very interesting centennial discourse, delivered on the 4th inst., and considering it of great historical value, we are very desirous that it should be published for distribution and preservation; and we would respectfully request you to furnish a copy for the press.

H. G. ROOT.	HILAND HALL.
GEORGE BENTON.	A. B. GARDNER.
M. C. MORGAN.	SAMUEL CHANDLER.
STEPHEN BINGHAM.	GEORGE LYMAN.
S. F. HARRIS.	I. W. VAIL.
M. G. SELDEN.	H. H. HARWOOD.
F. C. WHITE.	WILLIAM WEBB.

PREFACE.

HE foundation of this volume is the discourse delivered at the Centennial Celebration of the organization of the Bennington First Church, the publication of which was requested by the note on the preceding page.

The first nine chapters are, without essential modification, the discourse. Some account of the centennial celebration and the conclusion of the discourse make up chapter twenty-six.

In view of publication, four subjects presented themselves for a more complete consideration than the writer had given to them, namely: the land-title controversy; the Bennington battle; the individual men and women of Bennington in the past times; and the Separatist antecedents of many of the first inhabitants, together with their promotion of civil liberty as to public worship. Hence so many pages devoted to these subjects, and a volume instead of a discourse.

The writer has been in various ways much assisted by numerous kind friends of the work. He would make particular mention of his indebtedness to William Haswell, Esq., clerk of the church, now deceased, for reminiscences, documents, and labors upon the church records, without

which these memorials would be far more imperfect than
they are; to the Rev. R. C. Learned, of Plymouth, Conn.,—
an esteemed college classmate, deceased April 19, 1867,—for
information respecting Separatism in Connecticut; to S. F.
Plimpton, Esq., of Boston, Mass.,—also an esteemed college
classmate, deceased April 22, 1867,—for extensive and accurate researches amongst the laws of Massachusetts in their
bearing upon the Separates; and to the Hon. Hiland Hall,—
the able late president of the Vermont Historical Society,
writer of the historical account of Bennington (so comprehensive as to be in itself a history of the town) in Miss
Hemmenway's "Vermont Historical Magazine," and author
of "The Early History of Vermont." Almost the entire
manuscript of these "Memorials," before their final completion for the press, had the benefit of his careful revision.
His valuable aid in many ways, and active interest in the
success of these labors, demand grateful acknowledgment.

Thanks are also due to those who have encouraged the
undertaking by subscribing for copies of the volume in advance, who belong to other churches and parishes in the
town, and who, though now many of them prominent in the
community, have not by early settlement here, or by genealogical descent, any connection with its early history, and it
may be their names do not occur in the following pages.

And finally the author feels under obligation to the experienced judgment and kind co-operation of the publishers.

BENNINGTON CENTRE, VT., April, 1869.

CONTENTS.

CHAPTER I.

TOWNSHIP.

CHAPTER II.

FIRST MEETING-HOUSE.

CHAPTER III.

THE CHURCH.

CHAPTER IV.

SEPARATISM.

CHAPTER V.

INTERNAL PERPLEXITIES OF THE CHURCH.

CHAPTER VI.

THE CHURCH IN THE WORLD.

CHAPTER VII.

REVIVALS.

CHAPTER VIII.

THE FIRST SEVEN PASTORS.

CHAPTER IX.

TRANSIENT MINISTERS.

.

CHAPTER X.

THE LAND-TITLE CONTROVERSY.

CHAPTER XI.

THE LAND-TITLE CONTROVERSY, CONTINUED.

CHAPTER XII.

THE BENNINGTON BATTLE.

CHAPTER XIII.

PERSONAL NOTICES — SAMUEL ROBINSON, SEN., ESQ., AND MRS. MARCY L. ROBINSON.

CHAPTER XIV.

PERSONAL NOTICES — FIRST IMMIGRATION.

CHAPTER XV.

PERSONAL NOTICES — SECOND IMMIGRATION.

2

CHAPTER XVI.

PERSONAL NOTICES — SECOND IMMIGRATION, CONTINUED.

CHAPTER XVII.

PERSONAL NOTICES — 1762.

CHAPTER XVIII.

PERSONAL NOTICES — 1763-1765.

CHAPTER XIX.

PERSONAL NOTICES — 1766–1769.

CHAPTER XX.

PERSONAL NOTICES — 1775–1776.

CHAPTER XXI.

PERSONAL NOTICES — 1777–1784.

CHAPTER XXII.

PERSONAL NOTICES — 1785-1800.

CHAPTER XXIII.

PERSONAL NOTICES — 1803 AND AFTERWARD.

CHAPTER XXIV.

EDUCATION.

CHAPTER XXV.

CHURCHES ORGANIZED IN BENNINGTON SUBSEQUENTLY TO THE ORGANIZATION OF THE BENNINGTON FIRST CHURCH — 1762-1862.

CHAPTER XXVI.

THE CENTENNIAL CELEBRATION.

CHAPTER XXVII.

SUPPLEMENTARY.

CHAPTER XXVIII.

INFLUENCE OF THE EARLY SETTLERS OF VERMONT ON FREEDOM OF PUBLIC WORSHIP.

3*

NOTES ON CHAPTERS IV., AND XXVIII.

APPENDIX.

MEMORIALS OF A CENTURY.

CHAPTER I.

TOWNSHIP.

THE FIRST SETTLEMENT of Vermont, and the early struggles of its inhabitants not only in subduing a wilderness, but establishing an independent government," says Sparks, in his "American Biography," "afford some of the most remarkable incidents in American History." If this is true of the State in general, it is especially true of Bennington, the cradle of its infancy; and no less true of Bennington's religious than of its secular life; for as it was the first town chartered, so its First Church was the first also in the territory afterward Vermont, and the antecedents and early career of this church, which for sixty-four years was the only one in the town, furnish a subject second to no other in interest and importance in the history of Bennington.

To present the *religious*, side by side with the *secular* early life of the town, to gather up remarkable incidents of both, to extend careful research in directions heretofore neglected, and to combine the whole in a permanent form for perusal and preservation, is the design of the following pages.

On January 3, 1749, parties, many of them from Portsmouth, New Hampshire,[1] obtained a grant from the New Hampshire governor, Benning Wentworth, Esq., in the name of King George II., of a township, six miles square, situated six miles north of the Massachusetts line, and twenty miles east of the Hudson. According to the provisions of this charter, these purchasers first divided off acre homesteads in the centre, to the number of sixty-four for a village plot, and then divided the remainder into sixty-four equal parts, and cast lots for the same. Each original purchaser is believed to have sold his share without perhaps ever seeing it, except upon paper, certainly to have never settled upon it or improved it. It should have been said that, of the sixty-four shares, two went to Governor Wentworth, one to the first settled minister, whoever he might be, one for schools, and the remaining sixty to as many different individuals.[2]

The township remained an unbroken wilderness for thirteen years, though men thus cast lots for it, and appropriated it to be some time a town under the name of Bennington, in honor of the Christian name of the New Hampshire governor. Captain Samuel Robinson, returning to his home in Massachusetts from one of the campaigns of the Continental army in the French war, mistaking his route, passed, by accident, this way; and, impressed by the attractiveness of the country, resolved to obtain others to join him and come up and settle here. His resolution was carried into effect. Others agreed to accompany him. They searched out the owners of the land; they purchased the rights of the original grantees, or of those to whom they had sold, and removed hither.

1 The grantees of Bennington were many, probably most, of them from Portsmouth. Col. Williams, the first-named proprietor in the charter, was from Massachusetts, and afterward settled and died in Pittsfield. Probably some others were from Massachusetts.

2 Vermont Hist. Mag.

The purchasers of the rights were termed proprietors; and the whole purchase in common, or township as related to its purchasers, a propriety. The proprietors had business meetings before a town was organized, and for some years afterward; they settled boundary lines outside of the whole, and between one proprietor and another; they located and worked some of the roads; they re-located some of the proprietors who were not pleased with their original purchase. Some who found their purchase lying on the east side of the township desired to be re-located on the west side, and the change was authorized in the proprietors' meetings. The proprietors' meeting had its moderator; and the propriety, its clerk. Samuel Robinson, Esq., was moderator of the first proprietors' meeting and John Fassett was clerk of the propriety. Records were kept, — not folio volumes bound in calf and deposited with dignity in an iron safe; a few leaves sewed together after the fashion of a school-boy's home-made writing-book sufficed. Those records are interesting now. That little collection of eight-inch square leaves, now time-worn, — for it is a century old, — is bound in the first part of the first volume of the town records, and one can soon read it through; but the transactions recorded there are full of importance.

The first public meeting in Bennington, whose minutes are preserved, — a proprietors' meeting, — was held on Feb. 11, 1762, — one year lacking a day before the treaty was signed ceding the province of Canada to the British Government, and so ending the formidable French war. Therefore, anticipating the termination of this war, immigration had begun to press upward along the western slopes of these mountains. The first immigration had reached here seven months and twenty-three days before this proprietors' meeting, June 18, 1761. It consisted of the families of

Peter Harwood, Eleazer Harwood, Samuel Pratt and
Timothy Pratt, from Amherst, Mass.; Leonard Robinson
and Samuel Robinson, Jr., from Hardwick, Mass. The
party, including women and children, numbered twenty-
two. During that summer and fall other families to the
number of twenty or thirty came into town, among whom
were those of Samuel Robinson, Sen., and John Fassett,
from Hardwick. Mass.; Joseph Safford, John Smith, John
Burnham, and Benajah Rood, from Newint, Conn.; Elisha
Field, and Samuel Montague, from Sunderland, Mass.;
James Breakenridge, Ebenezer Wood, Samuel and Oliver
Scott, Joseph Wickwire, and Samuel Atwood. In that
winter, January 12, the first child was born in the settlement, Benjamin Harwood, a very worthy and intelligent
citizen, whose death did not occur until January 22, 1851,
at the advanced age of eighty-nine years, connecting vividly
that distant period with our times.

Our early immigrants had apparently to themselves
travelled much further to reach the place of their destination than the present generation would have to do to go
over the same ground. One of the descendants of the
Montagues, a resident in Sunderland, Mass., whence the
original inhabitants in this town of that name came, in answer to an inquiry, suggests that his relative did not
probably remove to Bennington, but farther north toward
Canada. There can be no reasonable doubt that the relative was the same Samuel Montague who was the moderator of the first town meeting here of which we have record.
The mistake, it is probable, originated in an impression,
prevalent in the communities our immigrants left, that
they, in removing to Bennington, were proceeding not only
to an unknown but also to a very far-distant northern
clime. The first year of the settlement must have been one
of much privation and hardship; the tenements, huts with

logs for walls, and bark and brush for the roof; the settlers numerous the first winter, — a part women and children. In a tavern-bill preserved of Samuel Robinson, Esq., at a tavern in Charlemont, Mass., about midway on the route from Hardwick, Mass., to this place, there is also a charge for wheat as early as April 9, 1761 ; and the inference may be that he was then on his way here, some two months in advance of the removal of families, to prepare as much as possible for their comfort. The seed for sowing the land must be brought upon horses for many miles ; also provisions for subsistence before crops could be grown here. The season, however, appears to have been uncommonly mild ; the setting in of winter providentially postponed to an unusually late period.

CHAPTER II.

FIRST MEETING-HOUSE.

HE first public meeting, according to the proprietors' records as preserved, has been incidentally mentioned. The first transaction at this meeting, after electing the proper officers, was as follows: —

"Chose Deacon Joseph Safford, Esq., Samuel Robinson, John Fassett, Ebenezer Wood, Elisha Field, John Burnham, and Abraham Newton, a committee to look out a place to set the meeting-house."

By the record of an adjourned proprietors' meeting, February 26, 1762, we find the place to set the meeting-house determined by the following vote: —

"The north-east corner of the right of land, No. 27, as near th corner as may be thought convenient."

No public plot had then been laid out; it was evident assumed that the place for the meeting-house should first be selected, and then that roads and other public improvements should adjust themselves somewhat to that. May 14, 1766, it was

"*Voted*, To give six acres, out of the sixty-four acres called the town-plot, for three acres where the meeting-house now stands, for public use."

"*Voted*, That the road from the meeting-house to Samuel Safford's will be the main road, and shall be four rods wide."

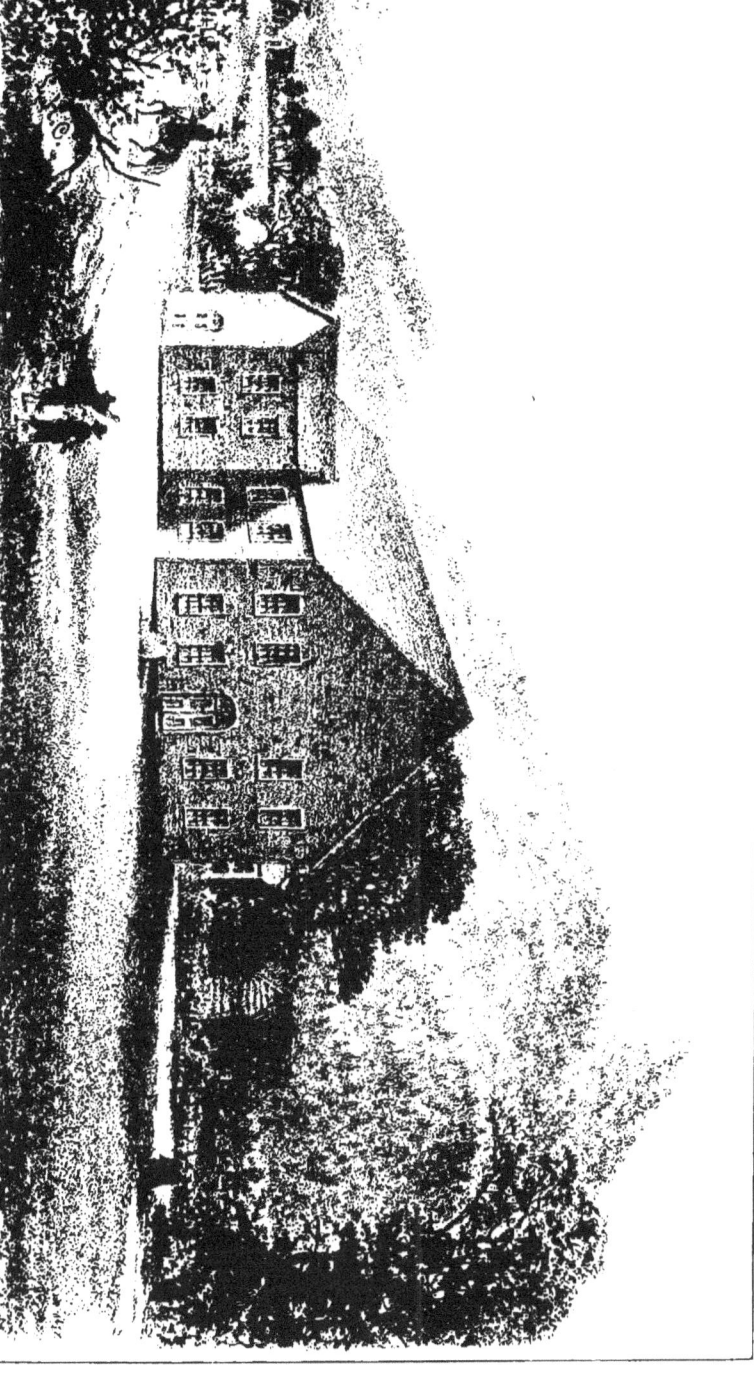

FIRST MEETING HOUSE ERECTED IN VERMONT.
BENNINGTON, 1763

A. Meisel, Lith. Boston.

We find subsequently in the records the three-acre lot on which the meeting-house stood, termed the meeting-house plot; and at a still later date the widened road northward designated as "The Parade." The first meeting-house, stood somewhere midway between the site of the present one and the Walloomsac House.

The precise date of the building of the first meeting-house is not known. It was built in time to be occupied on or before the year 1766. The cost of it, in the first instance, appears to have been met, in part, by a tax upon the several rights of land, and in part by a subscription. A vote is recorded,

"To send a petition to the General Court of the province of New Hampshire to raise a tax on all the lands in Bennington, resident and non-resident, to build a meeting-house, and school-house, and mills, and for highways and bridges."

In a meeting of later date, May 9, 1763, it was

"*Voted*, To raise six dollars on each right of land in Bennington for building a meeting-house and school-house."

The sixty-four rights of land, according to this tax, would raise three hundred and eighty-four dollars. The following minute upon the town records will show that the meeting-house was in an unfinished state, and that a subscription had had something to do with its erection: —

"October 22, 1768. — This may notify all persons who have signed a subscription for building a meeting-house in this place, to meet at said meeting-house, to see if they will do anything further toward the finishing of the meeting-house. To see if they will lay out the pew ground, and dispose of the same by public vendue."

There is preserved, in the possession of Dewey Hubbell, a subscription list to further finish the meeting-

3

house. This undertaking was in 1771, some ten years
after the building of the house. In this subscription list
are some one hundred and sixty names, and subscriptions
as high as ten pounds, others as low as ten shillings. The
agreement was, that if the finishing and repairing cost
more than the aggregate subscription, the additional
amount should be paid by the subscribers in the proportion of their subscription, and if less, the balance should
be deducted from their subscription in the same proportion.

The size of this meeting-house was fifty by forty, with
the addition of a porch twenty feet square. There was no
steeple. The porch extended upward to the roof, and in the
upper story a school was kept for some years. In 1797,
Miss Sedgwick, sister of the Rev. Job Swift, D. D., taught
school there; in 1798–9, Miss Thankful Hunt, sister of
Jonathan Hunt, was the teacher; she afterward returned
to Northampton, Mass. There were galleries on three
sides of the house; and square pews ornamented with little railings in the place of a top-panel, the balusters of
which would be occasionally loose so as to turn round in
their places, and furnish a little diversion for listless young
worshippers. There was a sounding-board over the pulpit;
three doors for entrance and exit, — one, through the porch
on the east side, toward the burying-ground and opposite
the pulpit, which was in the middle of the west side; and
two other doors opposite each other on the north and south
sides respectively. The building lengthwise stood north
and south, with the roof sloping to the east and west;
there was a main aisle through the centre from the pulpit
to the porch running east and west, and aisles from the
north and south (end) doors going round and so arranged
as to leave a tier of wall pews all round the house, and
two tiers of square pews on each side of the main aisle in

the body of the house. In the front seat of the gallery opposite, and on either side of the pulpit, sat the singers. That there was not always due order in the house in time of worship appears from an entry in the town records. March 26, 1777 : —

" *Voted*, That such persons as do continue playing in the meeting on the Lord's day, or in the worship of God, be complained of to the committee of safety for said town, who are hereby authorized to fine them discretionary."

In this meeting-house proprietors' meetings were repeatedly held ; also town meetings ; even after the erection of the court-house, town meetings were held occasionally here. In this first meeting-house the people met to worship God and give thanks after the taking of Ticonderoga, when that redoubtable fortress obeyed the summons of Ethan Allen "to surrender, in the name of Jehovah and the Continental Congress." Col. Allen being a resident of Bennington, and having returned with other officers to be present at the services, this circumstance gave peculiar interest to the occasion. From the pulpit under that sounding-board the Rev. Mr. Dewey preached a war sermon the Sunday preceding the Bennington battle. To this meeting-house the Hessians and others, prisoners captured in that battle, were brought for safe custody. It was as they were marching in solemn sadness hither, and while they were passing the Catamount Tavern, near by, that " Landlord Fay " stepped out, and with a gracious bow informed the prisoners that the dinner was then ready, which their officers, confident of gaining the victory, had haughtily ordered by a message sent in the day before. In the same meeting-house the first Legislature of Vermont held its June session, 1778. The General Assembly of 1779, also that of 1780, and in some instances successive Legislatures, met here.[1]   On the journal of the General Assembly of 1778, under date of June 5, is the following record : —

"*Voted*, That the Rev. Mr. Dewey be presented with the compliments of this House, to desire him to pray with the Assembly at their opening in the morning, for this present session."

In this first meeting-house, also, for want of room in the court-house, was conducted the famous trial of Whitney and Tibbits for the alleged wanton murder of the Indian, Stephen Gordon, — in which trial Pierrepoint Edwards was successfully employed for the defence, coming all the way from New Haven, Conn., for that purpose.

But not alone for secular transactions and scenes was this primitive sanctuary memorable. Of its spiritual history there shall be a more full relation hereafter. Let it suffice to say that from beneath its sounding-board the Rev. Mr. Dewey preached during his ministry here; also the Rev. Mr. Avery and the Rev. Dr. Swift. Within its walls the fathers and mothers of the church, and of the churches, in this town, met together for public worship; and here were witnessed signal displays of the reviving and converting grace of God. In it was held for long the Friday prayer-meeting, a weekly meeting held in the afternoon, and remembered with interest, and often alluded to, by aged inhabitants of the town familiar with the memorable days of the old first meeting-house. A few incidents connected with this Friday meeting will be found in subsequent pages of this volume.

1 The first Legislature of Vermont was organized and held a session in March (1778), in Windsor, and adjourned to hold another session in Bennington. It met according to adjournment, and opened in form (June 4, 1778) at the house of Captain Stephen Fay, the Catamount Tavern, and adjourned to meet the next morning in the meeting-house where the remainder of the session was held. The Bennington session of the General Assembly of 1799 was held also by adjournment of a Windsor session of the Assembly.

Soon after the close of the Rev. Dr. Swift's ministry here, and before the installation of his successor, the old meeting-house was superseded by the new one, and removed away. The following is an extract from the sermon of the Rev. Daniel Marsh, preached at the dedication of the new meeting-house : —

"We can say of the new meeting-house, it far exceeds the former in magnitude, riches, and elegance; but can we hope the glory of the latter house shall be greater than that of the former in the gracious presence of God? Though the latter Jewish temple was far inferior to the former in its earthly splendor and glory, yet the latter exceeded the former in glory in being honored with the personal presence of Christ, and his promising that in that place he would give peace. But can we, my brethren, hope for greater special blessings in this latter house than your fathers and yourselves have experienced in the former? You can look back to the ancient building and remember the many precious showers of divine blessing which have there been shed down from the Father of mercies. You can remember the gracious outpourings of his Holy Spirit, which fired the hearts of his people with love, which caused sinners in Zion to tremble, and many souls in captivity to sin and Satan to be set at liberty, and shout the praises of Zion's King! You can remember the many joyful hours you have spent in the demolished house of God, and take your final farewell. But never, no, never, will it be erased from your remembrance how often your blessed Jesus hath met you, mingled with you, and communed with you there; how often you have sat under his banner of love with great delight, and his fruit was sweeter than the honeycomb to your taste. With mingled emotions of joy and sorrow, do you not now take your last leave of yonder spot of earth which had been devoted to the service of your God for this more spacious building?"

There appears to have b en, f. e portion of the time at least, a place of common resort, apart from the meeting-house, for social religious services between the preaching services on the Sabbath. A communication in the " Vermont

Gazette" of May 3, 1803, mentions such a place, where, during the intermission, " the church generally convened to pass that period in suitable exercises and prayer." It is related that Mrs. Samuel Robinson, Sen., had such meetings in her house, and also the Friday meetings, if not constantly, for a period at least, on frequent occasions.

CHAPTER III.

THE CHURCH.

I. ORGANIZATION. — It is time we leave the external house, and turn our attention to the body of believers, to the efforts, and the divine blessing upon them, to gather, maintain, and perpetuate the ordinances, the assembly of saints and the body and succession of Christian people. The high use of the house of worship is as a home for the family of brethren and sisters in Christ, and the sphere of their concentrated spiritual labor for the salvation of souls. Hitherto I have consulted more prominently the proprietors' records and town records; let us turn now to the church records.

We find that the church of Christ in Bennington — which was the original designation, without any denominational epithet, of the first church organized within the limits of the present State of Vermont — came into existence on December 3, 1762. — The next was the church in Newbury, organized in September, 1764. — As we have seen, early in February, 1761, the committee was appointed, by vote in proprietors' meeting, to select the site for the meeting-house; early in December of the same year the first church was organized.

The entire minutes of the record of organization are as follows : —

" BENNINGTON, *December* 3, 1762.

"The church of Christ from Hardwick, and the church of Christ from Sunderland, met together and after prayers agreed upon and voted : —

"1. That said church from Hardwick and said church from Sunderland join together and become one body, or church of Christ in Bennington.

"2. That John Fassett shall be the clerk to keep the records of the aforesaid Hardwick and Sunderland churches, and also now Bennington church records.

"3. It is agreed upon and voted by the church of Christ in Bennington, that they make an exception in the fourth paragraph, in the eleventh chapter in Cambridge Platform, in respect of using the civil law to support the gospel; and also the ninth paragraph in the seventeenth chapter, in respect of the civil magistrate's coercive [co-hersive] power.

"4. *Voted*, To receive in Joseph Safford and Anne Safford his wife into full communion with this church.

"5. *Voted*, To receive Stephen Story into full communion with this church.

"6. *Voted*, To receive Bethiah Burnham, wife of John Burnham, into full communion with this church.

"7. *Voted*, To receive Eleanor Smith, wife of John Smith, into full communion with this church."

Antecedents. — Of these Sunderland and Hardwick churches more is to be said hereafter; it is now chiefly to be noticed that there were already churches existing here, though not here organized; and it is to be inferred that church privileges were here enjoyed. Capt. Samuel Robinson, Sen., and James Fay were or had been deacons of the Hardwick Church.[1] According to tradition, John Fassett was or had been deacon, probably of the Hardwick Church. Joseph Safford, who came here in the summer or fall of 1861, had been deacon of a church in Newint, Conn., as appears by records of that church preserved by his descendants in this town. By these records it also appears that Bethiah Burnham, Ann Safford, wife of Joseph S. or, John Smith and Eleanor Smith, who united with the Bennington church at the time of its organization, were from the

[1] Hardwick Centennial Address of the Rev. Mr. Paige.

church in Newint. The attorney for Redding was John
Burnham, Jr., a lawyer evidently of some influence and force
of character, and we find upon the Newint church records
the name of his father, John Burnham, and also of Bethiah
Burnham, Jr. Stephen Story, one of the original members
of the Bennington church, and deceased 1766, in the seventieth year of his age, had, as appears upon his grave-stone
in our burying-ground, been a deacon somewhere. From
records now in Sunderland, Mass., we learn that Experience Richardson, Elisha Field, Jonathan Scott, and Samuel
Montague were members of the Sunderland church before
its removal to Bennington. Preparatory, therefore, to the
organization of the Bennington church, there must have
been a stalwart community of Christian men and families,
who had arrived a twelvemonth, more or less, before; and
who from the first of their arrival had been recognized mutually as the followers of Christ, meeting together on the
Sabbath and at other stated times for religious worship, and
celebrating together the communion of the Lord's Supper.

Original Members. — Of the members of the Bennington
church, at its organization, so far as the names are preserved, there were thirty-two males and twenty-five females,
making a total of fifty-seven. —The number indicates a large
influx of people the first year and a half of the settlement
of the town. — The names are as follows : George Abbott,
George Abbott, Jr., James Breakenridge, William Breakenridge, David Doane, Jonathan Eastman, John Fassett, Daniel Fay, James Fay, James Fay, Jr., Elisha Field, Jacob
Fisk, Benjamin Harwood, Eleazar Harwood, Zechariah Harwood, Aaron Leonard (Martha, his wife, was one of the
separating members from the old church in Sunderland),
Samuel Montague, Samuel Pratt, Jedidiah Rice, Oliver Rice,
John Roberts, Samuel Robinson, Silas Robinson, Joseph
Safford, Simeon Sears, Jonathan Scott, Jonathan Scott, Jr.,

Elijah Story, Stephen Story, Samuel Tubbs, Benjamin Whipple, Ichabod Stratton, Martha Abbott, Rebecca Abbott, Pearce Atwood, Bethiah Burnham, Elizabeth Fay, Lydia Fay, Mehitable Fay, Elizabeth Fisk, Bridget Harwood, Elizabeth Harwood, Martha Montague, Marcy Newton, Baty Pratt, Elizabeth Pratt, Hannah Rice, Experience Richardson, Elizabeth Roberts, Marcy Robinson, Ann Safford, Elizabeth Scott, Eleanor Smith, Sarah Story, Hepzibah Whipple, Prudence Whipple, Martha Wickwire.

Of six of the names in this list, it may be interesting to know the number of individuals of the same name on the church roll for the first century of its existence. This enumeration is as follows: Sears, twelve; Fassett, thirteen; Safford, sixteen; Fay, seventeen; Scott, twenty; Harwood, fifty-one; Robinson, fifty-six. Of names not on the list of original members, instances of highest enumeration of individuals are as follows: Hubbell, and Nichols, each, twelve; Bingham, thirteen; Hinsdill, sixteen; Hathaway, nineteen; Henry, twenty-one; Hicks, twenty-five.

II. THE WESTFIELD CHURCH AND PASTOR. — At the first business meeting of the church after its organization, a standing committee was appointed.

"Chose brethren Joseph Safford, Elisha Field, and John Fassett as helps to examine into persons' principles who offer to join themselves unto this church; and also to provide preaching."

At the business meeting May 24, 1763,

"Gave the Rev. Mr. Jedidiah Dewey a call to the work of the ministry among us."

Ministers were not so numerous then as now. Of Mr. Dewey they had heard, and that there was a possibility of obtaining him, and for him they sent.

But they were in pursuit not only of a minister, but of more members also; they had already absorbed two churches, and now they essayed a third, the church at Westfield, Massachusetts. They, however, preferred to take minister, church, and all.

Westfield Council. — That they might proceed very orderly, an ecclesiastical council was employed. The particulars of this council will be sufficiently given here by inserting the minutes respecting it, preserved upon the Bennington church records. They are as follows : —

" *The act of the Council at Westfield, August* 14, 1763.

" At a council convened at Westfield by letters missive [1] from the church of Christ at Bennington : Present, John Palmer, pastor of the church of Christ in Scotland (Connecticut); Israel Hawley, pastor of the church of Christ in Suffield (Connecticut); Jonathan Underwood and Stephen Remington, messengers of the church at Suffield; the church at Bennington being present by three delegated brethren ; together with the church at Westfield. The council was received into fellowship. Chose John Palmer for moderator, and, after solemn prayer to Almighty God for divine assistance and direction, proceeded : —

" The first thing laid before us was the proposed contract between the church at Westfield and the church at Nine Partners, respecting the church at Westfield removing to Nine Partners, and becoming one church with them; and in the consideration thereof the council found said contract was made void by consent

1 The assembling of this council was a laborious undertaking. Carrying letters by post was then unknown in these parts. In 1783, the Governor and Council of Vermont established a weekly post (twenty years after the summoning of the Westfield council) between Bennington and Albany, N. Y. The next year the Legislature established five post-offices; one each at Bennington, Rutland, Brattleborough, Windsor, and Newbury. Between these several places a mail was transmitted once a week each way, and Anthony Haswell, Esq., of Bennington, was Postmaster General.—(Thompson's Vermont.) By a church record of 1780, of Bennington church, a council was called, and a messenger appointed to go in person and carry the letters missive. The messengers of the Westfield council must have gone in person with the letters missive to the invited Connecticut churches.

both of the church at Westfield, and the church at Nine Partners.[1]

"Second, the request of the church at Bennington to the church at Westfield, namely, that the church at Bennington and the church at Westfield unite and become one church under Mr. Jedidiah Dewey, pastor of the church at Westfield; and, in consideration of the circumstances of both churches, the council thought advisable for the church at Westfield to answer the above said request, which they did by solemn convenanting according to the above proposal.

"1. The church at Westfield consented to join with the church at Bennington by solemn vote; 2. The church at Bennington did the same by vote; 3. Both together signified their consent to become one church under the pastoral care and charge of said Jedidiah Dewey, pastor, with uplifted hands before God.

JOHN PALMER.
ISRAEL HAWLEY.
JONATHAN UNDERWOOD.
STEPHEN REMINGTON."

The following further minute touching these proceedings is on the Bennington records: —

"September 12, 1763. — The church of Christ, in Bennington, being legally warned, met together; and, after prayers, the committee which was sent to Westfield made their return with their doings; and the church unanimously voted their concurrence with the above said council, and the doings of the above said council, with uplifted hands."

III. EARLY GROWTH OF THE CHURCH. — The Bennington church was now fairly on its way. The Sunderland brethren, the Hardwick brethren, the Westfield brethren, and those here from Amherst, Mass., Newint, Conn., and other parishes, — who in those parishes respectively felt feeble and doubtful, and here also in the infancy

---

[1] A family tradition has Mr. Dewey preaching to the church at Nine Partners temporarily at this time.

of the settlement and the embryo state of its institutions
had but just made a beginning — were now united together in one church, in the land of their choice and where
many of them expected to pass the remainder of their
days ; where the whole land was theirs, and the future invited them to labor and hardship, but with the prospect
of enlargement and ample reward. They had obtained a
minister in whom they had great confidence. At once we
see in the brief and imperfect church records new life-
startings. In the same month, September, 1763, after the
ratification at Bennington of the doings of the council at
Westfield, we find a record of the return to full agreement
and fellowship with the church of a brother who had been
under discipline. He had departed from his profession
of faith and covenant with the church " by denying its
article of baptism and rejecting his own infant baptism ; "
but he now returned, having surrendered his objections, —
or his objections having surrendered him, — and this breach
in the fellowship of the church was healed.

In the next month, " October 2, then Abraham Newton was received into full fellowship or communion with this church ; and
also the wife of Benajah Rude, from the church at Newint, was
received into this church."

Thus onward. Successive entries in the records, at short
intervals, inform us that the church grew ; there being frequent and ofttimes numerous additions to it. Take one
page of the records as an example : —

" Jan. 3, 1765. — Then Ebenezer Wood, Timothy Pratt, Mary
Story, wife to Stephen Story, and Margaret Harwood, wife to
Peter Harwood, were all received to full communion with this
church." " Jan. 11, 1765. — Then John Smith, Matthew Scott,
Thomas Henderson, Esther Pratt, wife to Samuel Pratt, and Mary
Fassett, wife to John Fassett, were all received to full com-
munion with this church." " March 3, 1765. — Then Peter Har-

4

wood was received to full communion with this church." "April 4, 1765. — Then Rebecca Robinson, wife to Leonard Robinson, Hannah Abbott, Bershaba Scott, wife to Oliver Scott, Joseph Richardson, Hepzibah Wood, Marcy Robinson, and Timothy Abbott were all received into full communion with this church."

There are preserved upon the records, imperfect as they must be, the names of seventy-two individuals added to the church during the ministry of Mr. Dewey. Of these, nearly half, thirty-six, were received in 1765. That must have been, therefore, a year of religious revival and great spiritual prosperity. This was the fourth year or there-about of the settlement of the town.

From lists extant there appear to have been by June, 1765, about one hundred men in the town. About fifty men, according to the records, became connected with the church. The condition of the community at this time is thus stated in the " Vermont Historical Magazine " : —

" By the year 1765 a large portion of the town had become oc-cupied by industrious settlers from Massachusetts and Connecti-cut, who had cleared much of the land, erected dwelling-houses and barns, with mills, opened and worked highways, and estab-lished schools for the instruction of children and youth, and were living in a comfortable and thriving condition."

Bancroft, in his "History of the United States," referring to a letter of Gov. Hutchinson to Gov. Pownal of July 10, 1765, speaks of Bennington thus : —

"Men of New England of a superior sort, etc., etc., had formed already a community of sixty-seven families, in as many houses, with an ordained minister; had elected their own munic-ipal officers; formed three several public schools; set their meeting-house among their primeval forests of beech and maple; and, in a word, enjoyed the flourishing state which springs from rural industry, intelligence, and unaffected piety." [1]

---

[1] Quoted in Vermont Hist. Mag.

The Rev. Mr. Avery, successor to Mr. Dewey, in referring to the time of his pastorate generally, says: —

"There have been seasons of especial awakening and attention here, and in the judgment of charity a happy number have been renewed and added to the Lord. This circumstance has contributed not a little to the gaining them respect, and even fame abroad as a religious people."

In the year 1765 the controversy of the inhabitants with New York about their land titles began to be a matter of public concern; this would naturally interrupt and prevent for a long time to come special attention to religion.

IV. ROLL OF THE CHURCH FOR ITS FIRST CENTURY. — With regard to the roll of the church for the first century, it must be stated that it is far from complete. A covenant has been found among some papers thrown into the street, which would seem to have been adopted and signed at or near the time of the first formation of the church. This paper doubtless got among the condemned pile entirely by mistake. So soon as it was discovered it was preserved with religious care. It is interesting and comprehensive, but too long to be inserted here. A portion of the document, as found, had been torn off and lost; perhaps one-third of the signatures were on this lost portion. Not all the names on the part of the covenant preserved were on the church records, so much of them as has been preserved. The same may be true of that portion of the sheet which had been lost. The names on that lost portion of this covenant may not have been placed elsewhere on any church record; and the fact, whether they were member of the church or not, it may now be impossible to asrtain. There are names, on the records of the ? Separate Church, of persons known to have be31.

here and yet not on the Bennington church records. Such persons, at least some of them, were in all probability members of the Bennington church, but because their names were on that part of the covenant torn off and lost, or for some other reason, they have never been put upon any record of the church. John Burnham, who was with the autumn immigration of families in the first half year of the settlement of the town, and on the committee appointed at the first proprietors' meeting to choose a place to set the meeting-house, and who was in the military company of Captain John Fassett in 1764, has his name among the Newint church signatures, but not on the Bennington church records. During the whole of the Rev. Mr. Marsh's ministry, a period of about fifteen years, no records were kept, so far as is now known, excepting some letters of dismission and recommendation of individuals kept on file, and some names of persons received to the membership of this church, jotted down here and there upon detached pieces of paper. All the names thus accessible have been gathered up, and arranged in order in a book. Every document that could yield any assistance has been laid hold of with incredible patience and zeal by Mr. Haswell, late clerk of the church, and so far as was thus possible the omissions in the records have been supplied. In this way many names are preserved which would otherwise have been lost.

The roll of members thus gathered yields the following analysis of statistics for the first century of the church : —

Number of members at the organization of the church, anccluding five members added on that day . . . 57
rural 1.

Admitted during the pastorate of the Rev. J. Dewey : —

1763	2	1768	3
1764	4	1773	3
1765	36	1774	2
1766	4	1775	5
1767	5	1776	8

Total 72

Without a pastor : —

1779	1	1780	7

Total 8

Pastorate of the Rev. David Avery : —

1782 1

Without a pastor, — Messrs. Burton and Wood preaching temporarily : —

1784	40	1786	3
1785	4		

Total 47

Pastorate of the Rev. Job Swift, D.D. : —

1786	5	1790	8
1787	4	1792	2
1789	9	1795	2

Total 30

Without a pastor, — The Rev. Messrs. Davis and Spaulding preaching temporarily : —

1803 93

Pastorate of the Rev. Daniel Marsh : —

1811	38	1817	22
1812	1	1818	1
1813	1	1819	, 1810.
1816	7		3.

Total . . . . 77 , 1816.
, 9, 1831.

4*

Pastorate of the Rev. Absalom Peters, D.D. : —

1820	33	1823	3
1821	13	1824	7
1822	10	1825	5

Total 71

Pastorate of the Rev. Daniel A. Clark : —

1826	5	1829	6
1827	101	1830	11
1828	3		

Total 126

Pastorate of the Rev. E. W. Hooker, D.D. : —

1832	18	1838	2
1833	14	1839	7
1834	90	1840	8
1835	5	1841	5
1836	7	1843	14
1837	2	1844	2

Total 174

Pastorate of the Rev. J. J. Abbott : —

1845	1	1846	3

Total 4

Pastorate of the Rev. R. C. Hand : —

1848	5	1851	10
1849	6	1852	10
1850	10		

Total 41

Pastorate of the Rev. Isaac Jennings : —

1853	11	1858	31
1854	12	1859	1
1855	17	1860	3
1856	7	1861	2
rural 1.	50	1862	

V. Officers during the First Century.

Jedidiah Dewey — became pastor of the Bennington church by the action of the Westfield Council, August 14, 1763 ; deceased December 21, 1778.

David Avery — was installed May 3, 1780 ; dismissed June 17, 1783.

Job Swift, D.D. — was installed May 31, 1786 ; dismissed June 7, 1801.

Daniel Marsh. — By town records, Society recommended " the committee to hire Mr. Marsh for the year ensuing," at a meeting on March 27, 1805 ; also at a meeting May 12, 1806, requested the church " to unite with Mr. Marsh in calling a council for his installation." He was dismissed April 25, 1820.

Daniel A. Clark — was installed June 13, 1826 ; dismissed October 12, 1830.

Edward W. Hooker, D.D. — was installed February 21, 1832 ; dismissed May 14, 1844.

J. J. Abbott — was installed April 26, 1845 ; dismissed August 17, 1847.

Richard C. Hand — was installed January 20, 1848 ; dismissed November 26, 1852.

Isaac Jennings — commenced his ministry here June 1, 1853, and was installed September 21, 1853.

ˉer Harwood, Safford,	} June 9, 1768,	Resigned Dec. 14, 1770. Died in 1775.
ˉinson, ˉd.	} May 22, 1789,	Died May 19, 1813. R'md to Malone, N.Y., 1810. Died March 13, 1813.
1810 .		ˉch 4, 1816.
	Total 77	ˉ9, 1831.

4*

Jotham French,	April 12, 1816,	Died April 30, 1825.
Stephen Hinsdill,	⎱ May 10, 1822,	Dismissed to Hinsdillville Pres. ch. Nov. 19, 1834.
Erwin Safford,	⎰	Removed to Philadelphia, Pa., Sept., 1830.
Noadiah Swift,	Sept. 23, 1831,	Died March 21, 1860.
Aaron Hubbell,	Dec. 15, 1834,	Died Dec. 26, 1844.
Samuel Chandler, John F. Robinson,	⎱ Sept. 19, 1845. ⎰	Died Jan. 25, 1862.
George Lyman, John W. Vail, H. H. Harwood,	⎱ Feb. 14, 1862. ⎰	

CLERKS.

John Fassett, Dec. 3, 1762.
Jeremiah Bingham, Jan. 13, 1779,
Jonathan Robinson, Jan. 28,1785.
Aaron Robinson, Jan. 24, 1820.
Wm. Southworth, Dec. 12, 1846.
Wm. Haswell, Sept. 28, 1849.

There is no record of the appointment of deacons at the organization of the church. There were deacons on the ground already, — deacons of the other churches which had removed hither, and were merged in the Bennington church, and also other deacons. Upon the church records no deacons appear for the period 1775–1789 ; Eleazer Harwood had resigned in 1778 ; Joseph Safford died in 1775 ; the next election, according to the records, was in 1789 ; the probability is, that during this interval, 1775–1789, Joseph Bingham and Nathaniel Harmon were either acting deacons, or had been elected and the election not recorded. They both bore the title of deacon, and were members of the church, and resident here at that time, and both excellent men. Deacon Joseph Bingham died November 4, 1787, in the seventy-seventh year of his age ; and Deacon Harmon, in November, 1792, aged eighty.

VI. Interesting Memoranda. — Of the fourteen adult persons who settled Bennington, all with the exception of

one, who died at an early age, were or became church
members. The fourteen were: Bridget Harwood, Zacha-
riah Harwood, Eleazer and Elizabeth Harwood, Peter and
Margaret Harwood; Leonard and Rebecca Robinson, Samuel and Hannah Robinson; Samuel and Baty Pratt, Timothy
and Elizabeth Pratt.

The other members of the pioneer company were eight
children whose united ages were less than twenty-seven
years. One of these, an infant child of Mrs. Hannah Robinson, died; of the other seven, two: Stephen Harwood,
and Persis Robinson (Safford), united with this church;
the other five married and removed from Bennington. Samuel Robinson, Sr.,—who appears to have brought his family
early in the first half year of the settlement, though not
with the very first immigration of families, —had six sons
and three daughters, all of whom became members of this
church. Mrs. Bridget Harwood's four sons, who came to
Bennington, became also, with herself, members of this
church.

Mrs. Bridget Harwood was the mother of nine children.
At the time of her immigration to Bennington her husband
had deceased; also one child in infancy. As already noticed, Samuel Robinson, Sr., had nine children, who came
to Bennington; these composed his family, one child having died at eleven years of age. One, Samuel, Jr., with
his family, preceded his father a little time in the order of
removal hither; his father, the real pioneer, being detained
as to actual removal with his family, a little, by important
business. Deacon Joseph Safford, the father of eleven
children, came with his family in the second company. In
1837 — seventy-six years afterward — a genealogical record
of these three families (the Harwoods, the Robinsons, and
the Saffords), and their descendants — including of course
such persons as married any of the list — was published

by Mrs. Sarah (Harwood) Robinson, one of these descendants. Upon this genealogical record — the count being made with perhaps not absolute accuracy, but nearly so — there is found an aggregate of some two thousand one hundred and thirty-six individuals.

CHAPTER IV.

SEPARATISM.

WHEN we learn by the records that the church in Bennington was formed by the union of the Sunderland church and the Hardwick church, and that soon afterward the Bennington church obtained a pastor by taking to itself the Westfield church and its pastor, we are curious to know if these churches of Sunderland and Hardwick and Westfield left no churches behind them. Upon inquiry we find that those towns, respectively, have, meantime, had churches bearing the same titles, which know nothing of any removal to Bennington. These churches date their origin far back of that of the Bennington church, and they have never ceased to bear the designation that they now do, and to occupy the places that they now occupy. How is it, then, that we find upon our Bennington records mention of churches of the same name removing hither and being swallowed up in the Bennington church? The explanation is, that the churches which removed to Bennington were "Separate" churches, irregularly organized in the view of the churches then and there existing, and therefore by them never recognized as churches of Christ. Some members of the old church believed that it had departed from its original faith and order, and on that account refused to commune with it, and established a separate church. The original churches in several instances excommunicated those separating members, and in all cases, it is believed, refused

to recognize the separate organization as a church of Christ.
A sad state of things, the reader will say, for a Christian
community. It could not have been otherwise than full of
trials to all concerned. But, as we shall see, God overruled
it for good. Let me adduce some portions of the records
of the church still at Sunderland, the original church
founded in 1718. The first introduction of the subject into
these records appears to have been in a vote on March 3,
1749 : —

"*Voted*, That those persons who have separated themselves
from this church, and absented themselves from the public worship and ordinances among us, be desired and required to appear
and attend upon a meeting of this church, that the church may
have an opportunity to know from them the reasons of their ab-
senting themselves from them; and also what doctrines they hold
and advance."

In compliance with this vote, a subsequent meeting was
held according to due notice. Some of the Separates attended, and asked more time; more time was given by
adjourning the meeting. At this adjourned meeting a paper
was read on behalf of some or all the separating members,
giving their reasons for their course, which, as was to have
been expected, were not satisfactory to the old church.
Others separated, and their reasons, too, were demanded by
more voting of the old church. Divers more meetings were
held, with no favorable results toward bringing back the
separating members. Under date of August 24, 1753,
some four and a half years after the first proceedings, we
find this record : —

"*Voted*, The following declaration agreeable to the advice of the
neighboring ministers, called in to discourse with persons separating, etc. : —

"Whereas, ―――― ―――― have gone out from us, renouncing
our communion, and thereby have made it manifest they do not
belong to us; and we, having used many means to reclaim them,

and waited long upon them, and they still persisting 'obstinately in their separation from us, we now declare : they are now cut off from all the privileges of this church, and are not to be esteemed members hereof, and that we have no further care of them as members of Christ's Visible Church."

At the same meeting it was also, —

"*Voted*, That we judge it to be unlawful and dangerous for persons to frequent, and make a practice of attending upon, and especially to join in worship at, the meetings of the Separatists, and a just matter of offence to this church." "Which votes on the Lord's day following were read before the congregation ; and the pastor, in the name of the Lord Jesus Christ, the great head of the church, publicly declared before the congregation, agreeably to the vote of the church, that all and every one of the persons whose names are mentioned in said vote are cut off from all privileges in this church, and are no more to be esteemed members of Christ's visible church — praying that the proceedings of the church may be, ' for the destruction of the flesh in them, that the spirit may be saved in the day of the Lord.' " [1]

Fifteen persons are named in the above vote of excommunication, four of whom appear upon the roll of the Bennington church.

Many of the old churches did not proceed to equal extremities. The church in Hardwick did not.[2] The church in Westfield did not, in the case of Mr. Dewey. But even without the additional hardships of excommunication, this process of separation must have been attended by many painful circumstances both to the old church and the separating members.

These ecclesiastical troubles were a principal cause, without which the early settlers of Bennington would not have

---

[1] The original Sunderland church records were destroyed, but the church appointed Deacon John Montague, a man of extraordinary memory, who had previously kept the records, to restore them. The above extracts are from the restored records.

[2] The Rev. Mr. Paige's Centennial Discourse.

come hither in the numbers and at the time they did, — as religious troubles were the principal cause of the Pilgrims coming from the Old World to the New, in the first settlement of New England. In saying this, it is at the same time not intended to ignore the interest of secular adventure encouraged by the prospect of fertile lands, the extensive possession of which in fee-simple might be obtained at a trifling pecuniary cost.

This Separate movement attained vast proportions in the country. It excited a profound concern at the time, and has been studied with deep interest by the ecclesiastical historian. There is space here for only a glance at it. It was a vital part of the Great Awakening of a century and a quarter ago. There had obtained in the churches a vast amount of formality. The "half-way covenant" had been extensively adopted by them. At length the numbers became formidable of those who viewed this innovation as a fatal departure from sound doctrine and true Christian order. Many were ready to welcome Whitfield, with his unwonted power in the pulpit as a revivalist and reformer of the churches, and many more were awakened by him and led to enlist with great zeal in the cause of religious reformation. Edwards irresistibly assailed the formality and laxness of church usage with strong doctrine and ponderous arguments from the Word of God.

Many extravagances, the natural result, under the circumstances, of so profound a religious excitement, came into vogue. James Davenport sought to imitate Whitfield, and then to go beyond him, and did surpass him, in intemperate zeal, much more than he surpassed moderate men. Many staid churches and many staid ministers opposed the revival movement as a whole. The churches were divided into two antagonistic parties, one for new measures, the

other against them, — the "New Lights" and the "Old
Lights." The question came up whether it was right for
these "New-Light" preachers to be abroad, in other ministers' parishes, stirring up so much excitement, and being
the occasion of discord.   It became the practice to perform
itinerant labors on the part of the more earnest pastors.
These did not confine their efforts to their own parishes,
but "went everywhere preaching the word." Also lay-ex-
horters were by the friends of the innovation encouraged, —
persons with gifts and zeal, but without liberal education
and without regular ecclesiastical license.

In Connecticut these disorders, so termed, were made
the subject of a prohibitory statute, enacted in 1742 by the
General Assembly of the Colony of Connecticut, — not
without the consent and approval of some of the clergy.
By this statute ministers were forbidden to preach in any
parish other than their own, without invitation of the pastor
or people, under the penalty of forfeiting all title to the
benefit of the laws for the support of the ministry.   And it
was provided that a regular information against any minister to this effect should, without trial of the fact, work such
a forfeiture, and bar the collection of rates for his support.
By another section of the act, all exhorters were forbidden
to exercise their gifts, unless permitted by the parish authorities ; and all strangers, of whatever ecclesiastical dignity from out of the colony (of Connecticut), presuming to
teach, preach, and publicly exhort without such permission
of pastor or parish, were to be sent as vagrants from constable to constable out of the bounds of Connecticut.[1]

The "New-Light" minorities in the churches would not
endure this.   They maintained their right to hear such
preachers and worship God in such a manner as they
deemed to be most in accordance with the word of God,

[1] Article of the Rev. R. C. Learned in the "New Englander" for May, 1853.

and they did this the more earnestly because they believed
themselves alone to adhere to the genuine principles and
order of the original New England churches. The number
of Separate churches increased rapidly under this treatment. A general meeting of the "New Lights" was called
at Stonington, Conn., in 1754; elders and brethren from
forty churches met there, namely: twenty-four in Connecticut, eight in Massachusetts, seven in Rhode Island,
and one in Long Island.[1]

It was not long before another enactment was adopted
by the General Assembly of Connecticut, which added
much to the burdens and embarrassments of the "New-
Light" party. There had been a law that all who soberly
dissented from the prevailing order might, upon taking
certain oaths, be allowed to establish separate worship un-
molested; though still liable to be taxed for the support of
the parish minister. This law was repealed. Thus the
worship in the original society came to be still more odi-
ously known as the Established worship, or the worship of
the Standing Order.[2] The Separates came at length to call
themselves "Strict Congregationalists."

In this notice of persecuting laws those of Connecticut
have been adduced. In Massachusetts the case was different. There no laws were specially enacted against
Separate itinerant preachers and lay exhorters, but the
existing laws did not exempt Separates from paying taxes
to the parish minister and for building and repairing parish
meeting-houses. Neither did the Massachusetts laws give
to Separate congregations any legal power to collect taxes
or subscriptions for their own expenses.

Moreover, while it is true that many of the members of

---

[1] Backus' History. See, also, Contributions to the Ecclesiastical History of
Connecticut.

[2] Mr. Learned's article.

the Bennington church, perhaps most, came, in its incipient history, from Massachusetts, its ecclesiastical affinities appear to have especially identified it with the Connecticut Separate churches and ministers. "Father" Marshall, who used to pass this way frequently, and appears to have felt quite at home here, was pastor of the first Separate church that was formed, that in Canterbury, Conn. The Rev. John Palmer, who was repeatedly on ecclesiastical councils in this town, was pastor of one of the Separate churches in Connecticut, that of Scotland parish, in Windsor township. He was member of the council that was convened, by letters-missive from this church, in Westfield, to consider and act upon the question of the union of that church with the Bennington church. He was member of the council called here in 1770 to give advice in the difficulty about the duty of communicating for the support of the gospel. He was here also either as member of a council or informally to advise in the difficulties concerning Mr. Avery. He was a worthy and excellent Christian minister. He officiated to the Separate church in Scotland parish, doubtless with acceptance, through the long period of fifty-seven years,—1750 to 1807,—when he deceased. Universally spoken of as a man of real piety, he was imprisoned under the Connecticut laws before mentioned four months in Hartford for preaching. The other Separate churches called to sit in the Westfield council, and their pastors, belonged to Connecticut: Plainfield, Alexander Miller, minister; and Suffield, Israel Holley, minister.

A large part of the First Church in Norwich, Conn., drew off from its minister and met for worship in another place.[1] Thirty male members, including one deacon and a large number of females, left the Old Standing Order Church at about the same time. Others soon followed.

[1] Backus.

5*

Among these were some of the most wealthy and influential men in the town. The Separates and their friends finally outvoted the old church in the town meetings, and declared that they would no longer pay the minister's rates, as they were conscientiously opposed to the union of church and state. But upon a complaint entered, the General Assembly interfered, and they were taxed, by a special act, to support the Rev. Dr. Lord and his society. Refusing to pay the tax, they were imprisoned. For this cause as many as forty persons, men and women, were imprisoned in a single year.[1] Many of the early settlers of Bennington were from Norwich and its vicinity. The Newint Separate Church, so prominently represented in Bennington, belonged to a part of the town of Norwich of that day.

Deacon Joseph Safford and some others among the earliest members of this church belonged to a Separate church in Newint, Conn., and brought, if not the church, at least the records of it, with them to this town.

---

1 Historical Notices by the Rev. F. Denison, quoted in a foot-note by Hovey. Life and Times of Backus, p. 42.

CHAPTER V.

FINANCIAL CONTROVERSY. — The first great trial of the church, and perhaps the greatest of an internal character, was occasioned by the question, — how to pay the minister?

The Bennington church, as a church, never took any position identical with Separate churches more extreme than the actual reformation which was finally accepted by the great body of the Congregational churches of the country. In this it evinced the shrewd indomitable common sense of its leading minds. There were, however, individual members of the church, who, upon some points at least, were extreme, even factious, relatively to the Bennington church. They were not without serious influence in the church, and yet they appear to have been always in a minority when it came to voting. They had the more influence on one point in particular, that of a church member's duty with respect to the pecuniary necessities of public worship, because the Separate theory on this point was susceptible of a pretty sharp definition. It may be stated in the words of the Separate Ecclesiastical Council convened here in 1770, on this subject : —

" The Society is by no means to be allowed to control or govern the church in the affair."

At the same time there was in the Bennington church that common sense or practical — or worldly — wisdom which saw that in the secularities of public worship the world would certainly have a hand, and which reasoned that there might be so much jealousy of bringing the church under bondage to the world, as to fail to obtain all that lawfully might be of co-operation both of the world's people and of the civil law.

But the *extreme* Separates had on their side the moral weight of the fact that the Bennington church was formed out of *bona fide* Separate churches; that many had joined its ranks from other churches of the same character; that its pastor was thoroughly of Separate origin, — its ecclesiastical councils were made up from Separate churches, and the council of 1770 rather sided with the extreme members than with the church. At any rate they were unceasingly active, and in several instances inflexible to the last.

That which appears to have brought the opposing parties to a decisive struggle was the action of an adjourned meeting of the congregation, Feb. 8, 1768. At this meeting the following resolves were voted : —

1. That the church and society should stand all in an equal right about proposing any method, or voting in any meeting about the support of the gospel for the present year. 2. Chose Moses Robinson clerk for the same meeting and for this year. 3. Chose Stephen Fay, Samuel Safford, and Moses Robinson assessors. 4. Chose Stephen Fay treasurer. 5. Chose James Walbridge and Henry Walbridge collectors; then made a subscription binding in common law in order to secure to Mr. Dewey fifty pounds for the present year."

This, it will be observed, was a meeting, not of the church, but of the congregation, but church members acted in it and with it; three out of five appointed to office in the meeting were church members. This course of members of the churches was not suffered by the extreme Separates to pass unchallenged. Against these members of the church active in this meeting a complaint was soon brought in church meeting, and the attempt was made to convict them of violating the principles of the Separate churches, with respect to their independence of the Society and of the civil power.[1]

Had the complaining party been above suspicion of sinister intent their case would have stood better. It was the refusal of some of these, and perhaps of some others, to pay their share toward the minister's salary, which was the proximate cause of the action complained of. The salary was not secured; and hence the effort in the adjourned meeting of the congregation to hit upon some expedient that should accomplish this result. Most if not all of the brethren who complained so bitterly of that action were themselves remiss. Their remissness dates far back upon the records, as appears by the following entry: —

"June 19, 1766. — Then the church being met by appointment acted on the following articles, namely, 1. To send brothers James Breakenridge, Henry Walbridge, and John Wood to those brethren that did not attend the church meeting, and had not settled or paid their proportion or sums for the year past with Mr. Dewey, that they forthwith settle the above said sum or sums; and that they appear on Friday the twenty-sixth day of this instant at the adjourned meeting at the house of Mr. Dewey to answer to their conduct. 2. Voted, that those persons who do not settle and pay the sums of their equality with Mr. Dewey for his support within the time appointed by the church and society forthwith give security for the above said sums, and it shall be no offence."

Here we have the party of the first part aggrieved because the party of the second part would not do their share to-

---

1 The probability is that the error of these complaining brethren was not in their professed anxiety lest the church should lose its proper control in spiritual affairs, so much as in their want of discrimination as to what was purely secular in the matter, and therefore not to be a bone of contention in the church.

ward the salary of Mr. Dewey ; and the party of the second
part aggrieved because the party of the first part had
secured the adoption of church *and society* measures, and
some aid, if necessary, of the civil law, to relieve the financial difficulties of the parish. The result was a long church
controversy.

It is believed by some of Mr. Dewey's descendants that
he, in consideration of the valuable property called " the
minister's right" being settled upon him, declined, for a
while at least, other compensation ; they have a tradition in
the family to this effect. If so, Mr. Dewey could not have
begun to receive any compensation from the church and
society until near the time of the above vote. To suppose
that brethren would refuse to pay their part toward the
small amount then proposed to be raised as a salary for
Mr. Dewey, and at the first attempt, or nearly the first attempt, reflects seriously upon their goodness of character.
Whether they were afflicted with the malady not unknown
to mankind, a chronic disinclination to part with one's
money for a public good object, or whether they deemed it
a violation of their consciences to contribute anything to
the treasury of the church so long as it adopted financial
expedients inconsistent with their notions of Christian
duty ; or whether their course was the result of both these
causes combined, there grew up an irreconcilable difficulty
between the church and these brethren. The leaders among
them were under church censure from time to time, and
finally were excommunicated. For a long time, however,
they remained in the church, as it knew to its cost. New
complaints were brought ; new grievances there were ; new
offences for church action. All their church meetings, and
all their debates as to what was according to their principles
of freedom of conscience, and the church's true independence of and separation from the world, availed nothing to

settle the difficulty, or to remove the main difficulty of the delinquency of these brethren toward the salary. Among other entries upon the records of a like character, let us notice one under date of August, 17, 1769 : —

"The church being met by adjournment, and the meeting being opened by prayer, took into consideration the case of those brethren who are behind in their communication to the support of the gospel, and voted that if they shall.pay thirteen shillings to fifteen it shall be satisfactory."

It would seem that the delinquent brethren did not all of them now pay the " thirteen shillings to fifteen," for there are recorded actions of discipline in their case under subsequent dates.

Glimpses in the records show us that the sacrament of the Lord's supper was not administered for some time on account of the progress of this war in the church. Infant baptisms, however, were not omitted, whatever the state of the church might be, whether cold or lukewarm or divided. Some stayed away from public worship because of grievances.

At length a council of churches was called, 1770. Its result is on the records. On the whole it appears rather to condemn the church for calling to its aid the society as prominently as it did, according to the action of the adjourned meeting of the congregation on Feb. 8, 1768. It was a council of Separate churches. Apparently no good effect followed. Matters waxed worse and worse. One and another became the subject of church discipline. Thus they went on until January, 1780, fourteen years after the first appearance of this difficulty upon the records. Then we find this hopeful indication : —

"The church being met by appointment, the meeting being opened by prayer, TOOK INTO CONSIDERATION THE CIRCUMSTANCE OF

THE COVENANT BEING VERY MUCH SHATTERED AND TORN. VOTED, TO SIGN THE COVENANT NEWLY DRAFTED AND TO RENEW COVENANT WITH GOD AND WITH ONE ANOTHER." This return to the solemn renewal of covenant obligation, and to the enjoyment of the presence of the Holy Spirit, must have been a relief as delightful as it was salutary.

The old covenant so " much shattered and torn" was probably the one among the papers of the church on file ; that newly drafted and signed, the paper in the possession of John Fay.

With regard to the ultimate result as to the method of securing the salary, it may be stated that no invariable rule was attained. Society meetings and town meetings for some years played an important part in this business. The extreme Separatist method was never adopted. The more usual way was, to obtain as many as would consent to bring in their tax lists, and let the society or town rate upon them a tax sufficient for the salary and other expenses of public worship. Those who voluntarily brought in their lists to be taxed were liable to have their tax collected by law if they neglected to pay it at the right time. Church discipline upon members delinquent in this matter fell into disuse ; so it is inferred from the fact that cases of discipline of this kind do not afterward appear upon the records. This financial question came up again on the building of the new meeting-house, and created again a profound excitement.

II. CASE OF THE REV. DAVID' AVERY. — There were also troublous times to this church in connection with the ministry of the Rev. David Avery. This difficulty followed fast upon the heels of the other ; and it is quite possible some of the disturbing influence of the old trouble remained. The settlement of Mr. Avery here was commenced with a foreshadowed opposition, which increased until the termination of his ministry, June 17, 1783. One person only was added to the church; the Lord's supper was celebrated once only, and that not without opposition on the alleged singular ground of the impropriety of the measure because of the divided state of the church.

A pamphlet of fifty-five pages is extant, with this title : " A Narrative of the Rise and Progress of the Difficulties which have issued in a separation between the Minister and People of Bennington, 1783. With a Valedictory Address by the Rev. David Avery, V. D. M." He was evidently a man of superior talents and accomplishments. Governor Tichenor — who was proverbial for his graceful politeness, so much so that, having come from New Jersey, he obtained the not very graceful sobriquet of " The Jersey Slick" — used to say that the opposition sent Mr. Avery away because he walked to church arm in arm with his wife. There is some reason to think, however, that with all his acquirements he lacked humility, and, therefore, was less fitted than otherwise he might have been to build up and unite the people. In his communication to them respecting his dismission he exalts his official prerogatives, lays all the blame upon the opposition, loftily pities their weaknesses, and rebukes their wrong-doing, inasmuch as they receive the word at his lips with no more meekness ; and, which is most galling of all, derides their Separate origin.

As a ceremony of installation, Mr. Avery adopted the novel method of pronouncing, in the presence of the council, an address, first, to the church, and then to the congregation, solemnly declaring his acceptance of the pastorate in accordance with their request. In the address to the church occurs this paragraph : —

"Inasmuch as I have been duly ordained an officer in Christ's kingdom by the laying on of the hands of the Presbytery, whereby

6

I am invested with full power and authority to administer sealing ordinances, and to do all the duties of a minister in God's house; and inasmuch as I can receive no new, nor even any accession of, power, by a re-ordination, I do now, without some of the usual ceremonies of an ordination, thus publicly acknowledge myself to be under the most sacred vows to exercise my office, and to do all the duties of the pastor of this church," etc.

The "re-ordination" refers to the doctrine which had some currency among the radical Separates that ordination by the laying on of the hands of the Presbytery was a violation of the power of the brotherhood, and therefore it was their duty to require one who had been presbyterially ordained, and who had come to be their pastor, to be re-ordained by the laying on of the hands of the lay-members of the church. The Bennington church, as such, never received this doctrine; but from Mr. Avery's narrative it appears that, in the course of the difficulties with him, this was seriously pressed by some of the members.

A mutual council, half of Strict Congregationalists and half of Standing Order Congregationalists, was first called upon the difficulties. The Strict Congregational half failed to come, and the council did not proceed. Next, an *ex-parte* council of Strict Congregationalists was called, and failed to come. At length, a mutual council of Strict Congregationalists was called, and came. In this council the aggrieved portion of the church appeared as plaintiff, and the church itself as defendant, on the side of Mr. Avery. The chief burden of the complaint was alleged departure from the faith by Mr. Avery in his preaching, three specifications being presented. The council sustained Mr. Avery and the church in every particular, — advising the church, however, to accept Mr. Avery's resignation if he should offer it; which he immediately did.

In his address of resignation, he says, " One half of this

church are divided from me without any prospect of my recovering them." This must have been meant in a numerical sense; a leading personal influence in the community sided with Mr. Avery, and had, or carried, the council with it.

Among his more ardent admirers here were some of the most influential members of the church or congregation,—such men as Governor Moses Robinson, Hon. Isaac Tichenor, Dr. Jonas Fay.

When he was dismissed from Bennington and left the place, the troubles here on his account appear to have ceased. Soon afterward the church was again blessed with a revival of religion, in which numbers were added to its communion, of whom the names of forty-seven are upon the records. Its wounds were doubtless healed, and it was once more in the enjoyment of health and vigor.

III. THE SLAVERY QUESTION. — Mr. Avery brought with his family to town a colored woman, and he insisted on his right to hold her as a slave. This was one of the serious objections urged against him, and which created much dissatisfaction in the church.[1] But the persons dissatisfied on this account appear to have been in the minority.

One who had been for several years an active and influential member of the church, being frequently on important committees, having his children baptized, etc., was placed under church discipline during the ministry of Mr. Avery: —

" For withdrawing himself from its communion for its affirming the position that it would commune with a brother who might have a slave."

Some five years afterward this brother was excommunicated for continuing in his refusal to walk with the church. Nothing of an immoral character appears to have been alleged against him ; he continued to be respected as an upright citizen. It is related that, after his excommunication, one of the members of the church, a carpenter, was employed by him to do a day's work, who had scruples about eating with him, because he had been excommunicated ; he, therefore, caused a table to be set very nicely in the parlor, and directed the brother to dine there by himself.

That the slavery question was somewhat agitated about this time in this vicinity may be inferred from a case preserved upon the town records of this town. It can be best given in the words of the record : —

"HEAD-QUARTERS, PAULET, *Nov.* 28, 1777.

"To whom it may concern, know ye : whereas, Dinah Mattis, a negro woman, with Nancy, her child of two months old, was taken prisoner on Lake Champlain, with the British troops, somewhere near Col. Gilliner's patent, the 12th day of inst. November, by a scout under my command, and, according to a resolve passed by the Honorable Continental Congress, that all prizes belong to the captivators thereof, therefore, she and her child became the just property of the captivators thereof. I being consci-hentious that it is not right in the sight of God to keep slaves ; therefore obtaining leave of the detachment under my command, to give her and her child their freedom ; I do therefore give the said Dinah Mattis, and Nancy her child, their freedom to pass and repass anywhere through the United States of America, with her behaving as becometh, and to trade and traffic for herself and child as though she were born free, without being molested by any person or person. In witness whereunto I have set my hand and subscribed my name.

"(Signed) EBENEZER ALLEN,"
' *Capt. in Col. Herrick's Regiment of Green Mountain Boys.*"

1 "Major Ebenezer Allen was a captain in Col. Herrick's battalion of State Rangers, and distinguished himself in the Battle of Bennington." — See Biographical Sketch in Hall's Early Hist., Vermont, p. 651.

CHAPTER VI.

THE CHURCH IN THE WORLD.

ITH the ecclesiastical life of the community there was also going on here in strong pulsations the secular life of a most energetic people. These men, a glimpse of whom we get from meagre but suggestive church records, shared in this secular life. It is impossible to form any just idea of the church's life, its trials, influence, and dangers, without understanding the secular history of the town. Church members had a large part in the establishment of a town, and then of a State, and meantime of a nation. Each several work crowded fast upon the heels of the other, or mingled one with the other. There was the wilderness to subdue, land titles to establish. There were legislatures to entertain, and their share of legislation to perform. They had highways and accommodations to keep up for the travelling public, on one of its then most important thoroughfares.[1] They had strong individuality; each would

[1] " Settlements had also (as early as 1765) been made to the northward as far as Danby, and extensive preparations were making for occupying other townships, as well as for extending the settlements in those already commenced, — the tillers of the hard New England soil then, as they have often been since, swarming for emigration to new and uncultivated lands." — Vt. Hist. Mag.

Mr. Samuel Fay, five years of age the day of the Bennington battle, and who distinctly recollected occurrences of that day, with other reminiscences, stated to G. W. Robinson the following, of public houses, all in apparent successful operation; the Catamount Tavern, kept by his grandfather, Stephen Fay; the Dewey Tavern, now Walloomsac House, then kept by Capt. Elijah Dewey; the Herrick Tavern, kept by Col. Herrick, now known as the Dimmick place; the Harmon Tavern, kept by Daniel Harmon now the old yellow buildin west of

6*

in a measure have his own way, and yet they must endure one another and be mutually helpful, for they had many common labors, hardships, and dangers, and common interests, ambitions, and expectations. They must help each other to be strong, while sometimes, doubtless, they yielded to the temptation, in this or that private mutual competition, to put down each other. So they grew; so their individual force of character was developed.

As before said, many of those thus situated as to their secular and social life were members of the Bennington church, many were unwearied in Christian efforts, habitual in their attendance upon public ordinances, some — doubtless at times a few — faithful to the Friday prayer-meeting. There were in particular two great public struggles in the history of the town, and which are no less prominent in the history of the State, and one of them of commanding importance in the history of the nation. I refer to the land-title controversy and to the Revolutionary War. The land-title controversy and the Bennington battle will have a place as separate topics. Let it suffice now to say, prominent was the part Bennington acted in the Revolutionary War. Here was held the council of Allen, Warner, Easton, and others, in which the expedition to Ticonderoga, which resulted, under the intrepid leadership of Allen, in the surrender of that fortress, was planned, May, 1775, and a considerable portion of the Green Mountain boys who joined the expedition were from Bennington. Ethan Allen came to the New Hampshire Grants about the year 1769,

---

Henry Baker's residence; the tavern kept by Zechariah Harwood, the late residence of Perez Harwood, Sen., deceased; the State Arms House, kept by Jonathan Robinson; the Brush Tavern, where now stands the residence of Samuel Jewett; the Billings Tavern, in whose stables he has seen one hundred horses at one time, — not an uncommon occurrence, — belonging to people emigrating from Connecticut and Massachusetts to the different parts of Vermont and New Hampshire; it now stands on the side hill west of the residence of Mr. Nichols, near the Bennington and Pownal line.

and made his home in Bennington while within the territory,
until he was taken prisoner at Montreal, Sept. 25, 1775.
Col. Seth Warner came to Bennington to reside in January,
1765, and remained here until the summer of 1784.

In the regiment of Green Mountain boys which was
raised under the advice of the Continental Congress in the
summer of 1775 for service in Canada, the town of Bennington was represented by Seth Warner, its lieutenant-
colonel and commandant, Samuel Safford as major, Wait
Hopkins as captain, and John Fassett, Jr., as lieutenant,
and by many others in different capacities. Among the
important services rendered by this regiment was the decisive defeat of General Carleton at Longuiel, which prevented his furnishing relief to St. Johns and caused its immediate surrender, and also the abandonment of Montreal
to the American forces under General Montgomery.[1] In
the next summer, July 5, 1776, the Continental Congress
was so well satisfied with the services in Canada of these
men, that a resolution was passed to raise a continental
regiment of regular troops from this territory.

Of this regiment, which continued in service through the
war, Seth Warner, the colonel ; Samuel Safford, the lieutenant-colonel ; Wait Hopkins, captain ; Joseph Safford,
lieutenant ; Jacob Safford, ensign ; Benjamin Hopkins,
adjutant, were from Bennington. In October of the same
year, upon notice of an expected attack upon Ticonderoga,
the militia of Bennington and neighboring towns turned
out *en masse* and moved to its relief, and for their exploit
were handsomely complimented by the commanding general, Horatio Gates.[2]

At the time of the evacuation of Ticonderoga and Fort

1 A brief manuscript letter of Mrs. Montgomery to a friend, alluding to the
death of Gen. Montgomery, is preserved among the papers of Gen. David Robinson.

2 Vermont Hist. Mag.

Mt. Independence, July 6, 1777, the convention for forming the constitution of the State was assembled at Windsor, but, on receiving the alarming news of the loss of these posts, they hastily adjourned, appointing a Council of Safety to administer the government until the meeting of the Legislature under the constitution. This Council of Safety met at Manchester July 15, and soon afterward adjourned to Bennington, where it continued in permanent session until after the close of the campaign by the surrender of Burgoyne in October following. The room which this body occupied during this trying period is still to be seen in the ancient tavern-house of Landlord Fay, with the words " Council room," cut in olden time on the mantel-piece.[1]

Throughout the war Bennington furnished the full share of men and supplies for carrying it on.[2] Bennington was for some time a depot for public stores belonging to the United States. To obtain possession of these provisions and stores was the principal object of Burgoyne in sending his expedition to Bennington.

The leading men in the town were leading men in the religious community. The innholder at whose house the first town meeting was held, the moderator of the meeting, the town clerk then appointed, the first four of the selectmen, the town treasurer, the two constables and the two tithing-men, and indeed all but four of the officers appointed, were or became members of the church under Mr. Dewey. The first town meeting was held March 31, 1762, at the house of John Fassett, when the following officers were chosen : —

" Samuel Montague, moderator; Moses Robinson, town clerk; Samuel Montague, Samuel Scott, James Breakenridge, Benajah Rude, and Joseph Wickwire, selectmen; Deacon Joseph Safford, town treasurer; Samuel Robinson, Jr., and John Smith, Jr.,

1 Vermont Hist. Mag.
2 See journal of Council of Safety in " Vermont State Papers."

constables; Deacon Safford and Elisha Field, tithing-men; Peter Harwood and John Smith, Jr., hay-wards; Samuel Atwood and Samuel Pratt, fence viewers; Timothy Pratt and Oliver Scott, deer-rifts."

Of the first company of militia organized, October 24, 1764, all the officers were or became members of the church under Mr. Dewey.

Muster Roll of the First Company of Militia, etc.

Officers: John Fassett, captain; James Breakenridge, lieutenant; Elisha Field, ensign. — Warrant Officers: Leonard Robinson, first sergeant; Samuel Safford, second do.; Ebenezer Wood, third do.; Henry Walbridge, fourth do. — Rank and File: Benjamin Whipple, first corporal; John Wood, second do.; Samuel Pratt, third do.; Peter Harwood, fourth.

Deacon Joseph Safford and Samuel Robinson, Esq., received from the proprietors' meeting and fulfilled the contract to build the first grist-mill and to keep it in repair ten years, that in the east part of the town. Samuel Robinson, Esq., was the first Justice of the Peace under the province of New Hampshire, appointed to that office within the limits of the State. In the summer of 1764, Esquire Robinson, as magistrate, came into collision with the New York officers in a controversy about jurisdiction in Pownal, and was arrested and carried to Albany jail.

In the time of Mr. Dewey's pastorate, though within two years of its close, the declaration of American Independence was adopted; also that of the independence of the State; also the State constitution, adopted in convention, and the officers elected and other necessary measures executed by which Vermont became, in her own name, a sovereign and independent State. The time of Mr. Avery's pastorate here — the whole period from the decease of Mr. Dewey, to the settlement of Mr. Swift — was filled up with

as much intense excitement of civil affairs as, perhaps, any
other period of like extent in the history of the town. It
is impossible duly to appreciate the church's position and
career at such a time without understanding the contem-
porary civil and military history of the town and of the
State. It is evident the spirituality of the church must
have been put to a severe test in the midst of such profound civil and social agitation, and so great and abound-
ing worldly cares.

But in such a community and at such a time religion did
not struggle doubtfully to maintain its foothold. It
struck its roots deep into the hardy soil. The tree still
flourishes. I speak not now of the First Church alone, but
of all branches of Christ's church in the town. The tree
of religion, which was planted in this soil at the outset of
the gathering of a community here, took deep root amid
all the struggles, commotions, and rude first essayings of
public enterprise and of individual will. It still flourishes,
and the vigor thereof is genuine and enduring.[1]

1 See, further onward in the volume, dates and statistics of the other churches,
down to Jan. 1, 1863.

CHAPTER VII.

REVIVALS.

THE late Rev. Dr. Hawes, of Hartford, said of the church of which he was pastor (the church first organized in Connecticut) : —

"This church has ever believed in revivals of religion, and owes all its prosperity to those oft-repeated visitations of mercy." [1]

The same remark may be applied to this the first church organized within the limits of Vermont. The operations of the Spirit of God in revivals are, to some extent, matter of human study, and have some general laws which appear to be discernible by human judgment; but at the same time they involve the profoundest, as well as the most momentous, of all the special exertions of the divine power of God in the world. It has been the sacred privilege of this church in repeated instances, and in no common degree, to witness these remarkable displays of divine power in the hearts of men and the assemblies of God's people.

Its Separate origin would warrant our ascribing to the Bennington church the approval of religious revivals. Samuel Robinson, Esq., was an attendant upon Whitfield's ministry while in London, and upon his decease was interred in the burying-ground attached to Whitfield's meeting-house. After Esquire Robinson's decease, Whitfield, being on one of his preaching tours in this country, sent

---

[1] Cont. Ecc. Hist., Conn., p. 90.

word to Bennington that he was charged with messages
from Mr. Robinson, but could come no nearer than Albany.
Moses Robinson, his son, afterward governor, went to
Albany to meet Mr. Whitfield, and hear him preach; his
mother accompanied him, riding upon a favorite mare.

From the number, thirty-six, known to have been received into the church in 1765, there must have been a revival at that time.   In 1784, while the church was without
a pastor, and Messrs. Wood and Burton preached here temporarily, forty are known to have been received into the
church, and that special awakening has received the name
of the Wood and Burton Revival.

I. THE REVIVAL OF 1803. — Let us go back and endeavor to recall somewhat of the revival of 1803.   From
June 7, 1801, to the fall of 1804, the church was without a
pastor, and the state of religion and morals appears to
have fallen surprisingly low.   The reputation of the town
for irreligion, both at home and abroad, must have become
quite the reverse of what it previously had been.   A Miss
Eleanor Read was at that time teacher of a select school
in the building, now occupied as a residence, first south of
the old academy.   She taught school in the upper story,
a saddler's shop being upon the first floor.   She enjoyed a
high reputation as a teacher.   In a letter to a friend, dated
September 1, 1802, she says : —

"My first beginning in this place was peculiarly trying. I had to
endure sickness and trouble, such as I never experienced before.
In the midst of greatness and grandeur, every face was new, and
seemed marked with haughty ostentation."

At length, as she says, she summoned all her fortitude,
and met with marked success.   Miss Read was one of the
converts in the revival, and she published a narrative and

letters. — (Press of Anthony Haswell). In one of these letters we have an account of a singular circumstance as the incipient occasion of her awakening, and also a glimpse of the religious and moral state of the community immediately preceding the revival. She mentions a letter she had received from a minister of Chelsea, —

"In which he observes that the degeneracy of Bennington was truly lamentable; that their depravity, infidelity, and heaven-daring wickedness had become a subject of lamentation to the friends of Zion." "He also observed that he thanked God I was with them to lead the dear young people in the ways óf piety and virtue. This expression struck me very forcibly and led me to reflect on my unworthiness, and insufficiency to teach them that which I had reasons to fear I was myself unacquainted with."

Whether the strong language of the Chelsea minister was warranted or not, there was doubtless some occasion for it.

The Indian, or Canadian, Gordon, was killed about this time (Aug. 8, 1802), and a notice of this affair in the "Vermont Gazette" of Aug. 16, gives us some glimpses of the state of society. Stephen Gordon was so injured by wounds received in an affray with two young men, named George Tibbets and George Whitney (on Sunday P. M.), as to die on Tuesday morning following, and on Wednesday his remains were interred and an affecting discourse was delivered to a crowded audience, from Psalm xix. 12, 13. The following is an extract from the notice referred to :—

"Never was greater solemnity observable in Bennington on any former occasion than prevailed during the exercises; at the close of which, Tibbets, one of the prisoners, in pathetic terms, warned the assembled audience, young and old, against the evil tendency of Sabbath-breaking, as exemplified in their unhappy situation.

In reflecting upon late occurrences in our vicinity, the contemplative mind necessarily looks for an appropriate cause, and exercises its faculties to discover a remedy. But a few days have elapsed since the inhabitants of Bennington could say that the crime of suicide and murder never existed among them. The scene is now dreadfully reversed."

The editorial recites a case of suicide which had recently occurred, then returns to the Whitney and Tibbets murderous affray, and proceeds thus : —

" Fellow-citizens, there is a moral and a natural cause for these things, and in the opinion of considerable numbers the moral cause is the declension of religion; the natural cause, the prevalence of folly, and the introduction of frivolous amusements, gambling and intemperance. Fathers of families, parents, consider the consequence of permitting your sons to attend unlawful games, cards, dice, and billiards, even within the restrictions of the licensing law of the last Assembly of Vermont, which was imposed upon us under pretence of interdicting such practices. At such places as card tables and billiard tables animosities are frequently engendered, and the trifling emoluments to the individual owning the table accrue through the debasement of numbers and the ruin of some of its attendants. Mothers, consider the consequences to your daughters: in proportion as gambling and irregularity engage the mind of a man, female attractions and virtue lose their charms, and lewdness and inconstancy become less odious than formerly in their eyes. Thus your sons become worse husbands and worse men, and your daughters more lonesome and unhappy women. A billiard table until within a short time past was as unknown in Bennington as suicide and the slaughter of man by man," etc.

This extract shows that the editor at least was a timely sentinel, and that the community had not yet become so familiar with scenes of gross immorality as to be unaffected with profound concern by the fact of their occurrence.

But so far as irreligion and immorality were becoming bold, we have illustrated more clearly the virtue of prayer, and the power of the grace of God, which triumphed over every obstacle. The affair, which called out the editorial quoted from, occurred in August, 1802 ; in the winter of 1802–3 came one of the most powerful revivals Bennington has ever witnessed. Three members of our church survive who were added to it among the fruits of that revival : Mrs. Betsey Edgerton, Mrs. Celinda Henry, and Mrs. Lucinda Hubbell.[1] There are not a few who recollect it. It made a vivid impression on the mind. It will be remembered by many with gratitude to God through eternity.

It was still the time of the old meeting-house. Those interested in the project of having a new meeting-house had been trying ten years, and in vain, to obtain a successful movement of the town to build one. In the winter of 1803–4 the movement under the new and less stringent law was successful. This was the winter immediately succeeding the revival, and we may infer the one event had something to do with the other. At the time of the commencement and during the height of the revival the old meeting-house was standing. But it was not at all times adequate to hold the numbers that then pressed to hear the word of God. It was in vogue at that time to hold protracted meetings in the open air. There was a three-days' meeting here in the open air.

The Rev. Mr. Davis preached here in that meeting, and at other places also in the town. A committee went down to Mendon, in Massachusetts, to obtain him. He was, according to the imperfect accounts we now get, an abrupt, uncultivated, ut ea rnest and successful, laborer here in that revival. A Rev. Mr. Nelson preached here also, who was more learned and methodical, "a very able man."

The Rev. J. Spaulding is remembered as preaching here, at that time, with great elevation and power of language, particularly upon the attributes of God, — the divine benevolence, — and in connection therewith illustrating with uncommon solemnity the obligations and guilt of sinners, as well as the blessedness of the heavenly state.

[1] All these have since deceased.

Elder. Caleb Blood, minister to the West Church in Shaftsbury, near the burying-ground, came, with his deacon, Jno. Downes. Elder Blood said to Mr. Haswell, "We have come down to warm by your fire, for our fire has gone out." Not that the church had become extinct, but its revival spirit had declined; and, by coming to the meetings in Bennington at that time, his people were warmed anew. The Rev. Solomon Allen, of Pittsfield, was here at the three-days' meeting; so also the Rev. Messrs. Jackson of Dorset, and Preston of Rupert, and the colored preacher the Rev. Mr. Haynes.

The three-days' open-air meetings were held on the side-hill, east of S. S. Scott's residence. At that time Gov. Moses Robinson was one of the deacons of the church; and possibly the place of meeting being on the road to his house and in its vicinity may be accounted for by that fact. The cluster of houses on that corner, namely, S. S. Scott's, Mrs. Raymond's, and Mr. Moses Harrington's, were not then built. During the meeting, a staging for the ministers and others broke down, — one of the few circumstances recollected by persons now living. No one was seriously injured, though some were much frightened.

Daniel Smith, afterward the Rev. Daniel Smith, of St. Louis, was one of the converts. Another was the Miss Eleanor Read, as already noticed. She was a consistent, happy Christian, and died a triumphant death. We find the spirit of the revival manifesting itself in the columns of the "Vermont Gazette," then published here; among other ways, in original stanzas, of great spirituality and fervency. Two stanzas are selected from a contribution of this sort to the "Gazette" of July 12, 1803, and introduced in a note to the editor, signed William Kinnis: —

"To meditate on heavenly things
Gives to my thought an angel's wings,
Bears my aspiring mind above,
And fills my breast with holy love.

"My flesh and bones exult with joy,
And holy zeal without alloy;
My inmost soul doth all rejoice,
Absorbed in Christ, my only choice."

Some stanzas from another hymn, "occasioned by the present evidently awakened attention of the town to the things of religion," are inserted here, not so much for poetic merit as a witness to the revival. — *Gazette of Nov.* 15, 1802.

"Oh, art thou passing by?
  And may we see thy face?
Let every blind Bartimeus cry,
  Lord Jesus, grant me grace!

"Let each Zaccheus flee
  To catch a passing glimpse;
With zeal ascend the gospel tree,
  And baffle Satan's imps.

"Restrain reviling tongues:
  Be thou the convert's stay;
Sustain their hopes, avenge their wrongs,
  And wipe their tears away.

"Let Bennington rejoice,
  Her church with joy be filled,
And every heart, and every voice,
  Exult in grace distilled."

The published account of Miss Read's conversion may not be interesting to all; but, doubtless, it reflects with considerable accuracy the spirit of the revival. For this reason, a somewhat lengthy extract is presented. Refer-

7*

ring to her attendance at an inquiry-meeting, where were present anxious inquirers and young converts, she proceeds as follows : —

"An aged man came forward, and, in trembling accents, declared what God had done for his soul. Then a girl of ten years old, in a manner the most animating, related her remarkable experiences. I began to reflect on the assertion of Mr. Spaulding that God is good. Surely, thought I, these happy souls can attest the truth of this assertion. Their salvation is really as important as mine ; and it is remarkable that I should rejoice in their happy deliverance from the bondage of sin. God has been long tendering me the same blessed deliverance. But I, fool indeed, with such a price to get wisdom, had no heart for it. Why, then, should I murmur? How can I repine? I am forever lost; but God is just. Upon this most hearty confession my long-pent tears flowed; and, while bursting sobs almost tore my heart asunder, I reviewed my desperately wicked exercises toward him, whom I now saw to be just even in my eternal condemnation. Surely, thought I, of all the unreasonable wretches in existence, I am the most deserving of hell. Here I experienced such unusual convulsions of body as induced me to take hold of a chair before me to enable me to keep my seat. I verily supposed that my soul was taking its final separation from my body. I attempted to arise, in order to go into another room, but found it impossible. I must expire, thought I, in the midst of this assembly, for an example of God's righteous displeasure. It is just that it should be so ; and every one present must rejoice in this expression of his righteous indignation against such a vile worker of iniquity. Here I viewed myself a criminal, justly condemned to all the tortures of endless despair. No gleam of hope beamed on my benighted soul. No fond expectations from creature aid whispered consolation. Against God only had I offended, and done this great wickedness, and he only could afford me help. My soul seemed humbled in the dust in view of my condemnation, while I was constrained to cry out in spirit, 'Even so, Lord God Almighty, true and righteous are thy judgments.' At this view of my wretched, hopeless situation, the following words passed sweetly through my mind, and with such delightful energy as thrilled through my whole soul, and filled me with rapture inexpressible : —

" ' Jesus, to thy dear, faithful hand,
My naked soul I trust.'

" At this most cordial disposal of myself into the hands of a glorious Redeemer, the thick cloud seemed to disperse, and give place to such a transporting view of the blessed Saviour as no words can express. With an eye of faith, I beheld his transcendent glory, more conspicuous than that of the natural sun in meridian splendor, when bursting from behind the thickest clouds. I could no more doubt of the being and divinity of Christ than of my own existence. He was presented to my spiritual view in such substantial glory as caused me to adopt the acclamation of the astonished Thomas : ' *My Lord and my God!*' Here all my distress subsided, and all my anxiety for beloved self was cured. I was astonished that I could ever have felt such anxiety for myself. The greatness of God's character, and the glorious scheme of redemption, filled me with wonder, admiration, and joy. I raised my head, and looked on Mr. Spaulding, who was zealously engaged in illustrating the righteousness of Christ; but, oh! how altered was his aspect! ' *How beautiful,*' thought I, ' *are the feet of him that bringeth good tidings, that publisheth peace, that saith unto Zion, Thy God reigneth.*' "

In conclusion of the account of this revival, the following anecdote of Ezekiel Harmon, familiarly told, but pertinent, may be introduced. It is preserved as related by Mrs. Austin Harmon, third wife of Austin Harmon, grandfather of the present Austin Harmon, and sister-in-law of Ezekiel. " Ezekiel Harmon called at the door of our house as he was returning from the Friday meeting. I inquired of him if he had been to the Friday meeting, and if it was a good one. ' *A glorious one!*' said he. ' How many were there?' I inquired. His reply was, ' *Four, — Gov. Robinson, Mrs. Judge Robinson, ——, and myself. We had a glorious meeting. We got the promise.*' I looked, and I thought brother Ezekiel's face fairly shone." This was a short time, the summer or fall, before the great revival of 1803.[1]

---

[1] This Friday meeting is noticed in two or three other instances in the volume. " The Friday P. M. prayer-meeting went back to the formation of the

The names of ninety-three are on the roll of the church as added to it at this time. But aged inhabitants have stated the impression that there were about two hundred hopeful conversions.

The moral and religious tone of society again became elevated. The new meeting-house was built; considered, as doubtless it was, in advance of any other church edifice in this part of the country, it added to the new impulse which public worship had received from the great revival. The town was distinguished for the intelligence and influence of its people. Hon. S. H. Brown relates some reminiscences by Col. Hinman, of Utica, N. Y., who was a visitor here some few years since. Among other things, that gentleman remarked that he could recollect the time, say 1808–1820, when there was the best society in Bennington he ever saw, — men of a superior order of talent, gentlemen in their manners, of eminent influence and position in political circles and in professional life.

II. OTHER REVIVALS. — In 1811 (during the pastorate of the Rev. Daniel Marsh), thirty-eight are known to have been received into the church. In 1820 (the year in which the Rev. Absalom Peters was ordained and installed over the church), thirty-three were added. In 1827 (the second year of the pastorate of the Rev. Daniel A. Clark), there was an accession of one hundred and one. In 1838 (the interval between the pastorate of the Rev. Mr. Clark and that of the Rev. Mr. Hooker), one hundred and sixty-eight were added to the church. In 1834 (in the pastorate of the Rev. E. W. Hooker), ninety were received into the church. Without pursuing the list further, it is apparent there have

church, and continued until three years after Mr. Hooker came. It was held in the meeting-house, in earliest times not uncommonly at Mrs. Samuel Robinson, Sen. I have known my father to go when there were but two or three." — *W. Haswell.*

been repeated seasons of special religious awakening, and large ingatherings into the church since the revival of 1803. That, in 1831, may be called, perhaps, the greatest revival, certainly next to that of 1803. In the revival of 1831, one hundred and thirty-one persons were received into the church at one communion.

The following graphic account of that occasion is from Dr. Peters' "Birthday Memorial," Appendix, p. 64: —

"I cannot close my reminiscences of the church in Bennington without recurring to a scene of surpassing interest, in which I was called to participate some five years after my dismission from its pastoral care. My immediate successor, the late Rev. Daniel A. Clark, had already closed his ministry there, and the church was without a pastor. But where his ministry had planted and watered, God was giving the increase. It was that wonderful year of the right hand of the Most High in many of the churches, 1831. In connection with the preaching of Rev. E. N. Kirk, then of Albany, and others who had temporarily supplied the pulpit, a great revival of religion had been wrought. A large number of the hopefully converted had been examined and accepted, and were awaiting a formal admission to the church at the next communion day, September 4th. I was present by invitation, preached on the occasion, presided at the administration of the Lord's Supper, and admitted one hundred and thirty-one persons, on confession of their faith, to their first communion at the Lord's table. Their ages ranged from thirteen to seventy years, and seventy-six of the number, not having been baptized in infancy, received the sacrament of baptism. . .

"The baptismal service alone, for seventy-six persons in succession, which was performed wholly by myself, occupied all of two hours. Yet this, with the other protracted exercises, produced no weariness in the congregation. A wakeful, earnest attention and a tearful interest pervaded the assembly, and indicated a divine presence above and around us."

CHAPTER VIII

THE FIRST SEVEN PASTORS.

THE Rev. Jedidiah Dewey. — Of the Rev. Mr. Dewey, the first pastor of the church, it is to be regretted that so imperfect a memorial has been preserved. Nevertheless the testimony which we have (being found here and there in relations so diverse from each other, and so foreign to any design of a formal eulogy) is the more conclusive to his worth. Of the extraordinary measures to obtain Mr. Dewey to the pastorship of this church mention has been already made in the account of the organization of the church.

Unquestionable evidence has descended to us of his fervent piety and ability, as well as fidelity. A letter from Westfield, Mass., from the pen of the Rev. Emerson Davis, D.D., pastor of the original church in Westfield (which Mr. Dewey left to join the Separates) is interesting; and some extracts from it may be presented here: —

"Mr. Dewey united with the church (the original church in Westfield) in 1737, at twenty-three years of age. Soon after this the church adopted the half-way covenant. . . . This was particularly offensive to some of the earnest and devoted members. They said the church had abandoned its principles and would admit unconverted persons to the church. Many absented themselves from the communion. They left the church. Mr. Dewey did so, in 1748. He was called to give account in 1749. In 1750 the church voted that, inasmuch as he had gone out from them, had

joined the Separates, and become their preacher, that they
would no longer regard him as one of their number. They
did not call it excommunication, but a withdrawal of fellowship. Mrs. Dewey was cut off in the same manner in
1751. Mr. Dewey had only a common-school education,
but he was intelligent and gifted. His Christian character
stood high. 'The church refused to excommunicate him, because it would imply something criminal, and so they only
withdrew fellowship.''

From these few but interesting particulars we can learn
somewhat as to the sort of man he was. He was an earnest Christian, and had a conscience of his own, and aimed
to do good, that his life should not be a blank. He had
learned the trade of a carpenter. When the first meeting-
house was raised the force was insufficient, and one of the
sides halted when partly up. Mr. Dewey stepped forward
and said to the builder, '' Do you take a pole and help to
lift with the men, and I will give the word of command.''
The builder complied. At that instant two men came
riding up on horseback from the south. They dismounted,
and also grasped the poles. Mr. Dewey gave the word of
command, and the side of the frame went up forthwith to
its perpendicular position, was fastened, and the raising of
the building was completed without further delay. He
also built or superintended the building of the house in
which he resided.

It is a proof of Mr. Dewey's sterling qualities that,
though a Separate and without liberal education, and
though a party was increasing in the church more in sympathy with the Standing Order Congregational churches, —
a reaction apparent in the controversy of the church respecting the method of raising the salary and other moneys for
expense of public worship, and which became decisive in
the character of Mr. Dewey's successor, and in the charac-

ter of the men composing the council which installed Mr.
Avery, — yet Mr. Dewey was as much esteemed by the
conservatives as by any portion of the church and congregation. An incidental paragraph in the Rev. Mr. Avery's
published narrative corroborates the estimate here presented. Referring to the history of the church under Mr.
Dewey's ministry, he says : —

"As a number of professors, not of the Separate order,
have become inhabitants of the town, and have great respect for the personal and ministerial endowments of the
Rev. Mr. Dewey, who was of catholic and liberal principles, they have, at different periods, joined the communion
here."

From the time of his first connection with the Westfield
church as its pastor to the close of his labors in Bennington was a period of twenty-nine years. His pastorate of
the Bennington church continued through a period of fifteen
years and four months.

In rude and boisterous times he built up the infant church
in its new home, and left it to his successor with a roll of
at least one hundred and twenty-seven names. (Inclusive
of those deceased and those dismissed.)

Mr. Dewey was also a patriot. With a warm love of his
people, and a profound interest in the future prosperity of
the infant settlement where he had cast in his lot, his energies were unavoidably taxed, not only by the spiritual
wants, but also by the secular exigencies of the community.
As early as January, 1770, he was indicted with others at
Albany as one of the leaders in the efforts of the settlers
to maintain their land-titles ; not that he was active in
any violent sense, but his counsels were understood at Albany to have weight with his fellow-citizens, on public
affairs. In May, 1772, in a spirited correspondence between the New York governor and the inhabitants of Ben-

nington, his name is foremost in the address of the governor's letter, and at the head of the signatures in the reply of the Bennington men to that letter. The following pas sage occurs in that letter: "I am told Mr. Dewey, a minister of the gospel, James Breakenridge, and Mr. Fay (Dr. Jonas Fay) are persons in whose judgment you have much confidence. I should therefore think they would be your proper messengers on a business in which you are so deeply concerned; especially Mr. Dewey, who has been favorably represented here since my appointment to this government."[1] As the result of this correspondence with Governor Tryon, in which Mr. Dewey took a leading part, the government of New York for a time quite modified its course; so much so that the settlers here thought their troubles connected with this controversy had come to an end. Guns were fired in Bennington, speeches made, and a vast concourse from this and neighboring places united in celebrating what they believed, or hoped, was the dawn of peace. These bright hopes were destined, however, to be blasted; but it shows that Mr. Dewey did what he could wisely, by peaceful negotiation, to bring an end to controversy, and that his influence with *Governor Tryon* was not inconsiderable.

But Mr. Dewey, it appears, understood and applied the maxim, that there are times when forbearance ceases to be a virtue; and hence he was feared as well as respected at Albany. He was, as all accounts agree, a man of stern force in the discharge of his duty according to his conscience. In 1777, when the Revolutionary War had commenced, and the enemy were descending the Hudson River with great force, and threatening to devastate the whole country, and had sent a detachment to capture the military stores at Bennington, he preached a war sermon. He told

[1] See State Papers, pp. 22, 23.

8

his people to take arms and go fight for their country. On the next Saturday the Bennington battle was fought and won. The two following anecdotes do not seem exactly credible, but they are among the traditional anecdotes of Bennington, and given as related to the writer : —

It is related that on one occasion, when Ethan Allen was in the congregation, and Mr. Dewey was preaching on the character of God, some remark in the discourse displeased Col. Allen ; he arose in his place at the head of a prominent pew in the broad aisle, and saying with an audible voice, " It's not so," started to go out of the pew, evidently with the intention of leaving the house. Mr. Dewey, lifting up his right hand, and pointing with his fore-finger directly at Col. Allen, said, " *Sit down, thou bold blasphemer, and listen to the Word of God.*" Allen, who had too strong a taste for that style of doing things not to like it under any circumstances, immediately resumed his seat, and gave respectful attention to the remainder of the discourse.

It is also related that at the public divine service of thanksgiving for the capture of Ticonderoga, in which Allen bore so heroic and so famous a part, many officers from Ticonderoga attended, and Allen was present. Mr. Dewey preached, and made the prayer, in which he gave to God all the glory and praise of the capture of the stronghold. Allen, in the midst of the prayer, called out, " Parson Dewey ! Parson Dewey ! Parson Dewey !" The third time of so pronouncing his name made Mr. Dewey to pause and open his eyes. Allen then raised both hands and said, " *Please mention to the Lord about my being there!*" Mr. Dewey, taking no further notice of the interruption, proceeded with the public devotions.

He could also be genial and pleasant. One or two characteristic anecdotes are proper to be introduced to illustrate this. When the house, now the residence of Aaron L. Hubbell, and built by his father, was raised, Mr. Dewey was present: also Joseph Rudd, who was engaged to be married to Sarah Wickwire, then living in a house nearly opposite. Mr. Dewey, who knew of the intention of marriage, said to Joseph, " If you will go and lead Sarah over here, I will marry you for nothing." The reply was, " It's a bargain." Joseph led the young lady to the place, some planks were laid down upon the timbers for a floor, and they were married.

It is related, there was a stupid and withal an eccentric or half-witted servant man in Mr. Dewey's house, who had the strange habit of arising in the night, and wandering from room to room with a lighted candle in his hand. Mr. Dewey, who was both a careful and an economical man, rebuked the individual, saying he feared his house would be set on fire by such proceedings, and moreover he did not like to have his candles consumed so uselessly ; but on the very next night he heard the noise of the man about the house again. Mr. Dewey, full of indignation, and designing to be very severe, proceeded to the room, and lo ! instead of one candle, the fellow had two, one in each hand, illuminating his nocturnal perambulations. Mr. Dewey, who had a sense for the ludicrous, suddenly forgot his anger, and retired from the scene, saying not a word.

If Mr. Dewey had any enemies, it has not been handed down. The valuable right of land called the minister's right was settled upon him by vote, as follows : —

" July 18, 1763. — *Voted,* To give the Rev. Jedidiah Dewey the lot of land called the minister's, in said Bennington, exclusive of the labor already done on said lot, in case said Mr. Dewey settles with us in the gospel ministry." " November 1, 1763. — *Voted,* To give the Rev. Mr. Jedidiah Dewey the lot of land called the minister's lot, for his settlement, as an encouragement for him in the work of the ministry."

He built and occupied the house, the residence of the late Major Aaron Robinson.

He was the son of Jedidiah and Rebecca (Williams) Dewey. He was born in Westfield, Mass., April 11, 1714, and died December 21, 1778. He married Mindwell Hayden Hopkins, of Windsor, Conn., August 4, 1736. They were published July 3 of that year. Of her were born to him : —

Mindwell, Nov. 29, 1737.	Eldad, Aug. 12, 1747.
Lucy, Nov. 16, 1739.	Lucy, 2d, Nov. 9, 1751.
Jedidiah, June 17, 1742.	Margaret, Nov. 28, 1756.
Elijah, Nov. 28, 1744.	Betsey, Dec. 16, 1759.

Mrs. Mindwell Hayden Dewey died May 29, 1760, before Mr. Dewey's removal to Bennington, in the forty-eighth year of her age. Mr. Dewey married his second wife, Betty Buck, February 20, 1761. Of her were born to him : —

Loan, May 15, 1765.	Claret, Oct. 6, 1773.
Tabitha, Feb. 16, 1768.	Phyana, Dec. 13, 1775.
Julia, Oct. 20, 1770.	Plina, Jan. 26, 1778.

Mrs. Betty (Buck) Dewey died June 29, 1792, in the fifty-fourth year of her age.

II. The Rev. David Avery was born April 5, 1746, in Norwich, a part of the town called Norwich Farms, now a part of the town of Franklin, Conn. His immigrant ancestor was John Avery, a Scotchman who settled in Truro, Mass. His parents were John and Lydia (Smith) Avery. He experienced religion under the preaching of Whitfield.[1] He was fitted for college in the noted Indian Missionary School of the Rev. Eleazer Wheelock, D.D., at

---

[1] Notes of the Rev. P. H. White.

Lebanon Crank (now Columbia), Conn. He was graduated at Yale College in 1769, and studied theology with his former preceptor, then President of Dartmouth College, (into which institution the Indian Missionary School had just been formed).[1] He was ordained as missionary to the Oneida Indians, Aug. 29, 1771, as colleague with the Rev. Samuel Kirkland. This Mr. Kirkland was son of the Rev. Daniel Kirkland, pastor of the Newint (now Lisbon) church in Connecticut, from which the Newint Separate church, previously referred to in this discourse, separated. Mr. Avery did not, however, long remain among the Indians, but returned to New England and preached in various places until March 25, 1773, when he was installed at Gageboro' (now Windsor), Mass.

The Sabbath after the news of the battle of Lexington reached Gageboro', he preached a farewell sermon, telling the people that God would take care of them ; as for himself he was going to join the army. When ,the congregation was dismissed he took his stand upon the steps, and gave a soul-stirring address on behalf of his country, entreating his people " by every motive of patriotism, and as they valued liberty and abhorred slavery, not to turn a deaf ear to her cry." Twenty of his parishioners gave a quick response to his appeal, chose him captain, shouldered their muskets, and started on foot for Boston. In ten days from the battle of Lexington they were in their camp at Cambridge. They rested the first Sabbath at Northampton and attended public worship. In the afternoon, Mr., now Capt., Avery preached. His text was Nehemiah iv. 14,— " And I looked and rose up and said unto the nobles and to the rulers, and to the rest of the people, Be not ye afraid of them ; Remember the Lord, which is great,

[1] One hundred and fiftieth anniversary pamphlet of Columbia, Conn., by the Rev. F. D. Avery and others.

8*

and terrible, and fight for your brethren, your sons and your daughters, your wives and your houses." On the following Saturday, they arrived at Cambridge, and on Sunday Mr. Avery preached to the whole army from the same text. He received a commission as chaplain in the army, dated April 18, 1776, and was attached to Col. Sherborne's regiment. He not only faithfully performed the duties of his office, but occasionally volunteered to stand guard, or even to go into a battle. While holding his position as captain, he instituted daily religious services, going from tent to tent to read the word of God. At first he had leave of absence from his parish, the neighboring ministers supplying the pulpit two-thirds of the time; but his absence being protracted he was dismissed from Gageboro', April 14, 1777. He was at the battle of Bunker Hill; saw the defeat of our army at the battle of Long Island; was by the side of Washington in his melancholy retreat through the Jerseys; was present at the taking of Burgoyne, at the capture of the Hessians at Trenton, and in the battle of Princeton; was in the army during that terrible winter at Valley Forge; helped build the fortification at Ticonderoga; was by the side of Washington when he signed the death-warrant of André, and witnessed the execution of that ill-fated officer; and was very active in the efforts which were made to capture the traitor Arnold.[1] He resigned his chaplaincy Feb. 1, 1780, but continued to serve till March, 1780.

His ministry at Bennington was next in order. He publicly took charge of the church and congregation here, in the presence of the Rev. Messrs. Daniel Collins, Samuel Morrison, and Seth Swift, May 3, 1780. With the exception of church action in cases of discipline, and the doings of the councils in his own case, the records present little

---

[1] Anniversary pamphlet of Columbia, Conn.

clue to the nature and extent of his labors in this field.
Tradition has preserved still fewer particulars of his ministry here. A manuscript letter, written by him after he
left, to one of his Bennington flock, speaks of his earnest
endeavors to inculcate the doctrines of God's word, both in
his sermons and bible-classes. He was, undoubtedly,
active and laborious ; but what special fruits there were of
his labors here the judgment-day can only disclose. He
was dismissed at his own request, by vote of the church,
June 17, 1783.

He was settled at Wrentham, Mass., May 25, 1786, and,
after much difficulty there, was dismissed April 21, 1794,
but still continued to preach to a congregation in North
Wrentham. He afterward removed to Mansfield, Conn.,
and employed himself with preaching in vacant parishes in
Connecticut, Massachusetts, and Vermont. He also performed two missionary tours in the western part of New
York State, and one in Maine, under the patronage of the
Massachusetts Domestic Missionary Society. He afterward
gathered a church and society in Chaplin, Conn., to which
he preached for three years. In October, 1817, he went to
Shepardstown, Va., to visit a daughter, and while there received a call to settle in Middletown, Va.

He possessed superior talents and culture. Strange to
say, in two or more instances of disaffection toward him
in the parishes where he was, the openly alleged ground of
dissatisfaction was unsoundness of doctrine, " leaning
toward Socinianism ; " and yet all the reliable evidence
goes to show that he was a bold and discriminating preacher
of Orthodox doctrines. The principal charges against him,
before the council in this place, were with regard to the
doctrines which he preached. Three specifications were
presented in the complaint, wherein, as was alleged, his
doctrines were false. The council decided that the views

of doctrine which the complainants alleged he taught, and which they regarded as unsound, were correct.[1]

While here, Mr. Avery built and occupied the house late the residence of Judge Isham. He used to sign his name David Avery, V.D.M., — Verbi Dei Minister, — minister of the word of God. He is described as tall, portly, of commanding presence and strongly marked features ; a gentleman of the old school, frank, cordial, and dignified. He usually preached extemporaneously from short notes. He wrote with a very large, open, and graceful chirography, exceedingly pleasant to read. He had a clear, sonorous voice, and spoke so distinctly that every soldier in a brigade could hear all that he said.[2] His published discourses were, two funeral sermons ; a thanksgiving sermon ; and a sermon on holding the tongue.

When upwards of seventy, he received the call to settle in Middletown, Va. His installation was appointed, but never took place. It was prevented by illness, which proved fatal. The clergymen who were pall-bearers at his funeral were the same who were invited to his installation. The text on which he last preached, about two weeks before his death, was Rom. viii. 9 : "Now if any man have not the spirit of Christ, he is none of his." In the incipient stages of his last sickness, some evangelical ministers and elders of different denominations assembled by his request at the house where he was, and established a united monthly concert of prayer. One of the prayers he offered himself, sitting bolstered up upon his dying-bed. He died of typhus fever, Feb. 16, 1818.

III. The Rev. Job Swift, D.D., was born in Sandwich, Mass., June 17, 1743. His parents were Jabez and Abigail Swift, of Kent, Conn., to which place his father re-

---

[1] Church Records, and Mr. Avery's Narrative.   [2] Notes of Mr. P. H. White.

moved when he was very young. He was graduated at college in 1765. His mind became hopefully impressed with a sense of religion while engaged in the study of Pres. Edwards' writings at college. He was assisted in his theological studies by the Rev. Dr. Bellamy. He was little more than twenty-two years of age when he became a preacher of the gospel. In the following year he was ordained over a church and people in Richmond, Mass., where he labored seven years. After his dismission from the church in Richmond, he preached in different places for a twelvemonth. He then removed to the Nine Partners, in the State of New York, and remained there seven years. Thence he removed to Manchester, in this State. After a ministry of two years there, he removed to Bennington, and was installed here May 31, 1786.

His labors here were arduous and prosperous; but it was not a time of numerous and extensive revivals. The controversy respecting the claims of New York was not finally adjusted until Oct. 28, 1790, some four and a half years onward in his ministry here. The State was not admitted into the Union until March 4, 1791. The troubles had already commenced, growing out of the impoverishment of the people by the Revolutionary War, and the depreciation of paper currency. By the latter cause, Mr. Swift, previously to his removal to Bennington, had the misfortune of losing the chief part of his property. There were heavy taxes to meet the necessities of the national and State governments. There were serious disturbances in different parts of Vermont, and attempts to resist the collection of the taxes. The Shay's rebellion in Massachusetts, from the same cause, occurred at this time, — 1786, 1787. In Vermont, the attempts to overawe the courts and resist the officers of the government, though not in the end successful, showed how deep was the distress of the people because of the

poverty occasioned by the long and arduous struggle with
many and diverse enemies and dangers. The difficulties of
this time were aggravated fearfully in Vermont by its anom-
alous condition. It being yet unrecognized as a State by
neighboring States and by the Federal Union, and its
self-constituted regime being resisted and denied by some of
its own citizens, there was naturally an extraordinary influx
into the State of lawless persons, — individuals bankrupt in
character, as well as in finances. This was a source of dis-
order in the State of serious extent. The high part played
by Bennington in the civil affairs of the State was continued.
Twice during the ministry of Mr. Swift, the Legislature was
convened here, — in 1787, and in 1792. Also during his ministry here the party spirit of the two political parties, called
then Federal and Republican, waxed warm and was oftentimes at fever-heat. This excitement and struggle of political parties began as soon as Vermont was admitted into
the Union. Intensity of party contests in Bennington, it
would seem, could not have been surpassed elsewhere. Influential men, indeed the preponderance of influence in the
church and society, were committed to Jefferson and his administration. Mr. Swift is represented as a model minister for prudence. He was at all times careful of the interests of Christ's spiritual kingdom. He, however, without
doubt, sympathized with Pres. Dwight, of Yale College,
and the Rev. Dr. Emmons, of Massachusetts, and other
leading New England divines, who conscientiously believed
Jefferson to be infidel in religious opinion, and who gave
to this consideration great weight in their comparative estimate of the political parties of that time. It is represented
that Mr. Swift gave dissatisfaction because his prayers at
public worship were so worded as not to recognize Jefferson as a Christian, — it being the custom to pray particularly for both the President and Vice-President of the

United States. In 1792, six years after the installation of Mr. Swift, the subject of the erection of a new meeting-house began to be seriously agitated, and was carried into the town meetings. This agitation was continued during the remainder of Mr. Swift's ministry here.

It was a time of religious desolation throughout the land. A sermon to the ministers — one of the printed collection of his sermons — has this conclusion : —

"In a worldly view there are to all many discouragements. It is a time in which error prevails. It is a time of great stupidity and dark worldly prospects. But, cost what it may, let us preserve fidelity to our Lord and Master. You may be courted, on the one hand, to keep back the truth, and threatened on the other. But, oh, it is infinitely too great a sacrifice to gain the honors and riches of this world at the expense of fidelity to Christ! We are not, my brethren, to expect much from this world. This, however comfortable, would be but a poor reward. If we are faithful, we shall have an infinitely more important reward. A crown of glory awaits us from our Lord and Master, which may we, by our faithful labors, inherit, for the Redeemer's sake."

Upon the records of the church are preserved the names of thirty persons who united with the church during Mr. Swift's ministry here. Strange it would be if not many were added of whom no record is preserved, so imperfectly kept were the records.

There was no attempt in his sermons at quaintness, or antithesis, or merely rhetorical ornament. He chose an important subject of religious doctrine or practice, went straight through with it, and stopped when he came to a proper end. He enlarged upon his theme according to the Scripture, and that his audience might obtain as profitable an understanding of it as possible, and applied the same in a short, pertinent improvement. He preached on civil government to the Legislature convened at Manchester ; on the duties of ministers to the ministerial association. He preached on the duties of children, and duties of parents. A small volume of his sermons, and plans of sermons, was published after his decease, together with a biographical sketch, and the substance of a discourse to his memory by the Rev. Lemuel Haynes.

He reared a large family on slender means. He fitted his sons himself for college. At the same time, he was noted for his hospitality. Mr. Haynes, in his memorial discourse, says, "Mr. Swift's benevolence and hospitality often astonished those who came under his roof." Mr. Haynes had peculiar occasion to remember these traits. Mr. Haynes, it is well known, though highly gifted, and the pastor of three most respectable white congregations successively, was "the colored preacher." But he was never, by the least act of Mr. Swift, made to feel the difference. And when, on the occasion of many ministers being together over night, and so needing to be assigned two to one bed, Mr. Swift would anticipate all difficulty of allotting his brother of the darker skin by delicately saying, "Brother Haynes and I will go together." He ever possessed a deep interest in young men who were seeking an education, and in pious young men who had the ministry in view, and assisted many. Mrs. Hendrick, wife of Deacon Hendrick, of the Shaftsbury Baptist Church, residing where Perez Harwood, senior, deceased, resided, or near there, had a Baptist meeting at her house in a time of revival, and Mr. Swift came into the meeting. She said, "I am apprehensive, Mr. Swift, the young folks will be afraid of you; they are bashful." — "I think not," said he. He soon obtained their confidence, and they related their experiences very freely. They were young converts. At the close of the meeting, Mrs. Hendrick spoke to Mr. Swift of the success of the occasion. "One of the most interesting meetings," she said, "I have ever attended." Mr. Swift replied, " I do not know that I have more than the one talent; but I can feed Christ's lambs."

He was graduated at Yale College. He received the degree of Doctor in Divinity from Williams College. He was successively member of the corporations of Dartmouth, Williams, and Middlebury Colleges. He was sent for from far and near to eclesiastical councils. At his death he was called the Apostle of Vermont.[1]　　　•

He loved to do missionary work, and went sometimes to a great distance to preach the gospel to the destitute. His death occurred suddenly, while thus temporarily engaged in missionary labor. It took place at Enosburgh, in this State, Oct. 20, 1804. He had removed from Bennington to Addison, and his labors there were being much blessed. The town had been distracted with serious divisions; but after he commenced his labors there the moral and religious character of the people was soon entirely changed. A church was organized, and rendered respectable by the number of its members. "It is not easy," says the biographer, "to conceive the grief which the people there felt on learning the sorrowful news of his death." *He died in the triumphs of faith. When asked if he was willing to die, he replied,* "DEATH HAS NO TERRORS."

He resided in the capacious house now first south of the late residence of Gay R. Sanford, deceased; the same house or near to which in the earliest times here was the residence of John Fassett, clerk of the proprietors' meeting, deacon of the church, and innkeeper in that place.

He was a very large man. A lady,[2] with whom I was conversing on the subject, related to me that she was a child when he was pastor of this church, but that she recol-

---

1 Rev. Calvin Durfee. (See "Proceedings at the Centennial of the Berkshire Congregational Association.")
2 Mrs. Raymond.

9

lects him well. She recollects going to another town to
visit there; and, seeing a small man in the pulpit, she inquired if he was a minister, with some surprise. She had
always seen Dr. Swift in the pulpit, and supposed that
none but very large men were suitable to be ministers.

He was married Nov. 6, 1769, to Mary Ann Sedgwick
of Cornwall, Conn., sister of Hon. Theodore Sedgwick.
She died in February, 1826. Their children were:—

Sarah Gold,	Born,	Nov. 13, 1770.	Died, Oct. 23, 1853.
Clarinda,	"	July 18, 1772.	" April 12, 1851.
Serenus,	"	May 27, 1774.	" April 3, 1865.
Noadiah,	"	Feb. 24, 1776.	" March 21, 1860.
Erastus,	"	Feb. 9, 1778.	" April 14, 1848.
Benjamin,	"	April 9, 1780.	" Nov. 11, 1841.
Samuel,	"	Aug. 2, 1782.	
Mary Ann,	"	July 22, 1784.	" March, 1790.
Samanthe,	"	May 12, 1786.	" June 20, 1805.
Persis,	"	March 28, 1788.	" Sept. 5, 1815.
Laura,	"	March 6, 1790.	" April, 1790.
Heman,	"	Sept. 30, 1791.	" Jan. 30, 1856.
Job Sedgwick,	"	April 11, 1794.	" June, 1859.
Mary Ann,	"	Aug. 18, 1796.	

Of these children, Heman spent several months at Andover Theological Seminary, in the study of divinity, but
left for the profession of medicine. The only son who
became a preacher was Job Sedgwick, who, after gradua-
tion at Andover, preached several months in Maine and
Vermont; but, his health failing, he went to the South, was
employed some time in teaching in Georgia, and afterward
turned his attention to other pursuits. Two of the grand-
sons became ministers,—Alfred Brown Swift, son of Hon.
Benjamin Swift, and Henry Martyn, son of Dr. Heman Swift.

His second son, Noadiah Swift, M.D., became a deacon
in this church.

The following is the testimony of President Dwight to Dr. Swift's worth : —

"Dr. Swift was one of the best and most useful men whom we ever knew. Good men loved him, and delighted in his society. and the worst men acknowledged his worth. To the churches and ministers of Vermont he was a patriarch. He possessed an understanding naturally vigorous, respectable learning, sound theological opinions, eminent prudence, and distinguished zeal. combined in the happiest manner with moderation, benevolence. and piety; and wherever he was known he is remembered with the highest veneration." [1]

IV. The Rev. Daniel Marsh was born in New Milford, Conn., May 10, 1762. The first public school he attended was at Brunswick, New Jersey, in the time of the Revolutionary War. He served as militia man at various times, travelled on foot, to and fro, between Connecticut and New Jersey. He cut wood night and morning to pay for his board, and by his own exertions obtained his education. He studied divinity with the Rev. Dr. Bradford, near Boston. He received an honorary degree of M.A., from Williams College, in 1795.

He was ordained at Poughkeepsie, N. Y., June 30, 1790 : was pastor of the church there several years ; thence he removed to Catskill, N. Y.; next to Salisbury on the Royal Grant ; thence to Ballston and Saratoga ; thence to Bennington.

He succeeded the Rev. Job Swift, D.D. He preached in this town as early as 1805, and was the first settled minister after the great revival in 1802-3. According to records of the Congregational society — kept in the town records — of March 27, 1805, at a meeting of the Congregational society : —

---

1 " Dwight's Travels," vol. II., p. 443.

" *Voted,* That the society recommend the Committee of Supply to hire Mr. Marsh for the year ensuing."

The building of the new meeting-house was approaching to completion. By vote of the society, Mr. Marsh preached its dedication sermon. December 4, 1805, was first appointed for the dedication; afterward the time was changed, and the dedication took place on New Year's Day, 1806. The dedication sermon was published with the hymns sung on the occasion. A sermon by Mr. Marsh, subsequently preached before the Legislature, and a sermon on the sixteenth of August, 1809, were published.

" March 19, 1806, on application of seven freeholders, declaring themselves to be of the Congregational order, and also by particular request of the Congregational Church, all inhabitants of the town of Bennington, and especially of the Congregational society, are warned to meet at the court-house, to see if they will unite in calling the Rev. Daniel Marsh to settle over said church and society; to see if they will vote a sum of money for salary from year to year, or for the year ensuing; and to choose a committee, or in some other way to agree with him what he shall have." " March 31, 1806. —Met according to warning; *voted* affirmatively; *voted* to give four hundred and fifty dollars yearly, and so long as he shall continue with us in the gospel ministry." " May 12, 1806. — Adjourned meeting. *Voted,* It belongs to the church to call the installing council. *Voted,* It is our wish the church would unite with the Rev. Daniel Marsh in calling a council."

Mr. Marsh was accordingly installed, and remained pastor of this church until regularly dismissed by an ecclesiastical council, April 25, 1820.

When his labors closed in Bennington, he went out, a short season, as missionary into Central New York, aided by a missionary society in Massachusetts; then he preached in Rupert in this State; thence to a feeble church in Jamesville, Onondaga Co., N. Y. There he enjoyed a powerful

and extensive revival, in which his own soul was much enlarged, and the church greatly strengthened. This was the
crowning work of his ministry; for, after a few years of successful labor there, he suffered from inflammation of his eyes,
by which he so far lost his sight that he was unable to read
the remainder of his life. Although he gave up his charge,
he continued to preach occasionally until near the time of
his death.

Under his ministry, seventy-seven are known to have
been received into the church here. Among them, Hiram
Bingham, the missionary, Luther Bingham, Charles Cushman, Capt. Elijah Dewey (at seventy-four years of age)
Jotham French (afterward deacon), Henry Harwood,
Hiram Harwood, second, Seth Hathaway, Stephen Hinsdill (afterward deacon), James Nichols, James B. Nichols,
and others. Among the additions to the church, under his
ministry here, were several who were hopefully converted
while he resided as a near neighbor to them. The Bing-
hams, the Nicholses, Mr. French, were near neighbors to
him when he resided on the Charles Hicks farm. Also
Eunice (Mrs. Martin) and Lydia Bingham, Mrs. Uria
Edgerton, a neighbor, Mrs. Hinsdill, mother of Mrs. Geo.
W. Robinson. Also four female members of the Nichols
family. He was very sociable. When he moved into the
Hunt place, Capt. Burt lived near him. Capt. B. was not
favorable to ministers, and said he should "neither borrow
nor lend." Mr. Marsh heard of it, went to Capt. Burt's
and asked to borrow a saddle. Capt. B. lent him the saddle, and, in due time, became a great friend of Mr. Marsh.
He was a man of peace, and successful in settling difficulties
among brethren. On one occasion, being called, as a member of a council, to settle a difficulty in a neighboring
church, when the council had assembled, and while they
were organizing and preparing for business, he brought

9*

the contending parties together, and reconciled them before the council was ready to hear the case. His salary was small. He was obliged to work a farm, which he was enabled to purchase with property of his wife. While the horses were at work on the farm, he was accustomed to go from one side of the town to the other on foot, attending meetings, officiating at funerals, and visiting the sick. He subsequently bought a farm in Jamesville, in part with proceeds of the sale of his Bennington farm. He was gifted in prayer. On one sixteenth of August, at the celebration, he was designated to make the prayer. He introduced so much pertinent matter into the prayer, the orator of the day complained that there was nothing left for the oration.

In his last sickness he enjoyed much of the presence of his Saviour, and officiated in prayers in his son's family as long as his voice was audible. He died at Jamesville, N. Y., Dec. 13, 1843. A veteran of eighty-two years, he met death in peace, rejoicing in the hope of a glorious immortality.

In the early part of his ministry he married Miss Anna Jagger, daughter of Deacon Stephen Jagger, of Long Island. His wife was a remarkable woman. While residing in the north part of this town, hearing of Robert Raikes' Sabbath school, she organized one in her own house for the children in her vicinity. This, at the time, she supposed to be the first Sabbath school in the United States.[1] She

---

[1] A Sabbath school was organized in Middlebury, in this State, in 1813, and in Greensboro' in 1814. ("Vermont Chronicle," June 4 and July 30, 1864.) And in Connecticut, substantially, though not exactly, in the modern form, as early as 1764. (See Cont. Ecc. Hist. Conn., pp. 191-2.) It may not be out of place to introduce here the following notice of a *tract enterprise,* contained in the "Green Mountain Farmer" of August, 1811: "Excited by the example, and encouraged by the success of religious tract societies in different parts of the United States, and elsewhere in the world, a respectable number of persons in Bennington have subscribed and contributed to procure excellent cheap religious tracts for charitable distribution," etc., etc.

also drew up a series of Bible questions, which she had printed at the printing-office of Anthony Haswell. She also organized a cent society for contributions to the missionary cause, which continued a long time afterward in this parish.

They had nine children, — seven sons and two daughters. One of his sons, Edwards Marsh, became a minister of the gospel. One of his daughters became the wife of the Rev. Cyrus Hudson.

Two or three short extracts respecting Mr. Marsh, from Benjamin Harwood's diary, will interest those who remember either of these persons. Here is one to show that Mr. Marsh found some not smooth sailing early in his ministry here : —

"May 30, 1808. — This afternoon I attended a meeting of the Congregational society. The question to be tried was, Whether we should support our present minister or not? It was carried in the affirmative. There was some debate on the subject, which was conducted with candor and coolness, except in some instances where party feelings could not be suppressed. Judge Robinson intimated that, should Mr. Marsh be turned away through the influence of his enemies, he was of the opinion that another minister could not be had here. He meant to be honest about it, and said he should vote against settling any other man. He appears to be a pretty warm advocate for Mr. Marsh. I was on the affirmative."

Very Anti-universal. — "April 22, 1810. — Had the pleasure of being where I might have heard Mr. Marsh had sleep not blocked up my hearing channels. By this I do not mean I heard none at all. I understood of his preaching enough to know that it was very anti-universal."

Solemn and Impressive. — (Diary of Hiram Harwood.) — "May 28, 1813. — Mr. Marsh preached the funeral sermon of Governor Robinson in a solemn and impressive style."

March Meetings opened with Prayer. — "March 29, 1809. — A full meeting convened at the court-house, and, after an excellent prayer by the Rev. Mr. Marsh, proceeded to business."

V. The Rev. Absalom Peters, D.D., was born in Grafton County, New Hampshire, Sept. 19, 1793. His father was Gen. Absalom Peters, a graduate of Dartmouth College, and descendant of a brother of Hugh Peters, famous as an adherent of Cromwell, and who was beheaded on the restoration of Charles II., — a martyr to the cause of civil and religious liberty. The mother of Dr. Peters is claimed to be a lineal descendant of John Rogers, the Smithfield martyr of " catechism " celebrity.

Dr. Peters was graduated at Dartmouth College, in 1816 ; studied Theology at Princeton ; was ordained and installed pastor, at Bennington, July 5, 1820, and dismissed Dec. 14, 1825, to accept the secretaryship of the United Domestic Missionary Society, and as such to aid in the formation of the American Home Missionary Society, of which he was the first secretary, continuing such until 1837, — in these years also commencing and editing the " Home Missionary and Pastor's Journal ; " was editor of the "American Biblical Repository " for four and a half years, commencing January 1, 1838 ; on November 20, 1844, was installed pastor of the First Church of Christ in Williamstown, Massachusetts, and dismissed, at his own request, September 4, 1857. Beside these more protracted fields of labor, Dr. Peters' peculiar talent for originating and helping forward new instrumentalities in the cause of Christ has found scope in various engagements of lesser duration. Among these may be mentioned, his connection with the Union Theological Seminary, as one of its original projectors, and agent to collect funds for it, and in which he received appointment to the chair of Homiletics and Pastoral Theology ; also his connection with the " American Eclectic," as originator and editor for a brief time, and other temporary labors.

He was the immediate predecessor, in Bennington, of

the Rev. Daniel A. Clark. Under his ministry here, Articles of Faith and a Covenant were adopted by the church, — it having been before with no other instrument of this sort excepting the Cambridge Platform. The church records, too, were kept with remarkable neatness and care by Major Aaron Robinson, the clerk. Mr. Peters was warmly seconded, in his efforts to elevate the tone of morals and religion in the community, by intelligent and spiritually minded Christians. This was his youthful pastorate. With a graceful style in sermonizing, and great ardor in his work, he attracted large audiences, and was blessed with numerous additions to the church. He will pardon the insertion here of an anecdote related by himself to the writer. In the first days of his ministry here, sitting one day in his study, he was surprised by a loud and repeated knock at his study door, and, upon being bidden to enter, in rushed an entire stranger, of eccentric manner, and from the north part of the State, who took him solemnly by the hand, and proceeded to say, sadly, "Brother Peters, I have come to warn you, to pronounce a *woe* upon you — '*Woe unto you, when all men shall speak well of you!*'"

Not a very long time afterward the same individual paid him another visit in his study, but with a cheerfulness quite in contrast with his former aspect. He now grasped Mr. Peters warmly with both hands, and said, "This time, Brother Peters, I have come to congratulate you; you are all right now." The truth was, the wrath of some individuals in the community had been roused recently against Mr. Peters; the particular occasion of which was a sermon preached[1] September 29, 1822, aimed directly against public wickedness, which the week previously had

---

[1] The text was, "When the enemy shall come in like a flood, the Spirit of the Lord shall lift up a standard against him." — Is. xlix. 19. The sermon was published by unanimous request of the church.

assumed an alarming form in a devotion of a portion of the inhabitants, and of not a few congregated here from abroad, for nearly the entire week, to horse-racing and the performances of a travelling theatrical company. The zeal and efforts of Mr. Peters in this connection had no small share in the enactment of severe statutes against such evils, which, particularly with regard to travelling circuses, have for a long time not been inoperative in this State, until by an enactment, approved November 9, 1865, the bars, as to circuses, are again let down.

Dr. Peters was married, Oct. 25, 1819, to Miss Harriet Hinkly Hatch, daughter of Major Reuben Hatch, of Norwich, in this State. Of seven children, the issue of this marriage, three were born in Bennington. — George Absalom Peters. M.D; Harriet Adeline, wife of the Rev. William Clift; and Horace Hatch, deceased in infancy.[1]

VI. The Rev. Daniel A. Clark was born in Rahway, N. J., March 1, 1799. His father was David Clark, a relative of Abraham Clark, whose name appears among the signers of the Declaration of Independence. He was hopefully converted at the age of fifteen, and one year afterward united with the church. He was graduated at Princeton College in 1808; pursued studies preparatory to the sacred ministry at the Theological Seminary in Andover; and was ordained and installed pastor of the Congregational Union church of Braintree and Weymouth, Jan. 1, 1812. He remained in that charge until the fall of 1815. January, 1816, he was installed pastor of the Congregational church in Southbury, Conn., which field he left to be installed as pastor of West Parish, Amherst, Mass., Jan. 26, 1820.

[1] See "A Birthday Memorial of Seventy Years, with Memories and Reflections for the Aged and the Young; by Absalom Peters, D.D." New York, 1866.

From Amherst he came to Bennington, and was here installed June 14, 1826. His next and last pastorate was in Adams, Jefferson County, N. Y., where he was installed over the Presbyterian church July 17, 1832. He also labored for intervals before his ordination, and in repeated instances between his pastorates, in other places. He deceased March 3, 1840. "Without a struggle or a groan he calmly fell asleep in Jesus."

Mr. Clark's sermons and other productions have been repeatedly issued from the press. The last in two octavo volumes, with a biography.[1]

When thoroughly roused, which he often was, Mr. Clark delivered his thoughts from the pulpit with herculean force, nor did he disdain to flash the truth from a polished blade, or to cut a way for it to the conscience with a whetted edge. Sometimes his sentences disclosed a beauty rarely surpassed. A layman,[2] resident in Bennington during Mr. Clark's ministry here, states that of the many sermons of this divine which he heard, the one most impressed upon his own memory was marked by great beauty of style. The subject of this discourse was "The Beauty of Holiness." The discourse does not appear in the printed works. Of his discourse, "The Church Safe," the Rev. Dr. Sprague says,[3] "It is enough to immortalize the mind that could produce it."

Children listened with delight to his preaching, because of its simplicity and clearness. It is related[4] of a bright little girl, that, returning home from church one Sabbath day, she was inquired of who preached, and replied, with

---

[1] "The Complete Works of Rev. Daniel A. Clark," edited by his son, James Henry Clark, M.D., with a Biographical Sketch, and an Estimate of his Powers as a Preacher, in two volumes. Ives & Phinney, New York.

[2] Seth B. Hunt.

[3] Letter to J. Henry Clark, M.D., in Clark's Works, etc.

[4] By Mrs. Darius Clark.

marked signs of pleasure, "Nobody preached ; Mr. Clark talked to us." Mr. Clark had preached a sermon to children, and they, in their interest in what he said, forgot that it was a sermon.

The well-aimed labors of his predecessor, Mr. Peters, it is evident, had not wholly eradicated public sin from the community. A travelling theatre advertised to visit Bennington ; and the young men, some of whom knew better, had become committed to sustain the affair, and were quite determined to brave the opposition to it among good men. One of them, since a judge upon the bench of the Supreme Court in this State, has described the appearance of Mr. Clark when he entered upon the introductory exercises of the pulpit next Sabbath morning. There was a peculiar nervous excitement, and twitching of his countenance, and animation of his whole frame, which led his audience to anticipate what was coming. He preached two discourses that day, which made those respectable young men who had pledged their patronage to the travelling theatre wish they had taken a sober second thought before doing so.

Among outlines of discourses in his published works is one on the sinner's desperate depravity. The text is Jeremiah iii. 5 : "*Thou hast spoken and done evil things, as thou couldst.*" The discourse is thus introduced : "This passage evidently teaches the doctrine that *men are as depraved as they can be in present circumstances.*" The large comparative number of additions to the church during his brief ministry here — one hundred and twenty-six in four years and four months — and, it may be added, the powerful revival which occurred here the next year after his dismission, must have been due, in no small degree, to the divine blessing upon his faithful preaching of the doctrine of man's sinfulness, and dependence upon the sovereign mercy of God. Revivals attended and followed his labors elsewhere.

It was a time of powerful revivals in the country at large. It was a blessed time, indeed, in which to be an eminently talented and qualified preacher of the gospel, and in the prime of one's great physical and intellectual strength.

Mr. Clark aimed deadly blows at intemperance, Sabbath-breaking, dancing, card-playing, covetousness. If there was an infidel-club in the town, he discovered it, and poured his hottest fire into it. Like Samson, he was willing to pull down the temple of Dagon upon himself as well as the Philistines, if, otherwise, he could not destroy them. The temperance reformation had just commenced in the country at the time Mr. Clark was settled here, and he threw himself, with his accustomed ardor, into that movement. He began here by proposing to individuals to sign a pledge that they would, at the end of the year, report faithfully what amount of distilled liquor had been used in the family during the year. Many signers were obtained. Among the number, eight reported at the year's end they had used none; others reported the quantity they had used. We are amused at the report of one, whose figures went as high as ten gallons; he said it was for bathing purposes. At the time of the second annual report of this association it was resolved to practise total abstinence from distilled spirit. That was some years before the temperance reformation advanced to the point of abstinence from all intoxicating drinks. There were some earnest ones, who, at that meeting, anticipated the subsequent movement, and took a position in favor of including wine, beer, and cider, in the pledge. Mr. Clark thought it not then expedient, and reasoned as follows: "If wolves and bears were coming down in fury from your mountain sides to devour your flocks, would you stop to hunt out the rats and mice?"

10

Many were the large orchards in that day; and cider-mills, from early autumn until late in the winter, were busy night and day. And distilleries were not deficient, to which the hogsheads and barrels from the cider-press were constantly borne. These orchards were many of them cut down, under the powerful impulse of the temperance reformation. Mr. Clark also sought the promotion of intellectual improvement in schools, lyceums, and especially in the study of the word of God. The whole congregation was, at that time, engaged in Bible-class and Sabbath-school study during the intermission. His own success in preaching, and the great and multiplied revivals of those times, times in which Bible societies, Missionary societies, Temperance societies, and Sabbath schools were springing up as if by magic, on every hand, fired his expectations of the speedy advent of the millennium, and stimulated his ardor to the highest pitch. Every man here almost was a representative man. All were accustomed to move on in their purposes with more than ordinary energy and persistency of will. There were, nevertheless, leading spirits.

This place was, at that time, the scene of a remarkable competition between two rival seminaries of learning. The impulse of this competition drew crowds here from abroad to both schools; among them many talented youth. Bennington had once more become famous far and wide; and the Rev. Daniel A. Clark, was, for the time, among other noted ones, the most noted personage.

After all that has been said of Mr. Clark, in this short notice, it will not give surprise if it is added that he aroused much opposition against himself. His preaching and labors were the occasion of not a few in the community being "set at variance" (see Matt. x. 34, 35), not only from him but also from one another.

Abruptness and severity of dealing with ungodly men was not unknown to the preaching of those times; and Mr. Clark, self-trained to great terseness of expression, and by nature intense, sometimes manifested the fierceness of the lion rather than the gentleness of the lamb. The following incident, occurring in Amherst, Mass., was related to the writer of these sketches. It is easy to believe such a story would lose nothing by repetition in passing through lips unfriendly to Mr. Clark; still it is deemed proper to be given here as an illustration of the impression some of his labors made upon a portion of the community. Vehement controversy between two persons in a blacksmith's shop was overheard by another person, sitting in the open chamber-window of an adjoining house; and the person, thus an involuntary listener, went down to ascertain more definitely the character of the dispute, and found the two parties were the blacksmith, a profane man, and the Rev. Mr. Clark. Mr. Clark said to the blacksmith, "You will be damned if you do not repent." The blacksmith, enraged, with so personal and severe an application of the gospel warning, retorted upon Mr. Clark the same threatening, in similar language, though with probably more of it. The listening party returned to the house, and said, "The other man, no doubt, was swearing, and he should have said Mr. Clark was, also, if he had not known who he was."

One of his successors in the pulpit of the Amherst church, speaking of Mr. Clark to the writer, said, "He was a preacher of magnificent sermons; but he knew not how to take the kinks out of a Yankee's brain." It would seem, however, that he knew how to take out the self-conceit, and some of the delusions out of the sinner's heart. It may be said, too, that, as time wears on, the words of censure of Mr. Clark become infrequent and faint, and his admirers speak their warm praises, with few, if any, to call in question the fitness of the eulogy.

There was noticeable in him, as the infirmities of disease and a disabled frame gathered upon him, a rare childlikeness and humility.

He deceased at sixty-one years of age; but his remarkable powers began to give way under the influence of disease some eight years previously; so that his ministry in Adams, N. Y., where he was last installed, continued little over a year. " From that time he failed gradually, till God called him home." His disease was one of rare occurrence, — the ossification of the arteries of the brain.

He was married June, 1812, at Portland, Maine, to Miss Eliza Barker, daughter of Dr. Jeremiah Barker, of Gorham. The offspring of this marriage are, James Henry Clark, M.D., Hon. Horace F. Clark, LL.D., Rev. Frederic G. Clark, D.D., Edward Clark, Esq., Mary, wife of Rev. Livingston Willard, and Sereno Clark.

VII.   THE REV. EDWARD WILLIAM HOOKER, D.D., was born in Goshen, Conn., Nov. 24, 1794. By his paternal ancestry, he traces his descent back (seven or eight generations) to the Rev. Thomas Hooker, that "light of the New England churches, and oracle of the colony of Connecticut;" the Puritan father, who, with others of like religious character and aims, came to this country from England in 1633; first settled at Newtown, now Cambridge, Mass.; and in 1636 removed to Hartford, Conn., and was one of the founders of the first Connecticut churches, and pastor of the first church in Connecticut, that now the First Congregational Church of Hartford.[1] By his maternal an-

---

[1] In the life of Thomas Hooker (by Dr. Hooker), in the Appendix, are the names of forty-two ministers of the gospel descended from him, and of forty-one married to his female descendants, — among them some of the brightest lights of the American pulpit.

cestry, Dr. Hooker is descended from the Elder President Jonathan Edwards.

Dr. Hooker was fitted for college at Goshen Academy, and Addison County Grammar School; graduated at Middlebury College in 1814; studied theology at Andover 1814–18; was pastor of the Congregational Church in Green's Farms, Fairfield, Conn., 1821–29; associate general agent of the American Temperance Society, and editor of the "Journal of Humanity," 1829–31; pastor of the First Church in Bennington, 1832–44; Professor of Sacred Rhetoric and Ecclesiastical History in the Theological Institute of Connecticut, at East Windsor, 1844–48; pastor of the Congregational Church, South Windsor, Conn., 1848– (the date to which is not given); pastor in Fair Haven, Vt., 1856–62; since which time he has resided with his son, Rev. E. C. Hooker, at Newburyport, Mass., and at Nashua, N. H.

Dr. Hooker has published several sermons and pamphlets, and, at least, two thick volumes, — one the life of Thomas Hooker, the other memoirs of Mrs. Sarah Lanman Smith, and has also contributed, with more or less frequency, articles to the periodical press. With an intellect of superior excellence, having extensive knowledge of men and individuals at home and abroad, and wielding a racy and vigorous pen, he has possessed peculiar talents for writing for the press. But his heart has ever clung to the *preaching of "the glorious gospel of the blessed God"* as his great life-work. Loving the evangelical and Calvinistic doctrines, and zealous for the faith once delivered to the saints, he has uttered no uncertain sound, and occupied no doubtful position as a preacher of Christ and him crucified. And a life-long example of high-toned Christian courtesy and conscientious Christian circumspection has added weight to his words.

His was one of the longer of the Bennington pastorates, —

10*

twelve and a half years ; and probably none of the ex-pastors of this parish have gone away with warmer attachment to them of families left behind than has continued to exist between the Rev. Dr. Hooker and some families of his old Bennington pastorate.   Many were added to the church during his ministry here ; one year — that of 1834 — the number rose as high as ninety.   He was here in an important period of the history of the church and the town, and enjoyed relations of mutual respect and friendly intercourse with leading members of the church and community, and is therefore eminently fitted to furnish valuable reminiscences of the times of his residence here ; and it is hoped he will not fail to do so.

His first wife was Miss Faith Trumbull Huntington, of Norwich, Conn., daughter of Jabez Huntington, Esq., and grand-daughter of Gen. Jedidiah Huntington, of New London, Conn. ; and, on her mother's side, in the line of the Trumbull family, tracing her ancestry back to William Robinson, who came from England to Dorchester, Mass., in 1641, and is believed to be a descendant of the venerable Puritan, *John Robinson, of Leyden.*

The children of this marriage are : Mary Lanman, wife of the Rev. Anson Clark ; Faith Huntington, wife of the Rev. E. J. Montague ; Elizabeth Peck, deceased in 1841, at the age of twenty-two, — all of whom became members of the Bennington church ; the Rev. Elias Cornelius Hooker, Miss Sarah Huntington Hooker, and the Rev. Edward Trumbull Hooker, — these last three, natives of Bennington.

Dr. Hooker's second wife was Mrs. Elizabeth Shelden Lyman, of Troy, New York, sister-in-law of our Deacon George Lyman ; she died in Fairhaven, Vermont, in 1856. His present wife was Miss Lucy Bagley, of Newburyport, Massachusetts.

NOTE. — In introducing notices of two living pastors, the writer has felt he was executing a delicate task. He would not have done so but for the fact that the lapse of years has already separated their labors in Bennington to quite a distance from the present. With regard to the remaining ex-pastors of this church, and the pastors of the other churches in the town, the time of their labors here falling into the more recent past, is the writer's apology for omitting any other than the briefest statistical mention of them, which will be found elsewhere.

CHAPTER IX

TRANSIENT MINISTERS.

THE Rev. Mr. Burton. — In the interval be-tween the pastorates of the Rev. Mr. Avery and the Rev. Job Swift, D.D., there was a revival un-der the labors of the Rev. Messrs. Wood and Bur-ton. It is believed, though upon what evidence can scarcely be stated, that the Mr. Burton was the Rev. Asa Burton, afterward distinguished as the Rev. Dr. Burton, of Thetford, in this State, author of the "Taste Scheme in Divinity," and instructor of many students in theology. He was at that time the young pastor of Thet-ford. He was a close reasoner, and a difficult antagonist in controversy. The following characteristic anecdote has been told of him. Some people, called Christ-ians, set up a Sabbath evening meeting in a school-house in one corner of his parish, the town of Thetford, and it was the custom of their preacher to give opportunity after his sermon to any who might desire it to ask questions. These new-comers were esteemed to be not sound in divinity. Dr. Burton thought it his duty to attend their meetings and hear for himself. He did so, and when the opportunity was given to ask questions, he plied the stranger with such diffi-cult ones as caused him to cease holding any more meetings in that town.

FATHER MARSHALL has already been mentioned as a Con-necticut Separate pastor, who was accustomed frequently to pass this way. He is described as possessing ardent piety, but marked by eccentricity. A biographical sketch of him in the "Vermont Evangelical Magazine" for July, August, 1815, contains a graphic account in brief of his character and life; also affords a glimpse of the Separates of Father Marshall's time. He was, when a lad, brought under deep conviction of sin, which ofttimes returned upon him with great power after he obtained a Christian hope. His zeal in warning the impenitent and the lukewarm would brook no restraints, whether as an exhorter, being yet a stripling, or as a Separate minister, which he became a considerable time before his twentieth year. For violating the new laws against exhorting in other ministers' parishes, or the prevalent notions of propriety, — exhorting in season and out of season, — he was arrested, tried, set in the stocks, bound out to a farmer two months to pay the costs of prosecution; tried again, and for a time confined in Hartford jail. He was twice settled, — his longest pastorate being over the Separate church in Canterbury, Conn. When nearly seventy years of age he removed to Starksborough, in this State. He preached temporarily in Weybridge, Hinesburgh, and Westfield. When at home he regularly preached to the people in Starksborough until it became impossible for him to do so any longer because of the infirmities of advanced age. He often performed the devotional part of public worship until within a few weeks of his death, which took place at Starksborough Feb. 20, 1813, in the eighty-second year of his age.

Many anecdotes are told of him, of which three or four shall be given here. He tried for a time to conform to the demand for written sermons, but did so with an ill grace. On one occasion his little notes had got forward gradually to the outer edge of the pulpit-desk until they slipped off. He started back, and said, " There, go with your fetters ! "

Once preaching here with great earnestness, he cried out, " Where is Governor Moses Robinson's piety, and where is old Esquire Samuel Robinson's piety ? " — meaning, Is their piety reproduced in those who ought to imitate their good examples? At another time preaching here, he looked out of the window which was back of the pulpit and saw men harvesting grain on the Sabbath. The subject of his discourse was, " The Claims of God." Pointing backward to the men in the field, he said, " Bennington sinners can trust God to send them rain and sunshine, and ripen their crops for them ; but they cannot trust him, after the grain is ripe, to keep it for them twenty-four hours while they shall keep the Sabbath for him." Once when he was a guest at the elder Mrs. Samuel Robinson's, she lamented to him the loss of some religious privilege, occasioned by their removing from Massachusetts to this then wilderness. Father Marshall remembered her state of mind, with his wonted particularity, in his prayer at family worship, " that she might have grace to be more thankful for the mercies she still enjoyed, and not hanker so much for the flesh-pots of Egypt." It is related that she was never again heard to complain in that manner.

There is an anecdote relating to the " Oracles of Reason," an atheistical book of Ethan Allen, — the edition of which was consumed in the burning of the printing-office, — which has been, and not without appearance of truth, ascribed to Mr. Marshall. He was, so it is related, a guest for the night of Ethan Allen, and in the morning was duly called upon to attend prayers in the family. Such were the customs of hospitality of the place in those days. Col. Allen handed him his " Oracles of Reason," saying, " This is *my* bible. I suppose you have no objections to read out of my bible." His reverend guest replied, " Let us sing a few verses first ; have you any objection to the common psalm-book?"—"Not at all," said the host. Mr. Marshall, taking up the psalm-book which lay upon the table, selected, and proceeded to read, the psalm commencing with this stanza:—

> "Let all the heathen writers join
> To form one perfect book,—
> Great God, if once compared with thine,
> How mean their writings look!"

Allen, who, notwithstanding his infidelity, was characterized by great cordiality and frankness, interrupted him, and said, "Floored, Father Marshall; take your own Bible."

Father Marshall would be requested sometimes by the Baptists, when they were without a supply, to preach for them, and even to administer the communion, though it was not expected that he would himself commune. On one such occasion, a piece of the bread fell from the table to the floor; he picked it up, and ate it, saying, "The dogs eat of the crumbs that fall from the master's table."

THE REV. JOSHUA SPAULDING. — At a society's meeting, Dec. 13, 1804, a call was voted to the Rev. J. Spaulding, and a committee appointed to wait on him and inform him of the same. His answer is not on record. He was never settled here. He had preached here, it is said, for a year or more, just previously. This was immediately subsequent to his dismissal from the Tabernacle Church, in Salem, Mass., April 23, 1802,[1] and prior to his settlement over the Branch (now Howard Street) Church, in the same city. He was here during the revival of 1802-3. He is stated to have said that he had had a part in forty revivals.

---

[1] A printed farewell discourse of his, delivered at Salem, Mass., is advertised for sale in the "Vermont Gazette" of that day.

He was in the early part of his ministry styled a New-Light preacher. A two-volume treatise of his on Divinity is in print; also lectures on the coming of the Kingdom of Christ. He also compiled a hymn-book, which was published at Salem soon after his visit to this place. He was a millenarian. An interesting manuscript correspondence has been preserved, and is in the possession of G. W. Robinson, between Mr. Spaulding and others, and also between him and Judge Jonathan Robinson, on the second coming of Christ.[1] He was blessed greatly as pastor in building up the Tabernacle Church in Salem, and in promoting purity of church discipline and spirituality.[2].

He preached with great warmth and power. In Miss Read's narrative, as before noticed, after speaking of his singular unction, and elevation of countenance and manner in illustrating the righteousness of Christ, so as to bring forcibly to her mind the text, "How beautiful upon the mountains," etc., she says, upon a subsequent page, "The next day Mr. Spaulding preached in a most terrific manner. He showed forth the terribleness of Christ's coming to judgment, and treated of the confusion and dismay of his enemies at his glorious appearing."

He was a democrat in politics, and accustomed to speak and write his political sentiments with the same pointedness and freedom that he did those of divinity.[3]

Mr. Spaulding, while here, with his daughter, which was all the family he had at the time, enjoyed the large-hearted hospitality of Capt. Elijah Dewey.

---

[1] There appears to have been a considerable interest here and in the vicinity, in those times, in the Scripture prophecies. A printed sermon is at hand, by the Rev. John Griswold, pastor of the church in Pawlet, preached in 1804, and published at Bennington (Haswell and Smead), from Rev. xi. 10, taking the view that the " two witnesses " signified the two offices of the magistracy and the ministry.

[2,3] A discourse on the First Centennial of the Tabernacle Church, Salem, Mass., by Samuel M. Worcester, M.A., pastor of the church.

THE REV. JEDIDIAH BUSHNELL is remembered, by some of the old inhabitants in this town, as a Vermont minister, quaint, but able, and very much respected, and very useful. He was a classmate in Williams College, of David Robinson, Jr., Esq., and visited him while travelling through this part of the country with an invalid son. Returning home, and gratefully remembering the hospitality of his friend and classmate, he wrote an affectionate and faithful letter to Capt. Robinson, on the subject of his personal salvation. Capt. Robinson always esteemed this letter as a true expression of friendship, and a beautiful act of Christian fidelity, and to his dying day used to show the letter. It was, some few years since, at his request, printed in the " Vermont Chronicle." The following anecdote of Father Bushnell used to be related by the Rev. N. Hewitt, D.D., of Bridgeport, Conn. Mr. Hewitt, then a young preacher, happened, with his wife and first-born child, then an infant, to be in the company of Father Bushnell, who kindly noticed the child. Mrs. Hewitt made the remark, " Mr. Bushnell, I am afraid I shall love this child too much."

" No! no! madam," said Father Bushnell, " you cannot love it too much, if you will only love God a great deal more."

A recipe, that he once gave to Mr. and Mrs. P. M. Henry, at the outset of their married life, is worth preserving; it is as follows : —

"To Mrs. Henry. — 'Do you wish to know how to make Mr. Henry to be a good husband?'

" ' Yes.'

" ' Be a good wife.'

"To Mr. Henry. — 'Do you wish to know how to make Mrs. Henry to be a good wife?'

" ' Yes.'

" ' Be a good husband.' "

11

The Rev. Lemuel Haynes, the noted colored preacher, has been mentioned in the biographical notice of the Rev. Job Swift, D.D., as in that day one of the ministers of this region. It is related of him that, while a pastor in Manchester, he was called to preach a funeral sermon in this town, and introduced the sermon by saying, "If my hearers expect me to dwell upon the faults of the deceased, they will be disappointed; and if they expect me to dwell upon the virtues of the deceased, they will be disappointed; for I am not here to preach to the dead, but to the living."

There was a severe drouth in this town, and in the time of it came the day appointed for the ordination and installation of the Rev. Absalom Peters, then the youthful pastor-elect of this church and society. The venerable Mr. Haynes was present, and had assigned to him, as his part in the public exercises, the concluding prayer.

There were other able divines to perform the more conspicuous and weighty duties of the occasion, but a hearer[1] related to me that Mr. Haynes' concluding prayer was the particular part of the exercises that he retained a vivid impression of. Mr. Haynes made impressive remembrance in his prayer of the retiring pastor (Mr. Marsh), — of whom, doubtless without intention, the preceding speakers had omitted to make mention; also, he earnestly supplicated that the long-continued and distressing drouth might come to a speedy end. His words, as related by another hearer[2] were, "O God, wilt thou unstop thy bottles, and pour the waters upon the earth?" It began to sprinkle a little as the meeting was dismissed, and soon came the much-desired plentiful rain. On returning from the ordination exercises, Mr. Samuel Fay, at whose house he put up, and who was accustomed to relate this anecdote, said to him: "Well, Mr. Haynes, your prayer was answered." — "I *thought* it would be," was Mr. Haynes' laconic reply.

Another gentleman [1] recollects the following expressions of Mr. Haynes: In prayer, "O Lord, we are so selfish we spoil everything we do;" in a sermon, speaking of the power of temptation, and the distinction between temptations that are sinful and those that are not, "I acknowledge you cannot prevent a temptation entering your mind, at all times. Neither could you always prevent a bird flying down unawares upon your head, but you could prevent its making a nest in your hair."

THE REV. EDWARD DORR GRIFFIN, D.D., is remembered as one of the distinguished ministers who have occasionally occupied the pulpit of the Bennington First Church. His commanding form — being some six feet, seven inches in height, and of well-proportioned stoutness — need not be here particularly described. Pleasant anecdotes are related of his being duly mindful, upon his arrival in town to exchange, or to fulfil some special ministerial appointment, that in the respect mentioned he was not an ordinary man. Upon reaching the house where he was to be entertained, he was accustomed to see, first, that the faithful beast who had borne him hither was well cared for; secondly, that the place in the pulpit from which he was to deliver his discourse — that is, where the manuscript was to be placed — was, by such contrivances as could be extemporized, sufficiently elevated; thirdly, that the bed upon which he was to repose for the night was suitably supplemented, so as to be long enough for so tall a man to stretch himself upon it without discomfort, — for all which attentions he would

[1] Mr. Seth B. Hunt.

return graceful acknowledgments with a dignity peculiar to himself.

But when once in the pulpit, and engaged in his favorite work of preaching "the glorious gospel of the blessed God," who else could equal the majestic eloquence of Dr. Griffin? Of two or three excellent anecdotes illustrative of this, related to the writer of this notice, one shall suffice. It shall be given in nearly the same words of the friend who related it.[1] Let him be, as it were, heard to speak: "In the fall of 1830, a most beautiful day in October, news came that Alonzo B. Stiles was dead. Men stood appalled at the suddenness of such an event; and one would say to another, 'Is Stiles dead? It is impossible!' But so it was. He had undertaken to drive a pair of high-spirited horses *tandem;* something gave away, he was thrown out, his head striking upon a rock, and killed. If not killed instantly, there was no consciousness after the blow. He was a young man of singular beauty, very accomplished, and very much admired, and had many friends. He was in the employment of the 'Old Furnace Company.' We had no settled pastor. His friends, and particularly the proprietors of the 'Furnace,' sent down for Dr. Griffin to preach the sermon. They appointed Sunday as the day, and as three or four days intervened there was ample time to spread the notice. Many from the adjoining towns were accustomed to have business at the 'Furnace,' and they knew Stiles; they all came. The meeting-house was crowded. Dr. Griffin took his text from Ecc. ix. 12: '*For man also knoweth not his time.*' The sermon was preached to the young. The lesson which he inculcated was, The duty and importance of youth preparing for death. As the sermon drew near its close, leaning his towering form over that old pulpit, — he had a way of lifting very gracefully

[1] Mr. Aaron L. Hubbell.

his glasses, — leaning over the desk, he said: '*My dear young friends, procrastination is a rock around which the bones of shipwrecked millions are whitening for eternity!*' As he spoke so impressively upon the subject of preparation for death, its duty and importance, it was astonishing to see the countenances of the audience. I sat with my back to the minister — the old square pews — and looking a large portion of the audience in the face. I have often thought, I have no doubt that many then and there fully resolved to lead a Christian life.

" That death seemed to make a great impression upon the young people; and there was seriousness all that winter. Along in June of the succeeding spring it was resolved to hold a three-days' meeting." The summer of 1831 will be remembered as the season of one of the two greatest revivals in the annals of this church.

The grave of Stiles is in the church-yard. On the slab is this inscription: " In memory of Alonzo B. Stiles, son of James and Abigail Stiles. Born at Cavendish, Vermont, September 9th, 1805; died in this town (in consequence of being thrown from a wagon), October 14th, 1830, aged 25 years 1 month and 5 days."

11*

CHAPTER X.

THE LAND-TITLE CONTROVERSY.

AT the time our first settlers purchased their lands in this town, probably they had no intimation that any claims would or could be advanced prejudicial to their titles as derived through the Governor and Council of New Hampshire. "A claim of New York had been asserted to Governor Wentworth by letter from Governor Clinton in 1750, ... but the correspondence which had taken place between the two governors does not appear to have been published, and was wholly unknown to the settlers." [1] The pretext laid hold of by interested parties for claiming jurisdiction for the Province of New York as far eastward as Connecticut River, was an "untenable" charter granted by King Charles II. to his brother, the Duke of York, in 1664. "Prior to the proclamation of Governor Colden," Dec. 28, 1763, "setting forth the claim of New York to extend to the Connecticut River by virtue of this charter, one hundred and twenty-four of the one hundred and thirty land patents granted by Governor Wentworth had been issued, only six of the whole number bearing date after Dec., 1763." [2] Our Bennington settlers, and others, had already made valuable improvements upon their lands when this proclamation took them by surprise.

"That prior to the king's order of July, 1764, New York had never for a single moment exercised jurisdiction to any part of

---

[1] Hall's Early Hist. Vermont, p. 76.　　　　[2] Ibid.

Connecticut River; that New Hampshire had been repeatedly recognized by the king and his ministry as extending westward to
Lake Champlain, and to a line running southerly from that lake
to the north-west corner of Massachusetts, the present boundary
of Vermont; that in all the English and American maps of that
period — and they are numerous — New York is represented as
bounded on the east by the last-mentioned line, and that such line
was universally understood, both in Old and New England, to be
the boundaries between the provinces of New Hampshire and New
York."[1]

As to the charter granted by King Charles II. to his
brother the Duke of York, in 1664, it was well characterized by Williams in his history of Vermont as an in-
adequate and blundering transaction. In evident ignorance of the premises, and without any attempt at exact-
ness, it really gave the Connecticut River as an eastern
boundary, and the east side of Delaware Bay as a western
boundary, within which the Duke of York could take what
was not already chartered away. Otherwise it would also
have given to the Duke of York portions of Massachusetts
and Connecticut; but these States never allowed this charter
to deprive them of a square rod of their territory. It also,
for other reasons, had no validity in law against the settlers on the New Hampshire Grants.

"*All the lands from the west side of Connecticut River to the east side
of Delaware Bay.*" "This grant was inconsistent with the charters
which had before been granted to Massachusetts and Connecticut;
and neither of them admitted it to have any effect with regard
to the lands which they had settled or claimed to the west of
Connecticut River; and there were no principles which apply to
human affairs by which this grant would bear a strict examination. If it be examined geographically, the bounds of it were
contradictory, indefinite, and impossible. If it be subjected to
a legal construction, the whole of it, upon James's accession
to the throne, merged in the crown; and at his abdication passed

1 Vermont Hist. Mag., p. 146.

to William, his successor. If it be considered as an instrument of government, it did not establish any colony or province of New York, or any power to govern any such province." [1]

That, however, which made the New York pretext much more formidable was the order in council, referred to in the above quotation, obtained by the New York interest from King George II., under date of 1764.

As to this order in council, it was extensively believed, though probably without foundation, to have been obtained by applications falsely represented to be in the name of the inhabitants of the grants. [2]

But this order in council was interpreted by the settlers as simply decreeing *prospective jurisdiction* to New York as far east as Connecticut River. This the king had a right to do ; as, in chartering these provinces of New York and New Hampshire, the right of altering the boundaries of jurisdiction was reserved to the crown. Had the New York officers so interpreted the king's order, probably all controversy would have been at an end. The settlers were not disposed to revolt against the jurisdiction of New York upon such an interpretation of the order in council, though such jurisdiction was not agreeable to them. [3] Certainly they at first appear to have had no thought of resisting it by force.

1 Williams's Hist. of Vermont, p. 213. See also Answer of Ethan Allen to Governor Clinton's Proclamation, State Papers, pp. 85-93; and Early Hist. of Vermont.

2 Williams's History of Vermont, 1794, p. 215. In a note on this page : "The inhabitants complained that a petition was presented to the king, signed with their names, but unknown to them." In their first petition to Congress (see State Papers, p. 62), Jan. 7, 1776, they give this account of this petition to the king. "We have often heard, and verily believe, it was in your petitioner's names." On the subject of the surreptitious names to that petition to the king, see also an article from the "Connecticut Courant," April, 1772, cited in Mr. Houghton's published address, delivered in Montpelier, Oct. 20, 1848.

3 "The petition of Mr. Robinson, in behalf of his constituents, to the king had not only asked for relief against New York patents, but also to have the jurisdiction of the territory restored to New Hampshire."—P. 98, of Hall's Early Hist. Vermont.

But the New York government were not satisfied with an immediately commencing jurisdiction, and with such emoluments as might arise from lands not previously sold; they insisted on their right to all the lands that had previously been sold in the territory in question by the New Hampshire government, and to retrospective jurisdiction, and, of course, to satisfaction and due punishment of offenders for all acts in the past that had been committed in violation of their claimed authority.

" By the principles of the English constitution, the lands in both New York and New Hampshire were vested in the king, both being royal provinces. Their boundaries, also, might be fixed and changed by him at pleasure. It could not be material to him or to the public through which of his servants his grants were made, and it would be difficult to find a reason why a grant obtained in good faith from the government of one province should be declared void merely because the land, by the subsequent settlement of a disputed boundary, should happen to fall within the newly established jurisdiction of the other." — Early Hist. of Vermont, p. 119. With regard to the legality also, see pp. 119, 120.

The settlers here resisted this claim with indomitable determination and spirit. Matters continued to wax more serious until they were resolved that all the claims of New York, both to retrospective and prospective jurisdiction, should be resisted to the end. The result was, they came ere long to the determination to have an independent State; and they pursued this determination with a purpose and vigor which, under the circumstances, were natural, if not at all times legal. But that they had law and equity on their side in the main, there are many substantial reasons for believing. So Gov. Wentworth appears to have thought, for he reconfirmed their course by a new royal proclamation under date of March 13, 1764, counter to Gov. Colden's. That the king was displeased with the course of the New York government in respect to the Ver-

mont lands is evident from the fact that, notwithstanding
the preponderating influence of that interest at court,
Samuel Robinson, Esq., the agent of the settlers, without
prestige and without money, obtained an order in council
of his Majesty, of July 24, 1767, prohibiting the Governor
of New York,

"Upon pain of his Majesty's highest displeasure, from making
any further grants whatever of the lands in question, till his Majesty's further pleasure should be known concerning the same."[1]

Whether the settlers were able to fathom all the depths
of the subject-matters in controversy, or not, one has but
to read Gov. Hall's volume — so large a portion of which
is devoted to the exhaustive examination of its merits — to
see that the New York claim cannot bear the test of such
an examination either in law or equity. Not to attempt
any extended consideration of the question here, two or
three arguments of more obvious force to the minds of the
settlers may be stated, and reference is here more particularly made to the Bennington settlers, because it is of them
this volume more particularly speaks.

Their utter surprise at Gov. Colden's first proclamation
claiming their lands has been already alluded to. This surprise overtook them after they were well settled here, had
made many valuable improvements on their lands, having
first bought them in good faith, paying what was to them a
large price, for their means were generally scanty and they
had made great exertions and endured much hardship to
open to civilization and to plant with Christian institutions
this wilderness. These lands along their Green Mountain

---

[1] See Slade's Vermont State Papers, p. 20. That this order in council of his
Majesty was constantly and in a high-handed manner disregarded by the New
York officials, and as constantly and earnestly recalled to their attention by the
home government, see Hall's Early Hist. Vermont, pp. 94, 99, 105, 106, 108,
and elsewhere.

valleys were, with God's blessing, upon their sturdy exertions and sacrifices, putting forth signs of prosperity, progress, and wealth. Now all was to be swept away from them. They were to be left destitute, penniless ;[1] and, more than this, their prospects for the future were an utter blank. They would not know which way next to turn. Let it be borne in mind they were already a numerous and powerful community.. By that law of necessity which inheres in man's dependence, to a certain extent, with his choices and God's providence combined, upon the destiny he has already entered upon, they were compelled to accept as a logical conclusion the justice and expediency of revolt against the jurisdiction of New York, whatever that jurisdiction was as determined upon in the king's order of 1764. They did not accept this alternative until compelled to do so by a course of events which told them instinctively they could not err in so doing. They felt that justice on their side must be at the foundation of their cause. The lands under New Hampshire had been chartered in townships to numerous persons, holding some three hundred and thirty.acres each. The New York patents were employed to place oftentimes whole townships and even more in the possession of speculators, and fees in proportion into the pockets of officials. The covetousness with which the New York officials and speculators eyed the rich alluvials of the Green Mountain tributaries to the Hudson knew no bounds.

Some few statistics, which bear upon this point, may be noticed. Twenty-six thousand acres on the Battenkill, to John Taber Kempe, attorney-general of the New York province, James Duane, a prominent New York city lawyer, and Walter Rutherford, a merchant speculator. To said Duane,

---

[1] " And when the latter," the New Hampshire claimants, " applied to the New York governors for a confirmation of those not thus granted, such enormous patent fees were demanded as to make it impossible for them to comply." — Early Hist. of Vermont, p. 115.

afterward, fifty thousand acres more. Dunmore, colonial New York governor for eight months, contrived surreptitiously to make to himself a grant of fifty-one thousand acres of Vermont land, besides granting four hundred and fifty thousand acres to speculators, and getting the fees for the same. Tryon, his successor, provided himself, in like manner, with a township in Vermont of thirty-two thousand acres, besides making grants, and getting fees for the same, contrary to law, of two hundred thousand more. Afterward this Tryon was absent from his post for a little more than a year, and Lieutenant-Governor Colden filled his place. He at this time issued patents for about four hundred thousand acres of Vermont land, — fees to himself, not less than ten thousand dollars. "The whole quantity of Vermont land patented by New York up to the period of the Revolution, besides that embraced in confirmatory charters, exceeded two millions of acres, more than three quarters of which had been granted in direct violation of the king's order of July, 1767, and of the 49th article of the standing instructions of the crown." [1] Governor Colden, during one of the periods of his administration, which lasted little more than a year, by hurrying such land patents through his office, pocketed in patent fees twenty-five thousand dollars.

The New York provincial government was aristocratic in feeling and policy. It declared such sympathies at court — strongly siding with the king, against the republican character of the settlers on the grants, as matters were tending to a rupture with the mother country. Parties in the interest of the New York speculations upon the grants, contemptuously stigmatized the settlers as " fierce republicans," denounced across the water their " illiberal opinions and manners as extremely offensive to all loyal subjects of

[1] Vermont Hist. Mag.

the king." Had the New York jurisdiction, and the policy which the New York provincial government seemed determined to indissolubly wed with it, not been resisted, they would have established their lordly manors here, and become patroons of the Walloomsac and the Battenkill.

"All the officers from the highest to the lowest, — from the judges of the Supreme Court down to constables and superintendents of highways, were appointed, either directly or indirectly, by the central executive authority in New York city. The town meeting, that school and nursery of republican equality, in which the men of New England had been accustomed to elect all inferior officers, and to consult and legislate upon their local affairs, was an institution hardly known in that province." [1]

The measures by which the New York officials sought to accomplish their scheme were of the most arbitrary description. They divided the New Hampshire Grants into counties, and appointed county officers; sent men to survey the lands of the territory in question.

There was a long story of writs and trials of ejectment.

"If we do not oppose the sheriff and his posse he will take immediate possession of our houses and farms; if we do we are immediately indicted as rioters; and when others oppose officers in taking such, their friends so indicted, they are also indicted, and so on, there being no end of indictments against us so long as we act the bold and manly part, and stand by our liberty." [2]

[1] Vermont Hist. Mag.

[2] Letter of Ethan Allen and others to Governor Tryon; see State Papers, 24–29. "Silas Robinson is believed to have been the only settler in the Grants whom the Yorkers, as they were styled, were ever able to arrest and punish as a rioter, though great numbers were accused and indicted as such." He "resided on the main road about two miles north of the Bennington village, at the place now occupied by Stephen Robinson. Early in the morning of the 29th of November, the sheriff (Ten Eyck) and his party (John Munro and others) went to his house, and coming upon him when he was off his guard succeeded in taking him prisoner; and by returning with great speed, before notice could be given to his neighbors, they were enabled to carry him off to Albany, where he was detained in jail until released on bail the following October." — Vermont Hist. Mag.

These ejectment trials were appointed to be held in Albany.[1] In them the question of the validity of the New Hampshire charters was not allowed to be discussed; the charters were not allowed to be read to the jury. They were at the outset authoritatively judged to be null and void. The Vermont communities were pronounced to be a mob. In 1774 the government of New York passed an act of outlawry, "the most minatory and despotic of anything that had appeared in the British colonies,"[2] against those who had resisted the attempt to dispossess the settlers of the lands they had occupied and improved under grants from the New Hampshire government. All crimes committed on the Grants were, by a statute of the General Assembly of New York, subject to be tried in the county and by the courts at Albany. At the same time a proclamation was issued by the Governor of of New York, offering a reward of fifty pounds a head for apprehending and securing Ethan Allen, Seth Warner, and six others of the most obnoxious of the settlers.

To satisfy New York those who had bought and settled upon and improved lands under grants from the government of New Hampshire, must buy them over again from the Governor of New York, or from the speculators he had sold them to, at prices many times over more than they had paid for the original purchase. The fees to the Governor of New Hampshire for grants of townships were about one hundred dollars; under the government of New York they generally amounted to two thousand, or two

---

1 "The *integrity*, too, of the court in the above-named decisions (Albany trials of ejectment) may be questioned."—Early Hist. Vermont, pp. 120, 121.

2 Williams.—"An act which for its savage barbarity is probably without a parallel in the legislation of any civilized country."—Early Hist. Vermont, p. 180. See a full account of the act, and the responses it provoked on the part of the Green Mountain Boys.—Ib., pp. 180-186. See, also, Slade's Vermont State Papers, p. 48.

thousand and six hundred dollars. In instances not uncommon their possessions had been sold away to new purchasers by the New York officials before the occupants under the New Hampshire charters had time to rebuy them themselves of New York, if they would.

In addition to all this, there were for a time numbers of individuals and combinations of men on the east side of the Green Mountains, who lent their sympathies and aid to New York; some, doubtless, from the conviction that on account of having committed themselves in some way to the New York interest, they had little to hope for themselves if the cause of the settlers against New York should win, and others from the belief that the cause of New York was too powerful to be successfully opposed.

The following paragraph from the "History of Eastern Vermont," by Benjamin H. Hall, describes the serious division of feeling in Guilford (a town next to the Massachusetts line, and the easternmost but one in Southern Vermont) : —

"Houses were divided, — the father upholding the jurisdiction of New York; the sons maintaining the supremacy of Vermont. Friendships the most intimate were disturbed. The word neighbor carried no meaning with it beyond the idea of contiguity. The physician could not visit his patient in safety unless protected by a pass. The minister of the gospel failed to enforce the doctrine of Christian charity on the hearts of men who knew none for one another." [1]

It was in this state of things that, in the summer of 1783, General Ethan Allen was directed to call out the militia for enforcing the laws of Vermont, and for suppressing insurrection and disturbances in the county of Windham (southeast county). Allen proceeded from Bennington at the head of one hundred Green Mountain Boys, and on his

[1] p. 500.

arrival at Guilford he issued the following proclamation, concluding it (with an oath) as follows : —

"I, Ethan Allen, declare that unless the people of Guilford peaceably submit to the authority of Vermont, the town shall be made as desolate as were the cities of Sodom and Gomorrah."

These trials made the settlers here very determined, compacted them together, set them irresistibly against the jurisdiction of New York, caused all *tories* to become very odious in their sight, and bore them onward through inconceivable difficulties and hardships to the goal to which, under Providence, they were surely tending, — that of an independent State.

In this struggle the settlers exhibited some rare qualities of a superior understanding and character. With all their rude energy they were still more remarkable for shrewdness and tact, which failed not unfrequently to be identified as such, because it was clothed with a naive simplicity ; and yet it went as unerringly to its chosen mark, as ever did Locksley's arrow in the romance of Walter Scott. Full of interest are the accounts of their success in keeping the English forces from invading us on the north, for two years, and when we were in a manner defenceless, by simply permitting the English general Haldimand to believe that they could be cajoled to sell their country to the British crown ; and yet all the time the fire of patriotism burned as brightly on their altars as did the flame of their devotion to their more narrow interests as a commonwealth.[1] They kept the

_____

[1] The inhabitants of the Grants felt that they could not consistently join an association with the province of New York, so they formed and subscribed an association of their own in the following words: "We, the subscribers, inhabitants of the district of land, commonly called and known by the name of the New Hampshire Grants, do voluntarily and solemnly engage, under all the ties held sacred amongst mankind, at the risk of our lives and fortunes, to defend by arms the United States against the hostile attempts of the British fleets and armies, until the present unhappy controversy between the two countries

surrounding country, and every Tory and *Yorker* within their bounds, under fear of being hung and quartered by them if caught in any act of dereliction to their cause. "And yet during the whole controversy not a single life was taken by them, not a person was permanently maimed, and there is no evidence that a gun was ever aimed and discharged at any one."[1] Thus they were considerate of the rights and peace of others, although determined to maintain their own.

The New York government intimated a purpose to stop further hostile proceedings, though proposing to continue colonial jurisdiction over them, they grounded arms at once, and held public rejoicings over the prospect of peace. At a later period of the controversy, when they had a fair prospect of being able to incorporate with their declared new State all the towns up to the Hudson River on the west, and over the Connecticut River half way into New Hampshire as it now is on the east, upon the first intimation from Congress that they would be approved by that body if they would abandon the new acquisitions, they let them go; and when New York State offered to close the controversy upon their payment of thirty thousand dollars, they promptly accepted the terms.

But severely as they were, for more than a quarter of a century of unscrupulous and powerful opposition, put to the test, they triumphantly proved to the world that it was not in them to seriously yield the rights or advantages which were vital to their independence, and to their nobly doing

shall be settled." Subscribed by forty-nine of the fifty members of the convention held at Cephas Kent's, in Dorset, July 24, 1776, of which Captain Joseph Bowker, of Rutland, was chairman, and Jonas Fay, of Bennington, clerk; thirty-one towns on the west side of the mountains and one on the east side being represented by fifty-one delegates.—Early History Vermont, pp. 231, 2. The warrant for this convention was signed by James Breakenridge, Simeon Hathaway, and Elijah Dewey, — all Bennington men.

1 Early Hist. Vermont, p. 161.

as men and citizens.   They, therefore, organized their
companies of Green Mountain Boys, appointed general conventions of the towns, and town councils of safety, and
their far-famed State council of safety, adopted a declaration of State independence, enacted laws for themselves,
and put in operation the complicated machinery of an independent State government.

There is not space here to go much into the details of
this vigorous and effective struggle of more than a quarter
of a century. The hardy settlers were armed at all points.
They drove away the New York surveyors, even when
these came supported by the sheriff and his posse; if a
comrade was stealthily spirited away, when made aware of
the fact, they mounted horse and hurried to the rescue, and
that not without success; if a "*Yorker*" was discovered
among them, they applied the Beech Seal,[1] or some other
effective chastisement.   They sent able men to Albany to
remonstrate there against the proceedings of New York,
and, had they been permitted, to plead the causes of their
people in the courts there.   They sent agents to the court
of Great Britain.   When the question of their admission as
a State into the Federal Union had become a question for
Congress to act upon, and they were successfully opposed
for years by the powerful influence of New York in the
Federal councils, they sent petition after petition and their
foremost men to represent their cause occasionally or con-
tinuously at Philadelphia.

[1] *The moderation and justice of the settlers* have been referred to, and that the
severe language and threatenings were not so much for actual execution as for
rhetorical effect. With regard to the application of the beech-seal: "This
mode of punishment by the *beech-seal*, though much talked of and abundantly
threatened, was not often executed. There are, in fact, not more than two or
three well authenticated instances in which it appears to have been inflicted." —
Hall's Early Hist. Vermont, p. 162. See also his further remarks to show that
the Green Mountain Boys were not peculiar in inflicting corporal punishment
upon their adversaries, and that the colony of New York was "at that time by
no means an exception to that practice."

The continuance of this struggle was prolonged through a period of twenty-six years,—1764–1790. While they were fighting the battles of American independence, they were denied a place as a State among the United States.[1]

---

[1] The declaration of Vermont Independence was issued under date of Jan. 15, 1777. "The vote of convention to be an independent State, and the declaration of independence accordingly, was decisively brought about at last doubtless by the Declaration of American Independence. When the colonies declared themselves free of the British Crown, it was felt by the Vermont settlers that there no longer remained any earthly power recognized by the parties as a *superior* possessing the right of deciding the controversy between themselves and New York." — Gov. Slade in State Papers, p. 65. "Every part of the United States was, at that period, contending against oppression; and every consideration that could justify the proceedings of Congress was a reason why the people of Vermont should take that opportunity effectually to guard against their former sufferings." — Williams.

CHAPTER XI

LAND-TITLE CONTROVERSY, CONTINUED.

TO add to all their other difficulties, there sprang up in the course of them a protracted, painful, and very critical controversy with New Hampshire, and parties interested with New Hampshire in making the towns between the Green Mountains and Connecticut River a part of that State. There is not space here to notice that controversy further than to say that it had required the utmost possible vigor and address of the settlers to prevent it from finally destroying their hopes of becoming a State.

Bennington was, throughout this controversy, the head-quarters of the opponents of New York; the place where their plans of operations were generally devised, and whence issued their resolves and orders, and a large share of the physical force which carried them into effect.[1] Ethan Allen and Seth Warner, who bore a conspicuous part in the struggle, resided here.

Ethan Allen, being on one occasion in Albany, to aid, if an opportunity was granted, the defence in the ejectment suits, it is related that before he left Albany he was called on by the Attorney-General, who told him that the cause of the settlers was desperate, and urged him to go home and persuade his Green Mountain friends to make the best terms they could with their new landlords, remind-

1 For the composition of the Vermont Council of Safety (originally numbering twelve—(Gen. Stark),— and some notice of its spirit and measures, see Early Hist. Vt., pp. 258, 9.

ing him of the proverb, that *might often prevails against right*. Allen coolly replied to them, that *the gods of the valleys were not the gods of the hills;* and when asked by Kempe, the king's attorney, to explain his meaning, he only added, that if he would accompany him to Bennington the same would be made clear.

When James Breakenridge's farm, at one end of the town, and Dr. Fuller's at the other, were singled out to be forcibly wrested from their occupants and placed in the power of the New York speculators, the citizens of the town voted to take the farms of Breakenridge and Fuller under the protection of the town, and to defend them against the New York officers at all hazards. This resolve they effectually and thoroughly executed ; particularly, the attempt to obtain forcible possession of Mr. Breakenridge's farm was so systematically and deliberately organized, and yet so completely defeated, that it discouraged attempts of the like kind thereafter. The sheriff made a general summons of the citizens of Albany to accompany him, so that when he started on his expedition he found himself at the head of over three hundred variously armed men, of different occupations and professions, and he received additions to his numbers by new levies on the way ; but with all the sheriff found " the gods of the hills " too strong for " the gods of the valleys." [1]

Remember Baker, of Arlington, opposed to New York, was assaulted, with his family, in his house, before daylight Sunday morning, by John Munro, Esq., a New York justice, and ten or twelve of his friends and dependents, and forcibly carried off. News of the transaction was conveyed by express to Bennington. Ten men immediately mounted their horses, got upon the track of the banditti, intercepted them, and rescued Baker. The

[1] See a graphic account of this important affair in Early Hist. Vt., pp. 124-126.

names of the men were as follows: Gen. Isaac Clark, Col.
Joseph Safford, Maj. Wait Hopkins, Col. David Safford,
and Messrs. Timothy Abbott, Stephen Hopkins, Elnathan
Hubbell, Samuel Tubbs, Ezekiel Brewster, and Nathaniel
Holmes. (The men are designated by their subsequent
titles.)[1]

There was at one time a gleam of hope from Albany,
entertained, as before alluded to, by the settlers. A committee consisting of the Rev. Mr. Dewey and others wrote
a communication, and Ethan Allen and others also wrote a
letter. These were conveyed by Capt. Stephen Fay and his
son, Dr. Jonas Fay, to Governor Tryon; they had received
a safe-conduct for this purpose from the New York Governor. They were kindly received by him, and the letters
they bore appear to have had much weight with him at the
time; so much so that the council recommended and His
Excellency approved the suspension of all prosecutions in
behalf of the crown, on account of crimes with which the
settlers stood charged, until the pleasure of the king should
be known, and also suspension of civil suits. This slight
favorable turn moved the universal joy in Bennington and
vinicity. A vast concourse of people assembled at the
meeting-house in Bennington to give expression to the
general satisfaction. It was, however, shortlived; the
gleam of sunshine soon disappeared.

This was July 15, 1772. The year before military or-
ganizations were formed in the several townships west of
the mountains, for forcible opposition, when necessary, to
the New York patentees; one company was formed in
Bennington, with Seth Warner as captain; the whole body
of companies when acting together were commanded by
Ethan Allen as colonel. In defiant contempt of a reported
threat of the Governor of New York that he would "drive

1 Early History of Vermont, p. 137.

the opposers of his government into the Green Mountains," this military body took the name " Green Mountain Boys." The place where in Bennington the councils of the leaders were held, the Council of Safety, was the Green Mountain Tavern kept by Capt. Stephen Fay. It had for its sign the stuffed skin of a catamount, with teeth grinning toward New York, and hence came to be called the Catamount Tavern. Mention has been made of negotiations by Vermont statesmen, with other parties and powers, about the questions in controversy, and particularly at Philadelphia.

Prominent among them were Bennington men such as Jonas Fay, Moses Robinson, Isaac Tichenor, etc.

At the convention of the towns west of the Green Mountains, at the house of Cephas Kent, in Dorset, Jan. 16, 1776, at which it was voted " to represent the particular case of the inhabitants of the New Hampshire Grants to the honorable Continental Congress by remonstrance and petition," Dr. Jonas Fay was chairman of the committee to prepare the petition ; Lieut James Breakenridge, Capt. Heman Allen, and Dr. Jonas Fay were appointed to present the petition to Congress,— one of the most important documents to which this great controversy gave rise. Simeon Hatheway, Elijah Dewey, and James Breakenridge were appointed a committee with power to warn a general meeting of the committees on the Grants when they shall judge necessary *from southern intelligence.*

NOTES TO THE ABOVE TWO CHAPTERS.

" And we now proclaim to the public, not only for ourselves, but for the New Hampshire grantees and occupants in general, that the spring and moving cause of our opposition to the government of New York was self-preservation; namely, first, the preservation and maintenance of our property; and, secondly, since that government is so incensed against us, therefore it stands us in hand to defend our lives. For it appears, by a late set of laws passed by the legislature thereof, that the lives and property of the New Hampshire settlers are manifestly struck at. But, that the public may rightly understand the essence of the controversy, we now proclaim to these lawgivers, and to the world, that if the New York patentees will remove their patents, that have been subsequently lapped and laid on the New Hampshire charters, and quiet us in our possessions, agreeably to His Majesty's directions, and suspend those criminal prosecutions against us for being rioters (as we are unjustly denominated), then will our settlers be orderly and submissive subjects of government. But be it known to that despotic fraternity of lawmakers, and law-breakers, that we will not be fooled or frightened out of our property." [1] "At a general meeting of the committees for the townships on the west side of the Green Mountains, it was resolved, April 14, 1774, that for the future every necessary preparation be made, and that our inhabitants hold themselves in readiness, at a minute's warning, to aid and defend such friends of ours, who, for their merit to the great and general cause, are falsely denominated rioters. But that we will not act anything, more or less, but on the defensive; and always encourage due execution of law in civil cases, and also in criminal prosecutions that are so indeed, and that we will assist, to the utmost of our power, the officers appointed for that purpose."

"On the farm of James Breakeñridge the first serious attempt was made by the New York State Government to forcibly dispossess the occupants, and to divide up the property amongst New York claimants; and here they met with their first serious discomfiture; and this was their last attempt of that kind. Here, in fact, on the farm of James Breakenridge, was born the future State of Vermont, which, struggling through the perils of infancy, had, at the commencement of the general Revolution, acquired the activity and strength of adventurous youth, and at its close reached the full stature of manhood; and not long afterward had become the acknowledged equal of its associate American republics." [2]

[1] Remonstrances of Ethan Allen and others.—State Papers, page 49. See also proclamation of Gov. Clinton.—State Papers, pp. 52-4.

[2] Vermont Hist. Mag.

An Act for the admission of the State of Vermont into this Union.

The State of Vermont having petitioned the Congress to be admitted a member of the United States, —

Be it enacted, by the Senate and House of Representatives of the United States of America, in Congress assembled, and it is hereby enacted and declared, That on the fourth day of March, one thousand seven hundred and ninety-one, the said State, by the name and style of the State of Vermont, shall be received and admitted into this Union, as a new and entire member of the United States of America.

FREDERIC AUGUSTUS MUHLENBERG,
Speaker of the House of Representatives.

JOHN ADAMS,
Vice-President of the United States, and President of the Senate.

Approved Feb. 18, 1791.

GEORGE WASHINGTON,
President of the United States.

13

CHAPTER XII.

THE BENNINGTON BATTLE.

" Pliant as reeds where streams of freedom glide,
Firm as the hills to stem oppression's tide."[1]

IT is the aim of this part of the volume to view the battle from the Bennington stand-point, and at the same time to preserve the truth of history ; and the relation of the battle to general history will be presented at some length.

I. ANXIETY IN THE COUNTRY PREVIOUS TO THE BATTLE. — At the surrender of Ticonderoga by St. Clair, July 6, 1777, the anxiety of the country became universal. We had failed, under the brave and lamented Montgomery, to carry Quebec by storm. We had abandoned Crown Point. Our little navy, though handled with utmost spirit and resolution, had proved itself unable to resist the vastly superior strength of the British flotilla on Lake Champlain. We had, by mortifying negligence [2] in not fortifying Mt. Defi-

---

[1] Motto of the first paper printed in Vermont, 1781. — Thompson.

[2] " July 5. — It is with astonishment we find the enemy has taken possession of an eminence called Sugar Loaf Hill, or Mt. Defiance, which, from its height and proximity, completely overlooks and commands all our works at Ticonderoga and Mt. Independence. This mount, it is said, ought long since to have been fortified by our army; but its extreme difficulty of access, and the want of a sufficient number of men, are the reasons assigned for its being neglected." " July 14. — The abandonment of Ticonderoga and Mt. Independence has occasioned the greatest surprise and alarm. No movement could be more unexpected, nor more severely felt, throughout our army and country. The disaster has given to our cause a dark and gloomy aspect." Generals Schuyler and St. Clair are

ance, which commanded Ticonderoga and Mt. Independence, lost what was regarded, under the circumstances of the country at that time, as the bulwark of the North. The main body of our army, fleeing eastwardly into the New Hampshire Grants, had been hotly pursued by the enemy, and its rear-guard, under Warner and Francis, attacked at Hubbardton, and, though men never fought more bravely, Riedsell's advance with his Germans had decided the day against us. In our flight thence southward, being joined by that portion of the army which had charge of baggage and army stores, — and which had successively abandoned Skenesborough and Fort Ann, — Fort Edward, Moses Creek, Saratoga, were in a brief time occupied and then surrendered by our wasting troops.

Serious reverses in other parts of the country intensified the alarm. Public fasts were observed in some States.

spoken of in this entry as severely suspected, or, at least, complained of. "Time and calm investigation must determine." — Thacher's Military Journal. Palmer vindicates Schuyler and St. Clair from blame. "Both Schuyler and St. Clair were severely and unjustly censured;" but says also, "That a great error was committed in relying upon the supposed strength of the position at Ticonderoga, cannot be denied." — Palmer's History of Lake Champlain. Irving is an admirer of Schuyler. — Irving's Life of Washington. Bancroft appears to be about right. "Meantime the British were never harried by the troops with Schuyler, against whom public opinion was rising. Men reasoned rightly, that, if Ticonderoga was untenable, he should have known it, and given timely orders for its evacuation; instead of which he had been keeping up stores there to the last." — Bancroft, Vol. IX., p. 372.

Even Washington was oppressed by the tidings from Ticonderoga. He wrote to General Schuyler, on hearing of the disaster: "The evacuation of Ticonderoga and Mt. Independence is an event of chagrin and surprise not apprehended nor within the compass of my reasoning." He said, "As matters are going, Burgoyne will have little difficulty in penetrating to Albany." "Sir William Howe was promptly notified that Burgoyne had precise orders to force a junction with the army in New York." — Bancroft. "The rapid progress of General Burgoyne on the side of the lakes, and the unaccountable conduct of their (American) commanders in abandoning Ticonderoga, were events so alarming and unexpected that they could not fail to perplex their counsels, and considerably impede their defensive preparations in other parts." — An Impartial History of the War in America, etc. London, 1787. "There are many long faces, for the key of North America is lost and gone."

"At Albany, it is said, the people ran about as if distracted, sending off their goods and furniture; and this feeling pervaded the entire northern and eastern part of New York, and the adjacent portions of Vermont and Massachusetts."[1] The region of the New Hampshire Grants was profoundly stirred. The Rev. Mr. Noble, in his Williamstown centennial address, speaking of a dwelling-house then building (1777), — the Smedley house, — says, "The roof of it was no sooner in place than the house was crowded in every part by families flying from the terrors which darkened the whole region north and west of us, as the cloud of war rolled on from Canada to Lake George and Saratoga." East of the mountains the people of several towns crossed the Connecticut. In Stockbridge, Mass., they were "greatly burdened with people who had fled from the New Hampshire Grants." The settlers along the lake, and as far down as Manchester, had either submitted to Burgoyne and taken his protection, or were abandoning their possessions and removing southward.[2]

Gen. Howe had beaten us on Long Island and at New York, — taking forts. men and magazines, — and had also gotten possession of New Jersey, and Newport in Rhode Island.[3] Though this able British general spent much time contriving and executing manœuvres with his army and navy to deceive us as to his real intentions, Gen. Washington did not suffer himself to be successfully imposed upon, and entertained no doubt that his real design was to secure Gen. Burgoyne's junction with himself, by way of Hudson River.[4]

---

[1] Dawson's Battles of the United States.

[2] Butler's Address.

[3] "The British appeared now so far superior in their naval and military forces, and munitions of war, that whoever computed the issue of the controversy by the natural course of things could hardly avoid the conclusion that the Colonies would have to submit to the sovereignty of Great Britain."

[4] "The great battle-field of the Revolution" has been perhaps not inappropriately represented "as in the vicinity of Lake Champlain, — for the great purpose

Lieut.-Gen. Burgoyne brought to the campaign in the north a considerable prestige from over the sea, and this was now very much enhanced by his late achievements on Lake Champlain and in its immediate vicinity.[1] His men, officers, and equipments had been provided with great care by the Home Government.[2] Upon arriving in this country he entered promptly upon his work, and down to the time of his encampment on the banks of the Hudson, opposite Saratoga, his career had been an unvarying series of successes skilfully and vigorously pursued.

II. INDIAN TERRORS. — The early colonies of Massachusetts, Connecticut, and Rhode Island found added to their other hardships those of Indian hostility. Crafty and cruel tribes, who had preoccupied the soil, preyed upon them by night, and in ambush by day. The early settlers here were spared this severe experience: nevertheless the savage nature of the red man was sufficiently understood by them. Several of the inhabitants of this town had had

of the British Government was to sever New England from the South and West, thus rendering her incapable of assisting, or receiving assistance."

[1] He had concluded a campaign in Spain with great credit to himself. He then was elected to Parliament, where he served not without some distinction; he also used his pen with considerable success, before he was appointed a lieutenant-general to take charge of the campaign in America, in the North. — Introduction to Burgoyne's Orderly Book.

[2] " Lieut.-Gen. Burgoyne, an officer whose ability was unquestioned, and whose spirit of enterprise and thirst for military glory, however rivalled, could not possibly be exceeded." — Impartial History of the War in America, London, 1787. " The British general's well-known abilities and valor." — Andrews, London, 1783. " This part of the service " (a " powerful artillery ") " was particularly attended to, and the brass train that was sent over on this expedition (to America) was perhaps the finest, and probably the most excellently supplied, as to officers and private men, that had ever been allotted to second the operations of any army which did not far exceed the present in numbers." — Impartial History, etc. Account of the British preparations under Gen. Carlton, pending the arrival of Burgoyne from Europe. " Sir Guy Carleton, who had under him, Generals Burgoyne, Phillips, Frazer, Nesbit and Riedell; all men of acknowledged skill and ability." — Palmer's History of Lake Champlain, pp. 117, 134. See, also, Gordon, Thacher, Burgoyne's State of the Expedition.

13*

near relatives massacred or carried captives by the Indians.[1]

The murder of Miss McCrea, July 27, 1777, owing to some peculiar circumstances, was upon every tongue. She was a young woman of twenty, belonging to a patriotic family, that of a Presbyterian clergyman of New Jersey, but engaged to be married to one Jones, a commissioned officer in Peters' corps of loyalists. She was a guest at the house of Jones' mother, within the British lines, in the vicinity of Fort Edward, and started under an escort of two Indians to go to the house of Jones' brother, near the British camp, some three or four miles distant, to meet her betrothed. She esteemed herself under the protection of British arms. It is said a barrel of rum had been promised to her escort if she was delivered safely at the place of her destination; and that the Indians quarrelled about the reward. Some half a mile yet remained to the accomplishment of the journey, and one of the Indians sunk his tomahawk in her skull. The incident was not of unusual barbarity; but this massacre of a betrothed girl, on her way to her lover, touched the hearts of all who heard the story.[2]

Gen. Carleton (Burgoyne's predecessor in command) omitted to employ savages, " probably because, in a word, that their service was uncertain, their rapacity insatiable, their faith ever doubtful, and their actions cruel and barbarous." [3] Burgoyne hesitated for a time, but soon yielded

1 Major Wait Hopkins, father of Major Aaron Robinson's first wife, was killed by the Indians. Eliphalet Follet, father of Charles Follett, who married Hannah, daughter of Col. Samuel Robinson, was killed by them in a great massacre, June, 1777; Isaac Webster, who married Anna, youngest child of Samuel Robinson, Sr., was at one time previous to his marriage a captive among them. Mrs. Harvey, of Cleveland, is a grand-daughter of Mrs. Isaac Webster; Mrs. Rev. Henry M. Swift of Michigan, is a great-grand-daughter.

See Thompson's Vermont, p. 11, chap. 4, sec. 7.

2 Burgoyne's Orderly Book, Ramsey, Gordon, Irving, Bancroft.

3 An Impartial History of the War in America, etc.; London, 1787, p. 446. He was afterward ordered by the Home Government to employ the savages, and complied with his orders. — Ib., p. 447.

his scruples. He hunted out the assassin of Miss McCrea, and threatened him with death, but pardoned him on hearing that the total defection of the Indians would have ensued from putting that threat into execution.[1] Early in June he confessed to Germain, that, "were the Indians left to themselves, enormities too horrid to think of would ensue; guilty and innocent women and infants would be a common prey." He nevertheless resolved to use them as instruments of terror. He gave out that he would send them after arriving at Albany toward Connecticut and Boston.

"Let not people consider their distance from my camp. I have but to give stretch to the Indian forces under my direction, and they amount to thousands, to overtake the hardened enemies of Great Britain. If the frenzy of hostility should remain, I trust I shall stand acquitted in the eyes of God and man, in executing the vengeance of the State against the wilful outcasts." [2]

Every day the savages brought in scalps as well as prisoners.[3] Burgoyne had detachments from seventeen nations of Indians. The Ottawas longed to go home, but on the 5th of August, nine days after the murder of Jane McCrea, Burgoyne took from all his red warriors a pledge to stay through the campaign.[4]

III. BAUM'S EXPEDITION. — Upon leaving the lake and proceeding southward by land, Burgoyne found his progress greatly impeded by want of horses, carriages, and supplies. The country was a wilderness. He attempted to bring forward his artillery and stores, and to open the way from Skenesborough to Fort Edward. But, so effectually had the Americans blocked up and obstructed the road, that the British army was frequently twenty-four hours in ad-

1, 2, 3, 4 Bancroft.

vancing one mile. It was not until the 30th of July that he reached and fixed his head-quarters at Fort Edward.

Nothing could exceed their joy upon their arrival at the Hudson. They flattered themselves that their difficulties and toils were now ended, and that there was nothing before them but a safe and easy march to Albany, and thence to a junction with the British army at New York. But there was still much land carriage to be accomplished, and they had not the carriages necessary, nor the horses nor supplies. On the arrival of the army at Fort Edward, the great object of immediate attention was the bringing up the transports from Fort George. The distance was about sixteen miles, but the roads were out of repair, weather unfavorable, cattle and carriages scarce. Many of the latter had been detained to drag boats and provisions from Ticonderoga over the carrying-places between Lake Champlain and Lake George. In fact, there had also been serious delay in getting the different divisions of horses, collected in Canada, through the desert between St. John's and Ticonderoga.

It was soon found that, in the situation of the transport service. the army could barely be victualled from day to day.[1] Although at the fall of Ticonderoga Burgoyne obtained not less than 1,748 barrels of flour, and more than seventy tons of salt provisions, and also a large drove of cattle which had arrived in the American camp a few days previous to their retreat,[2] Glich (a German officer in the Bennington battle) referring to a time just before the setting out of the Baum expedition, says, " Though Burgoyne's troops had toiled without intermission during three whole weeks, there was in camp no greater stock of provisions than promised to suffice for four days' consumption."

[1] Burgoyne's State of the Expedition.
[2] Thompson's Vermont.

The idea of the expedition to Bennington originated in this difficulty. By intelligence through Gen. Riedsell, and from other sources, Burgoyne had learned that Bennington was the great deposit of corn, flour, store cattle, and wheel carriages; that it was guarded only by militia; "and every day's account"—so he states—"tended to confirm the persuasion of the loyalty of one description of the inhabitants, and the panic of the other." [1]

Besides, there was need of horses, not only for the transport service, but also for fighting. Riedsell's dragoons were without horses and needed to be mounted. [2]

Burgoyne, with the approbation of his officers, [3]—so he said before the Committee of the House of Commons,—resolved upon an expedition to capture the Bennington military stores. The particular purpose of the expedition, namely, Bennington and its storehouse, was to be kept secret as long as possible, and an impression was to be made that Burgoyne was about to break camp and start, with his army, for Boston, in order to conceal the main part of his general plan, which was to effect a junction with Howe, who was at New York. The true scope of the particular

---

1 Burgoyne's State of the Expedition.

2 "This want of necessaries" (in Burgoyne's camp) "was the more mortifying, as the Provincial (New England) camp was furnished with them in greatest abundance. . . . Here a copious magazine had been formed for the Provincial army."—Andrews, London, 1786. "The enemy" (Americans) "received large supplies from the New England provinces, which, passing the upper part of the Connecticut River, took the route to Manchester," . . . "until they were at length deposited at Bennington, whence they were conveyed, as occasion required, to the regular army." . . . "It (Bennington) was, however, at this time, beside being a store for cattle, a depot for large quantities of corn and other necessaries; and, what rendered it an object of particular attention to the royal army, a large number of wheel carriages, of which they were in particular want, were laid up there."—Impartial History of the War, London, 1787. See, also, Glick's Narrative.

3 Burgoyne's State of the Expedition.—The testimony before the Committee of the House of Commons shows that Burgoyne acted with the approbation of his officers, only that Gen. Frazer, a British officer, thought British soldiers better than German for the purpose.

expedition now in hand was not, however, merely to capture the block-house at Bennington, but also to scour a
wide circuit of the country. The instructions he gave to
the commander of the expedition were, to try the affections
of the country; to disconcert the counsels of the enemy;
to mount Riedsell's dragoons; to complete Peters' corps of
loyalists, and to obtain large supplies of cattle, horses,
and carriages; to scour the country from Rockingham to
Otter Creek; to go down the Connecticut River as far as
Brattleborough, and return, by the great road, to Albany,
there to meet Gen. Burgoyne. The number of horses to
be brought was thirteen hundred at least. They were to
be tied in strings of ten each, in order that one man might
lead ten horses.[1]

With all the elation of his hopes he fitted out this expedition with much care. He selected for its nucleus and chief
dependence a corps of Riedsell's dismounted dragoons, —
the same that had behaved so gallantly at Hubbardton,
— a company of sharpshooters, chosen with care from all
the regiments, under Capt. Frazer, — a most excellent officer; — Peters' corps of Loyalists, to be swelled as they
proceeded; a body of Canadian rangers; Hanau Artillerists with two cannon; a hundred and fifty Indians. He
placed all under the care of Lieut.-Col. Baum, a skilled and
thoroughly brave German officer. To these troops he,
after they had proceeded on their way a little, added fifty
chasseurs. There can be no doubt he expected his column
to be much increased by the accession of tories along the
route.

---

[1] Burgoyne's State of the Expedition. — " You will use all possible means to
make the country believe that the troops under your command are the advanced
corps of the army, and that it is intended to pass the Connecticut on the road to
Boston. You will likewise insinuate that the main army from Albany is to
be joined at Springfield by a corps of troops from Rhode Island." — Burgoyne's
Instructions to Baum. Also Burgoyne to Col. Skene.

To support Col. Baum in case of necessity, Gen. Burgoyne stationed Lieut.-Col. Breyman at Battenkill, twenty-two miles off from Bennington, with two cannon of larger calibre than those in charge of Baum, and a strong body of German regulars, Brunswick grenadiers, light infantry, and chasseurs.

To be himself more advantageously situated to render further support with his army, if there should be need, he moved it to a point on the Hudson opposite Saratoga, and encamped there on the side of the river toward Bennington. When Baum had started on his way, Burgoyne rode after him and gave him verbal orders.

IV. VERMONT AROUSED. — The weight of gloom at this time on minds devoted to the American cause must have been indescribable. But nowhere would this be true of patriots and brave men more than on the Hampshire Grants. It may be said this feeling would be intensified at Bennington.

In most, if not all, of the important actions recently at the North, both prosperous and adverse, Bennington had borne a part. Upon the fall of Montgomery and defeat of our troops before Quebec, Col. Warner, having, within a few weeks, honorably discharged his regiment of Green Mountain Boys, at the call of Gen. Wooster, again beat up for volunteers, and was at the head of another regiment marched to Quebec, endured the rigors of a winter campaign, and brought up the rear of the retreating American army in the coming spring. The northern portions of the Grants being then exposed, Bennington, at a town meeting, voted,

"To raise ninety dollars as an encouragement to those who may enlist in the service of guarding the frontier towns in the Grants."

It was also "voted to pay those who went a little time be-force on this service if the Continent did not." Ticonderoga was threatened on an occasion previous to its surrender under St. Clair. The militia of Bennington and the neighboring towns, under Col. Moses Robinson, turned out *en masse* and marched to its relief; the defence of the fort at this time was successful. Col. Robinson and his regiment received the official thanks of Gen. Gates.

At the same time flour was wanted for the subsistence of the army, and a letter on that behalf was addressed to Bennington. The next day it was returned for answer, that one thousand bushels of wheat were collected and being ground at the mills; though, as the militia had left, almost to a man, it would be difficult to get what they had on hand conveyed.[1]

Col. Ethan Allen was a British prisoner; Col. Seth Warner, as we have seen, had been defeated at Hubbardton.

The state of alarm in the country after the fall of Ticonderoga and the defeat at Hubbardton has been described; also the confident hopes of Burgoyne from the disaffection on the Grants toward the Yorkers, and the compromised situation of those inhabitants of the Grants who had sympathized with New York. There was an impression in Burgoyne's mind that the region of country through which he was passing, and especially the Hampshire Grants, because of their hostile relations to the new State of New York, and through the influence of New York with the general government, was ripe for defection to his cause.

Let not the reader, therefore, conclude that Burgoyne's impressions on this subject were correct; or even that our sturdy Vermont settlers had the first thought of shunning at such a crisis the post of danger. While women and children, and the infirm, and some timid ones, fled in large

[1] Vermont Hist. Mag.

numbers southward for safety, the profound anxiety of the
time carried with it this most significant of all its results:
the thorough arousing of the sturdy dwellers among these·
green hills of New England to the duty and necessity of
the hour.

*It is not too much to say that it was this spirit thus
thoroughly in earnest that turned the scale of victory on the
heights of the Walloomsac.*

To this spirit Burgoyne's menace of Indian hostilities was
rather an exasperation than a terror. " The murder of Miss
McCrea resounded throughout the land, counteracting all
the benefits anticipated from the terror of Indian hostilities.
Those people of the frontiers who had hitherto remained
quiet now fled to arms to defend their families and firesides. In their exasperation they looked beyond the savages to their employers. They abhorred an army which,
professing to be civilized, could league itself with such
barbarians; and they execrated a government which, pre-
tending to reclaim them as subjects, could let loose such
fiends to desolate their homes. The blood of the unfortunate girl, therefore, was not shed in vain. Armies sprang
up from it. Her name passed as a note of alarm along the
banks of the Hudson; it was a rallying word among the
Green Mountains of Vermont, and brought down all their
hardy yeomanry." [1]

V. GETTING A FOOTHOLD. — In estimating the influences which determined the result of the Bennington battle, one must not be overlooked, which was the growth of
all the previous history here of our early settlers, but did
not get complete maturity until about the time of Burgoyne's
invasion, *the motive of building up upon the New Hampshire Grants a separate and independent State.* An august

[1] Irving's Life of Washington. See Thacher.

14

crisis is that of the life of the nation, and it were well, perhaps, to pause longer and consider it; and to see how the zeal of the early settlers here was identical, to a degree, with their zeal for their country; but there was at this time, also, a crisis in the life of this community and this commonwealth.

To go back a little further, now, in our retrospect. Western Vermont, owing to its intermediate location between the French on one side and English on the other, in the times of the colonial wars had been a great thoroughfare and battle-ground for both sides, and so its permanent settlement had been prevented. The same course had prevented the permanent occupancy of this part of the country by Indian tribes at an earlier day; they crossed these valleys and roamed stealthily for prey up and down these mountain sides, but they established no permanent occupancy. The ground was common for battle and thoroughfare between tribes never for long at peace with each other.[1] The country here had remained comparatively destitute of Indian settlements, as it afterward was of French or English colonists.

A new order of things opened when our hardy immigrants of 1761 set foot upon this soil. *They came to stay.* They brought with them too much vigor and determination for any obstacle or foe whatever. It requires no stretch of imagination to see that, had not the Green Mountain Boys determined that Burgoyne should not cross this soil, their beautiful territory would have again become mere frontier;

---

[1] "The scantiness of the population cannot be attributed to any other cause than the local situation of Vermont with respect to the various Indian nations, which prevented its becoming a permanent residence for the red man in earlier times, and afterward prevented its being settled by the French and English during the colonial wars." — Mr. Houghton's Montpelier address on the life of Seth Warner. See Williams' Hist. Vermont, 1794, p. 211; also Palfrey's Hist. New England; also Thompson's Vermont, P. II., pp. 205, 207, 216.

a disputed territory no one can tell how long between inimical powers.

This appears from the address of the Council of Safety of Vermont to the Councils of Safety of Massachusetts and New Hampshire, requesting a concentration of patriotic troops for the defence of the Western Vermont border against Burgoyne. In that address the Council of Safety said : —

"This State in particular seems to be at present the object of destruction. By the surrender of the fortress of Ticonderoga, a communication is opened to the defenceless inhabitants on the frontier, who, having little more in store at present than sufficient for the maintenance of their respective families, and not ability immediately to remove their effects, are therefore induced to accept such protection as is offered them by the enemy. By this means those towns which are most contiguous to them are under the necessity of taking such protection, by which the next town or towns become equally a frontier as the former towns before such protection; and unless we can have the assistance of our friends so as to put it immediately in our power to make a sufficient stand against such strength as they may send, it appears that it will soon be out of the power of this State to maintain its territory."

Message after message came to New Hampshire from outraged Vermont in this style : — " When we are crushed and cease to be the frontier, you must be. There is no frontier, and will be none, except where there are sufficient troops with arms in their hands to defend it." [1] The action of the Vermont Council of Safety, boldly committing the State as a barrier of the bodies of her citizens against the further inroads of a powerful foe flushed with recent and uninterrupted success, was taken on the 15th of July, 1777 (the day that Burgoyne fixed in his proclamation for the affrighted towns and people to come in

[1] Butler's Address, referring to Stevens.

and make their submission to him). It was only six
months previously, Jan. 15, 1777, that the adjourned convention was held at the Westminster court-house, which
voted (N. C. D) : —

> "That the district of land commonly called and known by the
> name of New Hampshire Grants be a new and separate State,
> and for the future conduct themselves as such."

The author of that Declaration of Independence, Dr.
Jonas Fay, was a Bennington man and member of the
Council of Safety.

VI. PREPARATIONS TO MEET THE ENEMY. — The appeals
of the Vermont Council of Safety to those of Massachusetts
and New Hampshire have been noticed. Their efforts were
not relaxed ; nor were they the only ones that Vermont put
forth.

When the loss of Ticonderoga was known, agents were
appointed by the Vermont Convention to procure arms to
the amount of four thousand pounds sterling. Within a
week their agents had been in Connecticut, and, failing of
success there, had set out for Massachusetts. All arms found
in the possession of tories in Vermont were seized. Their
property also was confiscated to fill the military chest. One
hundred and fifty stand of arms had been recently presented
to Vermont by Massachusetts, and an equal number sold
among the Green Mountains by Charles Phelps, of Marl-
borough. Massachusetts had also furnished New Hampshire with five tons of lead and five thousand flints. When
news of the evacuation of Ticonderoga was brought to the
Legislature of New Hampshire, the speaker, John Langden,
thus addressed them : —

> "I have three thousand dollars in hard money. I will pledge
> my plate for three thousand dollars more. I have seventy hogs-

heads of Tobago rum, which shall be sold for the most it will bring. These are at the service of the State. If we succeed in defending our firesides and homes, I may be remunerated; if not, the property will be of no value to me."[1]

Stark was now a private citizen. The comrade of Putnam in the French war, and at the battle of Bunker Hill (where he defended light breastworks among the foremost in service); a brigadier with Washington at Trenton and Princeton, when the army went into winter-quarters at Morristown, he returned to New Hampshire on a recruiting expedition. Having filled his regiments, he returned to Exeter to await orders, and there learned that several junior officers had been promoted by Congress, while he was left out of the list. Soured with government, he had retired from service. He was upon his farm in New Hampshire;[2] and his name was a tower of strength among the Green Mountain Boys. The Legislature of New Hampshire offered him the command of the forces they were to raise. Laying aside his private griefs, he once more donned his armor, and went to the field; stipulating, however, that he should not be obliged to join the main army, but hang upon the wing of the enemy in our own borders, and strike when opportunity should offer. Joy pervaded the militia when their favorite commander was announced as their chief. They cheerfully flocked to his standard, which he raised first at Charlestown (No. Four, on the Connecticut River), and then at Manchester, twenty miles north of Bennington.

At Manchester, Gen. Lincoln met Stark, and had orders from Schuyler, then major-general of the northern department, stationed at Albany, to conduct him and his recruits to the Hudson. Stark positively refused to go, and exhibited the written terms upon which he had consented to ap-

---

[1] Butler, referring to Stevens's Papers, and Everett's Life of Stark.
[2] Irving's Life of Washington.

14*

pear in the field at all.   His refusal was communicated to
Congress; and that body resolved that the Assembly of New
Hampshire should be informed that the instructions they
had given Gen. Stark were " destructive of military subor-
dination, and highly prejudicial to the common cause;" and
the Assembly was desired " to instruct Gen. Stark to conform himself to the same rules which other general officers
of the militia were subject to whenever they were called
out at the expense of the United States."   Stark, however,
remained immovable in his purpose to pursue an independent course, and be at liberty to use his own discretion as
to where to go and when to strike.

The time upon which we now raise the curtain is antece-
dent to any definite knowledge of Burgoyne's designs upon
the storehouse.   At the head-quarters of Gen. Schuyler, no
doubt, there was profound ignorance on the subject; for, as
we have seen, he sent Gen. Lincoln to bring Gen. Stark and
his militia out of New England to the Hudson.   " After the
disaster at Hubbardton, Gen. Schuyler's first orders were
that the Vermont militia should repair to his camp; though,
when remonstrated with, he allowed them to remain for the
defence of their families, and said, ' I had forgotten to give
orders about the security of the people on the Grants.' " [1]

Gen. Stark's superior sagacity, or better means of information, appears in this, that he wrote, on July 29, from his
head-quarters on the Connecticut, that the destination of the
enemy appeared to be Bennington.   In fact, it was about
July 29 that Major-Gen. Riedsell conceived the purpose of
mounting his regiment of dragoons, and for this purpose
proposed the expedition under Col. Baum.[2]   " I am informed," says Stark, " that the enemy have left Castleton,
with an intent to march to Bennington."   How decidedly the

1 Butler's Address.
2 Burgoyne's State of the Expedition.

impression obtained that Bennington was an objective point with Burgoyne, or that his army, or any portion of it, would march through Bennington, does not appear. Up to the 13th of August Gen. Stark appeared to be still in some uncertainty whether his services would be needed in that locality, or he should rather be called at an early day to march elsewhere.

However, he came with his brigade, seven or eight hundred strong, to Bennington.[1] He was here as early as August 9, and encamped about two miles west of the meeting-house, near the then residence of Col. Herrick, more lately known as the Dimmick place, where he remained for five days, collecting information in regard to the position and designs of the enemy, and consulting with the Council of Safety, and with Col. Warner and other officers, respecting future operations.[2]

As time wore on, and the designs of the enemy were disclosed, the ever-faithful Council, holding its sessions at the Catamount Tavern, became still more anxious and alert; issuing orders for the effects of tories to be sold for the replenishment of the war treasury;[3] sending swift messengers

[1] Jesse Field to Gov. Hall.

[2] Vermont Hist. Mag.

[3] " But the new State had no funds or established credit; and to raise such a force " [" a permanent volunteer force to patrol the frontiers, and watch the domestic as well as foreign foes "], " without pecuniary means, was impossible. The difficulty was at once solved by a resolution of the Council " of Safety, " that the property of those who had fled to the enemy should be made to pay the expense of defending the persons and property of those that remained. In pursuance of this resolution, the Council, on the 28th of July, appointed ' commissioners of sequestration,' with directions to seize and dispose of the property, under certain prescribed regulations, of ' all persons in the State who had repaired to the enemy.' A proper fund for State use being thus secured, a regiment of rangers was soon organized, under Col. Samuel Herrick, which did efficient and valuable service to the State and country. ' This,' says Ira Allen, in his history, ' was the first instance in America, of seizing and selling the property of the enemies of American independence;' and such is believed to be the fact, though the measure was afterward pursued in all the States." — Early Hist. Vermont, p. 260.

in every direction for men and material ; even giving orders for the conduct of colonels of regiments.[1]

The first entry of their records as preserved, is as follows : —

> "Bennington. — *In Council of Safety,*
> August 15, 1777."
> (The day before the battle.)

"SIR : You are hereby desired to forward to this place, by express, all the *lead* you can possibly collect in your vicinity, as it is expected every minute an action will commence between our troops and the enemy within four or five miles of this place, and the *lead* will be *positively wanted.*

> "By order of Council."

(This order was sent with all speed in different directions.)

VII.   MOVEMENTS BEFORE THE BATTLE. — Baum encamped at Saratoga on August 11. That night at eleven o'clock he received a reinforcement of fifty chasseurs. On the 12th he started on his march at five o'clock in the morning, and marched a mile, when a messenger from Burgoyne ordered him to post his corps at Battenkill and wait further instructions. On the morning of the 13th, in consequence of orders from Burgoyne, he marched from Battenkill to Cambridge, and arrived at the latter place at four o'clock, P. M., a distance of sixteen miles. On this day's march he was joined by several of the country people.[2] During this march he also sent ahead thirty provincials and fifty savages to surprise an American army-guard with some

---

[1] "State of Vermont.—*In Council of Safety,* Aug. 16, 1777.
"To Col. John Williams,—
"SIR : You will proceed with your party toward the lines, and if the enemy should retreat, you will repair to the road leading from St. Cork to Hoosack, and, if you make any discovery, report to this Council ; at the same time, you are to pay proper attention to the road leading from Hoosack to Pownal.
"By order of Council,
"PAUL SPOONER, *D. Secretary.*"
[2] Glick.

cattle, of which he had received information. They took five prisoners, and continued their march, when they were fired on by a party of fifteen men, and returned the fire, the assailing party taking to the woods. At Cambridge they took some cattle, horses, carts, and wagons ; and Baum sent back from this place a dispatch to Burgoyne that he had been informed the Americans were eighteen hundred strong at Bennington.

The affair at Cambridge of the 13th was immediately reported to Gen. Stark, at his head-quarters, by two scouts in the employment of the Council of Safety, Isaac Clark and Eleazer Edgerton.[1] At the time of their starting homeward with this intelligence, however, the scouts were not apprised of the approach of Col. Baum, and merely announced the advance of a hostile party of Indians as far as Cambridge. Gen. Stark sent out two hundred men, under Lieut.-Col. Gregg, to stop them.[2]

On the morning of the 14th, Thursday, Col. Baum reached Van Schaik's Mills, and found Col. Gregg's party in possession. We will let him tell his own story with respect to what took place there : —

" SANCOIK, Aug. 14, 1777, 9 o'clock.

" SIR : I have the honor to inform your Excellency that I arrived here at eight in the morning, having had intelligence of a party of the enemy being in possession of a mill, which they abandoned at our approach, but in their usual way fired from the bushes, and took the road to Bennington. A savage was slightly wounded. They broke down the bridge, which has retarded our march about an hour. They left in the mill about seventy-eight barrels of very fine flour, one thousand bushels of wheat, twenty barrels of salt, and about one thousand pounds' worth of pearl and pot ashes. I have ordered thirty provincials and an officer to guard the provisions and the pass of the bridge. By five prisoners here they agree

---

1 Father of the late Uriah Edgerton, Esq.
2 Jesse Field to Gov. Hall.

that fifteen hundred to eighteen hundred men are in Bennington, but are supposed to leave it on our approach. I will proceed so far to-day as to fall on the enemy to-morrow early, and make such disposition as I think necessary from the intelligence I may receive. People are flocking in hourly and want to be armed. The savages cannot be controlled; they ruin and take everything they please.   " I am, etc.,

                                        " F. BAUM.

  " To Gen. Burgoyne.

  " Beg your Excellency to pardon the hurry of this letter; it is written on the head of a barrel."

At Sancoik, Baum began to be seriously molested. A party of Americans fired on them a good deal from the underwood, " causing them some loss in several of the most forward among the savages." " At last, however, they retreated, abandoning a mill which they had previously fortified, and breaking down the bridge, and, long before the latter could be repaired, they were safe from further molestation." " The Americans, though they gave way at last, fought like men conscious of their own prowess, and confident in the strength of the support which was behind them ; and this, coupled with the rumors which had reached us relative to the amount of the garrison at Bennington, failed not to startle Col. Baum, and the boldest of his troops." [1]

More complete information than the first report by the two scouts reached Gen. Stark, on the night preceding the 14th that a large body of the enemy were approaching in the rear of the Indians. On the morning of the 14th he rallied his brigade and what militia was at Bennington and vicinity ; sent to Manchester for Col. Warner's men ; issued orders for all the militia about to come to him with all speed, and forthwith marched to meet the enemy.

[1] Glick.

Some five miles on his way, he met Col. Gregg retreating before Col. Baum, and drew up his little army in order of battle.

When the enemy came in sight they halted on a hill or advantageous rise of ground. Gen. Stark sent out small parties in their front to skirmish with them, which had a good effect. He killed and wounded thirty of the enemy without any loss on his side; but the ground did not suit for a general action. He marched back about two miles and encamped; called a council, and agreed upon a plan of attack for the next day. But it rained the 15th, and he did no more than skirmish.

We will condense from Glick's narrative. Baum judged he could not reach the place of destination (Bennington storehouse) before sunset. " We bivouacked at the farm of Walmscott" (by Walloomschoik River). The 15th, Baum's outposts were attacked and driven in. He himself was among the buildings of the locality with his regulars. He formed them into close column, and sent provincials and sharpshooters to sustain the outposts. " On seeing us, our savage allies uttered a yell, which seemed to strike panic into the bosoms of their assailants; for the latter instantly paused, hung back, as it were irresolute, and finally retired." Americans kept up skirmishing attacks all day. Baum sent back for reinforcements, and commenced to fortify to await them. " Six or eight log-huts made up the farm of Walmscott, scattered here and there." " Baum kept the whole of his force, with the exception of a hundred men, on the north " (west) " side of the stream," " holding the road upon his flanks, and in front and rear, by the Indians." " To complete his arrangements, he occupied the entire day and some portion of the night of the 15th." " Rain of the 15th in torrents," " to afford shelter against which human ingenuity has as yet devised no covering."

The body of provincials and marksmen, who had advanced to assist in guarding the outposts, silently withdrew and joined the regulars in the breastworks, and there passed the night.

Baum was instructed by Gen. Burgoyne to keep his ranks always in order, with military precision, and, in case of meeting an enemy that threatened to be too strong, to post his regulars in the most advantageous position for defence, and throw up entrenchments. This he did, selecting an excellent position, and making the best possible preparations for defence.

He had the Walloomsac [1] River (a fordable stream, but liable to be swollen by rains) in front; across it, in front, a cleared bottom land and slope varying in width, and wilderness beyond, covering undulating hills, which rise to a general elevation of considerable height. Across these uplands, and hidden from Baum by intervening hills, was Stark's encampment, some two miles distant, and reached by a circuitous road. By Durnford's map [2] it appears the country in Baum's front, east of the river, was extensively cleared, also southward over the Cambridge road, and elsewhere in portions, but the breastworks on the hill had woods immediately in front and down to the river, also on the right down to the road, with the exception of a cleared lot, and an unbroken wilderness on Baum's left to the northward, and on his rear to the westward.

The hill selected for the main defence was high and abrupt, rising some three or four hundred feet, and washed at its base by the river, running here very nearly south. The Cambridge, or Sancoik, road from Bennington runs here nearly eastwardly, until it has crossed the run, making

---

[1] The same called Walmscott by Glick; Wallumscoik by others.

[2] Map of Lieut. Durnford, Col. Baum's Engineer, and published in Burgoyne's State of the Expedition.

nearly a right angle with the river, with a steep ascent from the road to the redoubt. Baum's main intrenchment was at the highest elevation on this hill.

According to Durnford's map, within the main fortification were Riedsell's Dragoons and a corps of Canadian Rangers ; some paces in advance, down the declivity, were also stationed some of Riedsell's Dragoons ; at the foot of the hill in front, by the river, chasseurs were posted. By the river to the right, at the bridge of the Sancoik road, and on both sides of the road, were minor fortifications, where were Canadian Rangers and German Grenadiers ; over the river, and less than a quarter of a mile distant on rising ground, were also considerable fortifications, and here Baum posted Peters' corps of Provincials. It was called the tory breastwork. Here Pfister, popularly known as Col. Pfister, a retired British lieutenant of the French War, is believed to have had immediate command.[1] This tory breastwork was nearly south-east of Baum's intrenchments on the hill, and at a considerably lower elevation.

According to Durnford's map he also had Canadians at the river *across the bridge;* and down the hill on his right, near the Sancoik road, and a quarter of a mile west of the bridge, some grenadiers. His fortifications and breastworks are stated to have been of earth and timbers, in perfecting which he employed much of the day and night of the 15th. The precise location of the artillery and cannon does not certainly appear. They were doubtless so disposed as to render most effective service. One or both of the cannon was within the main redoubt on the hill during the severest part of the struggle.

These were the defences and military preparations which Gen. Stark, with the advice of Col. Warner and the other officers, determined to attack on the 16th.

[1] Vermont Historical Magazine.

" His force consisted of three regiments of New Hampshire militia, respectively commanded by Colonels Hubbard, Stickney, and Nichols; a small body of militia from the east side of the mountains, under Col. William Williams, of Wilmington; a corps of rangers then forming under the authority of the Vermont Council of Safety, commanded by Col. Herrick; a body of militia from Bennington and its vicinity, Nathaniel Brush, colonel, of which there were two companies from Bennington, the one commanded by Capt. Samuel Robinson, and the other by Capt. Elijah Dewey. He had just been joined by part of a militia regiment from Berkshire County, under Col. Simmons, making his whole force to amount, probably, to about eighteen hundred men." [1]   This estimate would include volunteers.   Gen. Stark speaks of his *little army.*

The plan of attack was as follows: Col. Nichols, with two hundred men, taking a wide circuit through the woods northward of Baum's redoubt, was to get upon the rear of his left undiscovered to the last moment possible by him. Col. Herrick, with three hundred men, taking a wide circuit southward, was to get in like manner upon the rear of Baum's right. These two to join and commence the attack. Meantime, to divert attention from that proceeding, upon the success of which everything else very much depended, Colonels Hubbard and Stickney were to get before the tory breastwork, and one hundred men to march toward the front of Baum; Gen. Stark, with the remainder of his force, was, at the right time, to charge Baum's intrenchments in front.

VIII.   THE BATTLE. — The plan appears to have been carried out with remarkable completeness.   As the orders were given, and the several parties were about to enter

[1] Vermont Historical Magazine.

upon the performance of the duties severally assigned them, Gen. Stark in his saddle, pointing in the direction of the enemy, made this laconic address : " THERE ARE THE RED-COATS, AND THEY ARE OURS, OR THIS NIGHT MOLLY STARK SLEEPS A WIDOW."

On the map before mentioned the positions severally of Stark's men before the action had commenced, or before it had proceeded far, appear to be represented. Bodies of Americans are well advanced on the road leading south-westerly to Baum's front ; another body of our troops have approached near to the tory breastwork, advancing in a north-westerly direction ; a body of Americans are also near the grenadiers and tories, a quarter of a mile back on the Sancoik road ; and Nichols on one side, and Herrick on the other, have reached the coveted position in the rear of Baum's main intrenchments. After Nichols had started for his post he sent back to Stark for a reinforcement of a hundred men, and they were furnished him.

Gen. Stark says, " About three o'clock we got all ready for the attack." The time previously to this must have been improved by Colonels Nichols and Herrick getting round to the rear of Baum's works ; and by manœuvres and reconnoitering of Gen. Stark in front.

Silas Walbridge, who was in Capt. John Warner's (brother of Seth Warner) company and Col. Herrick's regiment of Vermont Rangers, and went with Col. Herrick, says [1] they went from Stark's encampment " west across the river (the Walloomsac flows northerly past the place of encampment, then curves westward, and soon takes a southerly direction past Baum's hill, and onward a short distance curves again westward, and so passes by Sancoik), crossed it again below Sickle's Mills (brick factory, now Austin & Patchin's paper mill, a mile and a half westward

---

[1] MS. statement communicated to Governor Hall.

from Baum's Hill, on the Sancoik road), and came in on the rear of the Hessian redoubt."

"Just before we arrived at the redoubt we came in sight of a party of Indians, and fired on them. They retreated to the north-west, leaving two killed. Our men came within ten or twelve rods of the redoubt, and began firing from behind logs and trees, and continued firing and advancing until the Hessians retreated out of their works and down the hill to the south. We followed on down the hill to the level land on the river, and some pursued on fur-ther."

Jesse Field, who was in Capt. Dewey's company of mi-litia, and went also with Col. Herrick, says [1] they " crossed the river over against the camp, went over the hills, forded the river again below the enemy, and came up on their rear."

"When we came in sight of the enemy's works we halted, and it seemed that the rear of our party had been detained for some cause. We stood but a short time when the firing commenced from the party on the north. I recollect hearing Lieut. —— ex-claim, ' My God, what are we doing? They are killing our broth-ers; why are we not ordered to fire?' In a moment our adjutant came up and ordered us to advance. We pressed forward, and as the Hessians rose above their works to fire, we discharged our pieces at them."

Solomon Safford states [2] that he turned out with Capt. Samuel Robinson's company, and encamped with them the evening of the 15th at the bend of the river, half a mile north of Stark's encampment, and was ordered to remain behind and guard the knapsacks and other baggage during the 16th. On the morning of the battle, after the company had started off with Col. Herrick, Gen. Stark and Col. Warner rode past him on horseback, and accosted him."

Thomas Mellen, the veteran whose statement is given in Mr. Butler's address, says : —

[1,2] From MS. statements communicated to Governor Hall.

"Stark and Warner rode up near the enemy to reconnoitre; were fired at with the cannon, and came galloping back. Stark rode with shoulders bent forward, and cried out to his men: 'Those rascals know that I am an officer; don't you see they honor me with a big gun as a salute?' We were marched round and round a circular hill till we were tired. Stark said it was to amuse the Germans. All the while a cannonade was kept up upon us from their breastworks. It hurt nobody, and it lessened our fear of the great guns. After a while I was sent, with twelve oth-' ers, to lie in ambush on a knoll a little north, and watch for tories on their way to join Baum. Presently we saw six coming toward us, who, mistaking us for tories, came too near to escape. We disarmed them, and sent them under a guard of three to Stark. While I was on the hillock, I espied one Indian whom I thought I could kill, and more than once cocked my gun, but the orders were not to fire. He was cooking his dinner, and now and then shot at some of our people."

Silas Walbridge speaks of the troops at Stark's encampment as parading early on the morning of the 16th for battle.

There was then no lack of activity on our side. All were on the alert from early morning, but there was little if any firing by our men until about three o'clock in the afternoon; but the enemy kept up firing all day upon us whenever we showed ourselves to them, and where they were not deceived to think we were tories advancing to join them.

Gen. Stark says, "The action lasted two hours." He appears to mean, from the commencement of firing by Nichols until the fight ended on the plain below. The manuscript statements of Safford, Walbridge, and Field do not, perhaps, conflict with this, though they seem to make the time shorter. If there is any real discrepancy, it probably shows that to unprofessional soldiers fighting so severely and with so much at stake, the time in the recollection of many years afterward appeared to be shorter than it really was. They had not anticipated getting their

15*

work done so quickly. When the order came to go over the breastworks it was then probably but a few moments ere the Hessians were dislodged. When that was done it seemed to our men as if really all was done.

Jacob Safford, orderly sergeant in Warner's regiment, afterward ensign,[1] says : —

"Should think the action at Baum's Hill one and a half hour of scattering fire, then twenty-five to thirty minutes of close work."

The onset upon all the works appears to have been simultaneous ; and the tory breastworks and other detached fortifications to have been carried early in the action, though particular accounts of this portion of the day's work are wanting. But if the outworks were carried with comparative ease, it was not so with the main intrench-ments, those on the hill, where was Col. Baum in person and his faithful veterans. They were slow to believe they were to be vanquished. They kept their cannon at work. They lined the breastworks. Nevertheless, our brave fellows, no less in earnest, pressed up upon every side. The instant or place of first entrance of the redoubt by our men does not now appear. It will assist to a more complete impression of the battle to introduce here further portions from Glick's interesting narrative : —

"The morning of the 16th rose beautifully serene. The storm of the preceding day having expended itself, not a cloud was left to darken the heavens, while the very leaves hung motionless, and the long grass waved not, under the influence of a perfect calm. Every object around appeared, too, to peculiar advantage; for the fields looked green and refreshed, the river was swollen and tumultuous, and the branches were all loaded with dew-drops, which glistened in the sun's early rays like so many diamonds. Nor would it be possible to imagine any scene more rife with peaceful and even pastoral beauty. Looking down

[2] MS. communication to Governor Hall.

from the summit of the rising ground, I beheld immediately beneath me a wide sweep of stately forest, interrupted at remote intervals by green meadows, or yellow corn fields, whilst here and there a cottage, or shed, or some other primitive edifice, reared its modest head, as if for the purpose of reminding the spectator that man had begun his inroads upon nature, without as yet taking away from her simplicity and grandeur."

" At the dawn, no note of military preparation forewarning an attack." Baum ordered his men to eat their breakfasts. Soon reports came that columns of armed men were approaching. Col. Baum was duped to believe that these were friendly tories, and called in his pickets. Capt. Frazer thought Baum was deceived, and so did most of the troops ; but not so Baum.[1]

" We might have stood half an hour under arms, watching the approach of a column of four or five hundred men, who, after dislodging the pickets, stood in the edge of the open country." " Then trampling of feet in the forest on our right."

A patrol sent. Encountered a discharge of fire-arms. Indians came in in dismay.

" Then we are surrounded on all sides."

Then firing and shouting. Then the column in front pressed up. Then traitors inside fired at the dragoons, and withdrew.

" We lined the breastworks and fired well ; the advancing columns fell back at first ; but fresh attacks developed themselves at every point." " All threatened with a force perfectly adequate to bear down opposition, and yet by no means disproportionately large, or such as to render the main body inefficient."

The Indians fled, when in the rear of right and left appeared the enemy's (Stark's) columns.[2]

---

[1] Gen Stark's plan of the day, to make no actual assault until all was gotten ready, probably favored this hallucination of Baum.

[2] When Col. Nichols commenced firing, coming up on the rear left, and Col. Herrick approached, firing on the rear right, the Indians, alarmed at the pros-

"The vacancy which the retreat of the savages occasioned was promptly filled up by one of our two field-pieces, whilst the other poured destruction among the enemy in front as often as they showed themselves in the open country or threatened to advance. In this state of things we continued upwards of three-quarters of an hour. Though repeatedly assailed in front, flank, and rear, we maintained ourselves with so much obstinacy as to inspire a hope that the enemy might even yet be kept at bay till the arrival of Breyman's corps, now momentarily expected."

The solitary tumbril containing all the spare ammunition exploded with great violence, shaking the earth. The enemy (forces of Stark), arrested a moment by the violence of the concussion, guessed the nature of the affair, then rushed up the ascent, sprang over the parapet, and dashed within the works, — bayonet, butt, and rifle in full play. A few moments finished the work. Glick, with thirty of his comrades, cut their way through, and he escaped.

It is presumed, not until all hope of recovering the day by further standing their ground was utterly lost. All accounts agree as to the strange valor of these German hirelings. The Royalists and Canadians, as many as could escape, had taken to the woods; but the Hessians, though their works were forced and their cannon captured, preserved their discipline and fought bravely until there was not a cartridge left, then drew their sabres and charged the Americans, with their colonel at their head. They were nearly all killed or taken with Col. Baum, who did not surrender until wounded fatally.[1]

pect of being surrounded, endeavored to make their escape in single file between the two parties, with their horrid yells and the jingling of cow-bells. — Thacher.

[1] Andrews. — The story of the impressment of these Hessians into the British service by the petty sovereigns of Germany is an affecting one. They were gathered by force, locked up in fortresses to prevent their desertion, marched to their place of embarkation without ammunition or arms, but under the com-

Jesse Field says : [1] —

They "ran down the hill to the south and south-east.[2] We ran over and round their works after them, and continued the pursuit until they were all, or nearly all, killed, or taken. The day was very warm, the Hessians were in full dress, and very heavily armed, and we in our shirts and trowsers, and without our knap-sacks, and thus had greatly the advantage in the pursuit. After we passed the redoubt there was no regular battle, — all was con-fusion, — a party of our men would attack and kill, or take prison-ers, another party of Hessians. Every man seemed to manage for himself, and, being attached by chance to some squad, either under some officer, or without any, would attack every party that came in their way. I should think I did not continue in the pur-suit over half a mile, though some parties went further,— probably nearly down to Runsellan's Mills."

Gen. Stark, in his despatch to Gen. Gates, referring to this action of storming the redoubt, says of it : —

"The hottest I ever saw in my life : it represented one contin-ued clap of thunder."

Again :—

"They were all environed with two breastworks with their ar-tillery; but our martial courage proved too hard for them."

He is also quoted as saying, "Had each man been an Alexander or a Charles of Sweden, he could not have be-

mand of trusty yagers who had both, and were ever ready to nip mutiny in the bud. Some did desert. Some attempted to mutiny, and were fired into. It was a measure of cruel and base tyranny and oppression. — Bancroft, vol. ix., pp. 316, 317. " England entered early in 1776 into treaties with the petty sovereigns of Germany to take into British service nearly twenty thousand German troops. Over four thousand of them were Bruswickers. Over these latter Col. Riedsell was major-general — a portion of them was Lieut.-Col. Baum's regiment of dis-mounted dragoons ; a portion, Lieut.-Col. Breyman's grenadiers. Of the four thousand Brunswickers, about twenty-eight hundred returned to Germany." — Burgoyne's Orderly Book, pp. 103, 104. See Irving's Life of Washington, ii., 196 Beside the subsidy exacted by the German princes, they were to be paid seven pounds, four shillings, and four pence, sterling, for every soldier furnished by them, and as much more for every one slain. — Irving.

[1] MS. statement.   [2] After being forced from their works.

haved more gallantly." A Hessian eye-witness declares that this time "the Americans fought with desperation, pressing within eight paces of the loaded cannon to take surer aim of the artillerists."[1] Andrews, the British author, says: "Gen. Stark advanced upon Col. Baum with the utmost diligence, and inclosed him on all sides. The defences he had raised were forced after a valiant resistance."

Immediately after their hard-earned victory, prisoners already captured were to be sent under guard to a secure place, and some pursuit, if possible, still maintained to effect more captures. The wounded were to be cared for, — persons still living speak of beds and bedding, sent out for this purpose, afterward bearing blood-stains. Our dead were to be reverently conveyed to their homes. Col. Baum and the tory Col. Pfister, both mortally wounded, were separately borne to a house a mile and a half this side of the battle-field, Col. Pfister, a part of the way on the back of Jonathan Armstrong, of Shaftsbury. They both died within twenty-four hours. Capt. Robinson, who guarded the house where Baum lingered in his last hours, and watched gently as a woman with him till he died, was wont to say, that "a more intelligent and brave officer he had never seen than this unfortunate lieutenant."[2] The spoils of victory, too, were to be gathered. Gen. Stark had promised, in his orders, that all the plunder in the enemy's camp should be distributed among the soldiers; beside all, many of our brave fellows, neither wounded nor slain, were scattered about, thoroughly exhausted by their exertions in the fight.

But we must return to the battle, which is not yet

[1] Irving's Life of Washington. — "New England sharpshooters ran up within eight yards of the loaded cannon to pick off the cannoniers." — Bancroft, quoting Schlözer's Briefwechsel. "The royal officers were astonished to see how undauntedly they rushed on the mouths of the cannon." — Gordon.

[2] Rev. S. Robinson's Address.

finished. Baum and the remnant of his forlorn hope had probably not yet ceased fighting, when Breyman arrived at Sancoik with his formidable *corps-de-reserve.* Each soldier had forty rounds in his pouch, and there were two boxes of ammunition on the artillery carts.[1]

Breyman left Battenkill at nine o'clock of the 14th, his order to march having been received by Sir Francis Clarke at eight o'clock. His guide lost his way at one time. On the evening of the 15th he halted seven miles before reaching Cambridge. The men lay upon their arms all night. He sent a message to Baum and got a return next morning. He started again, on the morning of the 16th, and reached the Sancoik mill at half past four, P. M., and found the advanced guard in possession, which he had previously sent on — (sixty grenadiers and chasseurs, and twenty riflemen) — and Col. Skene directing. "I had scarcely passed the bridge when I perceived a considerable number of armed men making for the hill on my left flank, some in jackets, some in shirts. Col. Skene said they were royalists, but they fired into us."[2] Here Col. Breyman's part in the Bennington battle began in earnest.

Gen. Stark's men, it is evident, were in no condition to meet this fresh and more powerful foe. It is said it was with great difficulty he himself could be roused to meet the new danger, so worn out and stiffened had he become. Contrary to his first impression, and on the earnest appeal of Warner, Col. Breyman was immediately resisted, instead of a retreat being ordered, to form the scattered forces in order of battle.[3]

They opened an incessant fire from their artillery and small arms, which was, for a while, returned by the Ameri-

1 Breyman's dispatch.
2 Col. Breyman's dispatch.
3 Vermont Hist. Mag.

cans with much spirit; but, exhausted and overpowered by numbers, we at length began slowly, but in good order, to retreat before the enemy, disputing the ground inch by inch.[1] Firing into their flank, and, at the same time, keeping in front of them, though retreating, and firing into them that way, so as not to be outflanked by them.

Early, however, in this unexpected encounter with Breyman, Col. Warner's men came upon the field, and most opportunely indeed for our cause.

Warner himself was already here; "was with Stark, at Bennington, for several days previously to, and remained with him until after, the battle, *assisting him in planning the first and conducting both actions.*"[2] His regiment (or, rather, the remnant of it, it having been sadly wasted at Hubbardton) was stationed at Manchester. At the summons of Stark, the men, about one hundred and thirty in number,[3] so soon as they could be collected together, started for Bennington. They marched the rainy night of the 15th, under command of Lieutenant-Colonel Safford; stopped, the forenoon of the 16th, to get rested and dried, and to put their firelocks in order, in Bennington, and, at the time mentioned, came upon the field.

Thus reinforced, it was some little time before we made a successful stand against the enemy. The day had been nearly lost;[4] nor was it rescued without the most arduous and critical exertion. We had Baum's cannon to turn upon them; but they had cannon of larger calibre; and our brave fellows were worn out, thinned in numbers, hungry, taken by surprise, and not in battle array.

The anxiety in the old village of Bennington grew in

---

[1] Thompson's Vermont.

[2], [3] Vermont Hist. Mag. William Carpenter of Swansea, N. H. — so his son Judge Carpenter, of Akron, Ohio, told me — used to relate, as what he himself heard, that the order was given, by Gen. Stark, to an aid, to retreat. Warner heard it, and said, "Stand to it, my lads; you shall have help immediately."

[4] Andrews.

intensity as the day wore away.[1] The Council of Safety remained in painful deliberation. A letter, still preserved, written by Secretary Fay, at Bennington, at six o'clock, and sent hither and thither, as a circular dispatch, says : —

"Stark is now in an action which has been for some time very severe. . . . . The enemy were driven; but, being reinforced, made a second stand, and still continue the conflict. But we have taken their cannon, and prisoners, said to number four or five hundred, are now arriving."[2] Gen. Stark, in his dispatch, says, "The battle continued obstinate on both sides till sunset."

But again "our martial courage proved too hard for them." Breyman's cannon, taken and retaken,[3] remained in the hands of the Americans. Breyman's "party were compelled to retire" as the British author [4] carefully says. They, however, so many of them as could, retired *at the last very hastily.* It was well for those who did escape that night was so near at hand. "We pursued them till dark," says General Stark ; "but, had daylight lasted one hour longer, we should have taken the whole body of them." The struggle of that eventful day may be said to have ended where it the day before began, at the Sancoik mill. Breyman got back that night (of the 16th) to Cambridge, and the next day (Sunday) got back to camp.[5]

IX. Some Extracts from an Oral Statement and MS. Communications.

From oral statement of Mr. Mellen.[6] — "Before I had time to fire many rounds, our men rushed over the breastwork, but I and many others chased straggling Hessians in the woods. We pur-

---

1 Thompson's Vermont. Upon the alarm of the approach of the enemy toward Bennington, the people of the border flocked to the centre ; as did also numbers from other towns. The place was crowded with fugitives. — Vermont Hist. Mag.

2, 3 Butler.   4 Andrews.
5 Col. Breyman's dispatch.   6 See Butler's Address.

sued till we met Breyman with eight hundred fresh troops and larger cannon, which opened a fire of grape shot. Some of the grape shot riddled a Virginia fence near me; one struck a small white-oak tree behind which I stood. Though it hit higher than my head, I fled from the tree, thinking it might be aimed at again. We skirmishers ran back till we met a large body of Stark's men, then faced about. I soon started for a brook I saw a few rods behind, for I had drank nothing all day, and should have died with thirst had I not chewed a bullet all the time. I had not gone a rod, when I was stopped by an officer, sword in hand, and ready to cut me down as a runaway. On my complaining of thirst, he handed me his canteen, which was full of rum. I drank and forgot my thirst. But the enemy outflanked us, and I said to a comrade, ' We must run or they will have us.' He said, 'I will have one more fire first.' At that moment a major on a black horse rode along behind us, shouting, ' Fight on, boys, reinforcements close by.' While he was speaking, a grape shot went through his horse's head and knocked out two teeth. It bled a good deal, but the major kept his seat and spurred on to encourage others. In five minutes we saw Warner's men hurrying to help us. They opened right and left of us, and half of them attacked each flank of the enemy, and beat back those who were just closing around us. Stark's men now took heart and stood their ground. My gun-barrel was by this time too hot to hold, so I seized the musket of a dead Hessian, in which my bullets went easier than in my own. Right in front were the cannon, and, seeing an officer on horseback waving his sword to the artillerymen, I fired at him twice; his horse fell. He cut the traces of an artillery horse, mounted him, and rode off. I afterward heard that officer was Major Skene. Soon the Germans ran and we followed."

From narrative of Jesse Field. [1] — " When the prisoners were collected, they were sent off under a guard to Bennington. Our men were scattered all over the field of battle, some resting themselves, some looking up the dead and wounded, and others in pursuit of plunder. An hour or two before sunset I heard the report of cannon, and news soon came that our men were attacked by a body of Hessians who had come to reinforce Baum. I with others went down on the side-hill north of the road. When we

---

[1] Communicated in MS. to Gov. Hall, and in his possession.

came in sight of the enemy, they were marching up the road this side the brick factory, their cannon in front clearing the way. Our men kept collecting in front and on the left. The party I was with took post with others on the side-hill above the road, within from twenty to thirty rods of the enemy, and kept up a constant fire generally from behind trees. The road appeared full of men, and it was like firing into a flock of sheep. The enemy kept firing upon us, but we were greatly protected by the trees. The battle continued till about dark, when the enemy retreated and were not pursued far."

From narrative of Silas Walbridge. [1] — "After the battle was over I went back with Captain Warner to where the action began, to look for the wounded, and while there we heard firing, the beginning of the second battle. We made all haste to the scene of action, and found things in much confusion. Some of the officers were ordering 'forward,' others saying 'retreat.' Our men retreated for some time, finally made a stand, and after hard fighting till about night we drove the enemy and took their cannon. This battle lasted an hour and a half or two hours. Warner's regiment, I believe, kept in order on the retreat, and served as a rallying point for the other troops."

Capt. Jacob Safford's statement, taken in 1828. [2] — (Jacob Safford after Bennington battle was an ensign in Col. Warner's regiment, as appears by a vote of Congress, accepting his resignation November, 18, 1779. — 3d vol. Jour. Cong., 395. He was a worthy man and died in Bennington in May, 1833.) Jacob Safford says that previous to Bennington battle he belonged to Warner's regiment and acted as orderly sergeant in Captain ——s company.

"After the battle of Hubbardton, by which our regiment was reduced to less than one hundred and fifty men, we were stationed at Manchester. On the 14th of August, I should think, information was received that we were wanted at Bennington, but, owing to the absence of a large scout under Captain John Chipman, and perhaps from some other causes, we did not march till the morning of the 15th. The day was rainy, but by marching till nearly midnight we arrived within about a mile of Bennington village and encamped. We were drenched with rain,

1 Communicated to Gov. Hall, and in his possession.
2 Communicated in manuscript to Gov. Hall, and in his possession; and the note at the head of the statement is his.

and our arms and equipments having been all day exposed to the weather, it took a considerable part of the forenoon of the next day to fit ourselves for a march. We were also short of ammunition, which occasioned some delay, and so much time was employed in making the necessary preparations for battle, that it was about noon, or perhaps a little past, when the regiment marched from Bennington village. While going down the Henderson hill [two miles from Bennington] a scattering fire of musketry was commenced in the direction of the battle-ground. We halted a short time at Stark's encampment [four miles from Bennington]; left our coats and knapsacks; and a gill of rum with water was dealt to each man. The weather was extremely warm, and after crossing the first bridge [about five and three-quarter miles from Bennington] we were halted while the men drank at the river. Two sergeants were now requested to volunteer to head the line, and I with another went in front. About this time the firing, which had gradually increased, became very heavy, and a general attack seemed to be made. We now began to meet the wounded, and when we arrived at the second bridge,[1] [three-quarters of a mile below the first], the Hessians were running down the hill, and the two pieces of cannon were taken. If we halted at all at this place, it was but for a very few minutes. Here I was put in command of the left flank guard, and the march was continued by the regiment down the road, and by myself and guard across the flat. There was also a flank guard on the right. We continued our march until we came to the top of the eminence next beyond where the brick factory now stands [one and a half miles below the second bridge], where I found the regiment had halted. On inquiring the cause, I was told that a reinforcement of the enemy was near. I mounted a fence, and saw the enemy's flank-guard beyond the next hill, say half a mile distant. We were then ordered to form a line for battle, by filing to the right; but, owing to the order not being understood in the rear, the line was formed by filing to the left, which brought many of our men into a sort of swamp, instead of on the hill above, where we should have been. We, however, waited the approach of the enemy, and commenced firing as they came up; but owing, as I think, to the unfavorable nature of the ground, we soon began a retreat, which was continued slowly and in good order, firing constantly for

1 Since known as Barnet's Bridge.

about three-quarters of a mile, until we reached the high ground west of the run of water, where we made a stand. The enemy had two pieces of cannon in the road, and their line extended a considerable distance both below and above the road. A party of Hessians undertook to outflank us on the right, and partly succeeded, but were finally repulsed and driven back. The action was warm and close for nearly two hours, when it being near dark the enemy were forced to retreat. One of their pieces of cannon was taken near the run, and the other a few rods below the brick factory."

X. RESULTS OF THE BATTLE. — In these two engagements the Americans took, according to Gen. Stark, "four pieces of brass cannon, seven hundred stand of arms and brass-barrelled drums, several Hessian swords, about seven hundred prisoners, two hundred and seven dead on the spot, the number of wounded yet unknown." [1] "Lieut.-Col. Baum, one major, seven captains, fourteen lieutenants, four ensigns, two cornets, one judge-advocate, one *baron*, one aide-de-camp, one Hessian chaplain, three Hessian surgeons." [2] "Our loss was inconsiderable; about forty wounded and thirty killed." [3]

Of the trophies, one Hessian gun and bayonet, one broadsword, one brass-barrelled drum, and one grenadier's cap, were presented to each of the States of Vermont, New Hampshire, and Massachusetts. Letters of thanks were returned by these States to Gen. Stark.

A broadsword, taken from Col. Baum on the field of battle, by Lieut. Thomas Jewett, of Capt. Dewey's company, afterward purchased by David Robinson, Esq., is now in the possession of G. W. Robinson. A set of draughting instruments, a map of the route from St. Johns, along the Lakes Champlain and George and the River Hudson, and

---

[1] Stark to Gen. Gates.
[2] Stark to the General Court of New Hampshire. — Dawson.
[3] Stark to Gates.

16*

a lieut.-colonel's commission of Col. Pfister, fell into the hands of one of his two capturers, Jonathan Armstrong, and are in the possession of his grandson, the Hon. L. B. Armstrong, of Dorset.[1] Of the cannon, two, doubtless those of Col. Baum, taken at the redoubt, rated by the War Department as three-pounders,[2] are in the State House at Montpelier.

The remains of Col. Baum and Col. Pfister, whose deaths have been already mentioned, were buried near the bank of the river, a few rods below the paper-mill of Messrs. Hunter & Co. There is nothing to mark the spot, and the place of their interment is not known.[3]

Of the Hessian prisoners who died, many were buried in a place still kept vacant in our church-yard.

The tory prisoners were marched into the village bound two by two. The women took down their bedsteads to get ropes to string them on. They were a care, and probably a vexation, to the Council of Safety for a long time. Capt. Samuel Robinson was chief overseer of them. There are many entries concerning them in the records of the Council of Safety; one to Capt. Robinson to detach ten of them, under proper officers, to tread and beat down the roads (drifted with snow in January) from this place through the Green Mountains to Col. William Williams' dwelling-house in Draper, alias Wilmington; and back again " in the same manner to this place, with all convenient speed." By an entry, September 4, 1777, it appears the prisoners were in Capt. Dewey's barn, or some of them. They were ordered to be removed to the school-house; "if there is sufficient room for them in the meeting-house" (probably with what are already there) " they are to be removed to the meeting-house in lieu of the school-house," — always with a proper

---

1 Vermont Hist. Mag. 2 Butler's Address.
3 Vermont Hist. Mag.

guard over them. Some were put on the limits of their own farms ; some were banished the town under penalty of death if they should return.[1] Some, it is said, were sent to the mines at Simsbury.[2] The number of tories taken prisoners has been stated as one hundred and fifty-seven.[3]

In after years the military reputation of Bennington rose high. The Rev. Mr. Avery says of the town, in his Narrative, 1783 : —

"In regard to military prowess Bennington is thought to be second to none on the continent."

The *general results* were of the highest possible importance. This is true of their bearing upon the infant State of Vermont.

Gen. Schuyler was a haughty, aristocratic New Yorker ; owing his place to social position, not to military talent, and despising New England ; refusing to answer an official letter of Ira Allen, Secretary of our State government, without addressing him as a private man.[4] Gen. Stark was ordered to report to Gen. Schuyler, and refused to do so, and was censured for it in Congress, where New York was all powerful, and Vermont unrecognized.[5] But some days before this vote of censure upon Gen. Stark, *he had fought and won the battle of Bennington.* The tidings had not reached Congress, because the post at that time required five days to get from Bennington to Philadelphia. So soon as the glad news did arrive, Stark's refusal to report to Gen. Schuyler was forgotten ; and a vote of thanks adopted, at length, and Stark was appointed a brigadier-general in the army of the United States.[6]

---

1 Vermont State Papers. 2 Butler. 3 Lossing. 4, 5 Bancroft.

6 Congress, on Oct. 4, 1777, resolved, "That the thanks of Congress be presented to Gen. Stark, of the New Hampshire militia, and the officers and troops under his command, for their brave and successful attack upon, and signal victory

Stark was, in spirit and action, and by association, a representative New Hampshire Grants man. He rose in estimation at Philadelphia, and the petition of the New Hampshire Grants to be recognized as an independent State obtained a more respectful hearing.[1]

The inhabitants of the Grants were reassured in their purpose; and, outside the limits of their territory, men reasoned that if the Green Mountain Boys could make of themselves a barrier of defence for the country, they had a right to self-existence as a commonwealth.

By this victory on the Walloomsac hope returned to the American people. The gift of trophies of the battle to Massachusetts was, and still is, suspended in the Senate Chamber at Boston, over the entrance, and opposite the Speaker's chair, and a copy of the letter of thanks is fastened to the wall just beneath the trophies, and is as follows : —

> " COMMONWEALTH OF MASSACHUSETTS,
> " BOSTON, Dec. 5, 1777.

" SIR : — The General Assembly of this State, take the earliest opportunity to acknowledge the receipt of your acceptable present, the token of victory gained at the memorable battle of Bennington. The events of that day strongly marked the bravery of the men, who, unskilled in war, forced from their entrenchments a chosen number of veteran troops of boasted Britons, as well as the address and valor of the general who directed their movements and led them on to conquest. This signal exploit opened the way to a rapid succession of advantages, most important to America.

" These trophies shall be safely deposited in the archives of the State, and there remind posterity of the irresistible power of

---

over, the enemy in their lines at Bennington; and that Brigadier Stark be appointed a brigadier-general in the Army of the United States." — Journal of Congress, iii., 327. Yeas and nays required and taken; but one dissenting voice, — M. Chase, of Maryland.

[1] Thompson's Vermont.

the God of armies and the honors due to the memory of the brave.

"Still attended with like successes, may you long enjoy the reward of your grateful country.

"JEREMIAH POWELL,
"*President of the Council.*

"Brigadier General JOHN STARK."

"The great stroke struck by Gen. Stark near Bennington," says Gen. Washington, in a letter to Putnam.[1] "The capital blow given the enemy by Gen. Stark," says Gen. Lincoln.[2] Bancroft pronounces this "victory one of the most brilliant and eventful of the war."[3] Baroness Reidsell, then in the British camp, wrote: "This unfortunate event paralyzed, at once, our operations." Clinton wrote: "Since the affair at Bennington, not an Indian has been heard of; the scalping has ceased. I do not apprehend, indeed, any great danger from the future operations of Mr. Burgoyne." The Indians, in particular, were so disheartened, that nearly all of them immediately left the British service, and about two hundred and fifty of them came over and joined the American army. The Canadians and tories also deserted in large numbers.[4]

The terror of Burgoyne, and his confidence in himself, alike departed. In his instructions to Baum, before the battle, he wrote : —

"Mount your dragoons; send me thirteen hundred horses; seize Bennington; cross the mountains to Rockingham and Brattleborough; try the affections of the country; take hostages; meet me, a fortnight hence, in Albany."[5]

[1] Irving's Washington, iii., p. 170.
[2] Bennington, August 18. To Gen. Schuyler.   [3] ix., 386.
[4] Thompson's Vermont.
    "At Bennington Stark gave the wound
    Which, like a gangrene, spread around."
                    —From a poem by the Rev. Wheeler Case.
[5] See, also, Evidence on the American War, given before the House of Commons, London, 1780, p. 77.

Four days after the battle, he wrote to England thus : —

"The Hampshire Grants, in particular, — a country unpeopled and almost unknown in the last war, — now abounds in the most active and rebellious race on the continent, and hangs, like a gathering storm, on my left." [1]

"The ideas entertained of the Americans, by Gen. Burgoyne, now experienced a total revolution, and he declared that it would be impossible for Britain to succeed in her views, and that he should, on his return to England, recommend the recognition of their independence." [2]

In what remained to be done, and in putting the finishing stroke upon Burgoyne's campaign, at Stillwater, on the 7th of the following October, the Green Mountain Boys bore their full share.

XI. COMPARATIVE STRENGTH OF FORCES. — Authorities differ as to the numbers, particularly of Baum's expedition and the reinforcement. As we are obliged to depend upon those who were beaten in the engagements, it is reasonable to assume that the numbers given will be too low rather than too high. Burgoyne, in his order of August 26, giving explanations for the unfortunate result of the battle, does not mention the great superiority of the enemy in numbers. [3]

Burgoyne felt that very much depended upon the success of the expedition. In addition to what has been stated, in the fore part of this article, of his threefold object, and of his carefulness in fitting out the expedition, it may be

1 Burgoyne's more private letter to Germain.

2 Introduction to Burgoyne's Orderly Book. "Their measures are executed with a secrecy and dispatch that are not to be equalled." — Burgoyne's more private letter to Germain. "Your funds of men are inexhaustible, like the hydra's head; when cut off, seven more sprang up in its stead." — Gen. Burgoyne to Gates, at dinner, after his surrender, at Gen. Schuyler's. Orderly Book.

3 Orderly Book, p. 82.

added. that he gave to Baum and to Col. Skene very carefully prepared instructions ; and when news came of the disaster, he set out, with the forty-seventh regiment, to cover
the retreat of the beaten detachments.   It is not to be presumed that he would trifle with the occasion by sending,
for an expedition of such importance in his estimation, an
inferior force.   He had high hopes, it is true, of the disaffection and number of the tories on the Grants ; but this
would not, in his mind, it is presumed, justify any careless-
ness.   The best troops he had were selected for the expedition.

Col. Baum wrote to Gen. Burgoyne, from Sancoik on
August 14 : —

" By five prisoners, taken here, they agree that from fifteen to
eighteen hundred are at Bennington.   .   .   .   I will proceed so
far to-day, as to fall on the enemy early to-morrow."

Had his own numbers been *very* inferior in the comparison, it is scarcely possible he could have sent back such
word.   Bancroft, who had access to German materials for
this portion of history, which other authors on this subject had not enjoyed,[1] says : " More than four hundred
Brunswickers, Hanau artillerists, with two cannon, the
select corps of British marksmen, a party of French Canadians, a more numerous party of provincial royalists, and a
horde of about one hundred and fifty Indians."   (This enumeration leaves out the fifty chasseurs added after Baum
had first started.)   At the first engagement, certainly, not
all the Hessians were killed or taken.   Glick speaks of
cutting his way through with thirty, a portion of whom
escaped.   The Hessians, after being routed on the hill, ran
to escape ; and, doubtless, some few of them succeeded.
The Indians made good their retreat from the first affair,

[1] See Bancroft's Preface to the ninth volume of his Hist. United States.

as did Capt. Fraser, with part of his company, and many
of the provincials and Canadians.[1] And yet, notwithstanding numbers did escape, the prisoners, in addition to the
number of killed of the enemy, in this action, was very
large. Aaron Hubbell made the following statement:
" Was in the first battle. We left the battle-field as one of
the guard placed over something more than six hundred
prisoners captured in the first engagement."[2]

With regard to Breyman's force, Stark, in his dispatch
to Gen. Gates, calls it " a large reinforcement." Thacher,
in his military journal, makes it to number one thousand
regulars. Butler, without giving his authority, adopts the
same number. This *corps de reserve* was ordered to march
after a true statement was sent back, by Baum, of the
number of the Americans. In a general enumeration of
the spoils of victory, more than one author says one thousand stand of arms, besides the dragoon swords. Burgoyne's Orderly Book puts the killed, wounded, and prisoners of the enemy at twelve hundred and twenty. On
the whole, the writer of this article would judge the number of the enemy, including tories and Indians, not to have
been much if at all inferior to the number of our men, the
aggregate of both engagements being considered.

XII. ESTIMATE OF GENERAL BURGOYNE. — Burgoyne's
prestige, after his defeat at Bennington and subsequent
surrender at Stillwater (17th of October), was gone, of
course, and the pompous style of his manifestoes, while on
the flood-tide of success, naturally caused him, afterward,
to be more reproached than were some of the other British
generals. But it is unfair, notwithstanding his failure, to
withhold from him the credit of an able and skilful mili-

---

[1] Burgoyne's letter to Lord George Germain.
[2] MS. in possession of Gov. Hall.

tary officer. He returned to England, of course, under a heavy cloud. But, in 1781, a committee being appointed to inquire into the conduct of the war, so far as it was shared in by Sir William Howe, Burgoyne obtained a chance to be heard; and henceforth the stigma upon his name appears to have been removed. He rose again into favor and influence. Before this committee, " every officer that was examined gave the strongest testimony to his bravery and superior talents. It did not appear that a single fault had been found with any of his plans or movements by the most enlightened judges who were on service with him; but it did clearly appear that he enjoyed the entire confidence of the army; and that, in situations of the most trying nature, in the face of disaster, of danger, and of death, he was looked up to, by his troops, with the utmost affection and the most undoubted reliance; that they were, at all times, ready to suffer, to fight, and to perish with him." [1]

These remarks are made as what justice to Gen. Burgoyne requires, and because to unreasonably disparage the foe is to detract from the just merit of our success in his defeat.

XIII. OUR MEN NOT TRAINED SOLDIERS. — In order to appreciate the valor of the Americans, in the Bennington battle, their general want of military experience and training at that time must be considered. When Stark ordered the cannon taken from Baum to the scene of action, upon the arrival of Breyman, the men whom he directed to load and fire knew not how to do it; the general dismounted, and taught them, by loading one of the pieces himself.[2] A glimpse at the destitution of Stark's New Hampshire re-

---

1 Burgoyne's State of the Expedition.   2 Thacher.

17

cruits is given us in a letter from his head-quarters at the
fort in Number Four, on the Connecticut River, July 30 : —

"We are detained by the want of bullet-moulds, as there is but
one pair in town; and the few balls sent on by the Council go but
a little way."

He also wrote, at the same time : —

"If some rum could be forwarded, it would oblige us very much;
for there is none of that article in those parts where we are going."

Many other things were wanting to Stark's little army;
he mentions kettles and cooking utensils; none of these
wants could be supplied from New Hampshire. Out of
eleven barrels of powder at Number Four, nine had been
condemned. The four cannon there had been dismounted,
and apparatus for putting on carriages could not be procured.[1]

After the battle, in all Stark's brigade there was but one
case of amputating instruments; there were no tents, and
few pails and canteens.[2] Doctor Henry Clark relates that
a resident of Bennington, who was a lad at the time of the
battle, told him of the vivid impression made upon his mind
by seeing the men hurrying past where he stood (he stood
upon the corner since occupied by Mr. Patchin's store),
with scythes and axes, as well as muskets and fowling-
pieces, to meet the enemy.

Some remarks of Mr. Everett, in his life of Stark, may
be appropriately adduced on this point : —

"Too much praise cannot be bestowed on the conduct of those
who gained the battle of Bennington, officers and men. It is, perhaps, the most conspicuous example of the performance by militia
of all that is expected of regular veteran troops. The fortitude
and resolution with which the lines at Bunker Hill were main-

---

[1] Butler.   [2] Sparks' Biography.

tained by recent recruits against the assault of a powerful army of experienced soldiers have always been regarded with admiration. But at Bennington the hardy yeomanry of New Hampshire, Vermont, and Massachusetts, many of them fresh from the plough, and unused to the camp, 'advanced,' as Gen. Stark expresses it, 'through fire and smoke, and mounted breastworks that were well fortified with cannon.'"

XIV. INCIDENTS. — Some facts and incidents may further illustrate the spirit of our men, and the character of the conflict; anecdotes of uncertain authenticity, but with verisimilitude in them.

On the rainy night previous to the battle the men were under orders to remain in the encampment. David Robinson, afterward Gen. David, being one of the volunteers, could not overcome the conviction that he might be true to his duty, and also improve the opportunity of the postponement of the attack until next day, to go home, and see how it fared with the dear ones there. He had a young wife, and two young children, and an aged mother there. On his way he overtook his captain, who appeared to have reasoned as he did on the subject of domestic duty, and who lived on the road to the encampment. The young volunteer intended to pass the captain unrecognized, pulling his slouch hat over his face; but he failed in this. The captain recognized him, and called out, "David, were you not under orders to stay in camp all night?" David replied, "I suppose a soldier's orders are to follow his captain."

When, on this occasion, he had reached home, he had not been there long before a neighbor came in, and said the tories and Indians were coming up the hill, from the valley east, and were in his cornfield. With his characteristic promptness and courage, that never knew fear, he proceeded to reconnoitre. Upon his hands and knees, it being pitch-dark, that he might get objects between himself and the sky, the better to discern what there might be, he soon ascertained that what had occasioned his neighbor's alarm were the fire-flies of that August night, and some oxen that had broken into his corn. As he was returning, he stumbled upon his old mother, who had started from the house, and already proceeded some distance, to be more sure of flight in case of an overwhelming attack from the enemy. She had with her a pillow-case full of valuable papers, and said to her son, " I thought I would try to save at least these, as they might be of more importance to you, some time, than other things." He said to her, " Go back, mother, to the house ; and, if we must die, let us all die together." [1]

Capt. Samuel Robinson, mentioned in the foregoing paragraph, was, no doubt, back to his post betimes. The following anecdote will illustrate how he was not wanting to his duty. The roll of the large company he commanded at that time will be given at the conclusion of this article. In the battle, he was loading and firing like the rest ; but a ball on one side of his head, singing just past his ear, made him dodge away from it. Soon came another on the opposite side, and the head jerked again, nervously, at the whistle. Mortified to think his neck was so limber, he turned around to his men, and said, " Boys, keep your eye on me ; and, if I dodge again, put a ball through me sideways." [2]

Has the kind reader patience for two or three more Bennington battle anecdotes ? Eleazer Edgerton, in the midst of the second engagement, was firing away from behind a tree, when suddenly he espied a very young man looking round anxiously for a standing-place alike secure. " Here, boy," shouted he, " take my tree ; you fight behind, and I'll fight before. The rascals daren't shoot me ; they know me."

1 Related to the writer by Miss Caldwell.
2 Mr. Robinson's Address.

And in an instant he had planted his giant frame back to the trunk of the tree; and there he stood firing until the Hessians did know him, and fear him, and fled beyond the reach of his bullets.[1] Leonard Robinson, whose aim was quick and deadly, declared that every time he shot he saw a man fall. "But," said he, "I prayed the Lord to have mercy on his soul; and then I took care of his body."[2]

What queer notions they had of some things in those days may be illustrated by an incident or two.

"Old Uncle Silas Robinson was somewhat peculiar in his way of telling a story; but his sharp voice used to give great effect to the account of his participation. 'I had heard,' said he, 'that these Robinsons were all cowards; and I rather thought, if any of them was, I was the man. But somebody told me that gunpowder was good for courage; so I took about a gill of gin, and thickened it up; and when I had drank that, I tell you, then I fought.'"[3]

Eleazer Hawks, whose reason for not coming early to the battle has been narrated elsewhere in this volume, made the more haste when he did come. He was, therefore, much parched and exhausted with running, and with the labors of the remainder of the battle. A pint of rum was handed him, and he drank it all, supposing it was water; and before the man who followed with water had time to offer him some, he said, "Now give me some rum." The liquor he drank appeared to produce no ill effect.

A hogshead of rum had been procured by General Stark, and with a little more time would have been distributed at the termination of the first action. It was prevented by the so sudden appearing of Breyman.

With respect to the exhausting effect of the fight, in the oral account of the surviving soldier to Mr. Butler, he says, "My company lay down and slept in a cornfield,

near where we had fought, each man having a hill of corn
for a pillow. When I awaked next morning, I was so
beaten out, that I could not get up till I had rolled about a
good while." [1]

Of the interest of the ministry and the pulpit in the
cause of patriotism, with respect to the Rev. Mr. Dewey,
and the Rev. Mr. Avery, mention is made elsewhere. The
zeal of the Rev. Mr. Allen in the battle has become
famous, partly from its naïveté. In accounts of the battle,
he is called "Parson Allen" or "the fighting parson." He
is believed to have been the Rev. Mr. Allen, pastor of
Pittsfield, Mass. He came with the Berkshire detachment
of militia, Col. Simmons. The story is thus told in Everett's Life of Stark. "Among the reinforcements from Berkshire County,[2] came a clergyman with a portion of his
flock, resolved to make bare the arm of flesh against the
enemies of the country. Before daylight on the morning
of the 16th he addressed the commander as follows : —

"'We the people of Berkshire have frequently been called upon
to fight, but have never been led against the enemy. We have
now resolved, if you will not let us fight, never to turn out
again.'

"General Stark asked him if he wished to march then,
when it was dark and rainy.

"'No,' was the answer. 'Then,' continued Stark, 'if the
Lord shall once more give us sunshine, and I do not give
you fighting enough, I will never ask you to come out
again.'

"The weather cleared up in the course of the day, and

---

[1] Mr. Butler's Address.

[2] The Rev. Mr. Noble, in his Williamstown Centennial Address, gives credit
to the volunteers from that town in these words: " Every man in this town,
except a cripple on crutches, shouldered his gun and rushed to the field of conflict."

the men of Berkshire followed their spiritual guide into action." [1]

In other parts of this volume mention is made of prayer-meetings held at the time of the battle, for the success of our army, by those who could not aid with weapons of war. In Mr. Butler's Address is narrated a prayer meeting for the same object, held also at Williamstown, whither many from the north had repaired for safety, women and children, aged and infirm, in the event of the battle issuing adversely.

" In my boyhood, my grandmother often related to me, how, on that day, she, with many other women of Williamstown, and their minister, resorted to their meeting-house, and there continued in prayer for their kinsmen, who were in the field of blood, till late at night, when a courier came announcing glad tidings."

The cannon peals were heard booming over the hills at Williamstown during the anxious hours.[2]

The joy of the people of Bennington at the great victory was not unmingled with sadness. Four of its most respected citizens had fallen on the field of battle. They were John Fay (son of Stephen), Henry Walbridge (brother of Ebenezer), Daniel Warner (cousin of the colonel),[3] and Nathan Clark (son of Nathan, and brother of Isaac). They were all in the prime of life, and all heads of families, leaving widows and children to mourn their sudden bereavement. The grief for their loss was not confined to their immediate relatives, but was general, deep, and sincere.[4]

---

[1] See also American Revolution from Newspapers and Original Documents by F. Moore.

[2] Mr. Noble's Centennial Address. It is said that the smoke of the battle was distinctly seen from Bemis' Heights, thirty miles distant. — Lossing.

[3] " Warner rode near us. Some one, pointing to a dead man by the wayside, said to him: ' Your cousin is killed.' ' Is it Daniel?' asked Warner; and when the answer was ' Yes,' he jumped off his horse, stopped and gazed in the dead man's face, and then rode away without saying a word." — Account of a surviving soldier.   [4] Vermont Hist. Mag.

The following are selected from some stanzas on the Bennington battle, written by E. H. Chapin, a native of Bennington (now the Rev. E. H. Chapin, D.D.), in 1837, and delivered by him in the "Old Academy," in Bennington Centre :—

.　　.　　.　　.　　.　　.　　.

"They came, as brave men ever come,
　To stand, to fight, to die;
No thought of fear was in the heart,
　No quailing in the eye;
If the lip faltered, 'twas with prayer,
　Amid those gathering bands;
For the sure rifle kept its poise
　In strong, untrembling hands.

"They came up, at the battle sound,
　To old Walloomsack's height;
Behind them were their fields of toil,
　With harvest promise white;
Before them those who sought to wrest
　Their hallowed birthright dear,
While through their ranks went fearlessly
　Their leader's words of cheer.

"My men, there are our freedom's foe,
　And shall they stand or fall?
Ye have your weapons in your hands,
　Ye know your duty all;
For we — this day we triumph o'er
　The minions of the crown,
Or Molly Stark's a widowed one
　Ere yonder sun goes down.

"One thought of heaven, one thought of home,
　One thought of hearth and shrine,
Then, rock-like, stood they in their might
　Before the glittering line.
A moment, and each keen eye paused,
　The coming foe to mark,
Then downward to his barrel glanced,
　And strife was wild and dark.

. . . .

"It needs no monumental pile
  To tell each storied name,
The fair, green hills rise proudly up
  To consecrate their fame.
True to its trust, Walloomsack long
  The record bright shall bear,
Who came up at the battle sound
  And fought for freedom there."

The 16th of August, ever since the battle, has been observed, in Bennington and vicinity, as a patriotic holiday; and, though not superseding the observance of Fourth of July, with the rest of the country, is celebrated with no less spirit than is that great national anniversary.

The roll of Capt. Dewey's military company, as it was constituted at the time of the battle, has not been preserved. Of Capt. Samuel Robinson's company, the following is a list of the men in the battle: —

Robert Cochran,
Gideon Spencer,
William Henry,
Henry Walbridge,
Rufus Branch,
John Larned,
Thomas Abel,
Nathan Lawrence,
Josiah Brush,
David Fay (fifer),
Leonard Robinson,
Daniel Biddlecome,
Levi Hatheway,
Abram Hatheway,
Reuben Colvin,
Eliphalet Stickney,
Daniel Rude,

Benjamin Holmes,
James Marivater,
Mr. Alger,
Ammie Fuller,
Jonah Brewster,
George Dale,
John Marble,
Ephraim Marble,
Aaron Hubbell,
Samuel Safford, Jr.,
Aaron Smith,
Ephraim Smith,
Samuel Henry,
Edward Henderson,
Jonathan Haynes,
Archelaus Tupper,
Daniel Warner,

Lieut. Simeon Hatheway,
Aaron Miller,
John Fay,
Elijah Fay,
Joseph Fay,
John Clark,
Jehoshaphat Holmes,
Moses Rice,
Benjamin Whipple, Jr.,
Silas Robinson,
John Weeks,
Moses Scott,
Alpheus Hatheway,
Solomon Walbridge,
Ebenezer Bracket,
Jehiel Smith,
Asa Branch,
Phineas Wright,
John Smith,
Jesse Belknap,
Silvanus Brown,

John Forbes,
Stephen Williams,
William Post,
David Safford,
Jared Post,
Jeremiah Bingham,
Samuel Slocum,
Josiah Hurd,
Ezekiel Brewster,
Solomon Leason,
Thomas Selden,
John Rigney,
Elisha Smith,
Solomon Safford,
Joseph Roe,
William Terrill,
Noah Beach,
Simeon Sears,
David Robinson,
Joseph Safford,
Isaac Webster.

Ode by Mrs. A. C. L. Botta.[1]

" Our patriot sires are gone ;
    The conqueror Death lays low
Those veterans, one by one,
    Who braved each other foe ;
Though on them rests death's sable pall,
Yet o'er their deeds no shade shall fall.

" No, ye of deathless fame !
    Ye shall not sleep unsung,
While freedom hath a name,
    Or gratitude a tongue :

1 " Mrs. Anna C. (Lynch) Botta. She edited, in 1841, the ' Rhode Island Book ; '
in 1853, published an illustrated volume of poems ; in 1855, was married to Prof.
Botta, of New York city. The last work of Mrs. Botta is the ' Hand-Book of
Literature,' published in 1860, and entitles the author to a handsome place among
the prose writers in America." — Vermont Hist. Mag.

Yet shall your names and deeds sublime
Shine brighter through the mists of time.

" Oh, keep your armor bright,
    Sons of those mighty dead,
And guard ye well the right
    For which such blood was shed !
Your starry flag should only wave
O'er freedom's home or o'er your grave."

CHAPTER XIII.

PERSONAL NOTICES.

SAMUEL ROBINSON, ESQ., AND MRS. MARCY L. ROBINSON.

AS the best method of preserving some interesting incidents of the early history of the town and church, and some illustrations of the position and influence attained in early days by this community, some personal notices, it is deemed, will be acceptable to the readers of these pages. These notices will be confined to persons who came here, or were born here, at least a half century ago, including a few who have deceased during the writer's pastorate in Bennington, but who were much identified with the earlier persons and times of this community.

The writer regrets a certain necessary injustice to individuals in a work of this kind, both through the unequal treatment of some who are noticed, and the omission, doubtless, of many who deserve to be commemorated. He can only say, that, though expending a great amount of labor upon this part of the volume, he has been still obliged, very considerably, to use such materials as have happened to get into his possession.

I. SAMUEL ROBINSON, SEN., ESQ., was the acknowledged leader in the band of pioneers in the settlement of the town; and continued to exercise almost a controlling authority in the affairs of the town, the remainder of his life.[1]

[1] Vermont Hist. Mag.

He was born at Cambridge, Mass., 1705. His father, Samuel Robinson, was born at Bristol, England, 1668. In the Rev. Dr. Hooker's printed sermon at the funeral of Gen. David Robinson, in a note, it is said that the elder Samuel Robinson is supposed to have been a distant connection of the Rev. John Robinson of Leyden (pastor on that side of the water to the Pilgrims of the Mayflower). Mr. Isaac T. Robinson stated to the writer that both Samuel (our Bennington pioneer) and his brother Thomas were confident they were descendants of the Rev. John Robinson. Our Samuel Robinson, Sen., resided in Hardwick, Mass., twenty-six years before removing to Bennington.

Many facts attest his ability : that he conceived, organized, and set on foot the settlement of this part of the country ; that he was so prompt and resolute to resist the claims of New York officials to the lands and jurisdiction of this territory. It is related, when the surveyors came from New York upon his lands, he cut their chain in two with his hoe, but when they desisted from their attempt he invited them into his house and treated them in the most hospitable manner ; that he was deputed to London, as representative of the settlers here, in the British Court, and enabled, as such, to gain the ear of His Majesty, and secure two very important and significant orders from the crown in favor of the settlers, and against the government of the province of New York.

Before his coming to Bennington he was an active and leading man in Hardwick. He was captain of a company in Col. Ruggles' regiment of provincials, and served as such on the frontier, in 1755, 1756.[1] He was at the head of his company in the battle of Lake George, when the French were defeated by Generals Johnson and Lyman. He was a dea-

[1] Early Hist. Vermont, p 85.

18

con in the old church, and afterward in the Separate church in Hardwick.[1]

"He was commissioned a justice of the peace by Gov. Wentworth, Feb. 8, 1762, being the first person appointed to a judicial office within the limits of the State.

"In the summer of 1764 a controversy in regard to jurisdiction arose in Pownal between claimants under New Hampshire, and others under New York, in which the authority of Esquire Robinson, as a magistrate, seems to have been invoked. Mr. Robinson being at Pownal was, together with Samuel Ashley, a New Hampshire sheriff's deputy, and two other persons, arrested by the New York sheriff and his assistants, and carried to Albany jail. This collision of officers produced a correspondence between the governors of the two provinces, which appears to have resulted in a sort of compromise, by which Mr. Robinson and those with him were released on moderate or nominal bail, and, though indicted for resisting the New York officers, were never brought to trial.

"In December, 1765, when it was ascertained by the settlers under New Hampshire that their lands were being granted from under them by Lieutenant Governor Colden, Mr. Robinson was deputed by those of Bennington and the neighboring towns to go to New York for the purpose of trying to persuade him to save their possessions from the grasp of the city speculators; but his efforts were unavailing."[2]

"There being no longer any hope of relief from the government of New York, the claimants under New Hampshire resolved to appeal for redress of their grievances to the conscience of the king. A petition was accordingly prepared and signed by over one thousand of the settlers and grantees,

1 Hardwick Centennial Address, by the Rev. Lucius R. Paige.
2 Vermont Hist. Mag., p. 167.

and Samuel Robinson, Esq., was appointed their agent to repair to England and lay it before His Majesty." [1]

" William Samuel Johnson, an eminent lawyer and statesman of Connecticut, was then preparing to leave for England, as agent for that colony to the home government, and the petitioners employed him to assist Mr. Robinson in his mission. They sailed in the same vessel from New York, the 25th of December, 1766, and landed at Falmouth, England, the 30th of January following, and reached London a few days afterward." [2]

Mr. Robinson was much hindered in his mission by the aristocratic prejudices at court against the republican settlers on the New Hampshire Grants, also by want of money and prestige; [3] nevertheless he was, though not completely, in a very important degree successful. He seems to have shrewdly discerned the situation, and to have given the settlers at home sound advice as to the wise course for them to pursue under their difficulties.

But, most valuable of all, " he so far procured the aid of the crown that Lord Shelburne, on April 11, 1767, addressed a letter to Sir Henry Moore, who had then become governor of the province of New York, forbidding him in the most positive terms from making any more grants of land in the disputed territory, and from molesting any person in possession under a New Hampshire title. And on the 24th of July following, upon a report of the case by the Lords of Trade, a formal order of the king in council was made commanding the Governor of New York 'upon pain of His Majesty's highest displeasure' to make no grants whatever of any part of the controverted lands, 'until His Majesty's further pleasure should be known concerning the same." [4]

1, 2 Early Hist. of Vermont, p. 85.　　　　3 Ibid., p. 96.

4 Early Hist. Vermont, p. 94. For a copy of the petition sent by the settlers for Mr. Robinson to present to the king, and other documents of the correspond-

The negotiations appear to have made no further progress beyond this point. On the 27th of October following Mr. Robinson died of the small-pox, in London. Whether, had he lived, he would have been able to prosecute his labors, as agent of the settlers, to a complete and successful issue, we cannot divine. His past success and his sound judgment and skill would seem to have warranted high expectations. His death was felt by the settlers to be a great calamity. Upon his decease Mr. Johnson wrote a letter of condolence to his widow. This letter shows clearly that Mr. Robinson was high in the esteem of Mr. Johnson and others in London; and, on that account, and as containing interesting particulars, it is inserted here. The original is in the possession of G. W. Robinson. The letter is as follows: [1] —

"LONDON, Nov. 2, 1767.

"MADAM: — It is with the deepest concern and grief that I find myself obliged to communicate to you the sad intelligence of your dear husband's decease. He had enjoyed very good health, since he left America, till at length the misfortune which I always feared for him overtook him. He was seized with the small-pox, which but too generally proves fatal to Americans in this climate, and his appeared to be of a bad kind and very severe. Yet he bore up against the distemper, in all its rage, with great fortitude and patience; and till the twelfth day, we had hopes of his recovery (as the pocks had begun to turn), but the next day it took a sudden and fatal turn, and it appeared that he had not strength of

ence between the crown and the New York government, and details of Mr. Robinson's efforts, see Early Hist. Vermont, pp. 85-97.

[1] Mr. Johnson was one of the three first chosen to represent the colony of Connecticut in the Congress of the Revolution. He was the first of the three delegates from Connecticut in the Convention which framed the Constitution of the United States, the others being Roger Sherman and Oliver Ellsworth. He was one of the Senators first appointed by the Legislature of Connecticut, under the National Constitution. — New Englander, April, 1866. He had been sent to England, as agent of the colony of Connecticut, to argue for it an important cause before the Lords in Council, and for five years remained there, entrusted with various public as well as private affairs. ·

constitution sufficient to throw off the disease; and, on the 27th of October, at half past ten at night, he was no more! Such was the will of God. He was sensible to the last; was calmly resigned to the will of Heaven, and died full of faith. We have, therefore, — which must afford you the greatest consolation, — good reason to believe that he has exchanged this life for a better, and rests in eternal felicity. He is much lamented by his friends and acquaintances here, who are many. You may rest assured that no attention, care, or expense was spared for his comfort, and to have saved his life, had it been consistent with the designs of Providence. He had two excellent nurses constantly by him. A skilful apothecary saw, and administered to, him every three or four hours. He was visited every day by an eminent physician, and his friends afforded him every consolation in their power. After his death, as the last act of friendship to his memory, I took care to furnish him a decent funeral, at which Gen. Lyman and the other gentlemen here from America attended with me as mourners. He is interred in the burying-ground belonging to Mr. Whitfield's church, where he usually attended public worship. A club of American merchants and gentlemen, to whom he was known generously contributed eight pounds sterling toward defraying the expenses of his funeral, etc.; and the remainder, as the accounts come in, — the amount of which I cannot yet determine, — I shall advance, not doubting that it will be, somehow or other, refunded me.

"I most sincerely condole with you in this great affliction, and pray God to give you comfort and to sanctify this melancholy event to you and all his family and friends, to whom I beg leave to present my compliments, and am,

"Madam, your most obedient

"And very humble servant,

"WILLIAM SAMUEL JOHNSON."

Mr. Robinson had ten children, all born in Hardwick, one of whom died there at eleven years of age. The other nine removed to Bennington, became heads of families and members of the church. Their names were Leonard, Samuel, Moses, Silas, Marcy, Sarah, David, Jonathan, and

18*

Anna. Of his descendants some are to be found in almost every State and Territory in the Union.[1]

II. Mrs. MARCY (LEONARD) ROBINSON, the wife of Samuel Robinson, Sen., Esq., was of Southbury, Mass., born in 1713.

The following is an extract from a letter respecting her to the writer by her grand-daughter: [2] —

"I suppose my grandmother was quite a business woman. She was accustomed to take one of her sons with her, and ride to Albany on horseback, transact business, make her purchases, and return. I believe she would be gone several days, for she usually attended meetings there."

When living in their log-house, while her husband was still living, but in England, and her children, David and Jonathan and Anna, were with her, the wolves came up at night and tried at the doors and windows to obtain entrance. She knocked upon the door to frighten them from the immediate proximity, then seized firebrands from the fire, opened the door and waved them and shouted with all her strength. The wolves fled away and were no more seen or heard by her.

She is remembered for her great consistency and power of a Christian conversation. The volumes of Hopkins' divinity, which she much read, and many passages of which she marked as worthy of particular attention, are preserved. It is matter of tradition that the Friday prayer-meeting, noted in the early history of this community, originated with her. It was first held, and for a long time, at her house. It was a custom, long continued by her, to have a prayer-meeting, at noon, on Sunday, at her house.

---

1 Vermont Hist. Mag.

2 Mrs. Allyn, daughter of Anna Robinson, Mrs. Webster, and in the seventy-ninth year of her age, residing in Cleveland, Ohio.

A traditional impression has been related to the writer, of religious services being customarily held in a log-house before the erection of the first meeting-house. This was probably her house, — the same impression locating the log-house where her house stood.

A manuscript obituary notice of her, for the press, has been preserved. The following are extracts from this notice : —

"It was remarkable of the deceased, that her profession of religion, even from early life, was regular, her piety the effect of investigation, and her hope the enlightened offspring of a firmly grounded faith. For the last ten years of her life she was singular for the enlargement of her views, the extension of her liberality of sentiment, and her reading in ancient and modern history, both sacred and profane. She retained her usefulness to the last evening of her life; and the Sabbath previous to her decease she called her children together, took an affectionate leave of them, and gave a succinct account of her own views as to religious concerns, and the reason of her faith. In this remarkably affecting interview, her narration and comments took up nearly two hours."

The following anecdotes were related of her by her son, Gen. David, to William Haswell : —

While sitting in church, in revolutionary times, when our mothers had resolved that they would not wear clothing of foreign manufacture, a lady, who sat in the pew forward of her, had a plaid neckerchief which she admired so much, that she determined to get the lease (a technical expression with weavers), and set herself to counting the threads. She felt rebuked, turned away, and fixed her eyes upon the minister; but the handkerchief was still before her, and more potent than her sense of duty; her mind recurred to the counting of the threads to get the lease, until, despite her good resolutions, the threads were counted and the lease obtained; then, after heaving a sigh, she said to herself, but so audibly as to be overheard, " Well, devil, you have had your way this time."

She was in the habit of conversing freely upon the subject of her own decease. Her daughter inquired of her if she had any fear of death ; she replied, " I am not afraid to be dead, but I am afraid I shall not honor my Saviour in the hour of death."

She died on the 4th of June, 1795. Her funeral was attended the Sabbath following,—it was sacrament day,— " by the greatest concourse of all since the town was settled." [1]

The following are two stanzas of a hymn, composed by Mr. Anthony Haswell, for the occasion, and sung at her funeral : —

> " She spake, and to her calm reproof
>   The hardened sinner lent an ear ;
> Blest were the tenants of her roof,
>   Taught by her voice the Lord to fear.
>
> " She's gone ; her pilgrimage is o'er ;
>   She slept and breathed her soul to rest ;
> Her warning lips shall move no more,
>   Nor pain for sinners heave her breast."

[1] Obituary Notice.

CHAPTER XIV.

PERSONAL NOTICES.

First Immigration.

MRS. Bridget (Brown) Harwood was in the first company of settlers in Bennington. She was a widow. She came with her children, Peter, Eleazer, Zechariah, Stephen, Abigail, and Hepzibah. She rode on horseback, as did the other ladies of the company. As they neared the line they raced their horses, each vying with the other to be the first to pass over into the Bennington township. Thus they brought their effects on horseback, and came by the guidance of marked trees. She must have been a resolute mother. Her husband had deceased not quite three years before, — Benjamin Harwood, born April 30, 1713, in Concord, Mass., where, also, his father, Peter Harwood, was born; descended of English ancestors.

She was born April 20, 1715, at Concord. After the birth of their first child, Peter, they removed to Hardwick, Mass. All of their children, with the exception of the oldest and youngest, were born in Hardwick. They then removed to Amherst, Mass., and thence to Bennington. They were married in May, 1733.

Peter Harwood, her oldest son, at the time of the removal to Bennington was about twenty-six years of age, and came with his wife Margaret (Clark). She was born July 8, 1740, in Coleraine, Mass. (daughter of Matthew Clark, of Scotch origin). They were married June 9, 1759; settled in Amherst, and removed thence to Bennington, with one child named Clark.

This Peter Harwood set out the first apple-tree in this town, and it is still living and bears fruit. Theirs was the first son born in this town. Their mother, Mrs. Bridget Harwood, was the first person among the settlers who died here, November 8, 1762; Mrs. Margaret Harwood was the first hopeful convert added on profession of her faith to this church; and the house upon the old homestead, now occupied by a descendant, — H. Hopkins Harwood, now junior deacon of the church, — has been pronounced " to retain more of the shape and appearance of the first frame houses built in Bennington, than any other dwelling-house now standing." [1]

SARAH HARWOOD, daughter of Peter and Margaret Harwood, married Samuel Robinson, son of Col. Samuel Robinson, Jr., and Esther, daughter of Deacon Joseph Safford. She was the mother of Uel M. Robinson, Esq. She compiled the Genealogical History of the Families of Robinsons, Saffords, Harwoods, and Clarks, — a work of immense labor, and great accuracy, and very valuable. It has been constantly consulted in the preparation of portions of this volume. She was born October 3, 1775; married May 5, 1796; united with this church in July, 1803, and died September 10, 1854.

ELEAZER HARWOOD, second son of Mrs. Bridget Harwood, and who came with his mother, was nearly twenty-four years of age, and accompanied by his wife, Elizabeth Montague, to whom he was just married, May 19, 1761.

---

1 Samuel Fay, Esq.

She was daughter of Samuel Montague, believed to be one of the immigrants hither from Sunderland, Mass.; moderator of the first town-meeting in this town, and cousin to John Montague, deacon and clerk, and his son, also deacon of the old First Church in Sunderland.

Eleazer Harwood and Joseph Safford were elected deacons, at the first election of deacons in this church, according to the records. He became a preacher of the gospel, and resigned the office of deacon in this church to remove to Pittsford, in this State, where he became pastor of the church, and was blessed with extensive and powerful revivals.[1] One in particular is mentioned, — that of 1803. He died in 1807, " much beloved by all that knew him." [2] A grandson of his, by the name of Kellogg, is a minister of the gospel. Mrs. Eleazer Harwood's mother accompanied them to Pittsford, and died there in January, 1816, aged ninety-five years and three months.

Zechariah Harwood was unmarried when he came with his mother to this town. He was at that time nineteen years of age. He married Lovina Rice, daughter of *Oliver Rice*, of Hardwick, and born in 1751.

The names of Jedediah, Oliver, and Hannah Rice are on the old covenant, also on the roll of this church at its organization. The name of Oliver Rice is on the list given in Paige's Hardwick Centennial Address of those who from Hardwick served in the French war, commencing in 1756.

Mr. Harwood settled near the north border of the town on the road now the main road to Shaftsbury. In early times vaccination had not yet been introduced into the town, and on occasion of the prevalency of small-pox, the town gave permission for innoculation with the small-pox,

---

1 See Vermont Evang. Mag. of that day. — P. H. White.
2 Vermont Chronicle.

and appointed pest-houses, to which patients with this disease should be restricted. In 1800, such a house was established in the north-east part of the town, under the charge of Mr. Harwood, who, though not a regular physician, was believed to have peculiar skill in the management of the disease.

A Benjamin Harwood is recorded as a member of this church in 1762. If this is correct, it must have been the son of Mrs. Bridget Harwood, of that name.

BENJAMIN HARWOOD, son of Peter Harwood, mentioned in another place as the first male child born in Bennington, united with the church late in life, January 3, 1836. A diary which he kept has been preserved, dating back to 1806, and continued for some four years, from which extracts have been introduced into these pages. His son, *Hiram Harwood*, continued this diary down to 1836. It is comprised in some dozen volumes, most of them quite large, very legibly and neatly written, — a minute record of every day of life for thirty years.

The Zechariah Harwood above mentioned was a member of this church at its organization, and became a Universalist, said to be of the Winchester type.

This Mr. Winchester had been a preacher of Calvinistic doctrines, and became an advocate of universal restoration, preaching in Philadelphia, and afterward in various parts of America and England; and died in Hartford, Conn., in 1797. He published several works.[1] He came to Bennington and preached. Individuals of prominence went to hear him. It is said that Judge Jonathan Robinson went to hear him, but would not let his children go, and did not say at home what was his opinion of the preacher's sentiments.

[1] Encyclopedia of Religious Knowledge — Art. Winchester.

General Ebenezer Walbridge, an early settler in Bennington from Norwich, Conn., and highly distinguished in the civil and military annals of this town, and previously a member of the church, adopted Winchester sentiments.[1]

This case of Zechariah Harwood is introduced to bring to notice the fact that his third son, *Perez*, who had adopted his father's Winchester sentiments, became, after having arrived at adult age, and having reared a large family of children, converted to the faith of his ancestors. He embraced the doctrines of this church and united with it, January 5, 1834. Four of his children and a daughter-in-law had previously, at one time, united with the church, September 4, 1817.

All his children, and very nearly all his grandchildren, resident in this town, have become members of the church. One of them, James H. Harwood, is a minister of the gospel. Thus the stream of descendants, turned aside temporarily from the faith of the ancestors, turned back again in solid body to that faith.

---

[1] A communication in the "Vermont Gazette," of May 3, 1863, evidently from the pen of an admirer of Mr. Winchester, shows him to have had an insinuating and popular address. "The sentiments of the late pious Mr. Winchester, in coincidence with the above liberal mode, were once delivered in an agreeable manner in this town," etc. On his last visit to Bennington, "he happened to arrive within a few miles on Saturday evening; laboring under some disease, but anxious to hear the reverend and pious Mr. Job Swift on the Sabbath ensuing, he rode several miles, across an exceedingly bad road." When arrived and in the service, he gave exceedingly fixed attention to Mr. Swift's sermon; at noon he "walked with some difficulty to the house where the church generally convened, to pass that period in suitable exercises and prayer" (doubtless at "Grandmother Robinson's"). Here he was recognized by "a leading church-member" "who had formerly had a slight acquaintance with him in Philadelphia;" and a dialogue ensued, of which, as described, the following is a part. "Mr. Swift said," . . . — stating some doctrinal observation, — "and I conceive you could not fully coincide with him in those sentiments." — "Truly," resumed the worthy man . . . . . "while plenty abounded and no one felt a lack, what need had I to repine at your helping yourself to a slice that would not have been so savory to my taste, and while all have abundance, let each regard his fellow with complacency." . . . .

19

The remaining son of Mrs. Bridget Harwood, who came with her in the first company of settlers, Stephen, was at that time ten years of age.

The Harwoods, according to tradition, were, — as were so many others of the early settlers of this town, — Separates. The descendants of this family are very numerous; indeed, the most so of the three families (Robinsons, Saffords, and Harwoods), all so numerously represented in Mrs. Robinson's genealogical record. At present there are more members in the Bennington First Church of the name of Harwood than of any other.

A few extracts from the diary of Benjamin Harwood may interest the reader, as near-at-hand glimpses of a worthy man, such as cannot now otherwise be obtained : —

His honor. — "March 13, 1807. — Nathan Robinson received of me this day ten bushels of wheat at 7s. per bushel. Nothing but honor made me part with the wheat at the above price, for I can get 8s. 7d. at Troy for it. Mr. Robinson bargained for the wheat last fall when it went at the price which he now gives."

An eye for beauty. — "June 15, 1808. — Nothing about us seems more pleasant at this time than a view of Mt. Anthony, every tree from its base to its summit being completely covered with green leaves."

His hospitality. — "Jan. 30, 1809. — Uncle Zechariah, his son Abel, and son-in-law Hugh, and their wives, and Ruth Harwood, came and made us a visit. Next arrived Mr. Moses Donaldson on his way home to Coleraine; after him Mr. Stearns, wife, and daughter; and the last to come was our good friend, Mr. Case, of Hoosick, bringing with him brother and sister Stone, and their youngest daughter. Beside those I have mentioned, a considerable collection of the young people of the neighborhood spent the evening here. Except Uncle Zechariah and his people, who returned in the evening, those whose names I have mentioned tarried here all night."

Entries like the last of the above frequently recur in the diary.

Old folks' mowing match. — " May 31, 1808. — Late in the afternoon Governor Robinson and his lady came here on a visit. The old gentlemen felt pretty smart, talked upon religion, and read the Bible most of the time while he was here. I am requested to mention one circumstance which occurred this afternoon, though not of more importance than many others mentioned in this journal. My father commonly mows his door-yard about this time. It happened that he wanted to mow it to-day. So himself, Governor Robinson, and Mr. Warner, each took a turn at mowing, to see which one could cut his grass the most handsomely. The matter being left to themselves, each decided in his own favor. My father will be seventy-three years of age in July next, Governor Robinson is about sixty-nine, and Mr. Warner sixty-seven."

Of the above-named Perez Harwood, it may be said that, a son, Henry, two daughters, Lucinda and Ruhama, a brother, Hiram, and a brother's wife, Sylvia, and a second cousin, Hiram, 2d, united with the church Sept. 4, 1817. He himself, as above, Jan. 5, 1834. He died at the advanced age of eighty-nine, Dec. 9, 1859, — social and agreeable in conversation, firm in the faith of Jesus, and with a victorious hope. A grandson, *Isaac Harwood,* became deeply interested (1854) in an incipient missionary Sabbath-school movement in the north-east part of the town ; dying two years afterward, absorbed with prayer and desire for this school. His father, Henry, succeeded him, and has been succeeded by others in charge of the school. In the third and fourth years of its history it was blessed with a powerful revival of religion in the neighborhood, and many converts, among them the Rev. Simeon Knapp, a devoted and successful minister of the Baptist denomination, who has since died.

Of the above-named Benjamin Harwood, his wife was *Diadama Dewey.* They were married April 18, 1786. She was born Jan. 5, 1766, Stockbridge, Mass., daughter of Abner Dewey, born in Westfield, Mass., and married, 1776, in

Bennington. She united with the church Sept. 22, 1825, and deceased June 22, 1854, aged eighty-eight; clear-minded and bright-eyed to the last, and with vivid recollection of events occurring long since in the history of the town. A daughter and namesake, Mrs. Hiram Waters, united with the church Jan. 3, 1836, died Sept. 19, 1864; of superior loveliness, consistency, and excellence in all the relations of life.

GEORGE P. HARWOOD, son of Jonas, and grandson of Peter and Margaret Harwood, united with the church Jan. 3, 1836, died May 14, 1868; was one of the trustees of the First Church.

II.　SAMUEL AND TIMOTHY PRATT, with their wives, Baty and Elizabeth, came with the very first immigration. The names of all but Timothy are on the roll of the church at its organization; Timothy Pratt is on the records as uniting with the church, with others, Jan. 3, 1765; also, "Esther, wife" — it is to be inferred second wife — "of Samuel Pratt."

The names of Samuel Pratt and Timothy Pratt are on the "muster roll [1] of the first company of militia in the town of Bennington, organized Oct. 24, 1764," of which John Fassett was captain. Their names are also among those of officers appointed at the first town meeting held March 31, 1762, at the house of John Fassett.

The names John Pratt and Silas Pratt are on a "list of the persons settled in Bennington prior to June 1, 1765, prepared from recollection, by Samuel Robinson, Esq., in New York city, in December of that year, and furnished the governor of that province." [2]

---

[1] Found among the papers of Capt. Elijah Dewey by his grandson, E. D. Hubbell, Esq.

[2] Vermont Hist. Mag., p. 144.

The first settlers of this name came from Amherst, Mass., and settled in the easterly portion of the town. Among their descendants Stephen Pratt resided in what has since been raised and is now the Stark House. E. S. Pratt, residing where was the house of Roger Booth, is a descend ant.

ELISHA BILLINGS PRATT, who married Clara, daughter of Samuel and Aurelia (Mather) Safford, was son of Stephen Pratt.

III. LEONARD ROBINSON was the oldest child of Samuel Robinson, Sen. He came here, with his family, in the first company of settlers. He was born in Hardwick, Mass., July 27, 1736. He married his first wife, Rebecca Billings, in Hardwick, and his first two children were born there. She united with this church April 14, 1765. He united with the church December 20, 1764. His frequently leading the Friday prayer-meeting, and "lining out the psalm" with a peculiar tone, has been spoken of as familiar to the old inhabitants. He was first sergeant in Capt. John Fassett's military company. He was forty-one years of age at the time of the Bennington battle, and in Capt. Samuel Robinson's company. From the Bennington battle anecdote related of him, among the incidents of that battle, in a previous part of this volume, his piety would seem to have been of that kind that "trusts God, *but keeps the powder dry.*"

Late in life he removed to Swanton, and died September 29, 1827. He had sixteen children.

IV. COLONEL SAMUEL ROBINSON was second child of Samuel Robinson, Sen.; "was born at Hardwick, Mass., August 15, 1738; was one of the first company of settlers

19*

who came to Bennington in 1761 ; married Hannah Clark, in Hardwick, Mass. ; and, for his second wife, in Bennington, Esther, daughter of Deacon Joseph Safford, and died in Bennington, May 3, 1813.

He was an active man in the New York controversy, and in the other early affairs of the town; in 1768 was chosen town committee, in place of his father, deceased ; commanded one of the Bennington companies of militia in Bennington battle; performed other important military services during the war, and rose to the rank of colonel. In 1777 and 1778, he had charge, as " overseer," of the tory prisoners ; and, in 1779 and 1780 represented the town in the General Assembly, and was for three years a member of the Board of War. He was the first justice of the peace appointed in town, under the authority of Vermont, in 1778, and was also, during the same year, one of the judges of the Special Court for the south shire of the county, and, in that capacity, sat on the trial and conviction of Redding.

Col. Robinson was a man of good natural abilities, and of much activity and enterprise in early life ; upright and honorable in all his dealings, possessing undoubted personal courage, and beloved by all for the kindness, generosity, and nobleness of his nature and conduct.[1]

" He was one of the eight persons who, in 1781, certified, in writing, their approval of the efforts of Ira Allen to prevent the invasion of the State by *finessing* with Gen. Haldimand.   His patriotism was never doubted."[2]

He left numerous worthy and respectable descendants, some of whom reside in this town, and others in different parts of this State and the United States.

Dr. Benjamin Robinson, son of Col. Samuel Robinson,

[1] Vermont Hist. Mag., p. 168.   [2] Early Hist. Vermont, p. 468.

became a physician, and settled in Fayetteville, N. C.; obtained a wide and eminent practice in his profession, and was highly respected as a citizen. He was born in Bennington, February 11, 1776, and died in his adopted place of residence, in 1857.

In the "Vermont Historical Magazine" is the following interesting account of the introduction of vaccination into Bennington: "Dr. Benjamin Robinson, a young physician, son of Col. Samuel Robinson, advertised, in the 'Vermont Gazette,' under date of December 17, 1800, that he was 'inoculating for the *kine*, or, as it is commonly called, the *cow-pox;*' and stating 'that he has the best European authority for warranting him in publicly declaring, that when a person has once had the *kine-pox*, he is forever infallibly secure against catching the small-pox by any possible exposure.' And he stated, in some detail, the evidence on which his declaration was founded. In a publication in the 'Gazette,' of the 2d of February following, Dr. Robinson, among other proofs of the efficacy of the kine-pox, states that he had inoculated Russell Haswell, Heman Robinson, and Samuel Follett, lads from thirteen to seventeen years of age, with the kine-pox; that after having it, they had entered the pest-house and been inoculated, by Mr. Harwood, with the small-pox, and 'were exposed to the contagion of ten or twelve persons in the various stages of the disease,' and that not one of them was in the least degree affected with the pest-house disease."

CHAPTER XV

PERSONAL NOTICES.

SECOND IMMIGRATION.

DEACON JOHN FASSETT was born April 1, 1720. He was one of the second company of settlers in Bennington, in 1761. At his house the first town meeting was held in March, 1762. He resided about half a mile south of the meeting-house, near what has been lately known as the Doctor Swift place. He kept a tavern, and the town meetings were at the house of "John Fassett, inn-holder," until 1767, when they were at the meeting-house. In October, 1764, Mr. Fassett was chosen captain of the first military company formed in the town (by which title he was afterward distinguished). He was one of the two representatives of the town in the first State Legislature. He died at Bennington, August 12, 1794, in the seventy-fifth year of his age.[1]

His name is upon "the old church covenant," and he was one of the members of the Bennington church at its organization, and the first clerk of the church. He took a leading part in its affairs. His name constantly occurs upon committees on business, in the church, from its commencement, and through the pastorates of the Rev. Messrs. Dewey and Avery.

He was leader of the choir, and, with very few exceptions, the leaders of the choir, through the first century,

[1] Vermont Hist. Mag.

have been from among his descendants.[1] He removed hither from Hardwick, Mass., and he was a staunch Separate, in principle and feeling, through life. A common saying, which has been handed down, illustrates his punctuality and strictness in religious duties: "It is as true as that John Fassett will be at prayer-meeting at such an hour."

His children were Sarah (wife of Dr. Jonas Fay), John, Jonathan, David, Nathan, Amos, Mary, Benjamin, and Hannah.

JOHN FASSETT, JR., united with this church under Mr. Dewey, August 29, 1765. He was one of the two representatives from Arlington in 1778, and was elected one of the Council in 1779, which office he held, with the exception of the years 1785 and 1786, until 1795; and he was also a judge of the Supreme Court for eight years, 1778–1786.[2]

COL. BENJAMIN FASSETT united with the church in the Wood and Burton revival, Nov., 1784. He was for some years leader of the choir. He came to Bennington with his father in 1761. He was a commissary in the war of the Revolution; and served in other capacities in civil and military life, was an active business man, and died in Bennington years since, leaving numerous descendants.[3]

He married Betty, daughter of Capt. Elijah Dewey. She united with the church at the same time with her husband. They had three daughters, all of whom became members

---

[1] The following are the names of the leaders of the choir for the first century of the church's history. Those in italics are descendants of Deacon John Fassett: Deacon John Fassett, Judge Jonathan Robinson, *Col. Benjamin Fassett*, *Col. Jonathan E. Robinson*, Nathaniel Dexter, *Gen. Henry Robinson*, Deacon Stephen Bingham, William Bates, *Deacon John F. Robinson*, Hon. S. H. Brown, *J. Seymour Merrill*, *John Fay*.

[2], [3] Vermont Hist. Mag.

of the church; Betsey (the second Mrs. Uriah Edgerton)
and Sarah, in 1803; and Ruth (Mrs. Samuel Fay)
Nov. 10, 1822.

Col. Fassett married his second wife, Mrs. Hetty Alvah,
who also united with the church in 1803. Benjamin
Schenck Fassett, Adeline, first wife of Edward H. Swift,
and Mary, wife of the Rev. Gordon Hayes, were the offspring of this marriage. A daughter of Mr. and Mrs.
Hayes, Lydia, became the wife of a missionary, and resides
in India. The last-named three children of Col. Fassett
also became members of the church.

Deacon Fassett's daughter, Mary (Mrs. Judge Jonathan
Robinson), and his son Jonathan, became members of this
church, under Mr. Dewey — the former, Jan. 3, 1765; the
latter, May 16, 1765, — and a daughter, Hannah, in the
Wood and Burton revival.

Of the above, John Fassett, Jr., "was one of the nine or
ten persons who were first concerned in endeavoring to
prevent Gen. Haldimand from invading the State." [1]   He
was father of *Col. Elias Fassett*, of the thirtieth United States
infantry, in the war of 1812. The following allusion to Col.
Fassett is taken from Hiram Harwood's Diary of 1812 : —

"*Monday, June 7*, 1813. — Many of us went down to where Col.
Fassett's regiment took its departure for Burlington, which they
did in a brilliant manner." [2]

1 See Biographical Sketches in Hall's Early Vermont, p. 463.

2 "Soon after the admission of Vermont, as a member of the Federal Union,
this town became and long continued to be a recruiting station for the army. In
the spring and summer of 1792, Gen. William Easton, afterward distinguished
in the war with Tripoli, then a captain, recruited a company here, and at its
head marched to Pittsburg and joined the army under General Wayne, then preparing for his campaign against the Indians. Men were also enlisted here for
the army and marine service during the administration of the elder Adams, on
the apprehended war with France. It was also a recruiting station during the
war of 1812, and in 1813 the thirtieth regiment of U. S. infantry, under Col. Elias
Fassett, was mustered and drilled here, preparatory to joining the army for actual service." — Vermont Hist. Mag., p. 136.

Col. Benjamin Fassett bought extensively upon the eastern border of the town and resided there, afterward building and occupying the Dr. Morgan house, opposite the court house.

RUTH FASSETT (Mrs. Samuel Fay) was the mother of Samuel, Benjamin, and John Fay — a devoted mother, kind neighbor, full of hospitality, and much attached to her relatives and friends ; died Aug. 14, 1862, aged eighty.

II. DEACON JOSEPH SAFFORD was also one of the second company of settlers in Bennington, 1761. At the meeting in which the church was organized, and immediately after that business was disposed of, it was voted : —

" To receive in Joseph Safford and Anne Safford, his wife, into full communion with this church."

He, with Eleazer Harwood, was elected to the office of deacon, at the first election of this kind in the church on record.

His wife was Ann Bottom, of Norwich, Conn., born in 1710. He was born in 1705, at Ipswich, Mass. At the first town meeting he was appointed town treasurer, and one of the tithing men. At a proprietor's meeting, March 31, 1862, it was voted : —

"To give Esquire Samuel Robinson and Deacon Joseph Safford five acres of land, with the privilege within the said five acres to build a corn-mill on, and forty dollars in case it be built by August next." "Also, voted to give forty dollars to any one on the east side of the town who should build a saw-mill by the first day of September next."

These men had the saw-mill done by the 16th of June ; and the time was, at proprietor's meeting, extended one month, in which they might finish the corn-mill and get the premium of forty dollars.

Deacon Safford brought with him to this town the records of the Newint (Conn.) Separate Church. These are still preserved by his descendants; and also a manuscript letter from the old church in Newint, signed by Daniel Kirkland, its pastor, to Joseph Safford and others, Separates, with a view to some further conference on the matters of difference between the separating brethren and the old church. These records are interesting, as containing the record of Joseph Safford's formal election and installation to the office of deacon in the Separate church; also their confession of faith, and covenant, with the signatures; also an important case of discipline, spread out at length, showing their strictness and success in maintaining discipline in the church.

His daughter *Esther* was second wife of Col. Samuel Robinson and mother of ten of his children; Hannah (Mrs. Follett), Esther (Mrs. Hyde), Samuel, Benjamin, Polly, Betsy (Mrs. Sears, mother of Hon. Benjamin R. Sears), Safford, Hiram, Lucy (Mrs. Montague),[1] Sarah (Mrs. Haswell). His daughter, Abigail, married Jonathan Scott, one of the early settlers here from Sunderland, Mass. His son, Col. Joseph Safford, married Marcy, daughter of Samuel Robinson, Sen.; Anna, his first child, married Henry Walbridge; Cornelius Cady, born in Norwich, Conn., married his daughter Elizabeth; David married Anna Brewster; his daughter Lucy married Samuel Montague (the Sunderland family), and was mother of Elizabeth, wife of Deacon afterward the Rev. Eleazer Harwood, of Pittsford; Jacob married Persis Robinson, daughter of Col. Samuel Robinson, by his first wife, Hannah Clark, of Hardwick; his daughter Harriet married John Fassett, Jr.

GEN. SAMUEL SAFFORD was the eldest son of Deacon

---

[1] Died Dec., 1868, æ. 79. — It was truly said of her, at her death, "All who know her must feel that they have lost a friend."

Joseph Safford. "He was born at Norwich, Conn., April 14, 1737, and was one of the early settlers of Bennington. He took an active part in the land-title controversy with New York; and on several occasions represented the town in conventions of the settlers for defence against the Yorkers; and also for forming the territory into a separate State.

When the committees of the several towns met at Dorset, in July, 1775, to nominate officers for the batallion of Green Mountain Boys, recommended by Congress, he was nominated for major, under Warner as lieutenant-colonel, and served as such in the battles of Hubbardton and Bennington and throughout the war. Before the close of the war he became a general of the militia. He was a representative of the town in 1781 and 1782, and, in 1783, was elected a State councillor, and served as such for nineteen years in succession. For twenty-six successive years, ending in 1807, he was chief judge of the County Court for Bennington County. He was an upright and intelligent man, of sound judgment and universally respected. He died at Bennington, March 3, 1813." [1]

"He was concerned with Chittenden and others in the Canada negotiations, and his patriotism was never questioned." [2]

He united with the church in the revival under the Messrs. Wood and Burton, 1784; and his wife, Mary Lawrence, some two years afterward, at the commencement here of the ministry of Mr. Swift. He was elected deacon in 1789, and continued in the office until his death in 1813.

He was distinguished for exact truthfulness and for strict observance of the Sabbath. Saturday evening was required to be kept, under his roof, as strictly as Sunday. Secular

1 Vermont Hist. Mag., p. 175.
2 Early Hist. Vermont, p. 468; see, also, ibid., pp. 212, 221, 261, 325, 363.

preparations for the Sabbath were required by him to be made before sundown of the day before.

His wife, Mary Lawrence, was the daughter of Jonathan Lawrence, who removed with his family to Bennington, 1772. She was born in Norwich, Conn., April 8, 1741.

Their children were Samuel (born in Norwich, Conn., June, 24, 1761; married Aurelia Mather, in Bennington, May 8, 1786, deceased in 1851; he was the father of Mrs. Cogswell Morgan), Mary, John, Ruth, Anna, Clara, Electa (Mrs. Webb), Amelia, and Jonas. He resided in the house, now the residence of Cogswell Morgan, — Mrs. Morgan being his grand-daughter.

A son of Mr. and Mrs. Benjamin Webb, William Webb, is, or was, until his removal to Washington, a deacon in the Second Congregational Church. Mary, daughter of Gen. Safford, married Nathan Fay, son of John Fay, who was killed in the Bennington battle.

III. DEACON ERWIN SAFFORD, was elected deacon May 10, 1822, and removed to Philadelphia in 1830. He was a descendant of John, brother of Deacon Joseph Safford.

IV. ELISHA FIELD was one of the members of the church at its organization. He was ensign in the military company organized in 1764, with John Fassett as captain. He and Deacon Safford were the tithing men, among other town officers, appointed in the first town meeting, March 31, 1762. He came into town with the second company of settlers in 1761.

He was a member of the Separate church which removed from Sunderland. There are seven persons of the name on the roll of this church. Four of them united in the revival in 1803. Jesse and Mrs. Nancy Field united with the church in 1784, in the revival under Messrs. Wood, and Burton. He was one of the building committee of the new meeting-house. He was a carpenter.

He was in the battle of Bennington, and some extracts from his manuscript communication have been given, in the account of the battle, in this volume.

V. LIEUT. JAMES BREAKENRIDGE was one of the second company of settlers (fall of 1761), and his name, and that of William, his son, are on the old covenant, and on the roll of members at the organization of the church.

He was a large landholder. His name became famous in connection with the important fact that a successful stand was made by the settlers of Bennington, on his farm and at his residence, against the first and only overt attempt of the New York claimants to dispossess, by the sheriff and his posse, the settlers in this town from their New Hampshire grants.

Mr. Breakenridge was a man of quiet and peaceable disposition and habits, though his property, being covered by the old patents of Walloomsac, necessarily placed him in a belligerent attitude toward the New York claimants. Although indicted as a rioter, and outlawed with Allen, Warner, and others, by the New York government, he does not appear to have ever taken any part in the active proceedings.

He was sent to England, by a convention of the settlers, with Jehiel Hawley, of Arlington, as his associate, in 1772, to ask relief from the crown against the New York claimants and government; but the ministry were too much absorbed with their project of taxing America to give their attention to the matter. Mr. Breakenridge was chosen lieutenant of the first military company formed in Bennington, in 1764, and is, therefore, frequently designated in the records of the town, by that title.[1]

[1] Vermont Hist. Mag.

The father of Lieutenant James, whose name also was *James*, was a native of Scotland, and removed thence to Ireland; and removed from Ireland to this country in 1727, and settled in Ware, Mass., whence Lieut. James Breakenridge removed to Bennington. There was a brother of Lieut. James, named William, who was a greatly respected, and very influential citizen, in Ware, for many years.[1]

DANIEL BREAKENRIDGE, son of Lieut. James Breakenridge, of commanding form, and great determination and decision of character, united with this church in 1803. Esther Breakenridge united with the church April 8, 1765, Hannah, Jan., 1803. A daughter of Lieut. James married Thomas Henderson. A daughter of this marriage, Phebe Henderson, married Harry Smith, Esq. Two of the children of this marriage became ministers of the gospel. Mrs. Phebe (Henderson) Smith married a second husband, the Rev. Joel Lindsley, D.D. A son of this marriage became a minister of the gospel.

The Breakenridge place is in the possession and occupancy of John Younglove Breakenridge, son of Daniel.

MRS. AZUBAH BREAKENRIDGE, wife of Daniel, — previously Mrs. Paine, mother of Cornelia, Mrs. Tubbs; then Mrs. Haynes, mother of Harriet and Martha Haynes, the first and second Mrs. Gen. Henry Robinson, — deceased Sept. 23, 1857, at an advanced age. She united with this church May 6, 1821. In a few of the last years of her life, by reason of the infirmities of age, not able to leave her house, but still with a refined and earnest welcome, received her kindred and friends and her minister to the enjoyment of her cheerful hospitality.

---

[1] Ware Historical Address, by William Hyde.

VI. Ebenezer Wood came into town the first year of the settlement of the town, though not with the first company. He was one of the committee, appointed in the first proprietors' meeting, to choose a place to set the meeting-house. He was third sergeant in Capt. John Fassett's company of militia. He united with the church Jan. 3, 1765.

Deacon John Wood was one of the officers of Capt. Fassett's company. He was received into this church Dec. 13, 1764. His name is also down on the old covenant. He was elected deacon May 22, 1789, at the same time with Gov. Moses Robinson, and Gen. Samuel Safford. He is represented as a severe, exact, and very determined man, and as very pious. He must have been considerably advanced in years when elected deacon. His name appears frequently upon committees, in the church records, at a very early day, — as far back as June 19, 1766. The wife of Deacon Wood, Hannah, united with the church June 20, 1765. John, a son of theirs, dedicated by them in baptism, Nov. 1, 1767, married Sarah, daughter of Joseph Safford, and grand-daughter of Deacon Joseph Safford. Joseph Safford married Marcy, daughter of Samuel Robinson, Sen. John Wood, Jr., removed to Malone, N. Y. Deacon Wood, probably then a very old man, removed to Malone, in 1810. He resided on the place where is now the residence of Elijah Fillmore. Ten individuals of the name of Wood are on the roll of the church; none of that name are now connected with the church.

VII. Governor Moses Robinson. — The biographical sketch of Governor Moses Robinson, by Governor Hall in the "Vermont Historical Magazine," could not be condensed

21*

with justice to itself and its subject, and it is too long for insertion here. The reader is referred to that article for important information of his public career; and this notice would confine itself to particulars not therein contained, save to say in brief, that he was chosen town clerk at the first meeting of the town, and for nineteen years; colonel of the militia, and at the head of his regiment at Mount Independence on its evacuation by Gen. St. Clair; member of the famous Council of Safety at the time of the battle of Bennington, and, during the campaign of that year; chief justice in the Supreme Court on its first organization, and for ten years; when he was elected to the office of governor of the State by the Legislature; in 1782 one of the agents of Vermont in the Continental Congress; and on the admission of Vermont into the Union one of the senators in Congress.

He was born in Hardwick, Mass., March 26, 1741, and came with his father, Samuel Robinson, Sen., in the summer or fall of 1761, to Bennington.

He was hopefully converted at twenty-four years of age. It was in the summer time; he was in the field at work when he received light. He was so overjoyed, he hastened across the field, forgetting his hat, to inform his pastor, Mr. Dewey, of the happy change his feelings had undergone. He was received into the church with six others, June 20, 1765. He was proverbial for the fervency and unction of his prayers, when leading others at the throne of grace, and for always guiding, when it was possible, the conversation into the subject of religion.

Judge Stephen Robinson used to say that when a lad at home in his father's house (the present residence of G. W. Robinson) he could hear the whole of Governor Moses Robinson's prayer at the meeting-house. It is related of him that being across the mountain, to attend to some business of settling an estate, and there being a prospect of some time elapsing before the preparations would be completed for proceeding with the business, he proposed, and it was agreed to, that the interval should be devoted to a prayer-meeting.

He is remembered as often repeating the expression, and with unction, " As for me and my house, we will serve the Lord." Persons still living remember him as leading the meeting in the absence of the minister, and " lining out " the psalm.

At one prayer-meeting which appeared rather dull, the two other gentlemen who were deacons with himself were present, and he led the meeting. He called on one of them to lead in prayer, who, after several ineffectual attempts by " hemming " to clear his throat, wished to be excused. Governor Robinson then called on the other, who also desired to be excused ; thereupon the governor undertook the duty himself, and gave the following vent to his thoughts : " O Lord ! thou knowest we have come up here this afternoon to worship Thee, and we are cold and lukewarm as it were, — *I fear at least some of us are.*" The associate deacons knew well enough who were meant, but conceived no offence.

Governor Robinson was possessed of great wealth. The town was noted in his day for the wealth of its inhabitants, and he was, perhaps, more distinguished than any other in this respect. It is affirmed that his liberality to the cause of religion here corresponded to his ability.

He was elected deacon May 22, 1789, and continued in that office until his death, May 26, 1813. In a letter, preserved by G. W. Robinson, of condolence, to Gen. David Robinson on the death of his second wife, a letter of that lady is referred to in which Mrs. Robinson " mentioned the happy death of Governor Robinson, and observed that if she could feel as he did, it would be worth ten thousand worlds."

He married Mary, daughter of Stephen Fay, who united with the church May 16, 1765, and after her death, Miss Susannah Howe, who united with the church May 5, 1811. By his first wife he had six sons and one daughter.

CAPT. MOSES ROBINSON, JR., first child of Gov. Moses Robinson, was born in Bennington, Nov. 16, 1763. He was a member of the Council in 1814; and was several times, in 1820 and afterward, representative of the town in the General Assembly.

He was appointed, Jan. 30, 1804, building agent in chief for the building of the new meeting-house. A building committee previously appointed was to draw plans and advise with Capt. Moses Robinson. He was to make contracts and draw on the treasurer. He married Ruth, daughter of Capt. Elijah Dewey, and grand-daughter of the Rev. Jedidiah Dewey. Two of his grand-children are ministers of the gospel, — Thomas Wright and Henry M. Swift.

MAJOR AARON ROBINSON, the second son of Gov. Moses Robinson, was born May 4, 1767. He united with this church in the revival in 1803. He was town clerk seven years, in 1815 and afterward; a justice of the peace twenty-three years; a Representative of the Assembly in 1816-17; and Judge of Probate in 1835-6; and died in 1850.[1] He was clerk of the church from Jan. 24, 1820, until his decease. His faithful entries upon the church records, in a remarkably clear and regular hand, are models to those who have similar duties to perform.

His first wife was Sarah, daughter of Major Wait Hopkins (killed by the Indians in New York in the Revolutionary

[1] Vermont Hist. Mag.

War [1]), and Mindwell, daughter of the Rev. Jedidiah Dewey. His second wife was Mary Lyman, daughter of David Lyman, of Connecticut, born May 3, 1778, died March 28, 1852. She united with the church in 1811, and possessed devoted piety, constant and fervent in prayer.

Major Aaron Robinson and his wife were warm friends of the Rev. Absalom Peters, D.D., while he was pastor of the church, and very averse to his pastoral relation with this church being dissolved. Mrs. Robinson addressed to him, in a few stanzas of poetry, the expression of her appreciation of him as her minister, which testimonial was highly prized by Dr. Peters, but became mislaid, and cannot be found.

NATHAN ROBINSON, Esq., fourth son of Gov. Moses Robinson, was the father of Gov. John Staniford Robinson.

Gov. JOHN S. ROBINSON was born in Bennington, Nov. 10, 1804; graduated at Williams College in 1824; admitted to the Bennington County Bar in 1827; was twice a representative of Bennington in the General Assembly; twice a member of the State Senate; in 1853, on the failure of an election by the people, was chosen governor by joint ballot of the two houses.

He belonged to the Democratic party, and was frequently supported by his political friends for member of Congress, governor, and other important offices; but his party being generally in the minority, he was unsuccessful except as before stated. He died in Charleston, S. C., April 24, 1860, while attending the National Democratic Convention, where he was chairman of the delegation from Vermont.

The legal attainments and high order of talent of Gov. John S. Robinson placed him at an early day in the front

[1] Mrs. Robinson's Genealogical History.

rank of his profession, which position he always maintained. Generous of heart, amiable in disposition, and with integrity undoubted, he, by his uniform courtesy and kindness, endeared himself to all with whom he had business or intercourse. His remains were brought for interment to his native town, where his funeral was attended by the members of the bar in a body, as mourners, and by a large concourse of acquaintances and friends, — an impressive funeral discourse being delivered by President Hopkins, with whom he had received his college education." [1]

[1] Vermont Hist. Mag.

CHAPTER XVI.

PERSONAL NOTICES.

SECOND IMMIGRATION, CONTINUED.

GENERAL DAVID ROBINSON was the eighth child of Samuel Robinson, Sen. He was born at Hardwick, Mass., Nov. 22, 1754, and came to Bennington with his father in 1761, being then a lad of seven years. He was in the battle of Bennington as a private in the militia, and afterward rose, by regular promotion, to the rank of major-general, which office he resigned about 1817. He was sheriff of the county for twenty-two years, ending in 1811; when he was appointed United States Marshal for the Vermont District, which office he held for eight years until 1819.[1]

He possessed a powerful constitution and great courage. A desperate individual had committed crimes and escaped the law, and all were afraid of him. He had fled to a hayloft, and General Robinson went in pursuit of him. The neighbors of the general warned him to be cautious in approaching a person so dangerous, and endeavored to dissuade him from ascending to the man's retreat. Gen. Robinson, however, paid no attention to these remonstrances, but immediately went up on the loft and arrested the criminal without harm. In the winter before the Bennington battle, the British had command of Lake Champlain by the destruction of the American fleet under Arnold. They had a

---

[1] Vermont Hist. Mag.

large force at St. John's. The Americans held only Ticonderoga; all north of that point was under control of the enemy, and tidings came that a company of defenceless women and children were there. It was two hundred miles away, and the snow from two to four feet deep. David Robinson, a young man about twenty-two, holding himself as a minute-man, went to the rescue of those helpless and imperilled ones; forming, with one Deming from Arlington, and a few others, a small detachment for this object. They accomplished their magnanimous purpose, and conveyed the women and children to a fort for safety on the Connecticut River. On his return he had at length one companion, a broad-shouldered six-footer. Mr. Robinson proved the most enduring of the two, — his comrade tiring out some day and a half before they reached home, so that Robinson carried, for the remainder of the way, his own gun and knapsack and his comrade's also.

He was fond of warming his blood, of a frosty morning, on his wood-pile, without coat or hat, only a good sharp axe in his hand. Mrs. Robinson would remonstrate: "You will surely catch your death by such exposure." His laconic reply would be: "Well, I can't catch it but once."

"Prompt" was a favorite expression with him, and when he placed a boy in the saddle to do an errand, he was accustomed to say to the lad, "Do you go, and come."

He was deeply interested in everything that concerned the prosperity of Bennington; ever ready to bear his full share of the burden and expense of public worship, and of every public interest. The Rev. E. W. Hooker, D.D., his pastor, preached a discourse at his funeral, which was published. Some extracts are here quoted: —

"The precise date of his connection with the church in this place is not to be ascertained, from their being in an imperfect state. He is supposed, however, to have made a profession of religion in his young manhood. . . . In his religious relations and character, if General Robinson was an Independent Congregationalist, so was he also a man sound in the faith of the fathers of New England. . . . The infirmities of advancing age in a few of the last months and years of his life of course rendered it many times difficult to obtain a very definite knowledge of his religious frame of mind. For some time previous to this, however, he seemed gradually withdrawing his thoughts from things temporal; disposed to converse seriously on his state and prospects, and to realize himself his nearness to the scenes of eternity, and their deep and affecting solemnity. In the intervals, upon his views and feelings in regard to eternal things, he spoke with a solemnity and tenderness indicating a deep sense of their superior importance, and such as should testify to the consciences of his fellow-men on their own concern in them, as also hastening forward to the judgment-seat of Christ.

In illustration of his religious submission, Doctor Hooker related to the writer the following anecdote : —

"By the death of his son, Heman, he was deeply afflicted. Others were with him, and myself also, at the time, in the north front room. Heman was dying in the room above. Some time had elapsed, and we were expecting the event. His brother Stephen came down to the foot of the stairs and said, ' He is gone, sir ! ' General Robinson did not seem to hear distinctly the announcement, and I said to him, ' Your son has breathed his last.' Rising from his chair, ' Oh ! ' said he ; and, proceeding to ascend the stairs, he repeated the words, ' Be still, and know that I am God.' "

In illustration of the great infirmity of his advancing years, to which allusion is made in the above extract from Dr. Hooker's discourse, let an anecdote be given, related to the writer by Miss Angeline Selden. She was in at the house of Henry Kellogg, Esq., where Judge Noah Smith resided formerly, and General Robinson came in during his days of mental decline, as he was passing away. He inquired if Judge Smith was in.   Mr. Kellogg replied in the negative.   He persisted in inquiring for Judge Smith, and then added, "I will go to the court and meet Judge Fay and Judge Brush."   Judge Smith had been dead some forty years, and the other gentlemen, one of them longer, and the remaining one perhaps nearly as long.   The old man was truly living in the past.

He died Dec, 12, 1843, at the age of eighty-nine.

By his wife, Sarah, daughter of Stephen Fay, Esq., he had three sons, who became heads of families.

DAVID ROBINSON, Esq., graduated at Williams College in 1797, and became a lawyer.   His second wife, Mrs. Sarah Shewel, daughter of Jesse Dickerson, of Morristown, N. J., a lady of refinement and intelligence, united with this church Sept. 7, 1817.   Before his decease he executed a deed, conveying his residence to this church and society for a parsonage.   He died in March, 1858, aged eighty-one.

HON. STEPHEN ROBINSON was successively a member of the Assembly for several years, a judge of the County Court, and a member of the Council of Censors in 1834.[1] He received hope in Christ, and gave satisfactory evidence of his conversion in his last sickness, — about a year before his death.   In his inquiring state of mind he took the Bible, and with Scott's and Clark's Commentaries studied it carefully.   He became convinced of the impropriety of general visiting on the Sabbath, and when old friends, accustomed to that way, called on Sunday, he expressed his pleasure in seeing them, but that he preferred they should come on some other day.   He was very positive in his opinions, and in his expression of them, but he was so candid and intelligent that he did not give offence.   He married Sarah,

[1] Vermont Hist. Mag.

daughter of Deacon Aaron Hubbell. She united with this church May 4, 1817, and died August, 1844.

Of seven children, the first-born died at six years of age. The others became members of this church.

EDMUND A. ROBINSON became a prosperous and highly-respected merchant in Albany, where he deceased suddenly. For some of the recent years before his death, having a summer residence here, and for a few years for both summer and winter, he was ever a valued friend of this society, aiding and encouraging us always in our work, — generous, intelligent, genial ; his sudden death affected this community with profound surprise and sorrow.

RUTH ROBINSON married Professor W. H. Parker, of Middlebury College, and deceased some years since.

DEWEY HUBBELL ROBINSON became a physician, and was settled in the practice of his profession in Michigan, and died in early manhood.

ANNE CALDWELL ROBINSON deceased Dec. 5, 1868. She was distinguished for her zeal, labor, and success as a teacher in the Sabbath school, and particularly of an adult ladies' Bible class. She possessed a rare intellect, and great firmness in adhering to right and truth as she viewed them.

MRS. STEPHEN ROBINSON, JR., deceased, daughter of Joseph Hinsdill, deserves note for the amiableness of her disposition, and the loveliness and consistency of her Christian character.

HEMAN ROBINSON was the youngest son of Gen. David Robinson. His death has been already noticed. It took place when he was fifty years of age. He married Betsey, daughter of Joseph Wadsworth, and had twelve children ; one of them, the oldest son, Judge Albert D. Robinson, another, George W. Robinson, who owns and occupies the residence and farm formerly the possession of General David Robinson. There the first Mrs. Samuel Robinson, as a widow, lived and died with her son David. The family have an excellent portrait of General Robinson. Gen. Robinson's third wife, Nancy, daughter of James Caldwell, and widow of George Church, Hartford, Conn., is upon the church record, as uniting with this church October 18, 1816.

II. JUDGE JONATHAN ROBINSON, the youngest son of Samuel Robinson, Sen., was born at Hardwick, Mass., August 11, 1756, and came to Bennington as one of his father's family. He was a lawyer, and was early in public life. He was town clerk six years; represented the town thirteen years; was chief judge of the Supreme Court from 1801 to 1807. He was then chosen senator to Congress, to fill the vacancy occasioned by the resignation of Israel Smith, elected governor of the State; and was also senator for the succeeding term of six years, which expired March 3, 1815. In October, 1815, he became judge of probate and held the office for four years, and in 1818 again represented the town in the General Assembly. He was a man of pleasant and insinuating address, and, by his talent and political shrewdness, occupied a leading position in the Republican party of the State for many years.[1]

He was averse to making aristocratic pretensions among his towns-people. In illustration of this, the following incidents have been familiarly related to the writer. There had a family come into the east part of the town by the name of ———. The young people of this family were awkward and unused to company; Judge Robinson made a party at his house, went over himself and invited

[1] Vermont Hist. Mag.

them, and made them promise to come; they came, and he spent the evening chiefly in entertaining them, and in every endeavor to make them feel at home.

When a senator in Congress, he came home on one occasion, and Sunday morning, as the family were prepared for church, his daughter Polly, afterward Mrs. Merrill, came into the room dressed handsomely in silk; he noticed the dress at once, and made inquiry about it; his daughter answered his inquiries, relating that her mother had purchased it of a peddler, calling his attention to its excellent quality, and seeking his approval of it as a good bargain. "I do not care about that," said he; "go, take it off, and put on your calico dress, or you shall not go to meeting with me; when your mates have silk dresses to wear, then you may wear one." Her mother, who was more aristocratically inclined, had bought the dress when he was absent at Washington.

He had great influence over the boys in the street; he was very kind to them. When they came into the street to play, he would let them stay until eight o'clock in the evening, and then would say, "Come, boys, now you must go home;" and they complied. On the 16th of August, they went to him with entire confidence for money with which to buy powder; and also on the 4th of July. He was very tender-hearted. Theophilus Harrington, at the time assistant judge, said to Judge Robinson: "Be you the judge, and Hyde the sheriff, and Spenser the State's attorney, and there will be nobody hung."

The following reminiscence gives a characteristic feature of those by-gone times. On one of the occasions of the return from college of Jonathan E., his son, some difference of opinion arose between them, upon some subject that had been introduced into their conversation at the table. Jonathan E. said, "I know it is so, and I ought to know; I am

21*

fresh from the schools." His father replied, "Well, if you
are fresh from the schools, I can throw you in wrestling."
"I think not, father," was the quick answer of the young
man; for he had returned fresh from wrestling as well as
from study. "Let us see," said his father. They arose
from the table; the order was given for it to be placed one
side, and the middle of the floor cleared. They grasped
each other, first at arms'-length, but the younger was the
more agile, and obtaining the right clinch was victorious;
Judge Robinson was thrown so effectually, and so far, as
nearly to overthrow the table and its contents. He admitted his son's superiority in wrestling. "I shall not try
with you again;" and so the discussion ended, with entire
good feeling however.[1]

He united with the church in the Wood and Burton
revival, 1784, at the age of twenty-eight. He was elected
clerk of the church, and continued so until his death. He
was fond of doctrinal discussion and study, and of hearing
leading ministers of the gospel preach, and used, when
they were temporarily here, to invite them to his house.
He was much interested in the prophecies, and corresponded with the Rev. J. Spaulding on the subject.

He married Mary (born in Hardwick, Mass., 1754;

---

[1] They were much given to wrestling. Governor Moses Robinson was over the
mountain in some place, and passed by where there was a raising. He stopped
and assisted, and when it was through they proceeded as usual to wrestle. After
wrestling awhile, he stepped up, they having found the bully, and took hold of
the bully, and threw him at once. The governor was long-legged, and they
looked at his legs and called him spindle-legged, and said that he took the bully
before he thought of it; so he tried the bully again, and threw him just as
quickly as before. They did not know him at the time, but soon after he made
himself known to them.

A bully came from Massachusetts, and inquired for the Robinsons, and they
set forward Jonathan E. He immediately floored the Massachusetts man. The
stranger looked at him, and said he could not do that again. He took hold again
and floored him as soon as before. He said he would not try again. They
had what they called "the Robinson lock."

united with the church, 1784; died July 15, 1822), daughter of Deacon John Fassett. Their children were Jonathan Edwards, Mary, Henry, and Isaac Tichenor.

JONATHAN E. ROBINSON, Esq., born August 4, 1777, was graduated at Williams College, 1797; married Alice, daughter of Deacon Benjamin Skinner, of Williamstown, Mass. Their daughter, May Alice, married Charles Manning, of New York city. These had a son, James E. Manning, died February 17, 1856, who was graduated at Williams College in 1848.

Mr. Robinson, after the death of his first wife, married Anna Storms, daughter of Thomas Storms, of New York city. He died April 27, 1831.

He united with the church in 1803. He was town clerk nine years; judge of the County Court in 1828; and resided in New York city for several years. His profession was that of a lawyer.

He was for some time leader of the choir in this church. He was distinguished for his tenor voice and superior excellence in singing. While residing in New York, the precentor in the congregation, where he attended public worship, was absent a Sabbath, and there was some perplexity as to what should be done. General Storms, the father of Col. Robinson's second wife, arose and said there was a gentleman there who would perhaps be willing to lead the singing, if agreeable to the congregation. Gen. Storms' proposal was readily assented to, and Col. Robinson stepped forward and took the precentor's place; he was very tall and graceful, and of commanding presence, and performed the service of leading the singing in such a manner as to astonish and delight the congregation. In fugue tunes, if any part faltered, he could at once strike that part and sustain it, were it *alto* or *treble*, and descend without delay to the *bass*, and so sustain the whole.

The following was told to the writer by the Rev. Hiram Bingham : " Dr. Yale, of Kingsborough, my classical tutor, used to say that Mr. Jonathan E. Robinson had the finest voice he ever heard. Jonathan E. Robinson was captain (afterward colonel), Stephen Robinson, ensign, — ensign and lieutenant were then one and the same. We were very proud of our captain. He was the most popular man in Bennington. He had a very commanding form and person."

The singing of the Bennington church choir, long noted for its excellence, was perhaps never more flourishing than when Jonathan E. Robinson was its chorister. Then the singers reached round the front seat of the gallery, from the east wall on one side of the pulpit to the same wall on the opposite side of the pulpit ; and it is said there were a score or more of persons, any one of whom was competent to lead. The old style of music was sung with great power and majesty.

MARY, born September 8, 1781 ; united with the church, 1803 ; died February 1, 1831 ; only daughter of Judge Robinson ; married Col. O. C. Merrill, born in Farmington, Conn., June 18, 1775 ; united with the church, 1831 ; died April 12, 1865. A son of theirs, James Seymour Merrill, has been leader of the choir of this church ; also of the Second Congregational Church ; also of the Methodist Episcopal Church.

GEN. HENRY ROBINSON was born August 26, 1778. He was successively paymaster in the army, clerk in the pension office, brigadier-general of the militia, and for ten years clerk of the County and Supreme Court." [1]

He united with this church in 1835. He was next but one to his father, Judge Robinson, as leader of the choir. Returning from Washington to pass the decline of life in

[1] Vermont Hist. Mag.

Bennington, he is remembered by the writer of this notice for his intelligent and genial conversation, his generous nature, and his interest in the public worship of the church of his fathers. He died in 1856.

He married Miss Harriet Haynes, and after her decease her sister, *Miss Martha P. Haynes*. She united with this church January 4, 1835, and deceased December 2, 1857, while residing with her son, the Rev. Charles Seymour Robinson, at that time pastor in Troy, N. Y. Unceasing in her prayers and toils and affection, she had the rare happiness, to a fond Christian mother, of living to see one of her sons an eloquent and successful preacher of the gospel. A younger son, Joseph Haswell Robinson, became, subsequently to his mother's decease, a minister of the gospel. He died March 4, 1868, aged thirty-two ; having commenced a professional career with every promise of a bright and useful future.

Isaac Tichenor Robinson, youngest child of Judge Jonathan Robinson, was born August 17, 1790 ; married Maria, daughter of Deacon Aaron Hubbell, and deceased in 1866. His son, John F., was a deacon of this church until his death.

Deacon John F. Robinson was born in Bennington, May 6, 1812, and deceased January 25, 1862, in the fiftieth year of his age. He was in the discharge of his duty as roadmaster of the Troy and Boston Railroad, and was in the cars passing up a little north of this town, when a gust of wind was encountered, so violent as to throw the cars from the track and down an embankment of some thirty feet elevation. He was mortally injured ; he had strength sufficient to ascend the bank and take his place in another car, and also to walk from the sleigh, in which he was conveyed from the depot, into his house. The accident occurred in the forenoon, and at about five o'clock, p. m., he died. The Rev. H. G. O. Dwight, D.D., missionary at Constantinople, of the American Board of Commissioners for Foreign Missions, was in the same car, sitting near Deacon Robinson, at the time of the overthrow, and was instantly killed.

Deacon Robinson was hopefully converted in the revival in 1831, and united with the church at the same time with Doctor Noadiah Swift. Upon the decease of Deacon Aaron Hubbell, he and Samuel Chandler were elected deacons of the church, September 19, 1845. He had also been treasurer of the society. For several years he was leader of the choir, until a disease of the throat compelled him to resign that office. Up to the time of his decease, and for some years previous, he played the double bass viol, whose mute presence in the gallery for years afterward, lying in its case unused, was a sad reminder that the hands which so carefully guided its tones had become motionless in death.

Deacon Robinson's acceptance of any duty was a guaranty that it would be well and faithfully performed. He was remarkable for a clear mind and a firm will, so that when once settled down upon any principle as true, or any course of action as a duty, it is believed no human power could swerve him. In adhesion to sound Calvinistic doctrine, in reverence for the Sabbath and sanctuary, and in sobriety of demeanor, he might have been regarded as no unapt representative of Puritan times.

When he became road-master on the Troy and Boston road, it was the custom to repair the bridges on the Sabbath, to avoid detention of the cars on week days. He, without any hesitation, determined that the repairs should take place on some other day than the Sabbath, or he would resign his post. Vigorous resistance to his proposed change was made, on the ground of a serious detention of the cars, to the great inconvenience of the travelling public. His unyielding determination, however, carried the point, and the bridges were repaired on week days, and the experiment proved it could be accomplished without a detention of the train, behind its regular time, of more than fifteen minutes.

This occasion furnished an incident illustrative of the moral weight of his words, when he felt called upon to take a decided stand in such a case. Having spoken of the concerns of the soul, involved in that question of taking the Sabbath or the week day to repair the bridges, to the foreman of the working party on the road, who was violently opposed to his view, the foreman replied, " It is no matter to you whether I lose my soul or not." Deacon Robinson rejoined with utmost sincerity and warmth, " *It is matter to me* whether *you* lose your soul or save it." The foreman replied no more, but remembered the words, and deeply felt their force as he afterward honestly stated, and conceived thenceforth a profound reverence for Deacon Robinson.

In the prayer and conference meeting his prayers and remarks were always *short*, and always to the point and impressive.

His natural temperament perhaps, added to much ill-health, made him distrustful as to his evidences, but he found comfort and motive to duty in the doctrine of justification by faith alone in Christ. When in dying, and from internal injuries scarcely able to articulate, he said, " I must trust in Christ and in him alone." From a child he was remarkably conscientious. There was a warmth, tenderness, and sincerity of friendship that attached his friends, and particularly his bosom friends, to him in an extraordinary degree. On his mother's side he was great-great-grand-child to Rev. Mr. Dewey ; on his father's side he was great-great-grandson of Samuel Robinson, Sen. ; and also, by his grandmother Robinson, great-great-grandson of Deacon John Fassett.

CHAPTER XVII

PERSONAL NOTICES.

1762.

STEPHEN FAY. — Next to Robinson, Harwood, and Scott there is the largest number of individuals on the roll of the church of the name of Fay. James, James, Jr., Daniel, and Lydia Fay are on the old covenant. Probably Lydia was the wife of James Fay, and James, Jr., and Daniel their sons. No other mention is made of these individuals afterward in the records of the church, nor do they appear on any of the lists furnished by Gov. Hall in the "Vermont Historical Magazine," nor upon the town records. Mention is made of James and his son Daniel in Mr. Paige's Hardwick Centennial Address, and that he was a deacon in the Separate Church there, and died there of small-pox in 1777, and that Daniel died in 1815, aged eighty-six. It is probable they came at an early day to Bennington, and returned again to Hardwick, and remained there. James was brother of Stephen Fay. Mehitable and Elizabeth Fay are also among the signers to the old covenant. Stephen Fay had a sister Mehitable, and also a sister-in-law Elizabeth (wife of his brother John), who became members of this church.

Among the early settlers, Stephen Fay (son of John Fay and Elizabeth Wilmington), who came to Bennington in 1766, occupied a prominent position as landlord of the Green Mountain House, afterward Catamount Tavern, as

22

father of an influential family; and as exhibiting a spontaneous instance of moral sublimity in connection with the death of his son John in Bennington battle, he has won for his name a bright place in the history of the town. He sent five of his sons [1] to the bloody rescue of his country on that eventful day. One of them was shot through the head, and died instantly. The following is the account in a Connecticut newspaper of Nov., 1777, three months after the battle, by an "*Eye-witness*": — "A good old gentleman who had five sons in the field at the celebrated action of Bennington, August 16, 1777, whose furrowed cheeks and silvered locks added venerableness to his hoary brows, being told that he was unfortunate in one of his sons, replied, ' What, has he misbehaved? did he desert his post? or run from the charge?' ' No, sir,' said the informant; ' worse than that, he is among the slain; he fell contending mightily in the cause.' ' *Then I am satisfied,*' replied the venerable sire; " bring him in and lay him before me, that at leisure I may behold and survey the darling of my soul;' upon which the corpse was brought and laid before him, all besmeared with dirt and gore. He then called for a bowl of water and a napkin, and with his own hands washed the gore from his son's corpse, and wiped his gaping wounds with a complacency, as he himself expressed it, which before he had never felt or experienced." Another account preserved by tradition gives the following additional expression: "I thank God I had a son who was willing to give his life for his country." He had ten children: John, Jonas, Stephen, Mary, Sarah, Elijah, Beulah, Benjamin, Joseph, David.

JOHN FAY was forty-three years of age at the time of his death. He left a widow and children, and many of his descendants are now living in the northern part of this State.

[1] John, Elijah, Benjamin, Joseph, and David.

Of the circumstances of his death the following have been related : [1] —

He was fighting behind a tree. His last words, as he raised his musket to fire once more at the enemy, were, " I feel that I am fighting in a good cause." And as his eye ran along the barrel, taking aim, his head just exposed from behind the tree, a ball struck him in the very centre of his forehead, and he fell with his gun undischarged. Quick as lightning ran the cry over the ranks of his townsmen, " John Fay is shot ! " Maddened to fury they sprang from behind the trees, fired their guns in the very faces of the foe, and, clubbing the breeches, leaped over the breastwork with an impulse of onset nothing mortal could resist.

Nathan, a son of this John Fay, united with this church in the Wood and Burton revival.

Dr. Jonas Fay was the second child of Stephen Fay. He was born at Hardwick, Mass., Jan 13, 1737. He was a man of great versatility, boldness, and determination, and of acknowledged ability and skill as draughtsman and composer of public documents.

His public career commenced at an early age, while the family still resided in Hardwick. In 1756, being then nineteen years of age, he was clerk to the military company of Capt. Samuel Robinson, Sen., in the campaign of the French war at Fort Edward and Lake George.

He was twenty-nine years of age when he came to Bennington, and at once took a prominent position among the leading actors who came upon the stage in that eventful period of the history of the town and State and nation ; and it is difficult to tell in which of these relations, if not in all equally, his services were the most important.

---

[1] The Rev. C. S. Robinson's Address.

" In 1772 when Governor Tryon invited the people of
Bennington to send agents to New York to inform him of
the grounds of their complaint, he, with his father, was
appointed for that purpose. He was clerk to the convention of settlers that met in 1774, and resolved to defend by
force, Allen, Warren, and others, who were threatened with
outlawry and death by the New York Assembly, and as
such clerk certified their proceedings for publication. He
served as surgeon in the expedition under Allen at the capture of Ticonderoga. He was continued in that position by
the Massachusetts committee who were sent to the lake in
July, 1775, and also appointed by them to muster the
troops as they arrived for the defence of that post. He was
also surgeon for a time to Col. Warner's regiment.

In Jan., 1776, he was clerk to the convention at Dorset
that petitioned Congress to be allowed to serve in the common cause of the country as inhabitants of the New Hampshire Grants, and not under New York, and also of that
held at the same place in July following. He was a member of the convention which met at Westminster in Jan.,
1777, and declared Vermont to be an independent State,
and was appointed chairman of a committee to draw up a
declaration and petition announcing the fact and their reasons for it, to Congress, of which declaration and petition
he was the draughtsman and author. He was secretary to
the convention that formed the constitution of the State, in
July, 1777, and was one of the Council of Safety, then appointed to administer the affairs of the State until the
Assembly provided for by the constitution should meet;
was a member of the State Council for seven years from
1778 ; a judge of the Supreme Court in 1782 ; judge of probate from 1782 to 1787 ; and he attended the Continental
Congress at Philadelphia as the agent of the State under
appointments made in Jan., 1777, Oct., 1779, June, 1781,

and Feb., 1782. . . . . In 1780, he, in conjunction with Ethan Allen. prepared and published in their joint names a pamphlet of thirty pages, on the New Hampshire and New York Controversy, which was printed at Hartford. Conn." [1]

His daughter *Lydia* married Uriah Edgerton, Esq. She became hopefully pious after she began to be crippled by rheumatism. She used to say that it was her becoming so great a sufferer that with God's blessing led to her conversion. Before, she was very worldly and ambitious; afterward, the cause and love of Christ was ever the theme upon her lips and warm in her heart. She united with this church during the ministry of the Rev. Mr. Marsh.

FAY EDGERTON, a son of Mr. and Mrs. Uriah Edgerton, was graduated at the Rensselaer Institute, in Troy, N. Y., assisted in the establishment of a scientific school in Utica, N. Y., and while engaged as lecturer on chemistry and botany in the medical school in Woodstock was taken sick and died. He was a bright and devoted Christian. He was born in 1803, and deceased in April, 1838.

Dr. Jonas Fay's daughter, *Sarah*, married Henry Hopkins, only son of Major Wait Hopkins, and grandson of the Rev. Mr. Dewey. These had a son, Deacon Fay Hopkins, of Oberlin, Ohio.

MAJOR HEMAN A. FAY, a twin son of Dr. Jonas Fay, graduated as cadet at West Point in 1808. He was appointed a lieutenant in the army, in which he served through the war in 1812, and soon after became military store-keeper at Albany.[2] He united with a Presbyterian church in Albany, and became one of its elders. He afterward returned to Bennington to pass the remainder of his life, and became a member of this church.

---

[1] See Vermont Hist. Mag., pp. 171, 172, and Early Hist. Vermont, pp. 463, 464, and elsewhere.   [2] Vermont Hist. Mag., p. 172.

22*

Mary, daughter of Stephen Fay, and first wife of Gov. Moses Robinson, and mother of his children, united with this church May 16, 1765. Two of her descendants in this town became ministers of the gospel.

BENJAMIN FAY, son of Stephen Fay, was the first sheriff in the county and State. He was born Nov. 22, 1750. He was sheriff from March 26, 1778, until Oct., 1781, and died in 1786.[1]

He married *Sarah,* daughter of Samuel Robinson, Sen. She united with the church at thirteen and a half years of age. After the death of her first husband she married Gen. Heman Swift, of Cornwall, Conn.

SAMUEL FAY, ESQ., a son of Sheriff Benjamin Fay, lived and died in the family mansion, which was formerly "the Green Mountain House," "the Catamount Tavern" and "Landlord Fay's," — the house in which the Council of Safety met; afterward, altered and added to. An obituary notice from the pen of Gov. Hall appeared in the "Bennington Banner" and was copied into the "Vermont Record," valuable for its historical reminiscences as well as a just tribute to Mr. Fay. Considerable portions of it shall be inserted here.

. . . . "Samuel Fay, Esq., was born in Bennington, Aug. 16, 1772, and died the 25th of Dec. 1863, in the ninety-second year of his age. The day he became five years old, — the 16th of August, 1777, — was fought the battle of Bennington, of which he retained through life a clear recollection, remembering well the noise of the guns, and the extraordinary confusion of the day. The scene at the execution of Redding was also fresh in his mind. He was appointed a deputy-sheriff under Gen. David Robinson. This was in 1793, when Thomas

[1] Vermont Hist Mag., p. 171.

Chittenden was governor, Elijah Paine, Samuel Knight, and Isaac Tichenor, judges of the Supreme Court. He held the office of deputy, with the exception of two years, until 1811, when he was chosen high-sheriff, and was annually re-elected for twelve succeeding years, until the year 1823 ; making twenty-eight years' service in the sheriff department of the county. During this period the position of sheriff was made more important, and its duties greatly more arduous and responsible than at the present day.

"The laws allowing imprisonment for debt were then in full force, and suits were some twenty or thirty times as numerous as they now are. Aside from the hazards that an officer incurred in the service of original writs, which were many, those in the collection of executions were very great. It was not uncommon for an officer to have fifty or more executions in his hands for collection at the same time, ranging in amount from three dollars up to several hundred dollars. If a debtor did not satisfy an execution, within its life of sixty days, it was the duty of the officer 'to commit him to jail, where he must remain until payment was made, unless he took the poor debtor's oath, which could only be done after a probationary imprisonment for twenty days, subsequently reduced to six days. If the officer saw the debtor for a moment and then suffered him to go at large, he became liable for the debt, unless he should afterward, within the life of the execution, arrest and commit him to prison. The performance of the sheriff's duty to the acceptance of both creditor and debtor, without incurring loss to himself, required a talent and skill which few men possessed. Mr. Fay was remarkably successful in the discharge of the varied duties of his position. While many of the sheriffs, in most of the other counties in the State, either became insolvent from the want of proper diligence and care, or rendered themselves unpopular, and even odious, by their extraordinary harshness and severity, Mr. Fay, by his promptness and energy in the right place, and his uniform kindness and care for the interest and convenience of those against whom he held process, was enabled, through the long period of his service, to preserve the confidence and affectionate regard of all parties. Among the many hundreds of debtors whose bare word he took to meet him at an appointed time to relieve him from his official responsibility, such was the good feeling and gratitude which his unvarying civility and kindness inspired, that instances of failure rarely occurred, and never to his services pecuniary loss. Few if any men in the State have ever performed the duties of so difficult and responsible a station, for so long a period of time, with such uniform success, and with such entire approbation of the public.

"His mental faculties seemed to continue to the last, in almost their original brightness. The unpretending dignity and courtesy with which he received the calls of visitors, and the cordial greeting which he gave them, always made a pleasant and agreeable impression, and would mark him, in the estimation of mere casual observers, as a favorable specimen of the old-school gentleman. Those who knew him well were fully assured that these pleasing outward qualities had their foundation and source in the natural goodness of his heart, and his integrity of purpose. Of him it may be truly said, that in all the affairs of life which his duty required him to perform, he acted his part worthily and well, and that his name is now, after the lapse of more than ninety-one years, enrolled upon the list of the dead, undefaced by any blot.

"Mr. Fay, in early life, married Ruth, daughter of Col. Benjamin Fassett. Their children were Samuel R., Benjamin Fassett, and John."

BENJAMIN F. FAY died Feb. 15, 1853, born Oct. 21, 1805. His death was the first in Mr. Fay's family, and gave to Mr. and Mrs. Fay a shock from which they never recovered. He was possessed of much business talent, and had been engaged in wide and extensive business operations.

SAMUEL R. FAY, born Nov. 5, 1802, died Oct. 13, 1860, united with the church March 4, 1827, and was a marked example of purity and conscientiousness of Christian character.

JOHN FAY born Feb. 1, 1815, died Feb. 25, 1866, was, at the time of his death, and had been, for many years, leader of the choir. He possessed a musical ear, so perfect as probably not to be surpassed ; a tenor voice singular for its musical purity and force, and the degree to which he could make it effective at his pleasure ; and superior common sense and leadership as a conductor of church singing. Besides there was peculiar to him unaffected simplicity and strength of social feeling, and a profound all-controlling attachment to the church and parish of his fathers. His warm and genial companionship was not confined to a few. He had a kind word and cordial greeting for all, whether of high or low degree. This was in part the secret of the large congregation — thronging the sanctuary — that gathered at his funeral.

His singing was never better than in the last year of his life ; his voice was never more tender, forceful, or impressive. Not only as leader of the singing, but also by personal efforts socially, he appeared to have received new measure of zeal for the unity and prosperity of the church and congregation.

His beloved choir were with him in his last moments, and received from him an affecting farewell. He united with this church July 4, 1858. He was married on his death-bed to Miss Alice Robinson, daughter of Col. O. C. Merrill.

BENJAMIN FAY, son of Sheriff Benjamin Fay, united with this church in the revival in 1803, and removed to Chicago, where he died in the eighty-ninth year of his age. He married Amelia, daughter of Gen. Safford. The following is part of an obituary notice of him from the "Bennington Banner" : —

"He warmly sympathized with those who are for maintaining and perpetuating the National Union, which his family's blood had been shed to establish.

"On receiving the intelligence of the recent decease of his only brother, — two years his senior, — at Bennington Centre, so great was the shock which he received therefrom that he could not rally under it. He lived an honest, truthful, and Christian life ; and, from the commencement of his last illness, had no desire to live, save to comfort and administer to the wants of his aged companion. His heart, during his sickness, seemed to overflow with gratitude to God for his goodness and mercy for sparing him so many years ; and the last audible expressions which passed his lips were those of prayer and adoration to him."

"COLONEL JOSEPH FAY, son of Stephen Fay, was born at Hardwick, about 1752, and came to Bennington, a member of his father's family, in 1776. He was secretary to the Council of Safety, and of the State Council, from September, 1777, to 1784, and Secretary of State from 1778 to 1781. He was the associate of Ira Allen in conducting the famous negotiation with Gen. Haldimand, by which the operations of the enemy were paralyzed, and the northern frontier protected from invasion during the three last years of the Revolutionary struggle. He was a man of very respectable talents and acquirements, of fine personal appearance and agreeable manners, and well calculated to manage such a diplomatic adventure with adroitness and ability. He built and resided in the house[1] afterward the residence of the late Truman Squier, next north of the court-house, but removed to New York city in 1794, where he died, of the yellow fever, in October, 1803."[2] He married Margaret, daughter of the Rev. Mr. Dewey.

Hon. Theodore S. Fay is their grandson. He was recently minister of the United States to Switzerland, author of one or more religious publications, and a popular writer.

Judge David Fay, youngest son of Stephen Fay, married Mary Stanniford (daughter of John Stanniford, Windham, Conn.), a member of this church. The following characteristic anecdotes are related of ˌJudge Fay : " He used to say to Gov. Moses Robinson, ' Brother Robinson, don't let the church go down ; you take care of the church, and I'll take care of the world.' To William Haswell, addressing him familiarly, ' Let the church be at peace, and there'll be no war with the rest ; the church has a great sway in this world, though there are a good many little men in it.' "

II. Nathan Clark " was a resident of Bennington as early as September, 1762. . . . He was a leading man in the controversy of the settlers with the New York land claimants, and his name appears in nearly all of their public proceedings prior to the Revolution, generally as chairman of their committees and conventions. He is said, by tradition, to have been ˎa pen and ink man,' and to have been the draughtsman of many of the published papers of the early time. He was chairman of the Committee of

---

[1] Since destroyed by fire.   [2] Vermont Hist. Mag., p. 172.

Safety, of Bennington, in 1776, and, as such, held corre-spondence with Gen. Gates, then commander at Ticonderoga, rendering him substantial and efficient aid in collecting and forwarding supplies for the army. He was representa-tive from the town in the first legislature held in the State, which met at Windsor, in March, 1778, and was speaker of the Assembly. He is said to have been of decided en-ergy of character and of very respectable talent. One of his sons, Nathan Clark, Jr., died of a wound received in Bennington battle. He had other sons in the battle, one of whom, Isaac Clark, was afterward known as 'Old Rifle,' and served as colonel in the war of 1812. Nathan Clark died at Bennington April 8, 1792, aged seventy-four, leaving many descendants.[1] Mrs. Salem White is a descend-ant and member of this church."

III. PHINEAS SCOTT first came here, at the age of seven-teen, with his father. They returned to Connecticut, whence they came. The old man died there, and Phineas soon returned. He died here June 6, 1819, aged seventy-four. A name, Phinehas Scott, is upon the roll of Capt. Fassett's military company in 1764. Phineas Scott had five sons, Samuel (married Lucretia Harmon), Henry, Hiram, John, Kinsley, and Martin ; also, daughters, Clara (Mrs. Squiers), Betsey (Mrs. Bingham), Mary (Mrs. Hawks), and Rhoda.

COLONEL MARTIN, son of Phineas, was born in Benning-ton January 18, 1788. He was a noted marksman, and many anecdotes are related of his extraordinary skill. It was not a difficult thing for him to kill one bird with one barrel of his gun, and another with the other, when a flock were on the wing. "He would drive a nail into a board part way with a hammer, and then, taking the farthest distance at which his eye could distinctly see it, drive it home with his unerring bullet." "April, 1814, he was appointed second lieutenant in the army, and rose to the rank of lieutenant-colonel, always sustaining the character of a brave and active officer." "He lost his life in Mexico, at the sanguinary battle of Molino del Rey, and his remains were brought to Bennington and interred in the old Centre burying-ground, beside those of his own family relatives." His death took place September 8, 1847. Of the inscription on the massive monument to his memory, the following is a part: "Brevet Col. Scott, of the 5th regiment of infantry, was thirty-three years in the service of his country on the western frontier; in Florida; in Mexico, at the battles of Palo Alto, Resaca de la Palma, Monterey, Vera Cruz, Cherubusco, and was killed at Molino del Rey. He commanded his regiment in nearly all these engagements, and received two brevets for gallant conduct. No braver or better officer fell in the Mexican war." [1]

[1] See notice of Col. Scott in Vermont Hist. Mag., pp. 177, 178.

23

CHAPTER XVIII

PERSONAL NOTICES.

1763 – 1765.

APT. Elijah Dewey was the son of the Rev. Jedidiah Dewey, and was born in Westfield, Mass., November 28, 1774, and came to Bennington with his father in the fall of 1763.

His name is found among the privates in the first military company formed in town, in October, 1764, he being then under twenty years of age. He was captain of one of the Bennington companies early in the war of the Revolution; was at Ticonderoga with his company in the fall of 1776,[1] and again at the evacuation of that fort by St. Clair in July, 1777. He was at the head of his company in the battle of Bennington, August 16, 1777; also in service at Saratoga on the surrender of Burgoyne in October following."[2]

Captain Dewey also served the public in various stations

---

[1] "Pay roll of Capt. Elijah Dewey's company, in Col. Moses Robinson's regiment of the militia in the service of the United States of America, Mount Independence, 1776: —

"Elijah Dewey, captain; Ebenezer Walbridge, 1st lieut.; Thomas Jewett, 2d lieut.; Nathaniel Fillmore, ensign; Joseph Rudd, Daniel Harmon, John Fay, sergeants; John Smith, Jedidiah Merrill, Thomas Story, corporals. Privates, — Samuel Cutler, Ezekiel Harmon, Joseph Wickwire, Daniel Kinsley, Jonathan Parsons, Andrew Weaver, Abner Marble, Phineas Scott, Aaron Haynes, Silas Harmon, Joseph Robinson, Ezekiel Smith, Seth Porter, David Powers, Hopestill Armstrong, Joseph Willoughby, Samuel Hunt, Joshua Carpenter, Othniel Green, Philip Matteson, Roswel Mosely." — Vermont Hist. Mag., p. 153.

[2] Vermont Hist. Mag., p. 176.

in civil life. At the convention of delegates of the inhabitants of the New Hampshire Grants west of the Green Mountains, at Cephas Kent's, in Dorset, January 16, 1776, it was voted that Simeon Hathaway, Elijah Dewey, and James Breakenridge, be a committee with power " to warn a general meeting of the committees on the Grants, when they shall judge necessary from *southern* intelligence." [1] •

He represented the town in General Assembly, in 1786–87–88, in 1796, and again in 1812–13 ; and was a member of the Council of Censors in 1792.

He was a Federalist in politics, and headed the list of presidential electors of this State in 1797, and also in 1801, voting on the first occasion for Washington, and on the second for John Adams.

Captain Dewey was a man of sound and discriminating judgment, and of undoubted integrity, who did well and faithfully whatever he undertook.[2]

He did not unite with the church until his last sickness. He deceased Oct. 16, 1818. He received the sacrament at his residence, and united with the church May 17, 1818. His active, earnest, and life-long devotion to the external religious prosperity of the community, entitles him to a prominent place among the supporters here of the means of grace. It was a common remark of his that no one lost anything by going to church. He was very wealthy, nearly as much so as Governor Moses Robinson ; and no one in the place, probably, except the last-named gentlemen, contributed more largely to the support of public worship.

There was great wealth in the place. Some one has stated Gov. Robinson's investments were estimated at over $90,000 ; Capt. Elijah Dewey's at $50,000 or $75,000. Capt. Dewey kept a public house during the first session of the Legislature, and as compensation for his services or attentions in

---

[1] Early Hist. Vt., p. 226.   [2] Vermont Hist. Mag., p. 176.

some way, they voted him the "Gore,"—a gore of land, not set off to any towns, in the north part of the State, which ultimately, and before it left his hands, became quite valuable. The ministers and councils used to receive accommodations and large hospitalities at Capt. Dewey's. He liked to see all things going on in good order, and church matters among the rest. The Rev. Mr. Spaulding and his daughter were his guests, while Mr. Spaulding preached here for a year and more.

His first wife was *Eunice Brush*, married March, 1766. She died March 7, 1788. His second wife was *Mrs. Mary McEowen*, and he was her third husband.

Three daughters, *Sarah*, *Ruth*, and *Betty*, married respectively Dea. Aaron Hubbell, Capt. Moses Robinson, Jr., and Col. Benjamin Fassett. As will be seen by reference to the notices of these gentlemen, four or five of Capt. Dewey's descendants became preachers of the gospel,—one a deacon in this church, one the wife of a minister of the gospel, and another the wife of a missionary, and as such is now in India, and many of his descendants members of this church.

An anecdote [1] of the Bennington battle connected with Capt. Dewey, and not known to the writer to be in print, is as follows: Benjamin Fay, afterward first sheriff of the county and State, resided at that time in the house now the residence of Norman Crosier, and had in his possession a punch-bowl, an article of British manufacture, on the bottom of which was the inscription, "SUCCESS TO BRITISH ARMS." Some of the men (who had just been fighting for victory over British arms, and those hired by Great Britain to keep America in subjection), and Capt. Elijah Dewey with them, passed that way, on their return from the battle, and stopped at Mr. Fay's well to drink. This punch-bowl was brought out for them to drink from. As the bowl, in

---

[1] Related by John Fay.

the hands of some one drinking, was turned bottom upward, one of the men espied the inscription, and shouted, " *These are tories; break the bowl; don't let us drink out of it.*" Capt. Dewey interposed and said, " Tut, tut; no, no! They are all friends here." The bowl is now in the possession of John Benjamin Calhoun, the son of Mrs. Sarah Calhoun, who was sister of Benjamin Fay.

ELIJAH DEWEY HUBBELL, a grandson, first son of Deacon Aaron Hubbell, inherited a valuable farm from Captain Dewey. The family also have in their possession a full-length portrait of Captain Dewey, said to be an excellent likeness.

The following Bennington battle anecdote is related of MRS. CAPTAIN ELIJAH DEWEY. They kept the tavern, now the Walloomsac; and she at the time of the battle had large kettles of meat boiling for dinner for the men when they should return from the battle. Captain Isaac Tichenor, then a young man, arrived in town late on that day on his business (commissary of the United States), by the way of Lebanon Springs and Williamstown, and stopped at the tavern. He ordered dinner, and was told by Mrs. Dewey he could not have any. He referred to the contents of the kettles boiling on the fire. The spirited reply of Mrs. Dewey was, " *That is for the men who have gone to fight for their country, where you ought to be.*" He quickly explained his business. He had been busy obtaining supplies for the army, and had rode hard on horseback all that day to get to Bennington, in the discharge of his duty. Upon learning the facts in the case, Mrs. Dewey relented, and gave the tired commissary some dinner.

MRS. CAPTAIN DEWEY was a remarkably good housekeeper; an anecdote illustrative of this, told of her, is as follows : A young gentleman, with white pants, was moving around amongst the utensils of her kitchen very circum-

23*

spectly, for fear of soiling his pants. She spoke up and said, "You need not be afraid of my pots and kettles. They are kept clean *outside* as well as within."

II. Deacon Hezekiah Armstrong and his wife Miriam united with this church in the revival in 1803. He was elected deacon of the church Sept. 6, 1812, and continued in the office until his death, March 4, 1816, aged seventy-one years. He is the first of that name on the roll of the church. He resided in Pleasant Valley, and has numerous descendants. The mother of W. E. Hawks, of North Bennington, was daughter of Deacon Hezekiah.

Zephaniah Armstrong, his son, united with the church in March, 1803. Mrs. Catherine, wife of Zephaniah, united with the church March 7, 1824, died May 12, 1862, at the age of eighty-seven. Of a strong constitution, high forehead, and fair countenance, and possessing great determination; left a widow at an early age, she reared up a large family, conducting her business with singular energy. She became hopefully pious under Mr. Peters' ministry here. The occasion was the sickness, and hopeful conversion in his sickness, of her youngest son, Hiram, and his death. He had great distress of mind until obtaining peace in Christ. He insisted on seeing Mr. Peters.

Mrs. Ruth Dickerson united with the church March 4, 1827, died Jan. 18, 1868, aged eighty-two; faithful in her attachment to the church, and in her consistent testimony for Christ; was daughter of Hopestill Armstrong, and Lydia Haynes, his wife. Their children were Azariah; Sarah, married Elijah Fillmore; David; Oliver; Ruth; Omindia, married Mr. Gerry. *Ethan Armstrong*, son of David, united with this church Sept. 4, 1841.

The names of John and Lebbeus Armstrong are on the

roll of the military company of 1764. The name Hezekiah Armstrong is on the list of persons settled here prior
to June 1, 1765.[1]

John and Hezekiah were brothers, and cousins to Hopestill and Lebbeus, who were also brothers. These four
came, as early as 1764, from Norwich, Conn., and settled in
town, — Hezekiah on the Brimmer place ; Lebbeus on the
Lyman Armstrong place ; John on the Dimmick place.
They were unmarried when they came. The mother of
John and Hezekiah gave them a bed, and directed that
whichever of them should be first married should surrender
his share of the bed to the other. In the time of the Bennington battle Hopestill lived in a log cabin, and was surrounded by a wilderness.

III. THOMAS HENDERSON, whose farm was near Irish
Corners, united with this church in 1765. He married a
daughter of Lieut. James Breakenridge, his next neighbor.
His daughter *Jennet*, a member of this church, married Dr.
Noadiah Swift, son of the Rev. Job Swift, D.D. His
daughter, *Phebe*, married Harry Smith, Esq., and after his
decease the Rev. J. H. Linsley, D.D. Two of her sons by
the first marriage became ministers of the gospel, — the Rev.
Albert Smith, D.D., and the Rev. Henry Smith, D.D., Pro-
fessor in Lane Theological Seminary. A son by Dr. Linsley,
Charles E. Linsley, is a minister of the gospel. Also, the Rev.
Abner Henderson was a grandson of Thomas Henderson.

Mr. Henderson was a man of the old Scotch type, — Calvinistic, strict in his religious notions, but of amiable disposition and incorruptible integrity. He threw away an
old sword, an heirloom in the family, saying that he was a
man of peace.[2]

---

[1] See Vermont Hist. Mag., articles Bennington and Dorset.
[2] Letter of the Rev. C. E. Linsley.

Lucy and *Thena Henderson* united with the church in 1803. Lucy Henderson's name is on the diagram as one of the proprietors of pew No. 2, with the Saffords.

IV. The Harmons were here at an early date in the history of the town. In the printed list of persons settled in Bennington prior to June 1, 1765, prepared from recollection by Samuel Robinson, Esq.,[1] are the names of Barnabas and Simeon Harmon. The latter name is on the old covenant. It is also among the names of those who united with the Bennington church during the ministry of Mr. Dewey, Aug. 28, 1766; together with that of Nathaniel Harmon, united with the church Sept. 6, 1776; Daniel Harmon, united with the church May 30, 1774; and Lucretia Harmon, united with the church May 30, 1774. There are seventeen individuals of this name on the roll of the church for the first century. Silas and Joshua united with the church Jan., 1780. Ezekiel united with the church June 20, 1790. His wife Grace united with the church Sept. 26, 1790. Their daughter Lucretia (wife of Samuel Scott, died 1832) united with the church Jan., 1803, Celinda (wife of James Henry, died Sept. 14, 1865, aged eighty-four) united with the church July, 1803; Elizabeth and Rhoda united with the church March, 1803.

Fisk Harmon is a minister of the gospel. He is the son of Austin Harmon, born Aug. 24, 1779, — a respectable citizen, who deceased a few years since at a great age, — and grandson of Austin Harmon, who settled here at an early day, and owned an extensive farm upon the western border of the town, born April 9, 1757.

Simeon Harmon united with the church Aug. 28, 1766. The following particulars concerning him are stated by a

[1] Vermont Hist. Mag.

grandson: [1] "Friday afternoon was set apart for the prayer-meeting at Grandmother Robinson's. He would not allow anything to interfere — leave plough and team, mount one of his colts and present himself in the midst of his beloved friends, and pray and praise God for one hour, the next hour at home diligently following his plough. . . The last days of his life he travelled from place to place holding religious meetings."

DEA. NATHANIEL HARMON was here at an early day. By the records of the town it appears he purchased a farm here in 1765. An anecdote, illustrative of his promptness and earnestness (related to me by Dewey Hubbell), identifies him personally with the Bennington battle. It was a rude transaction, but the time was urgent. It was better that the dead bodies of the slain foe should be buried in any manner than left to breed pestilence upon the surface of the earth. There were two large excavations for wintering potatoes — left open in the summer time until another harvest — near by; Mr. Harmon took his rope slip-noose halter from his horse's neck, and dragged the dead bodies of the slain enemy therewith into the excavations and covered them with earth. There were some sixty bodies thus buried in each of the two excavations. They were near where the Barnet house now stands; parts of the action of that eventful day were fought there.

Mr. Hubbell related another anecdote. Umbrellas were first brought for sale into the town in his day. Dea. Harmon, being asked to purchase one, declined, saying that a little of the Almighty's rain would not hurt him.

Dr. E. D. Harmon, of Chicago, furnishes the following reminiscence of him: "I recollect his acts of kindness to myself and other children when on our way to the school-

[1] Dr. E. D. Harmon, of Chicago.

house at Irish Corners. If he was present when we passed
by his apple-orchard or fruit-yard we were sure to receive
a bestowal of his bounty in some choice fruit."

He was possessed of ardent and active piety. He devoted
himself for some years to visiting from house to house, as a
modern colporteur, selling and giving away small printed
collections of religious verses and other matter, designed to
promote concern and diligence in religion. A portion of
a collection of verses, of which he himself was the author,
has been preserved. It is 32mo size, and bears the following title : "Poetical Sketches on various Solemn Subjects ;
composed by Dea. Nathaniel Harmon, late of Bennington,
of pious memory ; written a short time before his death.
Bennington : printed by Anthony Haswell, 1796." The first
three stanzas of one of the hymns in this collection is here
subjoined, on the necessity of works being joined to faith :

> " Faith without works is always dead ;
>   It occupies a room alone ;
> Much like the knowledge in the head,
>   Where grace of heart was never sown.
>
> " Works without faith can never save ;
>   But faith and works must strictly join ;
> Though faith be strong and works be brave,
>   Yet faith and works we must combine.
>
> " Faith without works is never true ;
>   Works without faith is poor enough ;
> They part the hoof, but do not chew,
>   Or chew the cud, and part no hoof."

Of the Dr. Harmon, whose letter is quoted from in the
above sketch, the following obituary notice is taken from
the " Bennington Banner," Jan. 13, 1869 : —

" DECEASE OF A NATIVE OF BENNINGTON. — Dr. Elijah D.

Harmon died at Chicago on the 3d inst. He was born in this town on the 20th August, 1782, and was, consequently, in his eighty-seventh year at the time of his demise. At the age of twenty-four, in 1806, he went to Burlington, and engaged in the practice of medicine, and he was an assistant surgeon in McDonough's fleet at the battle of Plattsburg. Dr. Harmon made his first trip from Vermont to Illinois in 1828, but he first went to Chicago to settle, as surgeon to the garrison at Fort Dearborn, in the year 1830, and he was for quite a while the only physician in Chicago. Dr. Harmon was already advanced in years when Chicago began its career of rapid growth, and he has spent his days in the midst of the bustling activity of the young and vigorous city, in comparative retirement, and like one belonging to a by-gone generation."

V. GENERAL EBENEZER WALBRIDGE came to Bennington in 1765. He was an officer in Col. Warner's regiment of Green Mountain Boys in the winter campaign of 1776, in Canada, and on the 3d of March, of that year, he was before Quebec, a lieutenant in Capt. Gideon Brownson's company, and adjutant of the regiment. He also served as adjutant in Bennington battle, where his brother, Henry Walbridge, was killed. In 1778 he was lieutenant-colonel in the militia, and, in 1780, succeeded Col. Herrick in the command of the Bennington regiment, and afterward became brigadier-general. He was in active service on the frontiers at several periods during the war, and in Dec., 1781, when troops were called out, by both New York and Vermont, to sustain their respective claims to jurisdiction over the "Western Union," as it was called, Col. Walbridge commanded those of this State. But for the decided superiority of the Vermont force, and a disposition to forbearance on the part of the Vermont authorities, it seems probable an actual military collision would have occurred. The matter was, however, compromised for the time being, through the mediation of Gen. Stark, who was then in command at Saratoga, and the troops on both sides were withdrawn. The correspondence of Col. Walbridge with the New York authorities, which is creditable to his intelligence and decision of character, as well as forbearance, is preserved among the papers of Gov. Clinton, in the State library, at Albany.

Gen. Walbridge also served the State faithfully and well in civil life. He was a representative of the town in the General Assembly, in 1778 and 1780, and a member of the State Council for eight years, — 1786–1795.[1]

His remains were interred in the old burying-ground, and a memorial slab, at the head of the grave, has upon it this inscription : —

"In memory of Gen. Ebenezer Walbridge, who departed this life Oct. the 3d, 1819, in the eighty-second year of his age.

"He was an affectionate husband, and indulgent father, and a friend to all mankind. He died in the full belief of a glorious resurrection in and through the atonement of Jesus Christ our Lord."

The Walbridge genealogy is traced back to Suffolk county, England. Miss Charlotte Walbridge, of Albany, has a copy of the coat of arms of the Suffolk Walbridges, on which are certain armorial bearings to show that "Sir William de Walbridge accompanied king Richard Cœur de Lion to the holy land, in the 4th crusade, and there greatly distinguished himself." He was "under one of the confederated ducal sovereigns of France."

Gen. Ebenezer Walbridge, born in Norwich, Conn., Dec. 20, 1738; Elizabeth Stebbins, his wife, born in Northfield,

Mass., Oct. 1736. One of his sons, Stebbins, married Betsey Denio, of Bennington. Their children: Sophia, married John L. Winne; Betsey, married Uel Hicks; Stebbins D., married Harriet Hicks (second wife, Eliza Ann Skinner, April 18, 1835); George, married Mary Ann Olin; Charlotte; Fanny, married Joseph N. Hinsdill; Ebenezer; Ebenezer 2d, married Mary Ann Hicks; Betsey W., married Chauncey Hopkins. Henry, the first child of Gen. Ebenezer Walbridge, had, among other children, a son, Henry, whose daughter, Mary, married Washington Hunt, one of the governors of New York. Hiram Walbridge, of New York city, is also his son.

24

CHAPTER XIX.

PERSONAL NOTICES.

1766–1769.

ELNATHAN HUBBELL. — On a petition of the settlers to the king, dated Nov., 1766, among other names is that of Elnathan Hubbell. He was also one of the ten rescuers of Remember Baker, captured, and attempted to be carried of, by Munro and his party in the interest of the New York land claimants.[1]

On his tombstone, in the burying-ground, is the following inscription : —

" The body of Elnathan Hubbell

" Beside this monumental stone
Consigned is, dust to dust.
Reader, perhaps a single hour
Shall make this fate thine own."

" He departed this life July the 21st, A. D. 1788, aged seventy-one years. He was converted in the sixty-ninth year of his age.

" Reader, accept the solemn call,
Instruction from the tomb receive;
Behold the certain fate of all,
And seal your pardon while you live."

1 Hall's Early History Vermont, p. 137.

The record of the date of his uniting with the church has not been preserved; probably it took place in one or two years after the revival under Messrs. Wood and Burton. The names of Aaron, a son, and of Bildad, another son (father of James Hubbell, Esq.), are on the records as uniting with this church about the time of that revival, and two years previous to the father's conversion.

JAMES HUBBELL, ESQ., was born in Bennington, Oct. 17, 1775; was admitted to the bar in Dec., 1806. He resided in New York for a considerable period, and held the office of magistrate under DeWitt Clinton, which gave him active and responsible employment. He afterward returned to Bennington, and died here April 24, 1840.[1] He was the father of Mrs. Henry Kellogg.

AARON HUBBELL, son of Elnathan Hubbell, was born in Old Stratford, Conn., Sept. 14, 1757. He was converted and united with the church as above. His wife, Sarah, united with the church when he did.

He was twenty years of age at the time of the Bennington battle, and a member of Captain Samuel Robinson's company of militia. He afterward became lieutenant of the company. After the first successful engagement of the battle, — that at Baum's redoubt, — he was placed as one of the guards sent over the prisoners captured in that action, as they were marched to the Bennington meeting-house. In a manuscript statement, in possession of Gov. Hall, Mr. Hubbell states that those prisoners numbered over six hundred.

He possessed great unaffectedness and simplicity of character. An incident related of him to this effect may be mentioned. He had a very large woodpile in a place deemed

1 Vermont Hist. Mag., p. 166.

too prominent by some members of the family, and they remonstrated with him, saying, " What will passers-by think of it?" His reply was, " Any man of sense, I am sure, would like to see a large woodpile ; and as for those who haven't sense I care not what they think concerning it."

He was more careful than some others not to speak against his neighbors and fellow-citizens. If aught was said ill of others in his presence, he was accustomed to say, " Well, *we* may be left to do the same or worse." He held for years the office of justice of the peace, which was in those days an honored office, and bore the appellation Esquire Hubbell. He was greatly respected for his integrity and good judgment.

He was seventy-seven years of age when appointed deacon, December 15, 1834. The church was divided upon two candidates, and there was much spirit on both sides, and evil consequences threatened. To avoid the perpetuation of strife in the church, both parties turned to Esquire Hubbell. He was nominated and elected without opposition. He arose and said, " I would not accept this responsible position, but I see in what condition the church is ; there are rival candidates, and there may be difficulty ; to preserve the church from this, I accept the office." There was intense feeling of relief, and many were in tears.

His first wife was *Sarah*, daughter of Captain Elijah Dewey and Eunice Brush, and grand-daughter on her father's side of the Rev. Mr. Dewey. She was married to him at the age of seventeen by the " Rev. David Avery, V. D. M.," June 27, 1782.

Their first child, *Sarah*, born June 20, 1783 ; united with the church, May 4, 1817 ; died August, 1844, was the wife of Hon. Stephen Robinson.

Their second child, *Betsey*, born February 24, 1785 ;

united with the church, September 4, 1831 ; died, September 6, 1845 ; married Daniel McEowen, and, after his decease, —— Harman.

Their third child, *Laura*, born March 18, 1787, married John Vanderspiegel, August 6, 1815 ; united with the church, May 2, 1863 ; died August 15, 1864, aged 77, deeply lamented by children and grandchildren, and much esteemed, by all her acquaintances and many friends, for her amiableness, sprightly conversation, and kindness of heart.

Their first son, and fourth child, was *Elijah Dewey Hubbell;* born May 8, 1790 ; married to Laura, daughter of Hon. Truman Squier ; died February 3, 1864 ; of an amiable and social disposition and of unblemished integrity. He was honored for many years with the office of first selectman in the town, and with other important public trusts.

He possessed a remarkably well-stored memory of dates, as well as facts and particulars of the early history of this town, and has been much consulted in such matters ; he had preserved many papers and documents of interest respecting the early history of this town.

He inherited a valuable farm from his grandfather, Captain Elijah Dewey, for whom he was named, and the family have in their possession a full-length portrait of Captain Dewey, said to be an excellent likeness. His daughter, Georgianna, married the Rev. Martin T. Sumner, a Baptist clergyman.

The fifth child of Deacon Aaron Hubbell, *Maria*, born October 27, 1792 ; married to Isaac T. Robinson ; united with the church, March 4, 1827, — ministry of the Rev. Daniel A. Clark, — died November 19, 1860. Sound in the faith, clear in her understanding of Christian truth, patient, cheerful, forgiving, faithful, she was a model woman in all

24*

the relations of life, and eminently so as a member of the church of God. Of her two children, one became a deacon of this church, and the other, Daniel Robinson, is a member and trustee of the Second Street Presbyterian Church, in Troy, New York.

Deacon Hubbell married for his second wife LUCINDA MOODY. She was born in Woodbury, Conn., Jan. 15, 1770. She came here from Farmington, Conn., in 1797. She retained vivid recollections of seeing Gen. Washington when, as commander-in-chief of the American forces, he, on one occasion, passed through Farmington. She was married March 11, 1798. She was hopefully converted in the revival in 1803, and united with this church at that time.

She deceased in the home of her daughter Catherine, and son-in-law Richard Smith, Esq., in Sharon, Conn., Oct. 3, 1864. She was at the time of her death in the ninety-fifth year of her age. She had bright eyes, a noble physique, and remarkable health and spirits, up to the last plying her knitting-needles, and keeping her information abreast of the times, particularly as to the affairs of the town, and to a great extent of the country at large.

Ever hospitable to all who came under her roof, she kept a bed exclusively for wayfarers who called for a night's lodging, however abject they might be, and personally attended to its being kept in order. She lived to see a large circle of descendants, and many great-grandchildren, all of whom remember with affection and gratitude her efficient care to promote their happiness.

Her first child, *Harriet, Mrs. Daniel Conkling,* perished in the wreck of the " Swallow," on the Hudson River, April 7, 1845. Affectionate and beautiful tributes to her superior worth appeared in the " New York Observer" and " Bennington Banner" of that day. She was, at the time of her decease, a member of the Presbyterian Church in Albany, N. Y.

D. Hubbell Conkling, a son of Mr. and Mrs. Daniel Conkling, died in Paris, Feb. 17, 1868. He possessed a noble and generous nature, and great executive ability. He had amassed wealth as a member of the firm of H. B. Claflin & Co., New York city, and gave with a liberal hand to many a worthy cause. He had returned to Bennington to reside, where, as a public-spirited citizen, he was becoming more and more widely loved and valued.

The intelligence of his death produced a profound sensation of surprise and sorrow. He had united with the First church.

Another daughter of Dea. Hubbell and Lucinda, his wife, *Caroline*, united with this church May 6, 1827, married the Rev. Hollis Read. They went as missionaries to India, and returned after some years to this country on account of her health. A son of theirs, Edward Read, is a minister of the gospel.

The above-named Elijah Dewey expressed in his last years a hope of salvation in Christ alone, but did not connect himself with the church; all the other children of Dea. Hubbell became, or have become, members of some church.

II. Joseph Robinson settled at Irish Corners in 1766. Of eight children, *Dr. Ebenezer Robinson*, born 1783, still living and resident in the same place, is the only survivor.

Peter Robinson, grandfather to the above Joseph Robinson, settled in Martha's Vineyard, Mass.; his son *Joseph* moved thence to Windham, Conn., where Joseph, the early settler in Bennington, was born.

The name Joseph Robinson is on the roll of Capt. Elijah Dewey's company, in Col. Moses Robinson's regiment of militia in the service of the United States, at Mount Independence, in 1776.

The ancestors of Mary Lucas, wife of Joseph Robinson,

were emigrants from Coleraine in Ireland, and were of Scotch descent. They settled in Coleraine, Mass., and saw the troubles of the French war. She when a child lived seven years in a fort.

III. Robert Cochran, Robert, Jr., and Mary Cochran united with this church in 1767. Robert Cochran owned the farm subsequently in possession of P. M. Henry; he sold it and removed westward, soon after the Revolutionary War. He is not the Robert Cochran famous in connection with the New York controversy.

IV. David Haynes settled here at an early day, 1768, on the farm now the residence of Dea. John Vail. He died 1776, and Ruth Paige, his wife, died 1796. Lydia, their daughter, was the wife of Hopestill Armstrong. Miriam, another daughter, married Dea. Hezekiah Armstrong. Abigail, another daughter, married Jonathan Armstrong. (He was one of the two persons who captured the wounded Col. Pfister, — a " volunteer from the vicinity of Bennington, and into whose hands there fell, as the spoils of war, a portion of his baggage, among which was found his commission, on parchment, as ' Lieutenant in His Majesty's sixteenth, or Royal Regiment of Foot,' dated Sept. 18, 1760, and signed by Sir Jeffrey Amherst; a set of draughting instruments, and a map of the route from St. John's, through Lakes Champlain and George, and along the Hudson, to New York. . . . These relics are in the possession of the Hon. L. B. Armstrong, of Dorset, a grandson of the soldier into whose hands they fell on the battle-field.") [1] Aaron, a son of the above David Haynes, was a Baptist preacher, married Molly, sister of Jonathan Armstrong.

David Haynes, Jr., was son of the above. Of his chil-

---

[1] Vermont Hist. Mag.

dren, the only one living and remaining in town is Mrs. Temmy, widow of the late Alvah Rice, and mother of Edward Rice.

V. REUBEN COLVIN was an early settler in Bennington, his name being found on a petition to the Governor of New Hampshire in 1769. He was in Bennington battle, as appears by Capt. Samuel Robinson's roll of those engaged in the action belonging to his company. His residence was near the place of the depot at the north village, where he died July 23, 1813, aged sixty-nine. He had three sons: David, who died Sept. 10, 1852, aged eighty-five; Thomas, who died July 23, 1856, aged eighty-five; and Reuben, Jr. Mrs. Eliza, wife of William E. Hawks, is the only child of Daniel Colvin now remaining in town. Of the children of Thomas; Sidney, John V., and Reuben, all with families, are now residents in North Bennington. Charles S. Colvin, of East Bennington, is the only son of Reuben Colvin, Jr. Dea. John W. Vail is a grandson of Reuben Colvin, Sen., whose daughter, Freelove, was Dea. Vail's mother.

VI. NATHANIEL FILLMORE united with this church in 1773, — ministry of Rev. Mr. Dewey. He was a reputable citizen; an ensign in Capt. Dewey's company in the battle of Bennington. His son Nathaniel, born April 19, 1771, father of President Fillmore, married here, and emigrated to Western New York about the year 1798, residing in Aurora, Erie County. Another son of Nathaniel, Sen., Elijah Fillmore, Esq., was representative of the town in 1839; lived and died, much respected by his neighbors and fellow-citizens, in the west part of the town, in 1853, leaving a numerous family of children.

VII. Simeon Hathaway, Jr., and Anne Hathaway united with this church during the pastorate of Rev. Mr. Dewey, May 3, 1776. The name of Simeon Hathaway, Sen., appears on a petition to the Governor of New Hampshire, dated October, 1769. Simeon Hathaway is also on the roll of Capt. Robinson's company in the Bennington battle as lieutenant. Levi Hathaway, Abram Hathaway, Alpheus Hathaway, are also on the roll. There are nineteen individuals of the name on our church-roll.

VIII. Thomas Jewett's name is on the petition [1] of the Bennington settlers to the Governor of New Hampshire, dated October, 1769. He came here from Norwich, Conn. He was active in the Bennington battle, and took the sword and hat from Col. Baum. He was a lieutenant of Capt. Dewey's company. The sword was afterward purchased by David Robinson, and used by him as a captain of cavalry, and subsequently as a field and general officer of the militia, and is still in the possession of his grandson, G. W. Robinson.[2] Lieut. Jewett tore off the ornaments from the hat and wore it, as he had lost his own. It is now in the possession of descendants in Weybridge. Thomas Jewett first settled in a log house, south of East Bennington. He has numerous descendants.

IX. Charles Cushman united with the church in 1784. A Charles Cushman was inn-keeper at an early day; in 1779, one of a committee, " as listers, to go round the town and take the lists of all who will pay their proportion of the above sum " (voted to supply the pulpit), " and to take the names of all those who refuse to give in the list." [3] John and Mrs. Cushman united with the church 1803. Charles and Anne united with the church 1817.

[1, 2] Vermont Hist. Mag.   [3] Town Records.

X. ELEAZER HAWKS united with this church January 29, 1786. He came here in 1774, from Deerfield, Mass., when a young man, drawn hither by the circumstance that John Kinsley had settled here, between whose daughter Rhoda and himself there was a tender attachment. He settled on land next to the Kinsley farm.

Some particulars of his connection with the Bennington battle assist to more vivid impressions of the event. He felt it his duty to remain near home as long as possible, on account of the illness of his wife ; and was pursuing his work in the field, when the noise of the firing, as the battle commenced, burst upon him over Whip-Stock Hill. He went for his musket, and proceeded with speed to join his neighbors and countrymen in the terrible encounter. He was not a member of either of the companies of militia. He was one of the volunteers, as were many others. One of his duties was to assist in conveying wounded from the battle-field into town, which he did on his father-in-law's ox-cart. Some died of their wounds on the way. The old meeting-house became packed full of prisoners, so full that fears were entertained lest it should break down. Some were let out in consequence, and some escaped.

When Mr. Hawks returned to his home (a log hut without chimneys and with but one room), it was empty. His wife, an invalid, had been conveyed, on a bed upon an ox-sled, by her father, for refuge, in case the result of the battle had been adverse to Pownal, to the town next south, whither many of the feeble and helpless had been conveyed for safety. Mrs. Hawks survived the fatigue and exposure of her flight but a short time.

The second wife of Eleazer Hawks, and mother of Capt. Ira Hawks, was *Anna* (united with the church 1803), daughter of Daniel Clark, of Shaftsbury, who was in the battle and wounded, and who died of his wounds soon after.

William E. Hawks, an officer in the Baptist church of North Bennington, is a grandson of Eleazer Hawks. A granddaughter, daughter of Capt. Ira Hawks, married the Rev. Mr. Palmer, deceased, pastor of the Baptist church at Hoosic Corners.

CHAPTER XX.

PERSONAL NOTICES.

1775 – 1776.

DEACON JOSEPH BINGHAM, with Jeremiah, the elder of his sons, united with this church May 3, 1776. They left Norwich, Conn., about the time of t e first settlement of Bennington, though they did not come here until a short time before the commencement of the American Revolution. On their removal from Norwich, they first settled in Charlemont, Mass., and came to Bennington from that place. Whether this was a family of Separates does not certainly appear. It is, however, quite probable, as they left Norwich, or its vicinity, about the time that a Separate church (that of Newint), or portions of it, left the same vicinity to remove to Bennington. In the records of the Newint Separate church, at the installation of Joseph Safford as deacon there, one Deacon Samuel Bingham was present from another Separate church, as delegate, and took part in the proceedings.

DEACON JOSEPH BINGHAM[1] was a lieutenant in a company of Provincials during the French war. At one time, when stationed with his men near Ticonderoga, his men were ordered to perform some fatigue duty. While engaged in this, one of them was taken sick. Lieut. Bingham

[1] The following notice of the Bingham family is chiefly condensed from an article in the "Bennington Banner" of December 28, 1855.

25

told him to quit work and lie down. Presently an English officer, accustomed to bear himself in a haughty manner toward the Provincials, began to cane the sick man because he was not at work. Lieut. Bingham saw this outrage and dared to interfere. He ordered the haughty English officer to desist, which the said officer thought it best to do, for Lieut. Bingham was a man of courage and of extraordinary muscular power, and he deemed he had the right to the control of his own men in such a case.

At the time of the Bennington battle, Deacon Bingham had been made lame by having one hip broken, but was able to walk with the help of a cane; it was not, therefore, expected that he would go into the battle-field. He went, with many others who were aged and infirm, to the meeting-house, or its vicinity, and while they were collected there, and while the battle was raging, he proposed that they should lift up their voices and their hearts in fervent prayer to the God of battles, that he would bless their sons, brothers, and friends who were in the battle fighting for their homes and for liberty; and that he would permit them to return again and peacefully enjoy their homes. The prayer was heard; at least, the blessings it supplicated were granted. The old man was allowed to return to his home and find it undisturbed.

Epitaph of Deacon Joseph Bingham :—

"'Tempus verax mortalium.'

" Sacred to the memory of Deac. Joseph Bingham, who departed this life Nov. 4, 1787, in the 79th year of his age. He left the church militant to join the church triumphant above.

"'Why do we mourn departed friends?'"

At the close of the war *Jeremiah* removed to Cornwall, in this State, where he trained a family of sons and daugh-

ters, and was loved and honored by his fellow-citizens to
the end of his days for his piety and manly virtues. He
lived to be almost a hundred years old.

DEACON CALVIN BINGHAM, the younger son, remained on
the farm with his father and mother while they lived, and,
after their decease, lived and died there. He united with
this church, and also brought forward his six children for
baptism April 19, 1789, during the ministry of Mr. Swift.
He was elected deacon in this church July 16, 1813, and
continued in the office until he died, February 23, 1831, aged
eighty. His regularity and punctuality in attending public
worship were proverbial. He was highly honored for his
fidelity as a Christian and an officer in the church, and in
all the duties of life.

He had seven sons and five daughters, who lived to the
age of maturity, and all became members of the church of
Christ. On Thanksgiving day, Dec. 6, 1855, the seven
sons and three of the daughters were still living, and
all met together in their native town ; the united ages of the
brothers amounted to four hundred and eighty-four years ;
average age sixty-nine years.

Asa, the first born, has been many years an officer in the
church where he resides ; *Stephen,* the sixth, a deacon
in the Second Congregational Church in this town. Two
became ministers of the gospel, — *Amos,* the second son (for
many years city missionary in Philadelphia), and *Hiram*
the fifth ; he was with his associate honored as a pioneer
missionary to the Sandwich Islands, 1819, where he labored
for about twenty years, and saw the wonderful Christian
transformations among that people. He is the author of a
history of the Islands. He found it necessary to return to
his native land on account of the illness of his wife. A son
of his, *Hiram Bingham, Jr.,* is now a missionary among

the Micronesian Islands; also two daughters have gone to teach native girls at Honolulu.

A son of Calvin, the third of the brothers, has been Governor of Michigan, and senator in Congress.

Rev. Amos Bingham was graduated at Middlebury College. He studied theology with the Rev. Dr. Burton, of Thetford. He soon became a domestic missionary, sometimes in the employment of some ecclesiastical body, and sometimes not. He was instrumental in the hopeful conversion of many souls. He preached in Peru, Winhall, and other places. He was so zealous as to be sometimes persecuted by those whom he had offended in his faithfulness. One who was converted under his ministry in Winhall removed to Virginia and married, and came into the possession of slaves. This man invited Mr. Bingham to enjoy his hospitality. Mr. Bingham was so much the lover of liberty, and spoke out so freely, that he was admonished to leave for his own safety. He went thence to Philadelphia, and remained and died there. He was employed by the city authorities to preach to the prisoners in the penitentiary. The prison is made into cells, arranged like the spokes of a wheel. The preacher stands, as it were, in the hub of the wheel, and preaches, not seeing into the cells. Mr. Bingham was very much engaged also in labors to promote the better observance of the Sabbath in Philadelphia.

II. Nathaniel Brush was here as early as 1775. He lived in the Judge Isham House. His sister was the first Mrs. Capt. Isaac Dewey. He was colonel of militia in the town, and in this capacity served in the Bennington battle. He was elected town clerk in 1782, in which office he continued for several years.

III. Samuel Blackmer moved here at an early day from Taunton, Mass. His name appears upon the town records as sealer of weights and measures, appointed March, 1776. He died in 1812, aged about sixty-four. His widow lived to be ninety-three. Their children were Samuel, Jason, Jesse, Ruby, — Mrs. Oliver Harwood, of Rupert, — Wilbur, Green, and Vesta, — Mrs. Joseph Harwood, of Rupert.

Hon. S. H. Blackmer, was son of Samuel, Jr. He deceased in Feb., 1861. He was for many years clerk of the court and judge of probate, and was highly respected. He gathered with much pains a rare collection of old volumes, now in the possession of his son, Frank Blackmer. One book contains a printed copy of the first sermon ever preached in New England, which was at Plymouth in 1621.

Hiram Blackmer was a son of Samuel, Jr. He was in mercantile business in Boston, Mass., and deceased there Aug. 2, 1860. He united with this church Sept. 4, 1831, and adorned his Christian profession by a consistent walk and conversation.

Jason, son of Samuel, Sen., was the father of Warren Blackmer.

IV. Mrs. Isabella Henry united with this church May 5, 1811 ; was the first of the Henrys, by the records. She was daughter of Mrs. Susannah Howe, afterward second wife of Governor Moses Robinson. She deceased Dec. 28, 1857. The writer of this notice had the pleasure of knowing her, and enjoying frequently her kind and graceful hospitality during the last few years of her life. She was a lady of superior personal presence, and of marked politeness, as well as of excellent Christian spirit.

David Henry, husband of the above, united with this church Sept. 4, 1831, and deceased Jan. 26, 1856 ; of few words, but of sound judgment, and great kindness.

25*

Their only daughter, *Mary Ann*, united with this church March 4, 1827; their only son, *P. M. Henry*, united with this church Sept. 4, 1831.

JAMES HENRY united with this church Nov. 6, 1831; his wife, CELINDA HARMON, in 1803. She was eminent for the purity of her Christian character, for her liberal support of the church, of which she was a member, and for large bene-factions to charitable and missionary institutions. Her daughter, *Persis F.*, Mrs. Alonzo Hinsdill, united with this church Sept. 4, 1331; *Celinda*, Mrs. Caleb Austin, died Sept., 1844; united with this church Jan. 5, 1834.

JOHN, son of John Henry, united with this church Sept. 4, 1831; at the same time WILLIAM G., son of Hon. William Henry.

The second among the Henrys to unite with this church was *Alice*, daughter of Hon. William Henry; united with the church Nov. 5, 1820. Her mother, *Anna Henry*, united with the church Sept. 4, 1831. Eight of the name of Henry, and one besides of the family, *Maria*, wife of James Hicks, united with the church at this date. Of the chil-dren of Hon. William Henry, four became members of this church; among them also *Lemira*, wife of Hon. Charles Hicks. She was one of those in whose blameless life and beautiful spirit the Christian virtues shine without alloy. A son, *Eli B.*, is deacon in the North Bennington Congre-gational Church. *Alida*, a daughter-in-law of John Henry, now Mrs. David Cross, united with this church Sept. 4, 1831.

HON. WILLIAM HENRY (born Oct. 5, 1760, died May 11, 1845) represented the town in the General Assembly for seven successive years from 1805, and was a justice of the peace for thirty-nine years in succession, ending with the year 1840, being a longer period than the office has ever been held by any other person in town. He was also judge of probate for two years, and, being familiar with legal forms of business, was the draughtsman of most of the deeds, contracts, and wills of persons in his quarter of the town for many years. He was a man of sound judgment and of undoubted integrity, and was universally respected. Hon. William, James, John, and David Henry were sons of William, one of several families of Scotch-Irish descent who came from Massachusetts and settled at an early day in the north-west part of the town ; from whom the neighborhood took the name of Irish Corners, which it still retains.[1] There are twenty individuals of the name on the church-roll.

V. JOSEPH HINSDILL was the first of the family to settle in Bennington, and came, it is believed, from Hardwick, Mass. He married Hannah Bingham. Their children were Norman, married Rhoda Harmon, sister of Mrs. Samuel Scott, and for his second wife a daughter of Gov. Galusha ; Daniel, father of Milo and Alonzo Hinsdill ; Joseph, father of Joseph, married Fanny Walbridge ; Eliza married Elijah Waters ; Amanda married R. N. Severance ; Caroline, Mrs. Samuel Weeks ;. Joanna, Mrs. Stephen Robinson ; Jane, Mrs. G. W. Robinson ; Chester ; Hannah married Mr. Tracy ; Stephen, Deacon Hinsdill, father of Mrs. Ballard, Lucretia, Mrs. Aaron Hubbell, Jennett, Mrs. Seymour ; Electa married Jonas Galusha ; Hiram married Roxanna Walbridge.

DEACON STEPHEN HINSDILL, with his wife Hannah, a sister of Uriah Edgerton, Esq., united with the church during the ministry of Mr. Marsh, May, 1816. He was elected deacon May 10, 1822, and removed his connection, with others, Nov. 9, 1834, to organize the Hinsdillville Presbyterian Church. He was the head of a manufacturing company in that place, and really almost the company itself,

[1] Vermont Hist. Mag.

which for a time was very flourishing, employing many operatives and sustaining numerous families. He possessed extraordinary enterprise and zeal in whatever he undertook. He was much gifted in prayer and exhortation, and much devoted to the cause of Christ. He was very strict in his observance of the Sabbath, and unbounded in his hospitality. Before the establishment of public worship in Hinsdillville, he chartered a four-horse team to bring up his neighbors and others to worship here. He prepared a room and seated it, in one of his buildings, for religious meetings, and was chiefly instrumental in the erection of the Hinsdillville church, — a very commodious stone edifice. The Rev. Daniel A. Clark was his warm friend, and he was a warm friend of Mr. Clark, who, during his ministry in Bennington, was frequently an inmate of his house. He gave his energies with great ardor to the prosecution of the revival which took place in that part of the town in connection with Mr. Clark's labors.

An extended notice of him would properly find a place in a more particular history of the church for the period during Mr. Clark's ministry here, and down to 1834, when the Hinsdillville Presbyterian Church was organized.

He eventually removed to Michigan and died there. He was one of the committee upon the last revision of the articles of faith and covenant of this church. One of his daughters married James Ballard, minister of the gospel. There are sixteen of the name of Hinsdill on the roll of the church.

VI. ELEAZER EDGERTON was here prior to 1775. As before mentioned, he was one of the scouts in the employment of the Council of Safety, who brought intelligence to Gen. Stark of the presence of a hostile party at Cambridge, on the 13th of August, three days before the battle; and an ·

an anecdote is related illustrative of his prowess in the battle.

He was the father of Uriah Edgerton, Esq., and resided a half a mile or so to the north of the late residence of the latter. His wife was a daughter of the Mr. Hyde whose family resided upon the place now owned and occupied by Giles Jewett. She was a relation of Chancellor Walworth. Mrs. Stephen Hinsdill was his daughter.

URIAH EDGERTON, ESQ., son of the above, deceased April 28, 1868, aged eighty-seven, having adorned old age, and made it attractive by his Christian conversation and his genial spirit, and having enjoyed the affectionate esteem of his numerous acquaintances and friends. He also united with the Bennington First Church, Sept. 4, 1831. He married a daughter of Dr. Jonas Fay.

VII. JOHN KINSLEY united with this church in 1773. There are seven individuals of the name of Kinsley, or Kingsley, on the church-roll. Nathaniel Kingsley united with the church 1784. There is a Nathaniel Kingsley on the Newint church records. Daniel Kingsley united with the church 1775. Eunice Kingsley united with the church 1780. Mrs. Nathaniel Kingsley united with the church 1784.

ABISHA KINSLEY, son of John Kinsley, a highly respected and worthy citizen of the west part of the town, deceased Aug. 9, 1859, born in Charlemont, Mass., March 18, 1766; removed to Bennington when four years of age.

VIII. CAPT. MOSES SAGE settled in Bennington as early as 1776; and, until 1805, was the most prominent business man at the north village, which bore the name of Sage's City, until the establishment of a post-office there, in 1828, when it was called North Bennington. "To his enterprise and energy of character it owes not only its first distinctive name, but its early growth and business.

"His business operations were not, however, confined to that village. For several years he had been either the sole or part owner of the blast furnace situated on what is still called Furnace Brook, two miles north of Bennington village, and. in 1804 he erected what was then called the new furnace east of that village. This, in 1811, was sold to Thomas Trenor, and in 1814 Mr. Sage removed to Chatauque Co., N. Y., and died in 1817."

Capt. Sage had a number of children, several of whom removed from town in early life. Mrs. Fanny Coney, his youngest daughter, is still living in Bennington village with her son-in-law, Charles S. Colvin. Mrs. Mary Anne, wife of Martin B. Scott, of North Bennington, is a granddaughter of Capt. Sage. Olin and Henry M. Scott, of Bennington village, are children of Mr. and Mrs. M. B. Scott.

IX. Simeon Sears appears on the tables prepared by Mrs. Haswell as having united with the church in the ministry of Rev. Mr. Dewey. His name is on the roll of Capt. Robinson's company in the Bennington battle. The name of Sears appears in the tables of Mr. Paige's Hardwick Centennial Address. He was one of the active opponents of the Rev. Mr. Avery. There are eleven individuals of the name on the roll of the church.

CHAPTER XXI

OVERNOR Isaac Tichenor was born at Newark, N. J., Feb. 8, 1754, and educated at Princeton College, then under the presidency of the cele-brated Rev. Dr. Witherspoon, for whom and whose memory he always had the highest veneration.

He first came to Bennington June 14, 1777. During the war of the Revolution he was deputy commissary-general of purchases for the Northern Department, having for his field of service an extensive portion of the New England States. After the war he was representative in the General Assembly; speaker of the House; agent of the State at Congress; member of the State Council; a judge, and then chief justice of the Supreme Court; member of the Council of Censors; thrice elected senator in Congress; governor of the State for eleven years in all; and called also to fill other offices of high distinction and responsibility.[1]

He gave his influence with great cheerfulness and liberality to the interests of public religion in this town. He bore a prominent part in the controversy about the Rev. Mr. Avery, and was his fast friend. His signature appears alone, on behalf of the congregation, to the address of that body, expressive of their regrets upon Mr. Avery's

[1] Vermont Hist. Mag.

dismissal. He took a warm interest in the settlement of the Rev. Absalom Peters. He had promised the parish, if they would get a minister who should fill the meeting-house, he would give them a bell. Mr. Peters was very popular and attractive, and Gov. Tichenor was as good as his word. The bell, which has been in the belfry ever since, has his name inscribed on it as its donor.

He used to marry people, but, not being a professor of religion, and never having assumed the Christian duty of personally leading others in devotions, he performed his marriage ceremony, likewise, without making any prayer. Deacon Bingham, on one occasion, remonstrated with him against his practice of solemnizing marriage without prayer; the governor replied, "Well, you come and make the prayer, and I will give you half of the fee."

Many anecdotes are related of him, illustrative of a certain painstaking on his part to kindly and cordially notice all. His manners and address were both impressive and very pleasing. William E. Hawks, whose home was on the second farm west of Aaron Hubbell's, relates that, when a boy, Gov. Tichenor used frequently to come that way hunting; he was accustomed to shoot game from his horse's back, and would ask William to go with him and pick up the game. A quarter of a dollar placed in his hand seemed to him, in those childhood days, a munificent compensation,—and very liberal it was. He thought, as did many other boys in the town and in the State, that he was a special favorite of Gov. Tichenor, and was ever de-lighted to see him come that way with his gun and his horse.

Gov. Tichenor was once sitting at his table, in the din-ing-room, which opened out into the yard in the rear of the house, and his attention was called to a bird, on one of the trees in sight. A friend was at table with him; and he

said, "I can shoot that bird without leaving my seat."
The friend doubted whether the thing could be done; the
governor sent for his gun, which was levelled and fired, and
the bird fell dead. He had tried hard, one day, to catch a
large trout in the Meach hole, and was obliged to come
away unsuccessful; a lad he employed to do chores, etc.,
was with him, and slyly went down the next morning to
try his luck, and was successful. As he came up toward
the governor's with the fish, Gov. Tichenor, quite excited,
said, "It is too bad to raise up eagles to pick our eyes
out."

When at Washington, at the presidential dinners, Mrs.
Madison had been led out to dinner repeatedly and rather
ostentatiously by a not very popular senator; and certain
of the others, who were piqued at that gentleman's pre-
cedence, agreed together to supersede him, and committed
the execution of the task to Gov. Tichenor. The obnoxious gentleman, on the next dinner occasion, engaged Mrs.
Madison, as before, in conversation, about the time of dinner; and those who were in the secret were quite impa-
tient at the unpromising aspect of affairs. But a moment
only before the announcement of dinner Gov. Tichenor
directly accosted Mrs. Madison; she arose to reply, he
added a word or two, and she politely listened; when the
call to dinner came, he immediately offered her his arm,
and the obnoxious Congressman was outwitted.

Governor Tichenor possessed a commanding form, a remarkably fine personal appearance, and accomplished manners. He was regular in his attendance at church; occupied
a seat in the large corner pew, which took up the space on
the south side of the pulpit; arose and stood reverently,
and yet with peculiar dignity, in prayers; gracefully recognized such persons as he met going and returning, — was,
indeed, quite a feature of the occasion.

26

He left no children. The present residence of Deacon George Lyman was his, and bears the name of Tichenor place. He died Dec. 11, 1838, aged eighty-four. At the time of his decease the Rev. Dr. Hooker was his pastor, and preached his funeral sermon.

The second Mrs. George Lyman was his adopted daughter. She united with this church May 7, 1843, and deceased Jan. 4, 1856 ; a lady of superior excellence, thoughtful, earnest, and conscientious, dignifying the social circle. Her sudden death was felt to be a severe bereavement in the household, the church, and the community. Her four children are members, and her three sons-in-law officers of churches.

II.   THOMAS HALL came to Bennington in the spring of 1779, and settled on the farm which has remained in the family, now the residence of the son-in-law of Governor Hall, Hon. T. W. Park. Mr. Hall was born at Guilford, Conn., Feb. 11, 1726, married Phebe Blachly, removed to Woodbury, Roxbury Parish, Conn., 1759, and thence to Bennington. He united with the Bennington First Church in 1785. He died Dec. 23, 1802.

NATHANIEL HALL, his son, was deacon of the old Baptist church in Shaftsbury, born March 4, 1763, died March 4, 1849, spoken of to the writer as " an Israelite indeed, in whom was no guile." His children were Hiland (Governor Hall), born July 20, 1795 ; Phebe, born March 24, 1797, married James Lazell, died May 27, 1860 ; Abigail, born March 13, 1799, married Nathan Bowen ; Nathaniel, born March 11, 1801, died Aug. 19, 1846 ; Anna, born Jan. 31, 1804, married Daniel C. Dyer ; Laura, born April 5, 1806, married Timothy Darling, died Nov. 25, 1854 ; Polly, born Sept. 22, 1808, married Sidney Colvin. The father of Mrs. Governor Hall, Henry Davis, was in the battle of

Bunker Hill, and served at West Point and other places during the Revolutionary War.

The ancestors of Thomas Hall were his father, Hiland Hall, born in Guilford, Conn., Sept. 20, 1703 ; his grand-father, Deacon Thomas Hall, born in Middletown, Conn., Aug. 29, 1671 ; his great-grandfather, Samuel Hall, born in England, 1626 ; and his great-great-grandfather, John Hall, born in Kent County, England, in 1584.

III. ANTHONY HASWELL was born at Portsmouth, Eng-land, April 6, 1756. He came to Boston when about thirteen years of age, and served his apprenticeship as a printer. He established the " Vermont Gazette " in Ben-nington. The first number was published June 5, 1783, and was continued, — not always, however, under the same name, — most of the time by himself or members of his family, until October, 1850, a period of over sixty-seven years. It had a much longer life than any other paper printed in the State. His enterprise led him to originate several periodicals, — among them, a paper in Rutland, also two monthlies, at different times, in Bennington. Numer-ous books and pamphlets were published by him on various subjects, some of which were reprints of valuable works, and others original matter. In the course of his life he furnished many articles for the newspaper press on moral, religious, and political subjects. For the most part he set up his original matter into type, when he composed it, with-out the intervention of the pen. He had for many years a share of the public printing of the State. Among his pub-lications may be mentioned an interesting memoir of Capt. Matthew Phelps, of three hundred pages, of which Mr. Has-well was the author. When the Legislature passed the act establishing post-offices at Bennington and other places, 1784, he was appointed postmaster-general, with extensive powers. He early imbibed the principles of the old Republican party, and was active and zealous in their defence and propagation.

Mr. Haswell was a kind and obliging neighbor, and a warm, ardent, and faithful friend.[1] He became possessed of the old meeting-house, after it ceased to be used for public religious worship, and had it removed and re-erected for his own residence, where now stands the residence of Hon. Benjamin R. Sears. His wife and others wished him to divide the frame, but he preferred to have it all. He desired a large house and a large table, and desired it full. He did not enrich himself, but he did much good. He was a man of extraordinary industry, and his labors for the public, through a whole life, were devoted with singular unselfishness.

In the revival in 1803 his zeal in politics abated, being overborne by a new consecration — to Christ. At that time he united with this church by a public profession of faith.

An anecdote will illustrate the high estimation of him, in connection with his zeal as a Christian convert, entertained by one of his neighbors, and an unconverted man. Mr. Nairne, a profane man, a Scotchman, but characterized by a certain heartiness and naïveté which is always attractive, resided then in the house now the residence of Henry Patchin. Mr. Nairne had the Rev. Mr. Spaulding and others at his house during the three-days' meeting, and with them, also, Mr. Haswell. Mr. Nairne whispered to his wife, " Let us have a prayer ; I'll call on Anthony Haswell." Mrs. Nairne, an excellent and lady-like woman (who united with the church in that revival), said to her husband, " Had you not better call on one of the ministers?" Mr. Nairne, with his Scotch bluntness, spoke out

---

[1] For these particulars, and others of his professional and public career, see Vermont Hist. Mag., p. 176.

so all could hear, using a profane expression which need not be repeated, " *I would as soon have Mr. Hóswell.*"

He not only required the Bible to be read at family prayers, but also had Watts' psalms and hymns read through at that exercise. He gave to his two daughters, Susannah and Eliza, each a copy of " Watts' Divine and Moral Songs for Children," as a reward for committing the songs to memory. He published many religious works, sermons, and collections of religious verses. A great variety of these publications are still extant, bearing his imprint.

Before any missionaries had been sent from this country into heathen lands he conceived a strong desire, and often expressed it, to have a son who should be qualified and willing to go and preach Christ to heathen nations. This desire was fulfilled in the person of his son James M., born subsequently to the time of Mr. Haswell's oft repeating this desire. His two sons, Thomas and James, the one born Sept. 26, 1807, the other Feb. 4, 1810, were clerks in the store of Messrs. Fassett & Selden, in Troy, N. Y., about the year 1830; and, during a revival in that city, were hopefully converted, and both resolved to fit themselves for the ministry. They alternately attended the Presbyterian and Baptist meetings for some months; both invariably attending the same meeting, until one Sabbath James said to Thomas, " Brother, I must be a Baptist and go to the heathen." Thomas replied, " Well, I will be a Presbyterian; we will both go into the field and see which can do the most good in the cause of our Lord and Master." Thomas became a minister of the gospel and home missionary, in which service he died. James went to Burmah as foreign missionary, translated the New Testament into a Burmese dialect, and, after some thirty-three years' labor in that country, has been compelled to retire by the failure

26*

of his health. James, a son, was sent to this country and graduated at college, and returned a preacher of the gospel to labor in Burmah, but was overtaken by failure of his health. Julia Ann Eliza became the wife of a missionary, and is still in Burmah. Another daughter, not married, is also doing efficient missionary service there.

Eliza, daughter of Anthony Haswell, married Hiram Harwood. James H. Harwood, minister of the gospel, is their son.

Susannah, another daughter, married Darius Clark. Their daughter Lydia drew the old meeting-house in the frontispiece in this volume — said to be a truthful representation of that sanctuary — from dimensions, shape, and position preserved in the recollection of old inhabitants.

WILLIAM HASWELL, seventh child of Anthony Haswell, was elected clerk of this church September 28, 1849, and remained so until his decease, December 16, 1864. He was much assisted in his labors as town clerk, and in other offices requiring a large amount of writing, by his wife, Sarah, daughter of Col. Samuel Robinson, born October 8, 1791; united with this church January 6, 1833; died December 14, 1850.

The following obituary notice of him is from the " Bennington Banner : " —

" William Haswell was appointed postmaster of this town June 6, 1813, and held the office until November, A. D. 1833, twenty years and over. He was also town clerk of Bennington from March, A. D. 1821, to March, 1849.

" He was register of the probate court under judges Artemas Mattison, Aaron Robinson, Jesse Blackmer, Jonathan Draper, Sylvanus Danforth, Orsamus C. Merrill, John M. Olin, — in all twenty-one years, commencing in 1826.

" For several years after 1820 the list of Revolutionary and invalid pensioners in Bennington county was very large, — the aggregate sums paid to them each year amounting to many thousands of dollars. These pensions were nearly all drawn and distributed by William Haswell, and he continued a pension agent until the time of his death. He was proverbially rapid and accurate in adjusting accounts and transacting public business.

" He was a kind-hearted neighbor ; a public-spirited, upright citizen ; a friend and benefactor to the poor, and an honest man. Thus he lived to exemplify the doctrines of the gospel, which, for many years, he professed to love.

" In his death one of the old landmarks of Bennington has passed away. He died December 16, 1864, in the seventy-fifth year of his age."

A large number of the descendants of Anthony Haswell have become members of this or of some other church.

His son, Anthony Haswell, born November, 1780, died December 10, 1856 ; an intelligent man and exemplary Christian, genial and social ; united with this church March 1803, and afterward removed his connection to the Baptist church.

Anthony Haswell, Sen., composed many hymns. Some stanzas from one, sung at the funeral of Mrs. Samuel Robinson, Sen., have been inserted in the notice of that lady. He also, it is said, composed one or two of the hymns sung at the dedication of the new meeting-house. One of the hymns sung on that occasion was, it is said, composed by Andrew Selden, Esq., and one by a gentleman from abroad. Four hymns are printed with the dedication sermon, but there appears to be no means of certainly identifying the authors severally.

He died May 26, 1816.

IV. THOMAS WEEKS and Catharine, his wife, removed to Bennington, from Hardwick, Mass., in 1783, and settled on the farm which has ever since borne the name of the Weeks farm. He died August, 1804, aged eighty-four; and Mrs. Weeks, October 14, 1819, aged ninety-seven.

The names David, Holland, and Thomas Weeks are on the list in Paige's Centennial Address of the Hardwick inhabitants who served in the French war.

DAVID WEEKS, son of the above, came with his father. He died October 4, 1836, aged eighty-three. *Elizabeth*, his wife, died April 2, 1822, aged fifty-six. Beside two that died in infancy, their children were Abigail, Betsey, Susan, David, Isaac, Samuel, Semantha, Willard, Maria. All have deceased except the eldest, Abigail. Willard died August 17, 1860; Betsey, Susan, and David in 1861, — the four within eight months of each other.

SAMUEL WEEKS died January 1, 1867, aged sixty-six; united with the church July 4, 1858; father of Mrs. Rev. Henry M. Swift. Called in the latter days of life to meet severe trials of bodily sickness and unexpected reverses of worldly fortune, these he bore with exemplary Christian meekness and fortitude.

ISAAC WEEKS united with the church January 5, 1862; died January 24, 1868, in the seventy-second year of his age. He was representative in the General Assembly in 1860; at different times and for several years first selectman and town treasurer, and held other important offices in the town. He was also, for many years, president of the Stark Bank. He possessed great kindness of heart, soundness of judgment, and fidelity to every trust, and was one of our most valuable citizens, and died enjoying, in an eminent degree, the respect and confidence of his acquaintances and friends and of the community.

V. ICHABOD PADDOCK came from Rhode Island, and settled, soon after the Revolutionary War, on the farm since the residence of Alonzo Potter. He had three sons, Daniel, Zechariah, and Thomas. Daniel was the father of Capt. Paddock, now residing in Pleasant Valley. Zechariah was the father of Daniel H. Paddock.

VI. WILLIAM POTTER came, about the time of the close of the Revolutionary War, from Rhode Island, and settled on Mount Anthony, on the farm east of the present residence of his grandson, Loan Potter. Three brothers came together, or nearly so. The two others were John and Amos; these settled a little over the New York State line.

VII. COL. MARTIN NORTON and his wife, Betsey, united with the church in November, 1784. They resided where S. H. Brown, Jr., now resides. Mrs. Col. Norton was a devoted Christian. Their son, Hon. Jesse O. Norton, late member of Congress and judge of the Supreme Court in Illinois, united with this church at thirteen years of age. Their grand-daughter, Sophia Love, became the wife of the Rev. S. H. Hurlbut, late pastor of the Congregational Church in New Haven. He died December 2, 1856, having been much prospered in his ministry, warmly beloved by his people, and giving bright promise of continued usefulness and success.

There are eleven of the name of Norton on the roll of the church.

CHAPTER XXII.

1785 – 1800.

R. NOADIAH SWIFT was the second son and fourth child of Rev. Job Swift, D.D., and Mary Ann Sedgwick. He was born in Dutchess County, N. Y., at a place then called Nine Partners, now known as Amenia, Feb. 24, 1776. He, with his father and the family, removed to Manchester, and thence to Bennington, when he was nine years of age. Here he received his academical education under his father's instruction, and pursued the study of medicine with Dr. Medad Parsons, at that time a practising physician. He continued in the practice of his profession here until prevented by the infirmities of age. He was possessed of a large and powerful frame, an iron constitution, and an iron will. Sound in intellect, and with a highly intuitive judgment, he was at once a master of books and of common sense. Plain-spoken and outspoken, of great frankness and simplicity of character, far-reaching in his perceptions of the public principles and measures which the progress of the future was to sustain, severe to his enemies in controversy, relentless to opposition, but confessing his faults and forgiving the faults of others in the subsequent reaction of tenderness and good-will, — he was a tower of strength to the church, the community, and the reforms of the day. No biography could do justice to him, unless it were a history of the times in which he lived. The revivals, the anti-slavery principles and measures, the temperance reformation, public secular struggles and enterprises of his day, — these must be written out in order to make a truthful sketch of the life of Dr. Noadiah Swift. It is not the purpose of the writer in this work to describe in detail the modern times of the church. Persons who were nearer the times and scenes themselves still live, and to them this interesting and important service is respectfully deferred. When the writer of this notice commenced his pastorate here, and first became acquainted with Dr. Swift, he was already in the seventy-eighth year of his age. His manly form was still erect and noble, and his independent and decided spirit exhibited enough of independence and decision still; but nearly fourscore years, so many of them years of toil, and with some share of life's heavy afflictions in the loss of beloved ones by death, had begun to disclose their effect. But no one could see him in his place in the house of God, or hear his trembling accents in prayer in the lecture-room, or witness his unflagging interest in the church's prosperity, without being convinced that he was still its friend tried and true, nor without being able to appreciate what a powful leader and helper he had been in his prime in every good word and work. Owing to his father's circumstances he commenced life for himself, to use his own expression, without a shilling, and the decease of his father taking place two years before his marriage, he assisted somewhat his younger brothers and sisters. At the same time his charges for medical practice were extremely low. He was wont to say that it was a wonder to himself that he came to possess so extensively as he did the means to do good. But a kind Providence smiled upon him. He rose to an extensive medical practice, reaching to a wide distance in the region round about. He was for three years a representative in the General Assembly of the State, and twice elected to the State Senate. He was also for many years successfully engaged in mercantile pursuits. His hopeful conversion took place in the great revival in 1831, and he united with the church on the same day when one hundred and thirty-one were received. One month afterward he was elected a deacon of the church, and continued in that office until his death, which took place in the city of New York, where he was temporarily residing in the family of his son, Edward H. Swift, March 21, 1860, in the eighty-fourth year of his age. His remains were brought home, and interred by the side of those of his wife, who had gone a few years before him.

He married *Jennett*, daughter of Thomas Henderson, March 28, 1802. She was a member of the church, but the date of her admission has escaped the records. She deceased Feb. 10, 1853.

Their children were Semantha, wife of Hon. Pierrepoint Isham, and Edward II., deceased. The following obituary notice of Mr. Edward II. Swift appeared in the "New York Independent" at the time of his decease : —

"Died, at Havana, Cuba, on the 21st of June, 1865, of yellow fever, Edward II. Swift, formerly of Bennington, Vt., and for many years a merchant in New York, in the sixtieth year of his age. Mr. Swift was a gentleman of liberal education and cultivated mind. Amid the cares of a most active and eventful business life he found time for various and extensive reading, and was singularly well-informed with regard to all the leading topics of the day. More than thirty years since, he made a profession of religion, and united with the church in Bennington, in connection with the ministry of the Rev. Daniel A. Clark, and throughout a life marked by no ordinary vicissitudes and trials maintained a high character for integrity and business capacity. Smitten by a fatal disease, and dying among strangers, his afflicted family were denied the consolation of soothing his last hours by the ministries of affection ; but one who knew his worth, and admired his intelligent and manly virtues, pens this brief tribute to his memory."

II. CAPT. SAXTON SQUIRE united with this church in March, 1803, born Jan. 4, 1758, removed to this place, 1786, from Kensington (now Southington), Conn. ; resided first near the residence of Esquire Hubbell, then, 1797, in the Centre Street, in the house which has for many years gone by his name, carrying on tanning, shoemaking, and also farming, subsequently removed into what is now Bennington village. He deceased July 25, 1825. His wife, Sylvia, united with this church Jan. 3, 1819, born August, 1765, died May 13, 1832. Their children : Dorcas, born May, 1783 ; Alson, born Jan. 25, 1784 ; Norman, born July 27, 1787 ; Fanny, born Feb. 27, 1789, united with the church May, 1803, married to Lyman Patchin July 22, 1810, died Sept. 17, 1834, — a Christian lady of exemplary piety, and in whose heart was a perennial fountain of benevolence. Many a poor person found daily charity at her door, and from thence no needy one was ever sent empty away. (Her daughter, Fanny M. Patchin, remarkable for the loveliness of her disposition, united with this church Sept. 4, 1831, married Samuel S. Scott, deceased May 27, 1851.) Buckley Squires, deceased, born May 4, 1791, — genial and generous, an officer in the Episcopal Church ; his funeral discourse was preached by his pastor, the Rev Dr. Manser, to whom he was greatly endeared for his warm and faithful friendship, and his zeal, tenderness, and efficiency as a member of the church ; Newell Squires, born July 4, 1794 ; Albert, born Sept. 6, 1796, and Eliza, born July 11, 1800.

27

III. Mrs. Mary Galusha united with this church in 1789. She was the first wife of Governor Galusha, and daughter of Governor Chittenden, married 1778, died 1791. By her, Governor Galusha had five sons and four daughters. Governor Galusha was not a member of any church, though, " in the estimation of those best competent to judge, a true Christian. He maintained family worship in all its forms, was known to observe private devotions, was an habitual attendant upon public worship and at social meetings, and frequently took an active part in the latter. In his daily life he was also such as a Christian should be, modest, amiable, upright, faithful to every obligation. . . . When nearly seventy-nine years of age, he attended a protracted meeting at Manchester, and took an active part in its exercises ; as the result of which he was aroused to a sense of the duty of making a public profession of religion, and announced his intention to do so, but was prevented from accomplishing his purpose by a stroke of paralysis, which he experienced soon after, and from which he never recovered. He was captain of two companies, consolidated into one, at the battle of Bennington ; and was in the detachment ordered to attack Baum's fortification upon the rear. His men were from Shaftsbury, where he resided. He was sheriff of the county, judge of the Supreme Court, and was appointed to other important offices in the State ; born in Norwich, Conn., Feb. 11, 1753 ; died Sept. 25, 1834.

By his first wife above mentioned he had five sons and four daughters. His children were well trained, and all of them who survived childhood became professors of religion ; one of them, Elon, an eminent minister in the Baptist denomination.[1]

A fourth wife of Governor Galusha, Nabby, united with this church in 1821.

[1] Memoir of Jonas Galusha by Pliny H. White.

IV. Rufus Barney came from Taunton, Mass., in 1790,
with Capt. Chace and Mr. Burt and Geo. Godfrey, and their
families, all from Taunton, Mass. They came in a vessel
which they had chartered up the Hudson to Troy. At that
time there was only a blacksmith shop, store, and one house.
Land could have been then bought there as cheaply as in
Bennington. *Elkanah Barney*, a younger brother of Rufus,
came from Taunton, Mass., in 1793. They bought lands
in the east part of the town. Elkanah Barney united with
the Bennington First Church Sept. 4, 1825; his wife,
Catherine, Aug. 6, 1820.

V. Capt. Ebenezer Chace came as above. His wife
was sister to Rufus and Elkanah Barney. His daughter, Mrs.
Roger Booth, retaining her faculties, and brightening with
the most genuine interest and feeling at the mention of the
olden times, an intelligent lady and a sincere Christian,
deceased in 1868, aged eighty-eight. Capt. Chace died
Jan. 20, 1832, aged eighty-eight. Hannah, his widow, died
Jan. 10, 1842, aged eighty-nine. They both united with the
Bennington First Church May, 1803.

They first lived upon the hill; then moved down where
Bennington village now is. Capt. Chace bought lands
there. He cut the timber for his house, and moved into it
in six weeks.

VI. Samuel Hicks and Charity, his wife, united with
this church Sept. 26, 1790, during the pastorate of the Rev.
Job Swift, D.D. His father was killed in the battle of
Lexington. The family were sent with other families to
Taunton, for safety.

Charles Hicks, son of Samuel Hicks, with his sons,
drove the first stages over the mountain, on the route
between here and Boston, and also southward in the direc-

tion of Pittsfield. His son, James Hicks, drove the first stage to Brattleborough about fifty years ago. The father drove a stage to Pittsfield many years before. He was the father of Hon. Charles Hicks and Uel M. Hicks, and William, deceased 1832, at twenty-five years of age, who graduated at Williams College with the appointment of valedictorian. Frederick, son of Uel M. Hicks, is a minister of the gospel.

George, also a son of Uel M. Hicks, born Oct. 3, 1840, united with this church May 6, 1855, entered Williams College 1862; was a lieutenant of Vermont volunteers in the late war, and was killed before Petersburg July 30, 1864. He was with a detachment which, after the explosion of the mine, made an unsuccessful attempt to pass beyond it within the enemy's line and capture the crest of Cemetery Hill. For gallant services, a commission of brevet captaincy was, by a vote of Congress, made out for him and sent to his parents. He was also in the battle of Gettysburgh. He was possessed of devoted piety, brave, noble, and good.

VII. Mrs. POLLY ROACH united with the church in 1790. She was the mother of Mrs. Fanny Raymond. An only daughter of Mrs. Raymond, Mrs. Seth B. Hunt, deceased in Feb., 1867. Mrs. Hunt united with this church Jan. 5, 1834, and at the time of her decease was a member of the Tabernacle Congregational Church, Rev. J. P. Thompson, D.D., New York city. Devoted as a daughter, sister, wife, mother, she was polite and attentive to her guests and acquaintances. Blessed with wealth, she dispensed her benefactions to the poor with a liberal hand, having car-loads of the produce of the Bennington farm at "Maple Grove" shipped to New York, to be there, by herself and family, distributed to the needy.

VIII. Dr. Micah J. Lyman came here from Troy, N.Y., in 1790. He was graduated at Yale College in 1785. He was postmaster here for several years — O. C. Merrill, Esq., being his successor. He was in business here as a druggist. He left here for Montreal about 1810 ; and removed thence to Troy, N.Y., on the declaration of war, and established himself in his business in Troy, taking his two eldest sons, Charles and George, as partners with him. " A family of great worth and excellent standing "[1] originally from Northampton, Mass. He came here to pass the remainder of life in 1851, but united with this church in 1843, while residing in Troy, because he was a Congregationalist, as a matter of principle, and so much so as to prefer to connect himself with that denomination in another town rather than with any other denomination where he was residing. His wife was Elizabeth Sheldon, a descendant on her mother's side of Ebenezer Hunt, one of the Northampton families of that name.

Charles Lyman, his son, married Elizabeth Sheldon, who after his decease became the second wife of the Rev. Dr. Hooker. *George*, his second son, is a deacon in this church.

IX. Col. Orsamus C. Merrill was born in Farmington, Conn., June 18, 1775. He came to Bennington, April 5, 1791 ; at sixteen years of age was apprenticed to Anthony Haswell, and learned the printer's trade. The first business he did for himself was to print an edition of Webster's spelling-book. The printing-press was in the kitchen part of the house, the residence of the late Gov. John S. Robinson. Mr. Merrill then studied law with Andrew Selden, Esq., and was admitted to the bar in 1805, and, in August of that year, was married to Mary, daughter of Judge Jonathan Robinson. In 1809 he was postmaster in this town,

---

[1] Genealogy of the Hunt Family, p. 225.

27*

and held the office about three years. He was a major of the army in the war of 1812, and afterward a lieutenant-colonel. He was a member of Congress 1817–1819, and afterward a member of the State Council for five years; also a representative to the Assembly and judge of probate. He was for several years, between 1826–1832, editor of the "Vermont Gazette." He made a public profession of his faith in Christ and united with this church September 4, 1831.

He was remarkable for great purity, elevation, and urbanity of character.

He was frequently the speaker of the day on public occasions. One of his orations of this kind, printed by request, with other literary exercises of the occasion, has fallen into the hands of the writer of this notice. He felt a deep interest and exerted himself much on behalf of common schools. His interested and careful labors as a Bible-class teacher also deserve mention.

His belief of the doctrine of justification by faith in Christ alone was scriptural and decided, and his Christian example characteristically conscientious and circumspect. He deceased April 12, 1865, in the ninetieth year of his age.

X. Dr. HEMAN SWIFT was born in Bennington, September 30, 1791. He was the sixth son and twelfth child of Rev. Job Swift, D.D., and Mary Ann Sedgwick. He was hopefully converted while a student at Middlebury College, which he entered at fourteen years of age, and united with the church there, graduating in 1811. He commenced the study of theology in the Theological Seminary at Andover; but his health failing, he was obliged to relinquish his purpose, and then chose the profession of medicine. He settled as a physician in this town in 1821, and connected himself with this church November 5, 1820. He deceased

January 30, 1856, in the fifty-sixth year of his age. He was a member of the Vermont Senate in 1837. His mind was cultured by education, and stored with theological and Christian truth, and with general scientific information. He was especially accurate and well versed in history, and he had extensive acquaintance with public men. He was a warm and valued friend of ministers, and for years conducted a large Bible-class with great interest and success. His forgetfulness of himself in his desire to promote the happiness of others, and his extended and varied information, made him ever an agreeable and instructive companion. He sustained his high professional reputation and was in active practice until his death. Acute sensibility and tender sympathy with the sick and suffering were remarkable traits in his character, and, in connection with his medical intelligence and untiring professional exertions, served much to establish that ardent attachment which existed between himself and those who employed him as a physician.

His decease was most sudden. He had just left the family and passed into another room, with the view of going out again to meet professional engagements. Some member of the family, having occasion to go through the same room a few minutes subsequently, found him sitting back in a chair dead. His prayer that morning, at family worship, had been particularly noticed for an unusual tenderness and fervency of his looking to Christ, supplicating for grace to cling to the Saviour as his only hope. He married Ruth Robinson, grand-daughter, on her father's side, of Governor Moses Robinson, and, on the side of her mother, of Rev. Jedidiah Dewey. The last few years of his life were attended by a heavy affliction in the decease of a daughter, the light and the joy of his house, — Jennett, wife of Hon. A. B. Gardner; and of a son, Dr. Heman Sedgewick Swift, of whom the following biographical sketch is contained in the "Vermont Historical Magazine" : "Dr. H. Sedgewick Swift was born June 16, 1827. He was graduated at Williams College, and, after receiving a thorough education as a physician and surgeon, acquired great practical knowledge and skill in the hospitals of New York and other cities. He was author of several treatises, which were published in the medical journals, some of which were translated into German and French, and by which he acquired much credit and distinction. He was a young man of great moral worth as well as of extraordinary professional promise ; but died of a disease of the lungs, September 23, 1857, at the early age of thirty years." Reserved and self-distrustful with regard to religious hopes, he left in a private journal evidence that, in view of the approach of death, his trust for salvation was alone in Christ.

Henry Martyn, a son of Dr. and Mrs. Swift, is a minister of the gospel.

XI. Samuel Brown came here to reside about the year 1794, with his wife and family, and the parents of his wife. She was Betsey, only child of Capt. Daniel and Annis Hinman. They came here from Charlotte, in this State, whither they had removed from South Britain, Conn. They purchased and resided on the farm now the residence of Mr. Paige, in the south part of the town. Capt. Daniel Hinman was a relative of Col. John Hinman, of Utica, Hon. R. R. Hinman, for several years Secretary of State in Conn., and of Gen. Hinman, Roxbury, Conn. He died here Dec. 8, 1807, aged fifty-five. Mrs. Hinman died Nov. 24, 1815, aged sixty-three. Samuel Brown died April 21, 1819, aged fifty-four. Mrs. Brown died May 8, 1811, aged thirty-six. They had two daughters who deceased in early life. Hon. S. H. Brown is the only surviving child.

XII. Roger Booth came in 1795 from Lanesboro', Mass. He married a daughter of Capt. Ebenezer Chace, mentioned above, and resided on the place where is the present residence of Edward S. Pratt. He deceased Aug. 2, 1849, aged seventy-six. He was the father of Asahel Booth.

XIII. Jesse Loomis settled upon a farm in Bennington some time previously to 1795. His name is upon the town records as surveyor of highways in that year. He died Sept. 13, 1839, aged eighty-five years and ten months. His children were Samuel, Ira, Lydia, Betsey, Clarissa, Jesse, Sally, and Emma. One of the above-named daughters married Hon. Luman Norton; another married Mr. H. E. Dewey. Samuel was the father of Mrs. J. F. Robinson and Mrs. Caldwell, deceased.

XIV. Capt. John Norton came from Sharon, Conn., and settled in Bennington about the same time with Mr. Loomis. He established himself here in the manufacturing of pottery ware. He died Aug. 22, 1828, in the seventieth year of his age. He was the father of Hon. Luman Norton, and grandfather of Mr. Julius Norton.

XV. Jonathan Hunt came to Bennington about the year 1795. He was connected with a furnace a part of the time, and more permanently in business as a jeweller. For the latter years of his life he resided where is now the country residence and grounds of his son, Seth B. Hunt.

He sang in the choir for forty years, commencing at eight years old. For many years he was leader of the bass in the Bennington church choir. He used to say, " When any persons expect to get better tunes than ' Old Hundredth,' or better hymns than those of Dr. Watts, they must go further than any whom I know of have gone yet." Isaac T. Robinson, a leading singer in the choir who stood near him, related the following reminiscence to the writer: " We sometimes discussed the comparative merits of old and new church tunes. Mr. Hunt strenuously advocated the old, I the new; but I now think he was right."

He married Miss Naomi Bliss, of Springfield, Mass. She deceased July 24, 1837. She was a faithful Christian. The Rev. Dr. Peters relates that, when, pastor here, he always believed that his preaching benefited Mrs. Hunt and was appreciated by her, and he felt supported by her interest in his ministry, and her prayers. She used to say, " It is as much a duty to be cheerful as to go to meeting. She abhorred selfishness, and assiduously trained her children to habits of benevolence. She was accustomed to quote a remark of Mr. Haines, the colored preacher: " Selfishness spoils all that we do." Their children who grew up to adult years have become members of some Christian church.

Ruth Hunt, their daughter, united with this church March 4, 1827, deceased Sept. 29, 1867, aged sixty-one. In her last years, afflicted with difficulty of seeing, and at length, owing to paralysis, with almost total deafness, and helplessness otherwise, but tenderly cared for by a brother's and a sister's affection, she ever expressed to the writer of this notice much gratitude toward them and to her heavenly Father.

Mr. Hunt was one of six of the same Christian name in direct succession, being himself the fifth. The first Jonathan was born in Salem, Mass., in 1637, married in Hartford, Conn., Sept. 3, 1662, and died in Northampton, Mass., 1691; the second in the direct succession, Lieut. Jonathan, was born in Northampton June 20, 1665, and died there July 1, 1738; the third Jonathan was born April 24, 1697, married Thankful Strong, and died in Northampton April 22, 1768; the fourth married Sarah Parsons, and died in

Northampton in 1791 ; the fifth, our Mr. Hunt, died in Bennington in 1843 ; the sixth Jonathan Hunt, of San Francisco, is still living. A Jonathan Hunt, descended from the first Northampton ancestor, cleared land in Guilford, Vt., in 1758, was much in public life, and in 1794 and 1795 was elected lieutenant-governor of this State. His son, Hon. Jonathan Hunt, of Brattleborough, was member of Congress, 1827–32. A brother of Lieut.-Gov. Hunt, Gen. Arad Hunt, gave five thousand acres of land to Middlebury College.[1]

Mrs. or Miss Thankful Hunt was in Bennington in the days of the first meeting-house, and taught school in the second story of the porch. She was from Northampton, and afterward became the second wife of Elisha Lyman, of Montreal.

XVI. ANDREW SELDEN, Esq., "was born at Hadley, Mass. When young he removed, with his father, to Stamford ; represented that town in the General Assembly for six successive years from 1790 ; came to Bennington about 1797 ; studied law with Hon. Jonathan Robinson ; was admitted to the bar in December, 1809 ; was register of probate several years, and died September, 1828, aged sixty-three."[2] He wrote verses. An ode is in print in connection with an oration of Hon. O. C. Merrill, delivered here on a celebration of the 16th August. It is said he composed one of the odes sung at the dedication of the present meeting-house, and printed with the discourse. Alonzo Selden, of Whitehall, and Mrs. Angeline Selden are children of his, and Marcius G. Selden, a member of the Methodist Church in Bennington village, is a grandson.

[1] See Genealogy of the Name and Family of Hunt, pp. 180, 182, 183, 189. This genealogical record exhibits pedigrees of individuals of this name in America to the number of ten thousand.

[2] Vermont Hist. Mag.

Clarissa Griswold, who united with this church May, 1803, was the first wife of Marcius L. Selden, and mother of Marcius G. Selden. *Minerva Griswold*, who united with this church November 5, 1820, was the second wife of Marcius L. Selden, and mother of Capt. Henry and Lieut. Edward A. Selden. Mrs. Alice Griswold, who united with this church September, 1784, was the mother of the first and second Mrs. Marcius L. Selden.

Betsey L., first wife of Alonzo Selden, in Whitehall, united with the church November 5, 1820. *Charity Selden*, wife of Andrew Selden, Esq., united with the church September 4, 1825. Lieut. Edward A. Selden united with the church July 4, 1858, was in Company A, fourth Vermont, in the Army of the Potomac, in its seven days' retreat before Richmond, and died soon after, and was buried in the church-yard of Westover church, near Harrison's Landing, Va., warmly cherished in the memory of his relatives and friends. Capt. Henry Selden, deceased, married Miss Manning, grand-daughter of Jonathan E. Robinson, Esq.

ALMIRA SELDEN was a native of Bennington. She united with this church November 5, 1820; was married to Mr. Edgerton, and died in Buffalo, N. Y. She published, in 1820, a 16mo volume of 152 pages, entitled "Effusions of the Heart, contained in a Number of Original Poetical Pieces on Various Subjects." She penned the following stanzas on the Bennington battle: [1] —

> "No Lethean draught can ever drown
>   The memory of that day of fear,
> When the wild echo of farewell
>   From parent, husband, child, and wife,
> Seemed sadder than the funeral knell
>   That tells the certain flight of life;
> Yet Freedom spake, Faith raised her rampart pure,
>   And holy confidence gave victory sure.

[1] Vermont Hist. Mag.

" Then firmer than the native pine
    That tops thy mountains ever green,
Led by Almighty smiles divine,
    Facing their foes thy sons were seen, —
As when the livid lightning keen
    Tears from the pine some stem away,
Yet still unmoved the trunk is seen :
    Thus Stark stood victor of the day,
And while the voice of triumph met his ear,
    He for the dying foe shed pity's tear."
    28

CHAPTER XXIII.

PERSONAL NOTICES.

1803 AND AFTERWARD.

DEACON JOTHAM FRENCH came from the vicinity of Boston. He was a shoemaker. Before his conversion he was a deist. He was hopefully converted, and united with this church July 1, 1811, under the ministry of the Rev. Mr. Marsh. In subsequent years, being inquired of by Mr. Peters (Mr. Marsh's successor in the ministry here) about the cause of his conversion, he replied, "The goodness of God leadeth to repentance." His wife had been dangerously ill and recovered. He afterward learned that Deacon Bingham, who lived not far from him, had made her recovery a subject of special prayer. He was elected deacon April 12, 1816, and continued in the office until his death, April 30, 1825. He resided in the house on the road to Esquire Edgerton's, and about half a mile this side; Deacon Bingham, about the same distance beyond Esquire Edgerton's, on the same road. He was familiar with the Scriptures. He had an excellent memory, and stored his mind with passages of Scripture to support his deistical principles in argument, of which he was fond. When converted, his knowledge of the Scriptures was employed in defence of the faith he had before sought to destroy. He died a happy death. Mr. Peters, his pastor, went to see him, and, when returning, some one asked him, "How is Deacon French?" The reply was, "On the borders of a better world."

II. Mr. HARVEY united with this church in the ministry of the Rev. Mr. Marsh, 1811. There are three other individuals of the name on the roll of the church; among these

REV. WILLIAM HARVEY united with this church in the ministry of the Rev. Mr. Peters, and became a minister of the gospel and missionary in India, where he fell a victim to the Asiatic cholera a few years afterward.

III. DANIEL NICHOLS united with the church in 1803. There are twelve individuals of this name on the church-roll, six of whom united with the church the same year, 1811, ministry of Mr. Marsh; *James, James B., Electa, Sophia,* died May, 1824 (wife of S. Hathaway, Jr.), *Rachel, Fanny,* died Dec. 23, 1862, a warm-hearted Christian, and faithfully attached to the old church.

IV. PARK. — Betsey Park, *Mrs. Wilson,* sister of William Park, united with the church in 1803. Sophia, another sister, *Mrs. Capt. David Lyman,* an earnest and exemplary Christian lady, mother of A. P. Lyman, Esq., and Mrs. Col. White, united with the church in 1817.

WILLIAM PARK united with this church Nov. 3, 1833, born Jan. 15, 1782, deceased April 18, 1867, in the eighty-sixth year of her age. He was a remarkable man. He possessed much intelligence, was thoroughly hospitable, and of singular honesty, sincerity, and firmness of principle; he was an early and life-long friend of the temperance and anti-slavery reformations, and a humble and devout Christian. The community in which he lived on Woodford hill felt in his influence the power of a daily life of godliness.

Several suggestive and valuable reminiscences of the early history of this town and church were received from him by the writer of these pages. He was a warm personal friend and great admirer of the Rev. Daniel A. Clark. His wife, *Sarah*, united with this church Sept. 2, 1827, and deceased July, 1854; esteemed and beloved by all.

Cynthia, *Mrs. Luther Park*, united with this church Jan. 6, 1833, — early in the ministry of Rev. Dr. Hooker, and their children were baptized by him. A son, Austin Park, is a minister of the gospel. (She removed her connection to the Second Congregational Church.) The Hon. T. W. Park is a son of Mr. and Mrs. Luther Park.

V. THAYER. — *Betsey* and *Nancy Thayer* united with the church in March, 1803; and *Clarissa* in July of the same year; Ruby Thayer, *Mrs. Lawrence*, in 1812; died Oct. 10, 1836. There are seven individuals of this name on the roll of the church. The Rev. Nelson Davis, of Lisbon, Conn., who preached here with others temporarily in the revival in 1803, was a relative of the Thayer family, and our townsman, Mr. Nelson Thayer, was named for him.

VI. JACOB POOL and his wife, Zeruah, united with this church March 4, 1821. He was born in Abington Feb. 2, 1767; he removed to this town Dec., 1805, and deceased April 1, 1864, at nearly ninety-seven years of age. The average age of his father and two brothers, at their deaths, was ninety-five. He was superintendent of the Sabbath school for a time during the ministry of Mr. Peters, and also that of Mr. Clark. He was possessed of a sound and clear intellect, and deeply attached to the Hopkinsian scheme of divinity. He had great muscular strength and agility, and in wrestling was a match for all competitors. He conducted family worship until a year and a half before his decease.

VII. CHARLES WRIGHT, Esq., son of Solomon Wright, of Pownal, was born in 1786, graduated at Williams College, studied law with Chancey Langdon, of Castleton, and was admitted to the bar of Rutland County in 1807. He soon after commenced the business of his profession in Bennington, in which he continued until his decease, Feb. 15, 1819. At the time of his death he had the largest and most lucrative practice of any lawyer in the county, and sustained a high reputation for professional talent and integrity.[1] He married Eunice Robinson, daughter of Col. Moses, and grand-daughter of Gov. Moses Robinson, and daughter of Ruth, and grand-daughter of Capt. Elijah Dewey.

VIII. LYMAN PATCHIN was born in the town of Half-Moon, Saratoga Co., N. Y. He came to Bennington in March, 1809, and entered into partnership with Mr. Vibard, under the firm name of Otis Vibard & Co. In the spring of 1812 he purchased the house and store belonging to the estate of Charles Nairne in Bennington Centre, one door south of the old court-house. He was a merchant in the same place forty years, and accumulated in his business for the times a large property. He possessed a remarkably firm will, and was very energetic, exact, and thorough in all business matters. He came into the town with an empty purse, and made his own way to fortune. He was married July 22, 1810, to Fanny, daughter of Capt. Saxton Squire. *Lyman* and *Henry Patchin*, and *Mrs. Samuel S. Scott*, deceased, are their children. Mr. Patchin was afterward married to Mrs. Sarah Maria Wells, his second wife. He deceased Aug. 16, 1857, in the seventy-second year of his age. He was regularly in his place in the sanctuary on the former part of the day, and an attentive listener.

1 Vermont Hist. Mag.

28*

IX.　John Vanderspiegel was born in New York city Sept. 30, 1773.　He came here from Lansingburgh in 1810. He was married to Laura, daughter of Deacon Aaron Hubbell, Aug. 6, 1815.　He deceased Nov. 24, 1848, in the seventy-sixth year of his age.　The following is an extract from an obituary of him, published in the paper at the time : " Mr. Vanderspiegel was a worthy citizen ; respectable as a magistrate, and gentlemanly in his deportment, generous and liberal in his intercourse with his neighbors, and kind and affectionate in all his domestic relations."

X.　" Hon. Trueman Squire came to Bennington to reside in 1810.　He was born at Woodbury, Conn., in Jan., 1764 ; was in the practice of law at Manchester for several years prior to and after the year 1800, where he held the office of State's attorney two years, judge of probate three years, from 1793, and was also secretary to the governor and council for several years.　He was a good lawyer and an upright man, and had the respect and confidence of all."[1]

XI.　Mrs. Betsey (Austin) Carpenter united with the church Aug. 6, 1820.　She was descended from Mr. John Austin, who settled in Bennington, it is believed, some time subsequently to the Revolutionary War.　Fond of religious reading, edifying in conversation, a pattern of cheerfulness, exemplary in life's various duties, she was an ornament to her profession as a disciple of Christ.　She died suddenly Aug. 23, 1862.

XII.　Robert Crossett united with this church Nov. 5, 1820.　*Isaac Crossett* became a member of this church March 4, 1827, and was subsequently a deacon in the Second Congregational Church in this town.　He has since de-

1 Vermont Hist. Mag.

ceased. He was much respected for his amiable virtues and his consistency as a Christian and an officer in the church. There are five individuals of the name on the roll of the Bennington First Church.

XIII. LEWIS CHANDLER and his wife united with this church March 7, 1824. He was the father of Dea. Samuel Chandler. They removed here from Bernardston, Mass. He died here at eighty-six years of age. For months before his decease, though naturally a strong-minded man, he ceased to recognize his neighbors and to take any connected interest in worldly affairs, but his mind was bright and steadfast with regard to his Christian hope. He had desired such a trust in Christ as would enable him to feel the assurance that all his sins were forgiven. This trust was vouchsafed to him, and he would frequently ejaculate, " Blessed Jesus ! " He had remarkable views of his Saviour and of heaven.

XIV. MRS. SUSANNAH WATSON united with this church Nov. 6, 1831. She deceased Sept. 15, 1862, quite advanced in years, having lived a life of remarkable cheerfulness and benevolence of spirit. She came to North Bennington to reside many years ago, and reared a large family of sons and daughters, who became Christian men and women.

Miss Nancy Watson, her daughter, resided with her mother in North Bennington, united with this church by letter, and deceased April 25, 1861. She was marked by enthusiasm and intelligence as a disciple of Christ and member of his church. She was much valued by her ministers and others as an efficient helper in every good work.

Mrs. Betsey Watson, wife of *Dea. Watson*, of the North Bennington Baptist Church, and daughter of Dea. Calvin Bingham, united with this church May 6, 1827, deceased

July 13, 1860; ever deeply interested in religion, and its institution and progress in the world.

XV. Dr. WILLIAM BIGELOW was born in Middletown, Vt., Nov. 7, 1791, and married to Miss Dorinda Brewster, of the same place, Oct. 9, 1815. He was hopefully converted to God in the summer of 1816. About this time he went to reside in Fairhaven, in this State, as a practising physician, and on the first Sabbath in 1817, with seventy or eighty others, he united with the church, and afterward was elected deacon there. He removed to Bennington in November, 1829. Though coming into a community of high social position, and where eminent physicians were already established, he at once took his place with the foremost in his profession, and ever maintained it.

On one occasion his fellow-citizens of this district elected him to represent them in the Senate of this State. His social powers, his observations upon men and events, his interest in public affairs and the prosperity of the community, his genial and generous nature, were alike remarkable. Owing to ill health he was not exempt from depression of spirits, but he learned the art of forgetting himself and so conversing as to cheer others. Those who prized him as a physician, or in any relation as a personal friend, did so with no common attachment.

He was an impressive speaker. Gracefulness of mind and person contributed to this. His manner was dignified, and his feeling genuine. This talent he frequently exercised in gatherings of his fellow-citizens, but more constantly in the prayer and conference meeting. He regarded the duty as sacred. To some it might have appeared unstudied with him, as he seldom suffered an occasion for the performance of it to pass unimproved; but his remarks were not unpremeditated, and were often prepared with much deliberation and care. In no place was his influence more happy than in business meetings of the church. There often occur in such meetings critical differences of opinion, or hesitancy on the part of brethren to act. At such times his counsels ever helped the good cause to move forward. He was on two or more occasions elected superintendent of the Sabbath school. He was one of the committee on the last revision of the articles of faith and covenant of this church.

When he first came to Bennington the great competition between the "Old Line" and the "Pioneer," as the two rival academies were termed, was at its height. It became necessary for his children, if they should go to the "Pioneer" academy, to pass by the "Old Line" institution, which was a thing then not pleasant to do. His children anxiously inquired of him to which of the schools he would send them. He replied, "It is not necessary for you to know until the time comes." When the time came he sent one to the "Old Line" and one to the "Pioneer."

At the same time there was a certain authority in whatever he said or did. He would never allow any one to speak disrespectfully of religion in his presence. Physicians whom he very much respected for their talents and professional acquirements, but who were irreligious, would sometimes let drop some irreverent expression; he never allowed such freedom to pass unrebuked, but would so reply that probably the person offending in that way would not repeat the offence.

When the Rev. Mr. Foot preached his revival sermons in Bennington, and took extreme ground in favor of human activity in conversion, Dr. Bigelow remarked, "He leaves nothing for me to pray for."

On Oct. 5, 1858, owing to ill-health, which obliged him to relinquish active professional duties, he went to Springfield, Mass., to reside with his son, Edmund Bigelow. He however continued, so long as his strength permitted, to practise as consulting physician, and received marked respect from the medical profession there.   He continued at Springfield his wonted labors as a member of the church, removing his church-relationship to that place.

At his funeral there his pastor, Rev. Mr. Parsons, said; " As I look around upon this assembly, I see ten physicians, and I wish to say to them that Dr. Bigelow always found time to attend church, and also to attend to his patients."

He revisited Bennington nearly every summer after his removal from this town, and passed a winter with his daughter, Mrs. John Squires, in Troy, N. Y. Upon his decease, according to his request, his remains were brought and interred here.   He died in Springfield April 13, 1863.

XVI.   GAY R. SANFORD, and his wife, HANNAH, daughter of Capt. Brown, of Southbury, Conn., united with this church Nov. 6, 1831 ; both invalids for years, and called to endure great bodily suffering, yet unflinching in resolution, proverbially cheerful, rejoicing in the prosperity of religion, devoted to the happiness and welfare of their children, and remembered with much affection and esteem for their generous hospitality and many virtues.   They came here to reside, from Harwinton, Conn., in 1829.   Mr. Sanford was successfully engaged in mercantile pursuits with his brother-in-law, Hon. S. H. Brown. Mr. Sanford deceased Nov. 9, 1853 ; his wife, Oct. 23, 1859.

XVII.   HON. JOHN H. OLIN was the son of Hon. Gideon Olin, of Shaftsbury, and resided in Shaftsbury.   He was born in Rhode Island, Oct. 12, 1772, and came to Shaftsbury, in his father's family, in 1776, and died. there June 17, 1860.   He was two years judge of probate, and eight, from 1817 to 1825, one of the judges of the County

Court. He united with the Bennington First Church March 3, 1839. A little more than a year before his decease he was with this church at its celebration of the Lord's Supper, and, thinking it might be the last time, as it was, he rose in his place, and, in a very feeling and appropriate manner, expressed his attachment to his fellow-members of the church, and testified to his faith and hope in Christ. He endeared himself to others by the warmth and frankness of his nature, and his intelligent and genial conversation, and was widely respected and esteemed.

In referring to the fact of joining the Bennington First Church, the writer finds there has been constantly an unconscious use of the terms, "the church," and "this church;" partly because he has written from his own stand-point as pastor of the church named, partly to avoid the more cumbrous repetition of the distinctive title, but chiefly because most of the instances adduced date back of the existence of other churches in the town.

In the above numerous personal notices it cannot be but that mistakes have occurred, which kind readers will be most likely to notice so far as their own families are concerned; these can readily correct such mistakes in their own copies, and the copies of others most interested.

In bringing the personal notices to a conclusion, the writer desires to express the sincere wish that it had been better done; but he has also to say that he has done what he could. This part of the volume has occasioned him more labor and anxiety than any other; particularly he regrets not to have been able to embrace to a greater extent, in these sketches, persons, who, since the organization of the other churches in town, have deceased in connection with those churches and parishes respectively. This he could not do without extending this volume and his labors beyond all practicable limits, nor even then to any good purpose, for want of suitable information.

CHAPTER XXIV

EDUCATION.

COMMON SCHOOLS. In the town plot granted by charter of the governor and council of New Hampshire, Jan. 3, 1749, one of the sixty-four lots was for schools. On Jan. 19, 1763, it was voted at a proprietors' meeting,

"To send a petition to the General Court of the province of New Hampshire, to raise a tax on all the lands in Bennington, resident and non-resident, to build a meeting-house and a school-house, and mills, and for highways and a bridge." "May 9, 1763, voted to raise six dollars on each right of land in said Bennington for building a meeting-house and school-house."

The first district school-house stood about four rods west of the present residence of Mrs. S. H. Blackmer. Mr. Bancroft, referring to a period of time as early as 1765, states that the inhabitants of Bennington, at that time, had provided "three several public schools." [1]

"As the settlements extended, new schools were opened, and they have been ever since kept in all parts of the town, so that a convenient opportunity has at all times been afforded to all the children and youth within its limits to obtain instruction in the common English branches of education." [2]

The earliest, as well as all the records, both of the town and the church, are remarkably free from those monstrosi-

[1] Vol. v., p. 291.   [2] Vermont Hist. Mag.

ties in spelling and grammar which are so apt to characterize the antiquarian documents of town and church histories.

II. EDUCATION IN THE STATE. — As it may be assumed that the Bennington early settlers, being also pioneers in Vermont, may have had some influence on the character of the educational institutions of the State at large, it may not be irrelevant to adduce the early history of the State with reference to this subject. In the first constitution (1777) is the following article : —

"A school or schools shall be established in each town, by the legislature, for the convenient instruction of youth. . . . One grammar school in each county, and one university in this State, ought to be established by direction of the General Assembly."

In accordance with this instrument, we find at an early date, and subsequently among the statutes of the State, efficient school laws. An act, passed in 1787, is at hand for example : —

"For the due encouragement of learning, etc. : that each town shall be divided, when necessary, into convenient school districts ; one or more meet persons, together with the selectmen, to be trustees of the schools in the town ; a district committee to be appointed at a meeting of the district, who shall be empowered to raise one-half of the money necessary for building and repairing a school-house, and supporting a school, etc., by a tax on the inhabitants of the district ; the other half of the expenses to be provided for in a meeting of the district, either by a tax, or by a subscription in proportion to the number of children any person shall send to such district school."

The following remarks, by Dr. Williams, respecting the interest of the early settlers of this State in education, are so creditable to them, and so intrinsically just, they are inserted here : —

29

"The aim of the parent is not so much to have her children acquainted with the liberal arts and sciences, but to have them all taught to read with ease and propriety; to write a plain and legible hand; and to have them acquainted with the rules of arithmetic, so far as shall be necessary to carry on any of the most common and necessary occupations of life. All the children are trained up to this kind of knowledge. They are accustomed from their earliest years to read the Holy Scriptures, the periodical publications, newspapers, and political pamphlets; to form some general acquaintance with the laws of their country, the proceedings of the courts of justice, of the General Assembly of the State, and of the Congress, etc. Such a kind of education is common and universal in every part of the State. And nothing would be more dishonorable to the parents or the children than to be without it. One of the first things the new settlers attend to is to procure a school-master to instruct their children in the arts of reading, writing, and arithmetic; and where they are not able to procure or hire an instructor, the parents attend to it themselves."[1]

From 1780, the time of the incorporation of Clio Hall in Bennington, until 1807, twenty-five county grammar schools and academies were incorporated in the State.[2] Vermont University was chartered in 1791, in connection with a donation of four thousand pounds from Ira Allen, but was not immediately organized. Middlebury College was chartered in 1800, and went into immediate vigorous operation. Vermont University was organized soon after at Burlington, the institution of learning at Norwich in 1820; Castleton Medical College, 1818; Vermont Medical College, 1827.[3]

The highly esteemed pastor of the writer in his boyhood, in Derby, Conn., Rev. Zephaniah Swift, was a Vermonter by birth, and received a portion of his academical, and, it is believed, his theological education in Bennington. A

---

1 Hist. Vermont, Walpole, 1794, pp. 224-25.

2 Tolman's Statutes, 1808, Appendix.

3 See lists of colleges and other seminaries of learning with officers, graduates, and students, in Thompson's Vermont.

subsequent pastor of the same church, while the writer's home was still there, the Rev. Hollis Read, the missionary and author, was a Vermonter by birth, and at the least came to Bennington for his wife. When the writer was settled as pastor in Stamford, Conn., every neighboring Congregational pastor, and at least two other pastors, distinguished members of the same ministerial association, were either graduates of Vermont colleges or natives of this State. This is by no means an isolated illustration of the fact that Vermont has nobly contributed to the clerical profession as well abroad as at home. If in Connecticut, how much more in the new States of the West? The following reminiscence, furnished to the " Bennington Banner" by Deacon Stephen Bingham, is so much in point, it shall be given here : " Mr. Sanders, the author of an excellent series of school-books, was at my house several years ago, in order to introduce some of his books into the schools. A minister of this town, formerly from Massachusetts, was there also. During the interview Mr. Sanders said, ' I have been through all the middle, the western, and south-western States, to introduce my books ; and I find more teachers from Vermont than from any other State.' The minister exclaimed in surprise, ' What ! more than from Massachusetts ? ' ' Yes,' replied Mr. Sanders, ' more than from Massachusetts. *For I seldom go into a place where there are two or three schools but I find at least one teacher from Vermont.'* "

III. Academies.—Clio Hall was the first incorporated academy in the State. The act of incorporation was passed Nov. 3, 1780. The building stood on the corner where the present meeting-house stands. It was for long in a flourishing condition. Mr. Eldad Dewey, grandson of the Rev. Jedidiah Dewey, was principal for several years. A notice of the celebration of the tenth anniversary of the Bennington

battle, in the "Vermont Gazette" of Aug. 20, 1787,
shows that educational interests, and Clio Hall in particular, were not forgotten in the making up of the programme.
A place in the procession was assigned to the rector and
students, and the quarterly examination of the students
was held both forenoon and afternoon, in connection with
the other public exercises, in the meeting-house.   In 1803
the Clio Hall building was destroyed by fire.

William S. Cardell, educated at Williams College, and
with scientific and literary acquirements of a high order,
resided in the North Bennington village 1805 to 1806,
and took pleasure in imparting instruction and promoting
a taste for learning among the youth of the village and
neighborhood.[1]

Union Academy, in the east village, was incorporated about 1816, and a building erected. The brick
building in the centre village, called Bennington Academy, was erected in 1821, " in which the higher branches
were successfully taught for many years." The institution
now called Mount Anthony Seminary was established in
1829. This and the Bennington Academy were rival
schools from 1829 until 1837. The teachers in the " seminary" have been Mr. — now Rev. — Addison Ballard, Rev.
Gurden Hayes, Mr. G. W. Yates, and now Mr. Yates in
partnership with Mr. S. Benjamin Jones. The list of
teachers in the Bennington Academy is not at hand, — Prof.
W. H. Parker, now of Middlebury College, was one. A
high school was commenced and a new academy building
erected in the east village in 1833. " It enjoyed the patronage of the Baptist denomination of the town and vicinity,
and was for several years in a flourishing condition under
the successive charges of Messrs. Adiel Harvey, Horace
Fletcher, Justin A. Smith, William G. Brown, and others."

[1] Vermont Hist. Mag.

Miss Eliza M. Clark and sisters opened a young ladies' boarding-school in the east village, Bennington village, in 1859.

In North Bennington a building, which had been erected for a Universalist church, was, in 1849, purchased by the citizens, and fitted up for an academy. Mr. Carpenter, Messrs. Knight and Gould, and others have taught the higher branches in this school.[1]

IV. COLLEGE GRADUATES AND OTHERS. — Eldad Dewey, Nathan Robinson, Esq., William A. Griswold, Esq., and one of the Harmons, are recollected by an old citizen as members of Dartmouth College, all at the same time. Jonathan E. Robinson, Esq., David Robinson, Esq., and Governor John S. Robinson were graduated at Williams College. Martin, a promising son of Jesse Field, went to college and died there. Governor Tichenor was a graduate of Nassau Hall. The successive pastors of the Benninton church, after the first pastor, have all been college graduates. We have not at hand materials for making out a complete list of college graduates, or of the sons of Bennington who have distinguished themselves without a college education, in the professions, in public office, and in mercantile or other business life. A great number of names will be found connected with some more or less particular notice of them throughout this volume. Bennington has a long list of sons, of whose talents, energy, and success in the world she may justly be proud. And her present impetus in enterprise, wealth, and taste, — an augury of a bright future, — doubtless, in no small degree, worthily represents the energy which, for forty years or more of her early history, made her a controlling town in the State, and an evidence that educational influences fitted to foster and promote energy of mind have not been wanting.

[1] See the article on Education in Vermont Hist. Mag., p. 103.

29*

CHAPTER XXV

CHURCHES ORGANIZED IN BENNINGTON SUBSEQUENT-
LY TO THE ORGANIZATION OF THE BENNINGTON
FIRST CHURCH.

1762 – 1862.

THE REV. J. HIBBARD AND HIS PEOPLE. — For a portion of the time during the ministry of Mr. Dewey, Rev. Ithamar Hibbard resided in the west part of the town ; and, for a short time, was minister of a congregation which assembled at his house. The site of his residence is well known as the Hibbard lot. It is on the north-western slope of Mt. Anthony. At that time a road wound round the mountain nearer its base than the road now does, and passed along the border of the Hibbard lot. There are few traditions and still fewer recorded particulars of this congregation. There is reason to believe that it was an attempt at a more radical Separatism than the Bennington church, as a body, approved. There are two brief entries, and only two, concerning it, in the Bennington church records: "November 12, 1772. The church being met by appointment, the meeting being opened by prayer, agreed to send for a council, on condition Mr. Hibbard and his people would drop Mr. Frothingham ; and, for ourselves, chose Mr. Miller and Mr. Park." This Mr. Frothingham might have been Rev. Ebenezer Frothingham, first pastor of the Separate (now South) church, in Middletown, Conn., 1747–1788. The Mr. Miller was, doubtless, Rev. Alexander Miller, pastor of the Separate church in Plainfield, Conn. The other, Rev. Paul Park, pastor of a Separate church in Preston, Conn. " December 31, 1772. The church having met by appointment, the meeting being opened by prayer, voted to send an epistle to the churches concerning Mr. Hibbard and his people; their setting up as a church in the manner they have done, and their conduct thereupon."

The following particulars of Mr. Hibbard's history are from a "Fiftieth Anniversary Discourse," delivered at Poultney, in 1852, by Rev. John Goadby: "This little church" (the Baptist church of Poultney) "in its infancy united with the Congregational church in supporting the gospel, in worship, and in *communion*, under the pastoral care of Ithamar Hibbard, who had been a chaplain in the army of the Revolution. He was the first settled minister in the town, and, it is supposed, came with an organized church from Bennington. In 1785 or 1786 some difficulty arose among the Congregationalists in relation to their pastor, some informality connected with his ordination being alleged as the ground of dissatisfaction. . . . . The result was the organization of another Congregational church." "It was expected by Mr. Hibbard's friends that the newly organized church intended to take advantage of the alleged informality in his ordination to dispute his right to the lands appropriated to the first settled minister. To preclude the attempt, a council was called about the year 1788, when he was ordained according to the Congregational order. His previous ordination was according to the *strict* Congregational order." In 1796 the two churches were united, and Mr. Hibbard, who had continued pastor of his own church up to this time, was moderator of the meeting at which the union of the two churches was effected. In 1798 he became pastor of the church in Hubbardton, and died there March, 1802. Before his dismission from the Poultney church "he became a free-mason, which was a trial to many."

Mr. Hibbard was a member of the Vermont General Assembly, in 1778, from Wells; also in 1779, as appears by the journal.

He is spoken of as an orthodox and sincere man, and of respectable attainments, with a voice which in preaching and prayer could be distinctly heard at the residence of Aaron Hubbell. Several verses, entitled "*The Death of the Saint desirable*," printed by Anthony Haswell in a collection of anonymous pieces, have been assigned by tradition to Mr. Hibbard as their author.

One of his sons was the first settled minister in West Haven, Vt.

With the above slight exception, if exception it can be called, the Bennington church was alone until April 11, 1827. It was not designated by any denominational title. Its simple name was The Church of Christ in Bennington. Up to this time the present house of worship in Bennington Centre and its predecessor were the only houses of worship for the whole town. At the close of this period the Protestant population of the town was nearly as large as it is now.

II. The First Baptist Church [1] was organized April 11, 1827; its first meeting-house erected in 1830, and dedicated July 7 of that year. Its pastors have been as follows: The Reverends F. Baldwin, June 28, to October, 1830; Thomas Teasdale, until February, 1832; Jeremiah Hall, for three years, until April, 1835; Samuel B. Willis, for one year, ending June, 1836; Stephen Hutchins, 1836–41;

---

[1] The following statistics are taken chiefly from the Vermont Hist. Mag., pp. 162-3.

William W. Moore, for one year, ending in 1843; Cyrus W. Hodges, from the fall of 1843 to that of 1848; Edward Conover, 1849–52; Mr. Conover was succeeded by the Rev. A. Judson Chaplin, and he by the Rev. Warren Lincoln; the Rev. E. B. Palmer preached one year; the Rev. William S. Apsey succeeded him. The number of members, at the close of the year 1862, was one hundred and forty-seven; the number at its organization, thirty-two.

III. THE METHODIST EPISCOPAL CHURCH, in Bennington Village, was organized in May, 1827; its meeting-house erected in 1833. The following named clergymen have been stationed here since May, 1827, for two years each: The Reverends Cyrus Prindle, John M. Weaver, Wright Hazen, Henry Burton, Henry Smith, —— Hubbard, C. R. Wilkins, Jesse Craig, J. W. Belknap, H. B. Knight, R. Wescott, C. R. Wilkins, Merrit Bates, H. R. Smith, Ensign Stover; 1856–57, J. E. Bowen; 1858–59, C. R. Morris; 1860–61, S. P. Williams; 1862–63, Jonas Phillips. The number of members at the close of 1862 was one hundred and seventy, and thirty probationers.

IV. ST. PETER'S CHURCH (Episcopal) was organized July 24, 1834, under the ministry of the Rev. Nathaniel O. Preston, and a church edifice built of brick in 1836, which was consecrated July 22, 1839. The Rev. Mr. Preston continued in charge of the parish until the fall of 1844, and was succeeded by the Rev. C. L. Todd for one year, and by the Rev. E. F. Remington for a few months. The Rev. George B. Manser, D.D., became rector in February, 1850, and deceased Nov. 17, 1862, aged fifty-nine years and three months. Dr. Manser was widely respected, and his death felt to be a public loss as well as a sore bereavement to his flock. His successor was the Rev. Duane S. Phillips. The number of communicants, at the close of 1862, was one hundred and twenty-six.

V.   THE HINSDILLVILLE PRESBYTERIAN CHURCH was organized Nov. 1, 1834, by a colony from the First (Congregational) Church. The Reverends Messrs. Kenney, Johnson, and Nott were successively pastors. The church ceased its active existence in 1842, and the members, who originally numbered seventy-five, mostly returned to the church from which they had colonized.

VI.   THE SECOND CONGREGATIONAL CHURCH, being also a colony from the old church, was organized April 26, 1836, and soon afterward the Rev. Aretes Loomis became its pastor. He continued in the pastorate until Nov. 6, 1850, and was succeeded by his son-in-law, the Rev. Andrew Beveridge, for a short time.

The Rev. Mr. Loomis, after his dismission, continued to preach in various places with acceptance and usefulness until a short time before his decease, which took place in Bennington, where he resided. He was logical, clear in his style, conscientious, and faithful, and enjoyed the highest confidence of all as a minister, a Christian, a man, and a citizen. Two of his sons and a son-in-law are ministers of the gospel.

The Rev. C. H. Hubbard commenced his ministry here in 1851, and still continues. The number of members, at the close of 1862, was one hundred and ninety-seven.

VII.   A UNIVERSALIST MEETING-HOUSE was erected in North Bennington in 1836. The Reverends Messrs. G. Leach, Bell, Warren Skinner, and others successively officiated as clergymen. In 1849 the building was purchased for an academy, and has been since occupied as such.

VIII. The Baptist Church at North Bennington was organized in July, 1844, and in 1845 a neat and convenient house of worship erected. The Rev. Justin A. Smith became pastor in 1844, and continued in that relation for nearly five years, until July, 1849. He was in a few months succeeded by the Rev. J. D. E. Jones, who continued in charge of the church until the spring of 1855. Then the Rev. William Hancock was the pastor for one year, and the Rev. Jay Huntington, for four years, 1856–60. His successor was the Rev. Jirch Tucker. The church numbered, at the close of 1862, ninety-five members.

IX. The Methodist Episcopal Church, in Hinsdillville, was organized in the spring of 1858, and the old house of worship, built in 1835 for the Presbyterian congregation, was purchased and repaired for their use. The Rev. J. E. Bowen was stationed there, 1858–59. His successor was the Rev. Mr. McChesney. The Rev. G. Cuyler Thomas, 1861–62, with a membership of ninety-four.

As long ago as 1836 a small chapel had been built about half a mile from the present church, which was supplied with preaching in connection with another Methodist Episcopal society in Hoosick. Among the clergymen who thus officiated here were the Reverends A. A. Farr, in 1840; F. D. Sherwood, in 1841–42; C. Barber, in 1843–44; William Henry, in 1845; A. Jones, in 1846–47; and J. Sage, in 1848–49. After this, regular preaching was suspended until the new organization in 1858.

In 1857–58 there was an extensive revival in the northeast part of the town, among the fruits of which were additions to the several churches, and a chapel built, where preaching is more or less regularly supplied by the pastors of the Methodist Episcopal denomination, and a flourishing Sabbath school maintained.

X.   For some years previous to 1850, Father O. Calli-
ghan, residing at Burlington, held occasional Roman Catholic meetings in the court-house in this town.   He was
succeeded by the Rev. Mr. Daley, who came regularly at
stated times.   He was succeeded, in 1855, by the Rev. Mr.
Druon, who resided here, and under whose administration
a convenient church building was erected the same year.
He remained about two years.   The Rev. Mr. Bayden, from
Rutland, then officiated until January, 1859.   Then the Reverends Messrs. Cloarce and Fitzgerald successively.   Father
Dennis A. Ryan is the present minister.   At the close of
1862 his congregation numbered some one hundred and
forty families in the town.

NOTE. — A Congregational church was organized in North Bennington in 1868.

CHAPTER XXVI

THE CENTENNIAL CELEBRATION.

THE celebration of the centennial anniversary of the church's organization, which in point of chronology would more appropriately have been held on Dec. 3, 1862, was appointed to the first Sabbath of January, 1863, — (Jan. 4.)

SOME EXTRACTS FROM AN ACCOUNT OF THE CELEBRATION, by Richard M. Green, M.D., in the "Bennington Banner," of a subsequent date, will not be deemed out of place among these records of the old church : —

"The weather was unusually fine, and it was in every way one of the most pleasant days that we ever have at this season of the year." It was so warm no fire was needed in the house, and some of the windows were a part of the time opened, — a remarkable circumstance for this latitude in midwinter. "Thus those who lived at a distance, — in particular many of the aged, and others whom it might have been expected would be detained at home under ordinary circumstances by the rigor of the season, were enabled to be present on this most interesting occasion. An invitation had been extended to the other and younger churches of the town to gather at this old house and join in the services of the day. The different choirs, also, had been invited to take part in the singing, which they did under the direction of Mr. John Fay, the beloved leader of the choir of the old church. For some time before the appointed hour the house was crowded to the extent of its accommodations,

30

and it was soon necessary to make use of all the seats and benches that could be placed in the aisles. It was easy to see that no feelings of mere curiosity had gathered together this large assembly, or any part of it, but a deep interest in, and sympathy with, the occasion. At the appointed time Rev. Mr. Phillips, of the Methodist Church, opened the exercises by asking the blessing of God on those present, and the object for which they had come together. 'Coronation' was then sung. After which, Rev. Mr. Hubbard, of the Second Congregational Church, offered a deeply impressive and appropriate prayer. After 'Old Hundredth' the discourse was delivered. . . . It was listened to by all with undivided attention from its beginning to its close, — a period of two hours and a half. . . . All present at the dedication of the present house of worship were asked to rise; only thirteen stood up. Prayer was offered by Father Beman, and the services were then closed by singing and the benediction. The members of the different religious bodies remained after the dismissal of the audience to celebrate together the Lord's Supper. Members of five different evangelical denominations were gathered about the table of their common Lord, and probably never before in this town had so large a number partaken together of the emblems of their Saviour's suffering."

II. Concluding Remarks of the Centennial Discourse. — "Even while I speak, how the scenes of the more recent past crowd upon my mind! and if upon mine, how much more upon yours, respected friends, who are ' to the manner born;' and whose profoundest emotions mingle to-day with cherished reminiscences of years recently, or long since, gone by. Venerated and beloved forms rise before you: actors and deeds when this church was still the only church in the town, and it was in the fulness and,

I may say, pride of its strength; the struggles in unscrupulous controversy of powerful wills, when subjects of controversy, or projects of innovation, had stirred up the whole strength of the parish to array the same, part on the one side and part on the other; individual events and transactions, assuming for some reason ineffaceable prominence in your recollections; the commanding and graceful person of Governor Tichenor as he used to come in and take his seat regularly, and with dignified propriety, in the sanctuary; the imperturbable regularity with which Deacon Calvin Bingham appeared over the hill with his sons and daughters, riding into the village street, and on to the house of God, to take their places in the pew and the singers' seat every Sabbath, in sunshine and in storm; the strong and earnest tones of Governor Moses Robinson in public supplication to God; the enthusiasm and power, and culture, too, with which sacred song has ever been maintained in this temple of God.

" Some of you will, to-day, I suppose, need not much assistance of mine to recall the feelings you have had while listening to the voices of leaders and other prominent singers who have occupied the seats in this gallery, — voices of exquisite melody and rare compass and control poured forth with the spirit and the understanding in the praises of God — alas! hushed in death. Some, even since my brief sojourn among you, have passed away from us, who were important actors in the scenes and career of this church; and than whom, if they were spared and were with us, there would be no more deeply interested participants in the exercises of this occasion, attached in bonds of enduring affection to this church of their ancestors and of their own intense care and unwearied labor; fathers and mothers in this Israel, and laborers with a will in this vineyard of the Lord, striving, alas! with human passion, and yet

where want of energy is treason to the cause, for these
altars of their God. Venerated and beloved ones! over
whose graves the tears of affection are still shed, and whose
vacant places we could easily pause to mourn over afresh
at this time, we may yet thank God for what you were
enabled to manifest of zeal for his house; and we will pray
that we may emulate that zeal, so far as it was worthy,
ourselves each in the church, and in that sphere in the
church where Providence has placed us.

"As a part of the more recent past of this church may be
reckoned the organization of other churches in the town, in
some more than others, I suppose, and yet in all instances
more or less, embracing those who have been members of
this particular communion. In the separation of members
of a church to join other churches in the same town, or to
assist in organizing such churches, there is apt to be a
little disagreement as to the line of propriety and duty in
such cases between those who go and those who remain.
But all now, I presume, feel that the course of population
into the valleys and plains demands there houses and means
of public worship; and all believe, too, that different denominations of Christians have a right, as to one another, to their
own opinions and preferences.

"It is in this spirit we welcome you, friends of the different
churches of the town, here to-day, and rejoice in the prospect of sitting down with you at the common table of our
Lord. We doubt not that you are sharers with us in the
interest we feel in the past history of a church of which
many of you were once particular members yourselves, and,
in the case of more of you, your ancestors were.

"Take the lessons of this occasion, if there is aught in
them to guide us, that we may act our part that remains
wisely and well; and, when we separate, go to your own
several fields of labor and privilege, leaving your blessing

with us, and taking our blessing with you, and with renewed zeal give yourselves to the duties which the best welfare of your several churches calls upon you to perform.   So may you for these churches help to make a history, which, when their hundredth anniversary shall come round, will make an occasion for their then living members as full of interest to them as this is to all of us who are here present."

30*

CHAPTER XXVII.

The Township in the Olden Time. — At the time of the Bennington battle there were rude tenements. Large portions of the town were covered with primeval forest, — Mt. Anthony, base and sides as well as top down to near the meeting-house. The land was, however, highly productive, and largely cleared and planted. There was great agricultural prosperity. The only village was what is now called Bennington Centre. There were also numerous frame dwellings.

Col. Seth Warner came to Bennington to reside in January, 1765, and remained here until the summer of 1784. He was a near neighbor of James Breakenridge. Ellwells and Strattons came among the early settlers and bought lands in that part of the town, where those families still are. Dr. Jonas Fay resided in a house on the "Blue Hill." Drs. Gaius Smith and Medad Parsons resided in the west part of the town. Dea. Joseph Safford located himself on a farm near the present residence of Thomas McDaniels. The Bingham homestead was on the commanding and beautiful eminence south of and near the present village of North Bennington. Jonathan Lawrence, whose daughter Mary was the wife of Gen. Samuel Safford, settled in the southeast part of the town. Gen. Ebenezer Walbridge was joint proprietor with Joseph Hinsdill in the first paper-mill erected in the State, 1786, where is now Paper-mill Village.

In Sager's City, now North Bennington, a saw-mill was erected in 1775. The mills, called "Samuel Safford Mills" as early as 1766, were built at the outset of the settlement of the town. Samuel Safford, afterward Gen. Safford, was the miller. It is related that on one occasion, when a committee waited upon him to inform him of his appointment to some important office, the spokesman remarked that they had found him an honest miller, and they therefore trusted he would make a faithful public officer. He built and occupied the house now the residence of Mr. M. C. Morgan, in 1774. Benjamin Webb, Sen., deceased Feb. 12, 1812, came from Windsor, Conn., about 1770, and settled where Benjamin Webb now resides, with his wife, Electa, daughter of Gen. Safford, ninety-two years of age, — bright and cheerful, and taking a deep and intelligent interest still in reminiscences of the olden time. Isaac Webster lived upon a farm west of Benjamin Webb.

Not until after the present century did the east and north villages gain much growth.[1] The road from Boston came over the mountain at the "Elbow." The first frame house in town was built by Capt. Samuel Robinson, near where is now the "Safford Robinson house." The first in the Centre Village was built by Gen. David Robinson, partly in front of the site of the present residence of G. W. Robinson. The house now occupied by Dea. H. H. Harwood was built in 1770.

The population of the town at the commencement of the Revolutionary War was, probably, about fifteen hundred. There is in the possession of the Vanderspeigel family a picture of Bennington Centre as it was in 1796, — a large oil painting by Earle.

---

[1] A particular account, by N. B. Hall, Esq., of the early progress of Bennington Village, and of the North Bennington Village, by Gov. Hall, will be found in Vermont Hist. Mag., pp. 136-142.

II.   EXECUTION OF DAVID REDDING. — He had been convicted of "enemical conduct," and sentenced to be executed.   The day of execution came, and with it a vast
concourse of people.   Ethan Allen had just arrived in town
from his English captivity, which added much to the excitement of the day.   In the mean time the fact, for fact it was,
that Redding had been tried by a jury of *six*, contrary to
the common law, was effectually employed by Redding's
counsel to obtain from the governor a reprieve until Redding
could be tried again.   The throng of people assembled to
witness the execution were much exasperated against Redding, and indignant that he should be so readily reprieved.
Ethan Allen, suddenly pressing through the crowd, as-
cended a stump, and, waving his hat, exclaiming, " Attention, the whole ! " explained the reason of the reprieve,
referred to the second day fixed upon by the governor and
council, bade them return on that day, and added, with an
oath, " You shall see somebody hung, at all events ; for, if
Redding is not then hung, I will be hung myself ! " [1]

III.   TIBBETTS AND WHITNEY.[2] — On Sunday, August 8,
1802, an affray happened on the farm of Roswell Moseley,
residing about a mile south of the meeting-house (Bennington Centre), the Paige place, where several men were engaged in harvesting grain, in which a transient person by
the name of Gordon, said to have been an Indian or Canadian, was so badly injured that he died the next day.   His
skull was fractured in several places, and trepanning, by
Dr. Porter, of Williamstown, was resorted to, but without
affording relief.   The injuries appeared to have been inflicted with clubs by George Tibbetts, of Pownal, and
George Whitney, from Stamford.

1 See a particular account of this affair, Vermont Hist. Mag., p. 159. See,
also, Slade's Vermont State Papers.
2 MSS. of Gov. Hall.

They were arrested, and brought to trial for murder at a special term of the Supreme Court, holden for that purpose in Bennington in November following, when they were convicted of manslaughter, and sentenced to three months' imprisonment, to pay a fine of four hundred dollars each, and to give bonds for their good behavior, each in five hundred dollars.

The trial excited great interest at the time, and the verdict and sentence appear to have created considerable dissatisfaction. Pierrepoint Edwards, of Connecticut, was sent for by the friends of the accused, and is said to have made a most eloquent and masterly defence.

The jury, on bringing in their verdict for manslaughter, were addressed by the three judges, Jacobs, Tyler, and Chief Justice Robinson, and sent back for a reconsideration. They, however, adhered to their first finding.

Mr. Mosely was a prominent and respectable citizen, a Federalist in politics, and is believed to have taken an interest in the fate of the deceased. For this reason, or some other, in the then excited state of party feeling, both the judges and jury were charged with being influenced by political bias in allowing the accused so easy an escape. It does not seem probable that the charge was well founded. It is more likely there were extenuating circumstances attending the occurrence which deprived it of much of its criminality.

IV. Jeffersonian Democracy. — The country was divided into two great political parties, at the head of one of which was Mr. Adams, and at the head of the other Mr. Jefferson. The former were called Federalists, the latter Republicans. Gov. Moses Robinson[1] was a political friend of Jefferson and Madison, and when in Congress united

---

[1] Gov. Tichenor, Capt. Elijah Dewey, and others were Federalists.

with them in their favorable views of the French revolution
and government, and in their hostility to Jay's treaty with
England.[1]   In June, 1791, Mr. Jefferson, then Secretary of
State, and Mr. Madison, a member of the House of Representatives, in making a horseback tour through New
England, stopped in Bennington, and spent the Sabbath
with Gov. Robinson, who had then been recently elected
to the Senate.   Judge Jonathan Robinson occupied a leading position in the Republican party of the State for many
years.   While in the Senate he was understood to have the
ear and confidence of President Madison, and to have a
controlling influence in the distribution of the army, and
other patronage of the administration within this State,
which, in consequence of the war with England, was then
very great.[2]

Previously to Jefferson's election, as President, and
during Adams' administration, Mr. Anthony Haswell published, in his paper, an article in relation to the imprisonment of Matthew Lyon, under " the Sedition law," and
another on the conduct of President Adams in making
appointments to office, which, though manifesting considerable warmth of feeling, would not now be noticed as possessing a criminal character.   For these he was indicted
before the United States Circuit Court, and in 1800, at
Windsor, was sentenced, by Judge Patterson, to two
months' imprisonment in the jail in this town, and to pay
a fine of two hundred dollars and costs.   He was allowed
to serve out his term of imprisonment, which term expired
the 9th day of July.   The celebration of the anniversary
of the declaration of Independence was postponed until
that day, when, his fine and costs being paid, he was lib-
erated from jail amid the roar of cannon, and the acclamation of his neighbors and political friends.   He was, by a

1, 2 See Vermont Hist. Mag.

large portion of the community, considered as a martyr in the cause of freedom"; and his prosecution, instead of strengthening the administration in this State, served greatly to increase the number and zeal of its opponents. The fine and costs have since been refunded to his descendants by Act of Congress." [1]

Throughout Vermont, at that period, party political zeal almost outran itself. The determined spirit, and individual independence, of the Vermonters, missing now the New York State controversies, and the Revolutionary War, exercised itself upon the subjects and measures in dispute between Federalists and Republicans. What was true of the State in general was certainly true of Bennington in particular.

The people read eagerly the newspapers of the day, discussed earnestly and comprehensively the public measures of the government, were intelligent, determined, and spirited in their conflicting positions almost beyond what we can now conceive of. The writer has been permitted to see an interesting glimpse of this in the MS. diary of Benjamin Harwood, and will take the liberty to favor the readers of these pages with one or two extracts : —

"Oct. 18, 1808. — In consequence of certain intelligence being received in town of Mr. Tichenor being elected Governor of the State of Vermont, there was wonderful rejoicing among the Federalists, which was demonstrated by firing the great gun, beating the drum, and playing the fife. . . . . Next year the Republicans will rally and defeat the Federal cause in this State," — *which they did.*

Mr. Galusha, one of the former judges of the Supreme Court of Vermont, was chosen governor of the State. His election was supported by the Republican party, which had managed so successfully as to secure a majority over

---

[1] See Vermont Hist. Mag., pp. 176, 177.

the old governor, who, for years, had served the State with fidelity and applause.

"April 29, 1808. — Mr. Parsons came here this evening and brought a couple of newspapers, dated April 26, "Lansingburgh Gazette," and "Farmer's Register." The "Farmer" contains some most bitter complaints against the embargo; but, after all they can say about it, they have not proved that it is not a wise measure. . . . . Mr. Parsons and I talk of taking a Federal paper between us, so as to see both sides, that we may the better judge."

V. Present Meeting-house of the First Church.—As early as 1792 the subject of a new meeting-house began to be agitated in town meetings. Every such attempt, however, was unsuccessful[1] until Dec. 12, 1803, then a vote was obtained,

" To build the meeting-house, and to tax the inhabitants to the amount of five thousand dollars for the purpose."

In 1801, a statute had been enacted requiring, instead of the certificate of belonging to a different denomination in order to exemption from the tax for religious purposes, only that persons should sign a simple statement of dissent. At the meeting which voted to build the meeting-house and tax the inhabitants, it was also voted,

"That the term of one month be allowed to the inhabitants to enter their dissent."

There were only a few who availed themselves of this provision. But, as appears upon the town records, one hundred and twenty-three persons, male and female, had signed such a dissent eight days before the warning pursuant to which the above meeting was held.

1 See town records for March meeting, 1792–1803.

The place for the new meeting-house was decided upon. David Fay, Esq., was chosen treasurer; David Robinson, Andrew Selden, William Henry, Jr., Esq., assessors; Jonathan Wentworth, collector; Isaac Tichenor, David Robinson,.Moses Robinson, Jr., Thomas Abel, and Jesse Field, the building committee. The work of building at once commenced, and was carried vigorously forward.

In the mean time only about two thousand two hundred and ninety dollars of the tax had been collected, and it was ascertained the house, according to the plan, would cost seven thousand seven hundred and ninety-three dollars and twenty-three cents. The taxing method became increasingly unpopular. Before the house was completed it was determined, in a meeting of the society, to surrender the plain of raising the money by tax; to refund to those who had paid their tax; and to sell the pews on the ground floor for sufficient to defray all expenses, — which was accomplished. In 1852 the square pews were removed and the church reseated with slips. A diagram of the pews of the house as it was dedicated Jan. 1, 1806, with the amount for which each pew was sold, and the names of the original proprietors of each pew, prepared by William Haswell, is in the keeping of the clerk of the society.

VI. ARTICLES OF FAITH OF THE BENNINGTON FIRST CHURCH. — The Cambridge Platform, with the exception hereinbefore mentioned,[1] was their standard of doctrine and discipline. They had no other articles of faith until July 1, 1820. Then a summary of fourteen articles of faith was unanimously adopted by the church, the same having been recommended by a committee previously appointed, — Rev. Mr. Peters, Deacon Calvin Bingham, Deacon Jotham French, David Robinson, and Aaron Robinson.

[1] See page 32.

31

In the interval between the dismission of Rev. Daniel A. Clark and settlement of Rev. Mr. Hooker, the subject of printing the articles of faith having been introduced into a church meeting, a committee was appointed to revise them, — Aaron Robinson, Deacon Stephen Hinsdill, and Dr. William Bigelow. This committee recommended new articles of faith, which were adopted unanimously Aug. 5, 1831, and are those still in use.

CHAPTER XXVIII.

INFLUENCE OF THE EARLY SETTLERS OF VERMONT ON FREEDOM OF PUBLIC WORSHIP.

LAWS OF MASSACHUSETTS AS AFFECTING THE SEPA-
RATES. — It is not denied that the civil power was, in
Massachusetts, applied to the Separates to compel them to support the public worship of the standing order. The principle, in the Cambridge Platform, that the civil magistrate was, when necessary,
to enforce conformity in doctrine and worship to the
word of God, was not repudiated. This principle made
the civil power, in some sort, a judge of what doctrine and
worship was agreeable to the word of God. But practically
that was esteemed to be such which was then prevailing.
And when the conformity to the word of God was not so
convincingly seen, or its force as an argument so irresistibly felt, the consideration — shown by experience to be not
always well founded — of the greater ease of supporting the
minister, and building the meeting-house, and keeping it in
repair, when all in the community united together in one
way, was readily accepted.[1] So late down as 1763 our
immigrants from Massachusetts to Bennington showed that
they understood the fourth paragraph in the eleventh chapter in the Cambridge Platform, in respect of using the civil
power to support the gospel ; and also the ninth paragraph
in the seventeenth chapter, in respect of the civil magistrate's " cohersive " power, to be in force, and that they had

---

[1] See the succeeding pages.

felt their force, when they, in their first church meeting, and as a fundamental act, voted to except to these articles, receiving the entire platform beside.

The law enacted in Massachusetts in 1760, requiring a university education, or the testimony of a major part of the settled ministry of the country that the minister is of sufficient learning, or making the assessment for his support void, was, it is quite likely, aimed at the Separates. With this — perhaps with some other — slight exception, the prevailing form in which, in Massachusetts, the Separates felt the civil magistrate's coercive power, was that of being obliged, under existing general statutes, to pay taxes to the regular ministry ; and of being incompetent to collect by law any assessment or subscription for their own minister. As Separate congregations, distinctively so known, there was no relief for them from this, in law, until the adoption of the constitution of 1780 ; and even then the instrument was so interpreted for years as to make it of comparatively little advantage to the Separates. For example, it was claimed by the dominant party that the privilege of minority worship, without liability to pay taxes for the support of the standing order, was, by this constitution, confined to incorporated societies, and in case of such incorporated society, if not the regular or established society of the town, they must pay their tax with the others to the collector, and, let it go for the parish minister, or recover back their portion for the payment of their own minister by suing it out, — so decided in 1808, by a decision of the Supreme Court.[1]

It is true there were exempting laws, so called (laws to exempt certain classes from the tax to support the established worship of the town), but no such law was ever passed for the benefit of the Separates. There was an exempting law as early as 1693, for Boston, by which all

---

[1] Montague *vs.* Dedham, 4 Mass., 269.

denominations and religious societies were as free, with
respect to public worship, as at this day ; and so it has ever
since been in that city. Exempting laws for five years,
seven years, eleven years, at a time, first began to be enacted for Episcopalians in 1727 ; for Baptists and Quakers
in 1728. The differing sects were then very inconsiderable.[1] But for the New-Light Congregational churches, in
towns where the old church remained and was in the majority, not only were no exempting laws in favor enacted,
but especial care was taken, in the re-enacting of such exempting laws as had been previously obtained, to so guard
them with new restrictions that the minority Congregational churches could by no means take advantage of them.
There was a portion of the New-Light churches which embraced Baptist views. It was inferred that many did this
to take advantage of the exempting laws for Baptists.
Probably this was true of some. It could not have been
true of all, for, in many instances, these persons refused to
comply with the exempting laws as Baptists, assuming that
they were wrong in principle, so that they could more conscientiously go to prison than give any countenance to
such laws by voluntary conformity to any of their require-
ments, — the laws requiring certificates that they were of
the Baptist persuasion, or that their names should be entered on a list to the same effect, by the proper authority.
With regard to the period we are now considering, we see

---

[1] First Baptist church in Massachusetts, in Swansea, 1663. One in Boston as
early as 1665. — Benedict. In 1737, but three Baptist churches in Massachusetts;
one in Swansea, one in Boston, one in South Brimfield. — Benedict. Backus
says there was a church in Sutton in 1735, though it afterward went down; was,
at the time of the New-Light stir, turned into a separate church. When religion
revived in 1741, there were but nine Baptist churches in all Massachusetts, and
none in New Hampshire and Vermont. — Backus. There was an Episcopal
church in Boston during the Andrus administration, 1686-9. — Barry. "The
Methodists made their appearance in the Commonwealth about 1720." — Mass.
Ecc. Law, p. 41.

an illustration of what has been here said in the titles of some of the enactments : —

"To the intent that the Anabaptists who are truly such may be distinguished from those who pretend to be."

To see the same thing in the enactment itself, take one for 1752 : —

"To exclude all Baptist churches from power to give legal certificates, until they obtain certificates from three other Baptist churches that they esteem such to be conscientiously Anabaptist."

The Separate churches, which had adopted immersion as the scriptural mode of baptism, had not generally denied the validity, in every case, of infant baptism and baptism by sprinkling, which is, perhaps, the meaning of Anabaptist. The regular Baptist churches might be as jealous of these Separate Baptist churches as the regular Congregational churches were. So it is plain what was the intention and force of such modifications as have been instanced of the original exempting laws.

It is probable that, in very many instances, the laws were not enforced upon Separates who refused to pay taxes to the Standing Order. As, in many churches (Hardwick and Westfield, *e. g.*), church discipline to the extreme of excommunication was not enforced upon separating members who seemed to be conscientious in their views. But there were instances sufficient to make manifest the animus of the-taxing laws themselves, at least as re-enacted from time to time. When enforced, the method was one, happily, unfamiliar to the present generation in this country, but then familiar in many relations of the application of the civil power other than that of the support of public worship. It does not appear that the Separates, as a class, objected, at that early day, to the laws of imprisonment for just debts, but they did object to laws of imprisonment for refusing to pay taxes to a church they did not in conscience approve, — laws which enforced the distraining, in some cases, of the necessary implements of household existence, for such taxes, from those who had nothing else the law could get hold of. In the records of the Newint Separate church is the following entry : " Joseph Read confessed the wrong he had done in paying his rates, and the church forgave him."

Backus, who was originally a regular Congregationalist, then a Separate, then a Baptist, in his three-volume ecclesiastical history, has preserved many cases of much hardship in Massachusetts, under the laws requiring the support of the regular Congregational Society. Among these sufferers were a few instances of Separates, and many instances of those who from Separates became Baptists. Some of these suffered according to law, and some without law. There were others whom the laws exempted, but they could not, as they alleged, in conscience comply with the conditions of the exempting laws. The historian of Chelmsford states that all separation and all following after itinerants and exhorters were effectually repressed there by church discipline. In many places the Separates, not having organized their church regularly, according to law, were harassed by taxation for the support of the ministers from whom they had seceded. At last the system of annoyance became too tedious to be continued and fell into disuse.[1]

II. LAWS OF VERMONT RESPECTING PUBLIC WORSHIP. — In respect of imprisonment or any other corporeal punishment as a means of compelling men to the performance

[1] Tracy's "Great Awakening," p. 417. See in the notes at the end of this volume.

of religious duty, Vermont has a clean record. Before the existence of the State, Christian people in Bennington, as we have seen, organizing the first church in what afterward became the State of Vermont, made express exception to the articles in the Cambridge Platform which affirm the duty of the civil power to see that religious matters take proper direction. This was while Massachusetts was re-enacting her exempting laws with new restrictions to force the Separates to pay taxes to the Standing Order, and whilst Connecticut was not quite through with imprisoning men for preaching within the bounds of other men's parishes, or for establishing new places of public worship without the consent of the old ones.

The tax of six dollars on each of the sixty-three rights of land, to build, not only the school-house, but, also, the meeting-house, might have been without any opposition from any of the proprietors. Indeed, whether this tax was ever collected does not appear, — neither does anything appear to the contrary, only a subscription list for building the meeting-house was also obtained. For the further finishing of the meeting-house, in 1774, or at least toward it, a subscription was also obtained. The moneys from time to time raised upon the tax lists were raised from those lists only which were voluntarily brought in for that purpose. The certificating laws in force for seventeen years, 1783–1801, came the nearest to compulsory support of public religion. These required every tax-payer to help in the support of the public worship favored by the majority of the inhabitants, who could not bring a certificate, signed by the minister, or deacon, or elders, or moderator of some meeting of another persuasion, that the tax-payer named was of that persuasion. In 1801, any person could be exempted from taxation for religious purposes by signing a paper on the records of the town, saying, "I dissent from

the worship of the majority." In 1807, even this require-
ment was abolished,[1] and ever since the people have been
free to support the public worship they prefer, or none, if
they so prefer.

The article on religious worship in the first constitution
is as follows : —

"That all men have a natural and inalienable right to worship
Almighty God according to the dictates of their own consciences
and understandings, regulated by the word of God; and that no
man ought, or of right can be compelled, to attend any religious
worship, or erect or support any place of worship, or maintain any
minister contrary to the dictate of his conscience; nor can any
man who professes the Protestant religion be justly deprived or
abridged of any civil right as a citizen on account of his religious
sentiment, or peculiar mode of religious worship; and that no authority can or ought to be vested in, or assumed by, any power
whatsoever that shall in any case interfere with, or in any manner
control, the rights of conscience in the free exercise of religious
worship; nevertheless every sect or denomination of people ought
to observe the Sabbath or Lord's day, and keep up and support
some sort of religious worship, which to them shall seem most
agreeable to the will of God."[2]

In the first constitution, and also in that revised by the
Council of Censors in 1785, the following declaration is required of the members of the House of Representatives : —

"I do believe in one God, the Creator and Governor of the uni-
verse, the rewarder of the good and punisher of the wicked. And
I do acknowledge the Scriptures of the Old and New Testaments to
be given by divine inspiration; and own and profess the Protestant religion."

In the revised constitution, adopted in convention at
Windsor, in 793, this clause was omitted.

[1] See Tolman's Revised Statutes, 1808.
[2] Article 3, in Declaration of Rights in the first constitution, adopted in general
convention at Windsor, 1777, never presented to the people to be ratified, but declared to have the force of law by the General Assembly at Bennington, 1779.

The public sentiment and understanding with regard to the liberty in this State respecting religion — though not exactly in accordance with the legislation of the State prior to 1801 — was thus stated by Dr. Williams, in his history, published in 1794 : —

> "To leave every man a full and perfect liberty to follow the dictates of his own conscience in all his transactions with his Maker." "The people of Vermont have adopted this principle in its fullest extent." "It is not barely *toleration*, but equality, which the people aim at." "That all denominations shall enjoy equal liberty, without any legal distinction or pre-eminence whatever." "The people are under no obligation to support any teachers but what they choose to lay themselves under."

It is absurd to ascribe the sole agency in a great step of progress in civilization to any set of men. Time prepares beforehand for its own changes. The reformers, so called, are but in advance of others in taking up, and giving expression to, the new convictions which generations have been slowly preparing for. It is the glory of reformers to be before others in discerning the advancing light, or in so feeling the force of the truth as to be constrained to utter it, to maintain it, when they have to do so alone, and even in the face of obloquy and persecution, because others do not see, or will not accept, the truth. So high a distinction with regard to civil and religious liberty in this country deserves to be shared, among others, by the Separates, of whom our Bennington pioneers were among the best examples.

NOTES ON CHAPTERS IV. AND XXVIII.

I. The Halfway Covenant. — By the halfway covenant persons could be, and were, admitted to the church without professing a change of heart, indeed, while professing not to have experienced this change, — such persons to come to the communion or not, as their duty should appear to themselves.[1] But all were required to assent to a covenant otherwise strict, and to bring their children to be baptized. The halfway-covenant members were capable of the elective franchise, and eligible to office where church membership was a requisite.[2]

"The effect of this method of proceeding in the churches in New England which have fallen into it is actually this. There are some who are received into these churches under the notion of their being in the judgment of rational charity *visible saints*, who yet at the same time are actually . . . , such as freely and frequently acknowledge that they do not profess to be as yet *born again*, but look on themselves as really *unconverted* . . . ; and, accordingly, it is known all over the town where they live, that they make no pretension to any *sanctifying grace* already attained;

---

[1] "*Also that it is your full purpose to obey God in the ordinance of the Holy Supper as God shall give you light and show you his will herein.*" — Cont. Ecc. Hist. Conn., p. 411.

[2] This law, making "free burgesses" of church members only, ceased in the New Haven colony by the merging of the colony with Hartford, Windsor, and Wethersfield in that of Connecticut, under the charter of Charles II., in 1662. By the charter of Massachusetts colony (March 4, 1629) the governor and assistants were empowered to say who should be freemen; in 1631, this privilege of freemen was limited to church members. The rule appears to have been strictly enforced until 1647, when some others beside church members might have the privilege of voting in some cases in the towns. In 1660, we find the original rigor again enacted in all its completeness by law; in 1664, the law was repealed and certain others beside church members admitted to the privileges of freemen, but so that very serious inequality existed still between church members and non-church members. In 1684, the colony charter was annulled, and probably the inequality of the law of 1664 between church members and non-church members then ceased. All such inequality was removed by the coming into force of the Province charter in 1692, which made all freeholders, etc., voters; by which, as Bancroft says, "in civil affairs, the freedom of the colony, no longer restricted to the members of the church, was extended so widely as to be in a practical sense nearly universal."

nor, of consequence, are they commonly looked upon as any other than *unconverted* persons." [1]

" In such churches (halfway covenant) neither their publicly saying that they *avouch God the Father, Son, and Holy Ghost to be their God, and that they give themselves up to him, and promise to obey all his commands,* nor their coming to the Lord's Supper, or to any other ordinances, are taken for expressions or signs of anything belonging to the essence of Christian piety. But, on the contrary, the public doctrine, principle, and custom in such churches, establishes a diverse use of these words and signs. People are taught that they may use them all, and not so much as make any pretence to the least degree of *sanctifying grace,* and this is the established custom. So they are used, and so they are understood." [2]

" But the fifth of those propositions (seven propositions affirmed by the majority of the Synod of 1662) reaffirmed and commended to the churches the crude expedient of the halfway covenant. It did not merely provide that baptized persons growing up in the church with blameless character, and without any overt denial of the faith in which they were nurtured, might offer their children for baptism without being required to demand and obtain at the same time the privilege of full communion; but it also provided that such persons, as a condition preliminary to the baptism of their children, should make a certain public profession of Christian faith and Christian obedience, including a formal covenant with God and with the church, which, at the same time, was to be understood as implying no profession of any Christian experience. . . .   The latter was a grave theological error hardening and establishing itself in the form of an ecclesiastical system." [3]

" It was what Davenport called the 'parish way,'—a system under which the local church, as a covenanting brotherhood of souls, renewed by the experience of God's grace, was to be merged in the parish; and all persons of good moral character living within the parochial bounds were to have, as in England and Scotland, the privilege of baptism for their households and of access to the Lord's table." [4]

1 Edwards' Qualifications for Communion, Part III., Obj. 15.
2 Edwards' Qualifications for Communion, Part II., Sec. 1.
3 Dr. Bacon, in Cont. Ecc. Hist. Conn., pp. 21, 22.
4 Ibid., pp. 28, 29.

The effect of the prevalency of this system is stated by a writer in the "Vermont Evangelical Magazine," August, 1815, as follows: "The engagements which were assumed were extensive and solemn, and were at first probably made with much seriousness. But the whole soon became an idle ceremony, which fashion so imperiously required all, generally upon their marriage, to observe, that the omission was deemed highly indecorous and almost inconsistent with a reputable standing in society. The prescribed formality having been heedlessly submitted to, nothing more was anticipated or exacted. Individuals having gained a sort of relation to the church, and the privilege of baptism for their children, became satisfied with themselves, and neither saw nor felt the necessity of anything beyond the customary and heartless attendance upon public worship on the Sabbath."

A citation or two will show the influence of this system upon the piety of the clergy. Dr. Chauncey, in his "Reasonable Thoughts on the State of Religion in New England," declared, "Conversion does not appear to be alike necessary for ministers in their public capacity as officers of the church,[1] as it is in their private capacity." Tracy, in his "Great Awakening," says, "Colleges received young men, without even the appearance of piety, to prepare for the ministry; if graduates were found to possess competent knowledge, and were neither heretical nor scandalous, their piety was taken for granted, and they were ordained of course."[2] "The extensively prevailing views of regeneration as a work attended by no ascertainable evidence discouraged all questioning concerning a minister's spiritual state."[3]

A movement to obtain approbation of this system with some other things in a New England Synod took place as far back as 1657.[4] A Massachusetts Synod, in 1662, went a little further, in giving the system an authoritative introduction into this country. "The church at New Haven, I suspect, yielded at, or soon after, the ordination of Mr. Pierpont in 1684. Near the close of the century, when Haynes and Whiting had been succeeded by Woodbridge in the First Church (Hartford), and Buckingham in the Second, we find both pastors and both churches united in the half-

---

1 "Ordinations in 1759 occasioned so much 'feasting, jollity, and revelling,' that the Council addressed the clergy a circular on the subject."— Mass. Ecc. Law, p. 23.

2,3 Ibid., pp. 393, 394.   4 Cout. Ecc. Hist., Conn., p. 19.

way covenant method of church discipline. The principles of the
Synod of 1662 were for the time victorious throughout New
England."[1] In 1704 the Rev. Solomon Stoddard, of Northampton,
Mass. (the grandfather of Pres. Edwards the elder, and with
whom at length Mr. Edwards became colleague pastor in the same
church), when he had been in the ministry at Northampton thirty-
two years, eminently respected, declared himself "of the opinion
that unconverted persons, considered as such, had a right in the
sight of God, or by his appointment, to the sacrament of the Lord's
Supper; that thereby it was their duty to come to that ordinance,
though they knew they had no true goodness or evangelical holiness. He maintained that visible Christianity does not consist in
a profession or appearance of that wherein true holiness or real
Christianity consists; that therefore the profession which persons
make in order to be received as visible members of Christ's church,
ought not to be such as to express or imply a real compliance
with, or consenting to, the terms of this covenant of grace, or a
hearty embracing of the gospel; so that they who really reject
Jesus Christ and dislike the gospel way of salvation in their hearts
and know that this is true of themselves, may make the profession
without lying and hypocrisy,"[2] on the principle that they regard
the sacrament of the Lord's Supper as a converting ordinance, and
partake of it with the hope of conversion. "We must remember
that the practice of admitting to the communion all persons,
neither heretical nor scandalous, was general in the Presbyterian
church, and prevailed extensively among the Congregational
churches."[3] If we place the time of the first foothold of this
system as early as 1657, we shall find it not wholly disappearing
from the Orthodox Congregational churches of New England for
more than a century and a half. From the church in Huntington,
Conn. (from whose halfway covenant a quotation is introduced
into these pages), it did not disappear until 1817. The Rev. Heman Humphrey was ordained in Fairfield, Conn., March 16, 1807.
"He found a state of things in Fairfield in regard to spiritual
religion that seemed to him to call loudly for reform. In addition
to the fact that such a thing as family prayer was scarcely known
in the church, there was nothing that he considered as amounting

---

[1] Dr. Bacon, Cont. Ecc. Hist., Conn., p. 29.
[2] Quoted from Dr. Hopkins in the Memoirs of President Edwards.
[3] Great Awakening, p. 391.

to a confession of faith; and there was the halfway covenant, which he regarded as nothing better than an organized provision for uniting the church and the world. The two latter difficulties he looked upon as entering vitally into the economy of the church; and he therefore made the removal of them a condition of his accepting the call; and the church, without much hesitation, acceded to his proposals."[1] The spread and influence of the half-way covenant probably culminated about 1740, or the time of the commencement of "The Great Awakening;" at that time it had borne fruit "after its kind" in a wide-spread and deep-rooted formalism in the churches; and, as we shall see in another place, in a fearful enlistment of the civil power in resistance to the "New-Light" men and measures that sought its overthrow.

A curious fact, illustrating the extent to which this false system became entrenched in society, is the book of the Rev. Dr. Chauncey, well known to have been prepared in opposition to the great religious revival then in progress. The friends of the prevailing spirit of religious society, and who were opposed to the "New-Light" movement, were quicksighted to see whither this awakening would tend; and the book referred to appeared upon the arena in their behalf. "A Treatise in five parts: 1. Faithfully pointing out the things of a *bad* and *dangerous* tendency in the *late* and *present religious appearances* in the land, etc., etc.; by Charles Chauncey, D.D., pastor of the First Church of Christ in Boston 1743," — a book of four hundred and twenty-four pages with a preface of thirty pages beside. With the book was bound up, as was usual in those days, a list of subscribers. This list contains over one thousand names, headed conspicuously with His Excellency William Shirley, Esq., captain-general and governor-in-chief over His Majesty's Province of the Massachusetts Bay in New England, for six; the Hon. Jonathan Law, Esq., governor of the colony of Connecticut; the Hon. Richard Ward, Esq., governor of the colony of Rhode Island and Providence Plantations; and so onward into the body of the list, — a proportion of honorables and reverends, and esquires, truly formidable, — in accordance with what is known to be the fact that, to a great extent at that time, the influence and learning and rank in the country was on the side of the halfway covenant and hostile to the reformation.

1 Dr. Sprague's notice of the Rev. Dr. Humphrey, President of Amherst College, etc., in "New York Observer" for May 7, 1868.

II. Special Cases of Hardship under the Laws of Massachusetts respecting Public Worship. — In 1744, Mr. Paine, of Connecticut, for preaching at Woodstock, in Massachusetts, within the bounds of another minister's parish, was imprisoned at Worcester, but the Worcester Court discharged him as being imprisoned without law.

The Sturbridge case is repeatedly adduced by Backus. It was doubtless an extreme case, and its repeated introduction would lead us to infer that it had not any other cases parallel to it. It will, however, so well illustrate some of the hardships which the Separates were liable to endure, it shall be cited here, as given in the appendix to the "Life and Times of Isaac Backus," by Hovey (p. 329), — or rather, portions of that version of the affair shall be given. "From the testimony of Henry Fisk, we learn that a New-Light Church was organized in Sturbridge on the 10th of Nov., 1747. The next year John Blunt was ordained pastor. A petition to be exempted from taxes to support the 'regular minister' was laid before the town by the members of this church; but their request was denied. On the 26th of May, 1748, a great part of the town got together, and laying hold of two brethren who came from other places (to attend the New-Light meeting) drew them in a hostile manner out of town. About this time some others were seized for rates, paid them privately and were set at liberty. As they went on to rate us from year to year, contrary to the royal act of indulgence and the Province laws . . . . . they stripped the pewter from the shelves of such as had it; and they took away skillets, kettles, pots, and warming-pans from those who had it (the pewter) not. Others they deprived of the means by which they got their bread; namely, workmen's tools and spinning-wheels. They drove away geese and swine from the doors of others. From some who had cows they took one or more of them; from some who had but one, they took that away. They took a yoke of oxen from one, and they thrust some into prison, where they suffered a long and tedious imprisonment. One brother was called from us, ordained pastor of a Baptist church, and came for his family, at which time they seized and drew him away, and thrust him into prison, where he was kept in the cold winter till somebody paid the money and let him out. A few specifications are condensed from the records of the church kept by Henry Fisk, clerk. In 1750 a spinning-wheel was taken from

A. Bloice; five pewter plates from D. Fiske; a cow from J. Pike; a trammel, andirons, shovel and tongs from John Blunt; a cradle from J. Perry; goods from John Streeter; household goods from Benjamin Robins, and also from H. Fisk; a cow from David Morse; goods from Phineas Collar and from John Newell; and during the same year John Corey, J. Barstow, Josiah Perry, Nathaniel Smith, and David Morse were imprisoned for ministerial rates. . . . . ." A narrative of cases, persons, and particulars of hardship at a subsequent period of this church's history is also given; but let this suffice. Somewhere about 1750 this became a Baptist church.

Two or three other cases of oppression of Separates shall be given. They are cited from Backus' three-volume history. " And among the many instances that discovered how tenacious our oppressors were of their taxing power to support worship, take the following : Esther White, of Raynham, had a small interest left her, for which she was taxed eight pence to the parish minister, from which she had withdrawn four years, and she seriously declared it was against her conscience to pay it. Therefore for no more than that sum she was seized Feb. 28, 1752, and was imprisoned at Taunton until March, 1753, when said minister's own people were constrained to go and release her, without her paying any acknowledgment to that taxing power. She soon after became a Baptist, and continued to give abiding evidence of true piety until she died in peace in 1774.[1] " The case of Framingham, twenty-five miles west of Boston, affords another demonstration of the iniquity of supporting ministers by ‚tax and compulsion. The Hon. Edward Goddard, Esq., formerly one of the council of this province, with other fathers of that town, could not concur with the majority in the settlement of a minister, and by the advice of other ministers they became an organized church by themselves in 1747, and wanted nothing but the sanction of the civil power to make them as regular and orthodox a religious society in civil law as any others were. But as they were zealous friends of the late revival of religion, such an incorporation was denied them. And they had been all taxed to a minister they never chose for six years " (before a publication on the subject quoted in the appendix to vol. I.). " Three years after, their minister left them, and

1 Vol. II., p. 194.

32*

a Baptist society was formed among them." The following lines are credited by Backus to this Hon. Edward Goddard, Esq.. [1]

> " Good conscience men allow, they say,
> But must be understood
> To say as they themselves do say,
> Or else it can't be good."

"In a place called Titicut, upon the river between Bridgewater and Middleborough, a powerful work was wrought in and after the year 1741." "After Titicut precinct was constituted, in Feb., 1743, ministers refused to dismiss the communicants therein, so as to form a new church, lest they should call a minister whom they did not approve of. They were thus denied the right which both the laws of God and man allowed them, until the brethren determined not to be restrained by such tyranny any longer, but came out and began to worship by themselves on Dec. 13, 1747. A church was formed Feb. 16, 1748, which increased to three-score members in ten months. But the opposite party met in March, and voted a large sum of money to finish their meeting-house, and to hire other sort of preaching, and assessed it upon all the inhabitants. Therefore, our society, on Nov. 21, drew up an address to them." — which was answered; "and they" — the respondents — "went so far as to call it 'gross ignorance and enthusiasm' for any to deny that Christian rulers have a right to compel their subjects to receive and support orthodox ministers. And Feb. 6, 1749, the author" (Mr. Backus) "was seized as a prisoner for thirteen shillings and four pence assessed upon him in said tax. But, as he refused to pay it, they, after about three hours' confinement of him, settled it among themselves. This was the best reward they offered him for preaching two months at their request." [2] "One of his brethren was imprisoned at Plymouth for said tax. But, when distress was made upon another of his" (Mr. Backus') "hearers, they were prosecuted therefor, and it was found upon trial that said money was voted at an illegal meeting. They therefore appealed to the Superior Court; and in the mean time, Dec. 14, 1749, procured an act of the Legislature, which says, 'That the proceedings of the meeting,

---

[1] Ib., p. 195.

[2] See this case spread out at large and more intelligibly in Hovey's Life and Times of Backus, pp. 67-71.

mentioned in the petition be, and they hereby are, held and
deemed good and valid in law, the defect of the notification, calling said meeting, to the contrary notwithstanding.' And, by virtue of said act, the case was turned against the appellee in the
next trial; which shows that a worship supported by tax is *partiality* established by law." [1]

III. Concluding Remarks on Separatism. — Separatism
played an important part in probably the most profound religious
movement hitherto in this country. The depth of the movement
appears in the fact that it embraced and agitated the whole
country. To New England, at large, it was what the local revival
is to a neighborhood or town. It was natural that such a movement should develop a party of revolution, and an antagonist
party of avowed and heated conservatism. It is not difficult to
see, from the circumstances of the origin of the party of reformation, that there would be some rudeness as well as force in it.
In putting forth the energy such exigencies require, human nature is not apt to stop before, in its vehemence, it sometimes slips
beyond the safe limit of law and order. It becomes more intent
upon the object than it is upon the character of the means by
which to accomplish the object. Festering corruption within is
compatible with much precision of outward manners, which reformers, who set themselves against the corruptions of aristocratic classes, come into opposition to. Such a thing has been as
declension in piety and justice, even when ecclesiastical institutions, human learning, and civil government of a high order are
enjoyed; and when there is such declension, they who rise up as
the leaders of reformation are tempted to undervalue these great
blessings. This was true of the Separatists of the seventeenth
century in Old England, and of those of the eighteenth century in
New England. We see this cropping out sometimes in the Bennington church, though always in the final action of the church
overborne by moderate counsels. We see the same thing in the
struggles of Vermont for State sovereignty, and in conjunction
with other States for a national existence in opposition to the
mother country. Patriotism, the purpose of manly independence,
was too much on fire to think just then of furnishing to the world
models of legal precision, and refinement in manners. Hence

1 Vol. II., pp. 205–208.

some features of barbarity in the first essayings of this State at legislation, soon, however, pointed out by wise statesmen in the Commonwealth, and soon removed. Hence, too, so much was energetically accomplished in the early history of the settlers toward order and independence, with only a modicum of legislation, as is amply illustrated by what is preserved to us of the records of the Council of Safety, — "the greatest political curiosity," says Gov. Slade, "which the history of Vermont can furnish."[1]

Moreover, while many would be attracted to the general movement of Separatism, because of its energy in reformation, others would join the Separates from less pure motives. Backus says, "Such evils had been practised under the name of learning, orthodoxy, and regularity, that many were prejudiced against the truth by what others falsely called by those names. Christian liberty had been so invaded that many ran into licentiousness to avoid tyranny. The right which the gospel gives to every saint freely to improve their several gifts for mutual edification had been so much denied, that frequent instances were now seen of persons putting themselves forward in exercises which they had not a gift for, being so earnest to maintain the liberty of speaking as not duly to regard others' right of judging."[2] The Separates were derided for their uneducated ministry. President Edwards complained of their extravagance, self-conceit, and zeal without knowledge, — particularly of their exhorters, — and of their preaching without license.

The duty or wisdom of "separating" remains an open question; how far, in what manner, and when, if at all, the minority or the aggrieved party is to go out, and organize a separate worship under the plea that they cannot in conscience any longer countenance the old church in its errors by remaining in it.[3] It is not the desire of the writer of these pages, in the case of the Massachusetts and Connecticut Separates, to say, whether, under their circumstances even, Separatism was the best conceivable method of promoting all needed reformation.

It must, however, be apparent that, as compared with any tame acquiescence in the growing evils in the churches, the Separates

[1] State Papers, p. 197.   [2] Vol. II., p. 185.

[3] See some remarks upon this question in the Preface to the Cambridge Platform.

are to have our approbation. They exerted an energetic influence for important reforms which in a sequel of remarkable success may be seen and read of all men.

It is to be remembered that the persecuting civil and religious power, and the unfriendly sentiment arrayed against the Separates, were in support of an innovation upon the Puritan principles and practice.[1] The halfway-covenant practice too nearly resembled the custom of the old country, which the primitive settlers of New England had intentionally left behind, — not without sacrifice. Strange to say, the doctrinal standards in the churches which adopted the halfway covenant had not been modified to suit it. The articles of faith of the Cambridge Platform, and of the Assembly's Catechism, were in form neither altered nor repudiated. The doctrinal formula was as sharp a statement as ever of the doctrine of regeneration.

So far as Separatism involved denunciation of the Standing Order churches as no true churches of Christ, in our opinion it was wrong. That in all cases the Separates were innocent of disregarding the rights and feelings of others, it is not here attempted to maintain. They, in many instances, perhaps, refused to those from whom they came out the same right of private judgment and liberty of conscience which they demanded for themselves. It is the want of discrimination and charity in condemning others which is wrong. The Separates were not by any means entirely innocent of this. Those especially who continued in the same place with the old church from which they had separated had a great temptation to uncharitableness. On the contrary, so far as the Standing Order churches assumed that the Separates were not responsible to judge for themselves whether they could best worship God in a Separate organization, the Standing Order was wrong. As to the question of the mutual fellowship of neighboring churches, — how intimate it shall be, — it must be decided very much by the circumstances. It has been well settled, and probably will remain so, that no party shall be compulsorily taxed for support of one religious society when there is another accessible which is preferred. This has now of a long time been settled this side of the Atlantic Ocean, though only just beginning to be accepted in the mother country. It has also been settled with us now

---

[1] See Preface to Cambridge Platform.

a good while that no party shall be taxed against his consent for the support of any religious society whatever; and this, too, is well.

President Edwards, in some passages of his writings, appears to disapprove the course of the Separates in separating; and, yet, in other passages to justify them.[1] He certainly disapproved the course of the majority, whensoever it sought to restrain the Separates by civil penalties or ecclesiastical discipline. There were some distinct results of reformation accomplished, which the Separates had the perspicacity to see, and the spirit to demand, in advance of the most zealous and spiritual, who, like President Edwards, preferred to remain with the old churches. President Edwards received his first convictions of the unscripturalness of the halfway covenant through the Separates.[2]

On the whole, the conclusion is forced upon us that Separatism, with other causes added, was, by the overruling providence of God made largely promotive of the interests of mankind.

Briefly to sum up the results: They were in sympathy with and did much to promote a revival acknowledged on all hands to be one of very remarkable greatness and power. We have seen how with regard to the progress of civil and religious liberty they were quite in the van.[3] Against the use of the civil power to enforce

[1] See his Qualifications for Communion, Part III., Obj. 20; also, his Letter to the Rev. Elnathan Whitman, Hartford, Conn.— Works of Jonathan Edwards, London, 1840, Vol. I., p. cxviii.; ib., pp. clvi., vii., viii.

[2] "It is certain that the conduct of the Separates (in not approving the halfway covenant) received his anxious attention." "He must, therefore, have seen their arguments against the admission of hypocrites into the church, and it was not in his nature to cast arguments away through prejudice without ascertaining what mixture of truth there might be in them."— Great Awakening, p. 406.

[3] "The expedition against Cape Breton, in which Louisburg was taken from the French, 1743,— Col. Pepperell commanding, — was favored by Whitfield; he gave them a motto, after much solicitation of Sherburne, the commissary, — 'Christo duce,' — upon which great numbers enlisted. Separates at Chebacco — separated from Pickering — enlisted. Whitfield preached to the troops upon their departure. Upon their victory Whitfield preached a thanksgiving sermon." — Notes in Great Awakening, p. 67.

The Bennington battle, as a successful contest of native spirit and vigor against odds of culture and of British prestige, was an example of the peculiar spirit and success which had marked the career of many of the early settlers of Bennington from the time they, as Separates, protested in Connecticut and Massachusetts against the aristocratic and domineering formalism of the Standing Order churches.

The resistance of the early settlers of Vermont against the attempts of the

religious conformity they successfully protested. In the midst of a serious declension in the mind and practice of the churches from the written standards, the Separates rescued, and practically re-established, every important doctrinal sentiment of those standards. One of the so-called excesses of the revivalists was their denunciation of the ministers as unconverted; but that there was too much reason for this has already been shown. The demand that a minister should be a converted man was made to appear reasonable. Public attention was so strongly fixed upon it that the churches and the community came soon to settle it correctly; and the correct settlement of this question has practically reached all evangelical denominations in the United States. "In some instances they were founded on separating from degenerate churches and an unconverted ministry, as even charity must admit, and were the means of establishing and preserving gospel ordinances in their life and power where otherwise there would have been only the dead form of religion. Some of them occurred where the Christian population was large enough to justify division. Some of them became regular and orderly churches and subsist to this day. President Clapp, of Yale College, who, in 1742, forbade his pupils to attend the Separate meeting at New Haven, became an attendant there himself in less than ten years," — now the North Church.[1]

In respect of every important position named, there has been a singular unanimity, on the part of the Congregational churches, professedly of orthodox faith, in coming over to the ground thus in advance taken by the Separates. When the objections to the old churches in their minds were thus removed, and there was felt to be no other need of the additional church, the Separates readily returned to the old church, excepting in those instance in which the Separate church had become Baptist. "They went out from us, but they were of us: their return was natural, pleasant to us, and honorable both to their candor and to our common religion."[2]

New York governors in council to establish their jurisdiction as far east as the Connecticut River, was a decisive struggle of republicanism against the spirit of aristocracy and monarchy.

1 Great Awakening, p. 390.

2 Rev. Dr. McEowen, in Cont. Ecc. Hist., Conn., p. 281. "The close of the Revolutionary struggle found many of the parish churches destitute of pastors, and in some of them the lack was not soon supplied. . . . The churches of the *Standing Order,* so called, gradually abandoned the practices which had

The removal of the Bennington settlers away from the vicinity of the old churches to new seats, would disembarrass them of the most serious evils of Separatism. They who came up hither had necessarily to found a new church. There was no room for any question about the expediency of this. They were under no temptation of uncharitable denunciation of any other church in the neighborhood, for there was no such church to denounce.[1] And to this day, the few principles they adopted as the basis of their church order have been sustained. The repudiation of the fellowship of the churches in common counsel and mutual advice, and the idea of lay ordination, were never practically adopted by the church. As has been seen, in less than a year after its organization, it invited a mutual council to convene at Westfield, Mass., to give advice upon the question of the removal of that church and its pastor hither. The duty of infant baptism was strenuously maintained from the outset.[2] Whatever impracticable peculiarities of extreme Separatism cropped out in the case of individual members gradually disappeared. The counsels of moderation and wisdom prevailed.

IV. LAWS OF MASSACHUSETTS AND CONNECTICUT RESPECTING FREEDOM OF PUBLIC WORSHIP, COMPARED. — That Massachusetts did not proceed to as great length as Connecticut in persecuting the Separates has been accounted for in part, and, doubtless, cor-

---

grieved the Separates, and, to some extent, adopted the very positions and courses which their former pastors had condemned. . . . . . The result was almost inevitable. Indeed, the reunion of churches began in Canterbury, Conn., soon after the close of the Revolution, though not at first completely successful. The same thing was accomplished, at different dates, in several places; the last, and one of the most successful instances, being that of North Stonington, where, for a number of years, Rev. Joseph Ayer was the minister, at once, of the old and of the Separatist church, until their happy union in 1827." — Rev. R. C. Learned in "New Englander" for 1853, p. 206.

[1] It is a familiar anecdote of the pioneer, Samuel Robinson, Esq., that when new-comers presented themselves to him as chief proprietors' agent for the lands in this region, he would inquire of them as to their religious persuasion: if Episcopalians, he would offer them lands in Arlington; if Baptists, in Shaftsbury; if no religious persuasion, in Pownal; but if Congregationalists, in Bennington. — Thompson's Vermont, Part III., p. 19. It may be questioned whether this slight partiality in the interest of a denomination was not really adverse to that interest and to the interest of true religion.

[2] See record of the first case of discipline after the organization of the church.

rectly, by the fact that the charter of 1691, obtained from King William III., termed in the account of the Sturbridge case "the royal act of indulgence," required toleration of every religious persuasion except Papists. "Liberty of conscience in the worship of God to all Christians, except Papists, inhabiting, or which shall inhabit or be resident within our said province or territory." This was interpreted to mean that men should not be imprisoned, or otherwise punished, for holding meetings by themselves; and was also interpreted *not* to prohibit some encouragement by law (as, for example, enforcing upon the Separates the payment of taxes to the Standing Order) of the religion professed by the majority of the inhabitants. To use the language of Mr. Bancroft: "In one respect the new charter was an advancement. Every form of Christianity, except, unhappily, the Roman Catholic, was enfranchised; and in civil affairs the freedom of the colony, no longer restricted to the members of the church, was extended so widely as to be in a practical sense nearly universal. The Legislature continued to encourage by law the religion professed by the majority of the inhabitants, but it no longer decided controversies on opinion, and no Synod was ever again convened."[1] Backus says: "King William intended by this charter (of 1691) to prevent their making any more persecuting laws, and it had that effect fifty years afterward, when Connecticut imprisoned men for preaching the gospel, but Massachusetts could not do so."[2]

It is necessary to a fair comparison between Connecticut and Massachusetts to say, and in justice to Connecticut to recall the well-known historical fact that, prior to the coming into force of this charter of 1691, Massachusetts had an unenviable distinction above Connecticut in punishing with fines, imprisonments, stripes, banishment, and worse, those who were not orthodox according to the Massachusetts way.

CONNECTICUT. — Of the original constitution of the colony of Connecticut Bancroft says (remarks that, of course, do not strictly apply to the colony of New Haven, which, however, was merged in that of Connecticut in 1662) : "Roger Williams had ever been a welcome guest at Hartford; and that heavenly man, John Haynes,

[1] Vol. III., p. 80.
[2] History Baptists in New England, 1602–1804, by Isaac Backus, Vol. I., p. 133.

33

would say to him, 'I think, Mr. Williams, I must now confess to you that the most wise God hath provided and cut out this part of the world as a refuge and receptacle for all sorts of consciences.' There never existed a persecuting spirit in Connecticut." Bancroft quotes Douglas, in a foot-note, as saying, "I never heard of any persecuting spirit in Connecticut. In this they are egregiously aspersed."[1] He adds, further on: "During the intervening century (Connecticut's first century) we shall rarely have occasion to recur to Connecticut. Its institutions were perfected. For more than a century peace was within its borders; and with transient interruptions its democratic institutions were unharmed. For a century, with short exceptions, its history is the picture of colonial happiness. To describe its condition is but to enumerate the blessings of self-government, as exercised by a community of farmers, who have leisure to reflect, who cherish education, and who have neither a nobility nor a populace."[2]

While the third article of the bill of rights of the new constitution (1780) of Massachusetts was not generally interpreted until an enabling statute (in 1811)[3] to give to every religious congregation, whether incorporated or not, their own taxes for the support of religion, Connecticut passed an unequivocal act to this effect in 1784. And whereas this third article of the bill of rights was not abolished in Massachusetts until 1833, Connecticut adopted a constitution, in 1818, which in principle left every one free to adopt some religion, or no religion, as they should be pleased to do; and pay a tax for public worship, only upon voluntary connection with some religious society, — thus obtaining complete religious freedom, the ground which the Separates took, and for which chiefly they separated from the Standing Order as far back as 1730. The constitution of Massachusetts was revised in 1820, and an attempt was made at that time to have the third article of the bill of rights abolished, by which Massachusetts would have been put on the same footing with Connecticut, but it failed. The attempt was again made in 1833, and was successful.[4]

---

1 Vol. II., pp. 56, 57. 2 Ibid., pp. 60, 61.

3 Buck's Mass. Ecc. Law, pp. 43, 45.

4 "So unanimous had the dissatisfaction become, that, in 1834, an amendment of the third article of the bill of rights was adopted, by which the ancient policy of the Commonwealth, derived from the mother country, steadily maintained for two hundred years, was entirely abandoned." — Buck's Mass. Ecc. Law, p. 64.

V. JUSTICE TO THE PURITANS OF MASSACHUSETTS BAY. — In what has been said in this volume respecting the laws of Connecticut and Massachusetts, in their bearing upon the Separates, the case has been stated strongly against them; not, however, with the least feeling of prejudice against the fathers of New England, but simply to account for the course of the Separates, to whom, as a class, so many of the early settlers of Bennington belonged.

With regard to the spiritual degeneracy of the churches, in connection with the culmination of the halfway covenant folly, the writer has no apology to offer for them. Such backslidings, however, have, from time to time, disgraced professed Christianity in all ages of its history; and the sad story of such degeneracies should be pondered by us, so as to impress the admonition of Scripture, "Wherefore let him that thinketh he standeth take heed lest he fall." But with respect to the principle of the enforcement of religious conformity, particularly in the matter of public worship, some words of explanation should be added, in justice to the Puritans; though they were but men, and, as such, to be seen in the light of their imperfections as well as their virtues.

The Puritans did not believe, did not profess to believe, in freedom of religious worship. They did not profess to be Separatists as to the Church of England. There were instances, indeed, in the mother country, of their standing in an attitude of severe antagonism toward the Separatists. (The Pilgrims who came in the Mayflower, and settled in Plymouth, were Separatists, of that day, and believed in entire freedom of conscience as to religious worship, and remained so while they lived, though the influence of the Plymouth colony was gradually overborne by that of the more powerful colony of Massachusetts Bay, and of the confederation, afterward, of the colonies of Plymouth, Massachusetts, Connecticut, and New Haven.)

Moreover, take them as they were, how far in advance were they of their times? Let such imperfections as there were in their knowledge and attainments be viewed in contrast with the greater imperfections and far deeper ignorance of the times at large, and of their own early education. *Their faults were not so much faults of the men as of the times.* Let it be remembered that the daylight of freedom of public worship, as to compulsory taxation, has not yet come in England, — only a faint twilight betokening, now at length the approach of day; and it may be the better understood how deep was the darkness a century and a half ago.

The purpose of the Puritan fathers, to maintain, as a parish, public worship, at all hazards, as a foremost duty and interest of the community, is to be charged with much of their proceedings toward the minority who refused to assist in supporting the public worship of God with the majority of the town. This principle has run through all the ecclesiastical legislation of Massachusetts, dominating every opposing principle and interest, until its power was felt, most seriously of all, by those who came to be in the minority, as against the Unitarians, and were themselves refused, in the courts, any of the property of the old society. This subject is fully set forth by Buck in his "Massachusetts Ecclesiastical Law." Our Puritan fathers believed it was necessary to compel unwilling ones to assist the willing; and they were slow to believe that a parish had become sufficiently large to maintain more than one meeting; and they felt no security that that meeting would be maintained unless severe measures of coercion were employed upon such as otherwise would refuse to co-operate with them.

"The confederate commissioners of the New England colony from 1643 to 1667, maintained a careful supervision of the religious condition of each colony. They distributed Bibles, they conducted missions to the Indians on a scale unknown before their time, beside settling the very difficult questions of public law relating to war, boundary, and jurisdiction, on high Christian principles, without precedents to guide them."[1]

"The General Court, as early as 1654, held it to be their 'great duty to provide that all places and people within their gates should be supplied with an able and faithful minister of God's holy word.'" "Presidents of county courts and grand juries were to present all abuses and neglects, and to attend to the orders of the General Court concerning the maintenance of the ministry, and the purging of their towns from such ministry and public preachers as should be found vicious in their lives, and perniciously heterodox in their doctrine. So strictly were these matters attended to, that we have, in 1800, the exact penalties which towns should pay for neglecting to supply good preaching to the people. If the neglect lasted for three months out of six, the penalty was

[1] Mass. Ecc. Law, p. 23.

from thirty to sixty dollars ; if repeated, the penalty was from sixty to one hundred dollars."[1]   The General Court also had a care over the attendance upon public worship. "At common law, it was an offence to be absent from public worship; and by statutes, 1 Elizabeth, ch. 2, absentees, without excuse, were liable to the censures of the church, and a fine of twelve pence." A fine might be imposed for delinquency until 1835.[2]

Some traces of this feeling of misgiving lest public worship could not be maintained without some assistance of the civil power is seen even in the first constitution and early legislation of Vermont.

It is even now claimed, by some authors for the infant colony of Massachusetts,[3] that the excluding of heterogeneous sects was a measure of necessity, on the principle that self-preservation is the first law of nature. Undoubtedly thus reasoned the fathers of the Massachusetts colony. The early history of Connecticut colony, and, indeed, of infant communities in the new States, in our own time, would seem, however, to disprove such reasoning.

Besides, if they degenerated, out of their own loins, from among their own churches and communities, came forth those who saw the truth, and led up the others and mankind to a higher plane.

The instances of exceedingly severe treatment — such as if inflicted now would be considered outrageous and diabolical in every sense — were sporadic cases, — effects of sudden and overpowering excitement in the community. They were not the normal and abiding results of the spirit of the people and the community as a whole.

In the "Massachusetts Ecclesiastical Law," p. 36, the author justly says, in a note, "It would seem that the harsh moods of our ancestors, in the case of the Quakers and witches, hardly lasted two years. We might look in vain for a swifter return to common sense, after a national excitement."

Another[4] has said of Massachusetts, "The wild excesses of the people in preventing witchcraft, in 1692, destroyed nearly every trace of belief in ghosts and such things."

Of the law of 1742, in the General Assembly of Connecticut, "For regulating abuses and correcting disorders in ecclesiastical

[1] Mass. Ecc. Law, pp. 26, 27.   [2] Mass. Ecc. Law, p. 27.
[3] See Palfrey's remarks on this point in his History of New England.
[4] Goodrich Hist. United States.

33*

affairs," and which imposed penalties on itinerant preachers and exhorters, it has been well declared, " It was a high-handed infringement of the rights of conscience, and in a few years fell and buried the party which enacted it in ruins." [1] The reaction against this persecuting course was as violent as the adoption of the course itself. It intensified the spirit of Separatism, and an accelerated progress of religious liberty ensued.

The constant tendency of human nature is to degenerate, while the church of God in the world, with all its reactions and backslidings, still brings forth from within itself those who lead mankind up to successively higher planes of civilization, goodness, intelligence, and happiness. " Even so every good tree bringeth forth good fruit; but a corrupt tree bringeth forth evil fruit." See the Pilgrims landing on Plymouth Rock, in 1620, and the Puritans settling in Salem and Boston, in 1630, and consider what New England is to-day, and what its influence in the world has already been.

In tracing, therefore, the course of legislation in the States named, with regard to freedom of religious worship, the object of the writer has been simply historical information upon an interesting, important, and little understood subject, and justice to all, while he still retains the most profound respect for our Pilgrim and Puritan forefathers.

---

[1] Great Awakening, p. 238.

APPENDIX.

A.

THE CHARTER OF BENNINGTON.

THE following is a copy of the original instrument in the town clerk's office. Upon the back of the charter are the names of the grantees, including the *minister* as one, and the *school* as another, and the name of Governor Wentworth occurs twice. Accompanying the charter is a plan of the township, in sixty-four squares, to designate the rights, with the name of its proprietor on each square, as the rights were severally drawn by lot " by the agents, for the proprietors in Portsmouth, Jan. 10, 1749; and were entered by the secretary of said province upon this plan; each man taking his chance whose name stands in the schedule annexed to the grant of said township."]

Province of
New Hampshire. }

        George the Second, by the Grace of *God*, of Great
        Britain, France, and Ireland, *King*, Defender
        of the Faith, &c.

§⸱⸱⸱⸱⸱§   To all persons to whom these presents shall come,
§ Seal. §   Greeting. Know ye, That We, of our especial grace,
§⸱⸱⸱⸱⸱§   certain knowledge, and mere motion, for the due encouragement of settling a new plantation within our said province, by and with the advice of our trusty and well-beloved *Benning Wentworth*, Esquire, our Governour and Commander-in-Chief of our said province of New Hampshire, in America, and of our Council of the said province, have, upon the conditions and reservations hereinafter made, given and granted, and by these presents for us, our heirs and successors, do give and grant in equal shares unto our loving subjects, inhabitants of our said province of New Hampshire, and his Majesty's other governments, and to their

heirs and assigns forever, whose names are entered in this grant, to be divided to and amongst them, into sixty-four equal shares. All that tract or parcel of land, situate, lying, and being within our said province of New Hampshire, containing, by admeasurement, twenty-three thousand and forty acres, which tract is to contain six miles square and no more, out of which an allowance is to be made for highways and unimprovable lands, by rocks, mountains, ponds, and rivers, one thousand and forty acres, free according to a plan and survey thereof, made by our said Governour's order, by Matthew Clesson, surveyor, returned into the Secretary's office and hereunto annexed, butted and bounded, as follows, viz. : Beginning at a crotched hemlock tree marked W.W., six miles due north of a white oak tree, standing in the northern boundary line of the province of the Massachusetts Bay, twenty-four miles east of Hudson's river, marked M. C. I. T., and from said hemlock tree west ten degrees, north four miles to a stake and stones, which is the south-west corner, and from said stake and stones north ten degrees east, six miles to a stake and stones, which is the north-west corner, and from said stake and stones east ten degrees south, six miles to a stake and stones, which is in the north-east corner, and from thence south ten degrees west, six miles to a stake and stones, which is the south-east corner, and from thence west ten degrees north, two miles to the crotched hemlock first mentioned; and that the same be and hereby is incorporated into a township by the name of *Bennington;* and the inhabitants that do, or shall hereafter inhabit the said township, are hereby declared to be enfranchised with, and entituled to, all and every the privileges and immunities that other towns within our province by law exercise and enjoy. And further, that the said town, as soon as there shall be fifty families resident and settled thereon, shall have the liberty of holding two fairs, one of which shall be held on the first Monday in the month of March, and the other on the first Monday in the month of September, annually, which fairs are not to continue and be held longer than the respective Saturdays following the said Mondays; and that, as soon as the said town shall consist of fifty families, a market shall be opened and kept one or more days in each week, as may be thought most advantageous to the inhabitants. Also, that the first meeting for the choice of town officers, agreeable to the laws of our said province, shall be held on the last Wednesday of March next, which said meeting shall be notified by Colonel William Williams, who is hereby also appointed moderator of the said first meeting, which he is to notify and govern agreeably to the law and custom of our said province. And that the annual meeting forever hereafter for the choice of such officers, for the said town, shall be on the last Wednesday of March annually.

To have and to hold the said tract of land as above expressed, together with all privileges and appurtenances, to them, and their respective heirs and assigns forever, upon the following conditions, viz. : —

Imprimis. That every grantee, his heirs or assigns, shall plant and cultivate five acres of land within the term of five years for every fifty acres contained in his or their share or proportion of land in said township, and continue to improve and settle the same by additional cultivation, on penalty of the forfeiture of his grant or share in the said township, and of its reverting to his majesty, his heirs and successors, to be by him or them re-granted to such of his subjects as shall effectually settle and cultivate the same.

Secundo. That all white and other pine trees within the said township, fit for masting our royal navy, be carefully preserved for that use, and none to be cut or felled without his majesty's especial license for so doing, first had and obtained on the penalty of the forfeiture of the right of such grantee, his heirs, or assigns, to us, our heirs or successors, as well as being subject to the penalty of any act or acts of Parliament that now are or hereafter shall be enacted.

Tertio. That before any division of the said land be made to and among the grantees, a tract of land, as near the centre of said township as the land will admit of, shall be reserved and marked out for town lots, one of which shall be allotted to each grantee of the contents of one acre.

Quarto. Yielding and paying therefor to us, our heirs and successors, for the space of ten years, to be computed from the date hereof, the rent of one ear of Indian corn only, on the twenty-fifth day of December, annually, if lawfully demanded, the first payment to be made on the twenty-fifth day of December next ensuing the date hereof.

Quinto. *Every* proprietor, or settler, or inhabitant, shall yield and pay unto us, our heirs and successors, yearly and every year forever, from and after the expiration of ten years from the date hereof, namely, on the twenty-fifth day of December, which will be in the year of our *Lord* 1760, one shilling proclamation money, for every hundred acres he so owns, settles, or possesses, and so in proportion for a greater or lesser tract of the said land, which money shall be paid by the respective persons above said, their heirs, or assigns, in our council chamber in Portsmouth, or to such officer or officers as shall be appointed to receive the same, and this to be in lieu of all other rents and services whatsoever.

In testimony whereof we have caused the seal of our said province to be hereunto affixed. *Witness*, BENNING WENTWORTH, Esq., our Governor, and Commander-in-Chief of our said provinces, the third day of January, in the year of our *Lord Christ* one thousand seven hundred and forty-nine, and in the twenty-third year of our reign. B. WENTWORTH.

By his Excellency's command, with advice of the Council.

THEODORE ATKINSON, Esq.

STATE OF VERMONT, SURVEYOR-GENERAL'S OFFICE,
SUNDERLAND, December 13th, 1785.

Recorded in the first book for charters of the New Hampshire grants, pp. 193, 194, 195. I. ALLEN, *Secretary-General.*

B.

ALLEN AND WARNER.

By successful acts of adventurous heroism, — foremost among which was the taking of Ticonderoga, with his small handful of men, "in the name of the Great Jehovah and the Continental Congress," — Ethan Allen has gained a conspicuous place in the annals of Vermont. He is fairly entitled to the admiration he has received, on account of the remarkable warmth of his nature, the irresistible popular force, for a time, of his writing and speaking, and his distinguished activity, daring, and enterprise in the public service. Two or three characteristic anecdotes are here introduced.

He was once sued upon a promissory note for sixty pounds, and as it was not convenient for him to meet a judgment, he employed a lawyer to procure a continuance. As the readiest means for this, the lawyer determined to deny the signature. The attesting witness would then be necessary, and as he lived in Boston, and could not be procured in season, a continuance would be inevitable. When the case was called, Allen happened to be present, and, to his astonishment, he heard his lawyer gravely deny the signature of the note. With long strides he made his way through the crowd, and, confronting the amazed attorney, rebuked him in a voice of thunder: "Mr. ——, I did not hire you to come here and lie. That is a true note; I signed it, I'll swear to it, and I'll pay it. I want no shuffling, but I want time. What I employed you for was to get this business put over to the next Court, not to come here and lie and juggle about it." It is needless to say he got the continuance.[1]

Two little girls, seven and four years of age, had wandered into the woods. Not returning, and night about setting in, the parents, fearing they had fallen a prey to the wild beasts then infesting the forests, with the aid of a few neighbors commenced a search, which was continued through the night, and the next day, joined by large numbers from that and adjacent towns, and was prosecuted until mid-afternoon of the third day, when, worn out by fatigue, and despairing of finding the lost wanderers alive, the men had collected together with the view of returning to their home; but among them was Ethan Allen. He mounted a stump, and, in a manner peculiar to himself, pointed first to the father and then to the mother of the lost children, now petrified with grief, and admonished each individual present — and especially those who were parents — to make the case of these parents his own, and then say whether they could go contentedly to their homes without making one further effort to save these dear little ones who were probably now alive, but perishing with hunger, and spending their last strength in crying to father and mother to give them food. As he spoke his giant frame was agitated, and tears rolled down his cheeks; and in the assembly of several hundred men but few eyes were dry; whereupon all manifested a willingness to return. The search being renewed, before night of the same day the lost children were found, and restored in safety to the arms of distracted parents.[2]

When Col. Allen was captured at Montreal, by the British, with his party of Canadians, order was given that thirteen of these

1 Vermont Record.   2 Vermont Hist. Mag.   Article, Sunderland.

Canadians should be thrust through with bayonets. "It cut me
to the heart," he says, "to see the Canadians in so hard a case, in
consequence of their having been true to me; they were wringing
their hands, saying their prayers (as I concluded), and expected
immediate death. I therefore stepped between the executioners
and the Canadians, opened my clothes, and told General Prescott
to thrust his bayonet into my breast, for I was the sole cause of
the Canadians' taking up arms; the guard in the mean time roll-
ing their eyeballs from the General to me, as though impatiently
waiting his dread commands to sheathe their bayonets in my
breast. I could, however, plainly discern that he was in a sus-
pense and quandary about the matter. This gave me additional
hopes of succeeding; for my design was not to die, but to save
the Canadians by a finesse."[1]

In the progress of the New York controversy, several pamphlets
were written by Allen, as well as letters of official correspondence
with the opposing party, exhibiting, in a manner peculiar to himself, and well suited to the state of public feeling, the injustice of
the New York claims. These pamphlets were extensively circu-
lated, and contributed much to inform the minds, arouse the zeal,
and unite the efforts of the settlers.[2]

When Col. Allen had been released from his long captivity, in
exchange for Colonel Campbell, Allen paid a visit to the American
camps at Valley Forge, where he had much to tell of his various
vicissitudes and hardships. Washington, in a letter to the President of Congress suggesting that something should be done for
Allen, observes: "His fortitude and firmness seem to have
placed him out of the reach of misfortune. There is an original
something about him that commands admiration, and his long
captivity and sufferings have only served to increase, if possible,
his enthusiastic zeal. He appears very desirous of rendering his
services to the States, and of being employed."[3]

Seth Warner, Allen's comrade in so many adventures, and in so
much public service, without attempting, perhaps incapable of,
rhetorical effects by his tongue and pen, possessed more breadth
of character, more prudence and judgment, and yet no less determination and courage, than Allen. When the peculiar occasions
for adventurous daring had passed by, Warner rose to a higher

1 Ethan Allen's Narrative, p. 36. 2 Gov. Slade, in State Papers, p. 36.
3 Irving's Life of Washington, Vol. III., p. 378.

degree of respect in the public mind, while Providence appeared
to have denied to Allen opportunity for achieving further renown.
" As a military leader, Warner was honored and confided in above
all others by the people of this State, and his bravery and military
capacity appear to have been always appreciated by the intelligent officers from other States with whom he served.   In the dis-
astrous retreat from Canada, in the spring of 1776, he brought up
the rear; and he was placed in command of the rear-guard on the
evacuation of Ticonderoga, by which he was involved in the
action at Hubbardton.   At Bennington he was with Stark for
several days before the battle, and was his associate in planning
the attack upon Baum, and in carrying it into execution; and it
was by his advice and contrary to the first impression of Stark
that Breyman was immediately opposed without first retiring to
rally the scattered forces." [1]

" It is evident that they "— Allen and Warner —" were far more
efficient and more useful in defending the New Hampshire Grants,
than they would have been, had they both been Allens, or both
been Warners; and it would not be extravagant to say, that, had
either been wanting, the independence of Vermont might not
have been achieved.   But in selecting a person to command a
regiment, the men of that day gave the preference to Warner.
Accordingly the convention assembled at Dorset to nominate
officers for a regiment of Green Mountain Boys, nominated Warner for lieutenant-colonel to command the regiment, by a vote of
forty-one to five.   And as Allen was candidate for the office, as
appears by his letter to Governor Trumbull, written shortly after
the officers were nominated, in which he says, that he was overlooked because the old men were reluctant to go to war, the vote
must be considered as a fair expression of the public sentiment
in relation to the qualifications of the two men for the office." [2]

[1] Vermont Hist. Mag.
[2] Quoted from Chipman's Life of Warner in Mr. Houghton's Montpelier Address.

34

C.

COVENANT OF THE BENNINGTON FIRST CHURCH.

[The greater probability is that this instrument was adopted and signed not at, but within two or three years after, the organization of the church. See p. 39 of this volume.]

We whose names are underwritten, apprehending ourselves called of God into church state of the gospel, do, first of all, confess ourselves unworthy to be so highly favored of the Lord; and admire that rich and free grace of his, which triumphs over so great unworthiness; and then, with an humble reliance on the grace therein promised for those who, in a sense of their inability to do any good thing, do humbly wait on him for all, — we now thankfully lay hold of his covenant; and would choose the things that please him.

We declare our serious belief of the Christian religion as contained in the sacred Scriptures, and with such view thereof as the Confession of Faith and Rules of Discipline in Cambridge Platform has exhibited, — heartily resolving to conform our lives unto the rules of that holy religion so long as we live in the world. We give ourselves unto the Lord Jehovah, who is the Father, and the Son, and the Holy Spirit, and avouch him this day to be our God, our Father, and our Saviour, and our Leader; and receive him as our portion forever. We give up ourselves unto the blessed Jesus, who is the Lord Jehovah; and adhere to him as the head of his people in the covenant of grace; and rely on him as our Priest, and our Prophet, and our King, to bring us unto eternal blessedness. We acknowledge our everlasting and indispensable obligation to glorify God in all the duties of a godly, a sober, and a righteous life, and very particularly in the duty of a church state, — a body of people associated together for an obedience to him in all the ordinances of the gospel; and we herein depend upon his gracious assistance for our faithful discharge of the duties thus incumbent on us. We desire, and intend, and with dependence upon his powerful grace we engage, to walk together as a church of the Lord Jesus Christ in the faith and order of the gospel so far as we shall have the same revealed to us, — conscientiously attending the public worship of God, the sacraments of the New Testament, the discipline of his kingdom, and all his holy institutions in communion with one another, and watchfully avoiding all sinful stumbling-blocks, as become a people whom the Lord hath bound up together in the bundle of eternal life.

At the same time, also, we do present our offspring with us to the Lord, purposing with his help to do our part in the methods of a religious education that they may be the Lord's. And all this we do flying to the blood of the everlasting covenant for the pardon of our many errors; and praying that the glorious Lord, who is the great Shepherd, will prepare and strengthen us for every good work to do his will, working in us that which will be well pleasing in his sight — to whom be glory forever and ever. Amen.

John Roberts	Mehitable Fay
Samuel Robinson	Hannah Rice
James Fay	Elizabeth Fay
Benjamin Harwood	Marcy Newton
George Abbott, Jun.	Hepzibah Whipple
Jedidiah Rice	Joseph Safford
James Breakenridge	Stephen Story
Oliver Rice	Bethiah Burnham
James Fay, Jr.	Eleanor Smith
David Doane	Aaron Leonard
John Fassett	John Wood
Daniel Fay	Zechariah Harwood
Ichabod Stratton	Timothy Abbott
William Breakenridge	Esther Breakenridge
Benjamin Whipple	Elijah Story
Eleazer Harwood	Mary Fassett
Samuel Pratt	Martha Wickwire
Jonathan Scott	Martha Montague
Elisha Field	Jonathan Scott, Jr.
Samuel Montague	Jonathan Eastman
Elizabeth Scott	Elizabeth Harwood
Experience Richardson	Daniel Scott
Rebekah Abbott	Silas Robinson
Lydia Fay	Elizabeth Eastman
Marcy Robinson	Sarah Story
Baty Pratt	Simeon Harmon
Bridget Harwood	Robert Cochran
Elizabeth Roberts	Mary Cochran
Elizabeth Fisk	Bettey Dewey
Elizabeth Pratt	Anna Walbridge
Peace Atwood	Daniel Mills
Prudence Whipple	Mindwell Hopkins
Martha Abbott	Rhoda Hopkins

[One quarter sheet of subscribers' names — probably thirty — was lost. — WILLIAM HASWELL.]

D.

ARTICLES OF THE NEWINT (CONN.) SEPARATE CHURCH.[1]

1. We believe that there is one only glorious God, a Being from Himself and for Himself, of Whom, and for Whom, are all things; Who is Infinite, eternal, unchangeable in power, wisdom, goodness, justice, holiness and truth.

2. That there are Three Sacred Persons in the Godhead. God the Father, God the Son, and God the Holy Ghost. Equally God, and yet but one God.

3. That God hath, from all eternity, foreordained what shall come to pass, and did not only foresee, but did foredetermine the eternal states of men and angels.

4. That there is a general Providence which is exercised about all things, and that there is a special government of God over all the rational Creation.

5. That God made angels and men in holiness; but some of the angels abode not in the truth, who are called devils.

6. That God gave to man, when he had made him, a rule of obedience for life, and threatened death in case of disobedience; which rule for obedience our first parents transgressed, by eating the forbidden fruit, and we transgressed in them, and so death passed on all men.

7. That the sin of our first parents is the sin of all mankind by just imputation and derivation, and from the whole, all descending from them by ordinary generation, do naturally choose and PRAC-TISE sin.

8. That God, having eternally elected some of mankind to life, did, in the fulness of time, send his Son to redeem them, and that God the Father and God the Son did send the Holy Ghost to sanctify them.

9. We believe that Jesus Christ, taking our nature upon him as Mediator between God and man, hath made full satisfaction to God for the sins of the elect, and purchased life for them by the merits of his active and passive righteousness, and having received all power from God the Father, doth, in the execution of his prophetical, priestly, and kingly offices, reveal unto, and work in, his elect, whatever is necessary for salvation.

[1] See p. 54 of this volume.

10. That in the new covenant, God hath promised life to all those that, with the full consent of their souls, believe in him through Jesus Christ, and that the object of justifying faith is Christ in his person and offices as he is revealed in the Gospel, and by union to Christ, by faith believers are made partakers of his Sonship, grace, and glory, so that through free grace in Christ they are justified, adopted, and sanctified, and shall enjoy eternal life.

11. We believe the Scriptures of the Old and New Testament to be the record of God, by the dispensation of which, and through which, with the co-operation of the Holy Spirit, conviction of sin and misery is given, a knowledge of, and a particular faith in Christ is begotten, repentance, love, and new obedience is caused in the elect.

12. We believe that the moral law in the hand of Christ is the rule of obedience for believers, and that the sum of this law is to love the Lord our God with all our heart, etc., and our neighbor as ourselves.

13. We believe that there are two seals of the covenant of grace, namely, Baptism and the Lord's Supper. That Baptism belongs to none but true believers who are received by faith and love, and their seed in their infancy, and is a sign of our entrance into Christ; and the Lord's Supper is a sign of our growth in grace.

14. We believe in the communion of saints, the resurrection of the body, and the life everlasting. Amen.

Our covenant with God and one with the other is as follows : —

1. We do each of us in particular unfeignedly resign up ourselves and our seed to the Lord Jehovah, Father, Son, and Holy Ghost, receiving Jesus Christ as very God and very man, and the only mediator between God and man, as our Lord and Saviour, freely given of God to each of us in particular and sealed to each of us in particular, by the Holy Spirit of promise. relying upon the free grace of God for that salvation and blessedness which he hath purchased, and we hope to have by faith in and dependence upon himself, and we do submit ourselves to the word and Spirit of God to be ruled and thereby to be sanctified.

2. We do acknowledge ourselves indispensably bound and

34*

will make it our great care to hold fast the doctrine of faith and good manners contained in the Scriptures of truth; that we will attend all those duties that are therein prescribed for the increase of our faith and growth in holiness, and of maintaining a good conscience, that is, gospel preaching, mutual exhortation, ordinances, discipline, prayer, singing of psalms, etc.

3. And, as God is the Author of order, beauty, and peace, we do solemnly promise that, by the assistance of God's Holy Spirit, we will labor mutually to watch one over the other, and to observe all Christian and brotherly offices one to the other, which Christ hath enjoined according to our respective places; that is, love without dissimulation, and real expressions thereof as occasion serves, in daily frequent exhortation to duty, and admonition in case of sin and falling, praying for one another, and sympathizing with one another in affliction and prosperous enjoyments, and using all possible means to promote the spiritual welfare and growth of each other in holiness.

4. *First.* We do submit to the discipline of Christ in this church,—the sum of which we do acknowledge as followeth, namely: That supreme and lordly power and authority over all churches doth belong only to Jesus Christ, who is King and Head thereof. He hath the government upon His shoulders; hath all power both in Heaven and in Earth, and it is exercised by Him first in calling the church out of the world to holy fellowship with Himself; (2), and in instituting the ordinances of His worship and appointing His ministers and officers for the dispensing of them; (3), in giving law for the ordering all our way and the way of His house; (4), in giving life to all His institutions and to His people by them; (5), in protecting and delivering His church against and from all the enemies of their peace.

Secondly. The power granted by Christ to the body of the church or brotherhood is a prerogative or privilege which the church doth exercise. 1st, in admitting their own members; (2), in choosing and ordaining their own officers: (3), in removing them from their offices and fellowship in case of scandal or anything that by the rules of gospel renders them unfit therefor; (4), in supporting and maintaining the gospel ministry, ordinances, and poor of the church, without using the civil sword or any co-*her-sive* means to force a man thereto.

5. We do also promise, by the grace of God, to oppose all sin

and error in ourselves as far as in us lies, and in others when they appear, to wit · all foolish talking and jesting, chambering, and wantonness, all vain disputing about words and things that gender strife and doth not edify to more godliness; also vain company keeping, and spending time daily at taverns, tippling-houses or elsewhere; also evil whispering or backbiting any person; also carnal and unnecessary discourse about worldly things, especially on the Sabbath day; unnecessary forsaking the assembling ourselves in private convenient conferences and especially on the Sabbath, and all other sins whatsoever both of omission and commission, etc.

6. We will teach all under our care, as far as in us lies, to know God, to fear him, and to live in his way. And now as a further . testimony of our hearty belief of the foregoing doctrine of faith and covenant, we not only call heaven and earth to record, but we subscribe and sign the same with our names.

E.

EXTRACT FROM RESULT OF A SEPARATE ECCLESIASTICAL COUNCIL HELD IN BENNINGTON, MAY 23, 1770. (See p. 59.)

" We see, then, from the general rules given in Scripture, Cambridge Platform, and from the reason and nature of things, the gospel ought to be supported by equality. The particular method of which we apprehend to be merely circumstantial where the essence of the duty is done and nobody injured, and we apprehend the church and society may warrantably unite in a method by mutual agreement to perform the same, with this reserve and caution : to guard the church from bondage. The society is by no means to be allowed to control or govern the church in the affair. Therefore we think this church in Bennington has made a mistake, or taken a wrong step, though perhaps inadvertently, in giving the members of society, without any reserve, an equal right of judging in this affair, which, when the society is in the majority according hereunto they may bind the whole church contrary to its own mind or judgment.

But as to the method of pursuing this equality, we suppose it may be varied so as to suit different circumstances; as, for in-

stance, if the circumstances are such as that by Sabbath contributions the thing can be done, very well; or if a community agree
to pursue a method of equality, as follows: Voluntary subscription for their mutual satisfaction; or that of equalizing a sum
among themselves, — very well. Or perhaps some other method
not mentioned may answer well in some circumstances. But in
none of these ways is the matter to be left without the care and
inspection of the church, which has the right of judgment concerning the duty, and when discharged by its individual members.
And when any of the agreed-upon methods is come into, and each
one's proportion is known, and any individual church-member will
not discharge the same, and will not give any satisfactory reason
why to the church, they have a right to use their discipline in the
case."

The "result" is signed,

JOHN PALMER,
ISRAEL HOLLY,
JOSEPH KENT,
ZACCHEUS WALDO,
} *Council.*

F.

A PAPER, WHEREIN THE SIGNERS AGREE TO BE TAXED TO PAY
THE MINISTER.[1]

We, the subscribers, inhabitants of the town of Bennington,
being desirous to have the Gospel preached among us, do bind
ourselves severally to bear our equal part in paying the cost of
sending for a minister of the Gospel, for the above purpose; and
also of supporting him for the term of six months, according to
our several lists in the year 1783. Witness our hands this seventh
day of January, 1784. The above proportion to be paid to Samuel
Safford, Esq., Jonathan Robinson, and Simeon Hathaway, Jr., a
committee chosen for the purpose of receiving said money and
settling with the minister.

Elijah Boardman	William Satterlee
Silas Robinson	Timothy Abbott
Daniel Kinsley	Samuel Tubs
Nathaniel Kingsley	John Wood

[1] Original in possession of G. W. Robinson.

Ephraim Smith
Joseph Robinson
Matthew Scott
Daniel Story
Nathaniel Harmon
Joseph Rudd
Daniel Rudd
Benjamin Fassett
Benjamin Hulburt
William Mather
Eldad Dewey
Samuel Safford
Simeon Hathaway, Jr.
Jonathan Robinson
Henry Walbridge
Simeon Harmon
Robert Blair
Joseph Wickwire
Timothy Follett
Simeon Hathaway
John Kingsley
Peter Harwood
Solomon Walbridge
Jonathan Scott
Simeon Harmon, Jr.
Daniel Harmon
David Robinson
Samuel Holmes
Ebenezer Walbridge
Stephen Hopkins
Robert Hopkins
Isaac Tichenor
Levi Hathaway
Jesse Field
Leonard Robinson

David Tracy
Thomas Henderson
Thomas Abel
Joseph Hinsdill

Names added by the committee.

Elijah Dewey
Nathaniel Brush
John Fassett
Zechariah Harwood
Joseph Farnsworth
Samuel Robinson
Joseph Willoughby
Calvin Bingham
Thomas Hall
Joseph Safford
Solomon Safford
Jacob Safford
Reuben Clapp
Loan Dewey
Joseph House
Gideon Spencer
Robert Cochran
Charles Cushman
Jonathan Fisk
Isaac Rice
Uriah Edgerton
Issachar Norton
Benjamin Demilt
Aaron Demilt
Joseph Tracy
Aaron Hubbell

G.

A Paper to Settle Indian Claims.[1]

Whereas the Stockbridge Indian tribe, Capt. Jacobs and others, challenge twelve or more townships of land, situate and being on the west line of the province of New Hampshire, as chartered by Benning Wentworth, Esq., governor of said province; and the said Indian tribe are willing, and will be ready on the first day of

---

[1] Original in possession of G. W. Robinson.

January next, to treat with us, or any of us, respecting their title, and will at that time likewise appoint a meeting, at which meeting they will make it appear that they are the sole owners of, and have the only proper and lawful right to sell and convey the same; and whereas, we, the subscribers, whose names are hereto annexed, being willing and desirous to make sure to ourselves and successors a good and sufficient title to the interests which we now possess, and to make such addition, or additions, thereto, as shall be thought proper and conducive to our moral interests by Mr. Jedidiah Dewey, Capt. John Fassett, and S. Fay, whom we depute and elect to treat with said tribe, or such of them as will be necessary to treat with, in order to the procurement of a proper title to such land and lands, lying and being as aforesaid.

In consideration of all which we severally engage for ourselves, heirs, executors, and administrators, to pay, or cause to be paid, to the said Jedidiah, John, or Stephen, the several sum and sums according to our proprietorship, as will appear by the charter aforesaid, both the sum and sums which he or they may give for said land, or lands, and the cost necessarily arising by means of the procurement of said title; and to pay such sum and sums of money unto the said Jedidiah, John, or Stephen, at such time and times as he or they shall agree with said tribe of Indians.

Witness each of our hands at Bennington, this thirtieth day of November, A. D. 1767.

John Fassett	Leonard Robinson
Stephen Fay	Samuel Montague
James Breakenridge	Timothy Pratt
Jedidiah Dewey	Thomas Smith
Joseph Safford	Jonathan Scott, Jr.
Elisha Field	Matthew Scott
Nathan Clark	Daniel Scott
Benjamin Whipple	Moses Robinson
Simeon Harmon	Ephraim Marble
Henry Walbridge	Samuel Cutler
John Wood	Stephen Hopkins
Lebbeus Armstrong	Joseph Smith
Samuel Tubs	Jonathan Fassett
Samuel Robinson	Josiah Barber
Jacob Fisk	* Benjamin Warner
Thomas Henderson	Samuel Robinson, Jr.
Josiah Fuller	Joseph Wickwire
Silas Robinson	Nathaniel Dickenson
Samuel Hunt	Daniel Mills

Jacob Hyde	Joseph Rude
Samuel Atwood	Thomas Story
Wait Hopkins	Hezekiah Armstrong
Joseph Willoughby	Benajah Rude
Ebenezer Wood	Benjamin Atwell
David Safford	Oliver Rice
Ebenezer Walbridge .	Daniel Warner
Cornelius Cady	Aaron Haynes,
Nathaniel Holmes	Henry Walbridge, Jr.
Zachariah Harwood	Ebenezer Robinson
Samuel Scott	Thomas Jewett
Elijah Story	Israel Hurd
Johnson Cleaveland	Jonathan Fisk
Nathan Clark, Jr.	Robert Wilcox
Jonathan Wickwire	Samuel Herrick
Ebenezer Allen	Jedidiah Merrill
. Nathaniel Holmes, Jr.	Abner Marble
Nathaniel Harmon	Elkanah Ashley
Joshua Harmon	Silas Pratt
Joseph Safford, Jr.	Benajah Storey
Samuel Harvey	John Wood
Joseph Robinson	Timothy Abbott
Daniel Story	Seth Warner
Elijah Wood	Simeon Hathaway, Jr.
Robert Cochran	—— Harmon
Nathaniel Fillmore	Brotherton Daggett
John Stewart	Charles Cushman
John Armstrong	Gideon Spencer

H.

EXTRACT FROM A LETTER OF GOV. HUTCHINSON, OF MASSACHU-
SETTS, TO GOV. POWNAL, THEN IN LONDON; DATED BOSTON, JULY
10, 1765.[1]

"Permit me while you are taking care of the interests of the
whole to mention to you that of a small part only. There came to
me yesterday one Robinson who was one of your officers, and
perhaps you will recollect meeting him upon the road when you
was travelling to or from Hartford. After the war was over, he
purchased from Mr. Wentworth a patent for a township which he
had laid out upon the New York line, as then understood, twenty

[1] Vol. II. of Hutchinson's Correspondence, p. 113, in the office of the Secretary
of the Commonwealth, Boston. Furnished by Gov. Hall.

miles distant from Hudson's River. The settlers have made great improvements, have sixty-seven families, and as many houses, — some of them, he says, of a superior sort to the common settlers' houses, — have a minister ordained, and their affairs in a very flourishing state. The town is called Bennington. Another township adjoining, which has nearly as many families, is called Pownal. Both these townships are lately laid out, together with many others, by Mr. Livingston, who, having purchased the claims of officers and soldiers, has obtained a patent from New York; and I suppose will have a second manor there. Robinson says he has expended more than a thousand pounds, lawful money, and that he shall be ruined; for he must either quit all or become tenant upon such terms as will be worse than quitting. The grantees from New Hampshire supposed their title as good to the west as to the east of Connecticut River, provided they did not go within twenty miles of Hudson's River, and it seems scarcely equitable that private property should be altered by the new settlement of the New York line. The people are unable to bear the expense of the controversy."

THE END.